SOCIAL MOVEMENTS

Ideologies, Interests, and Identities

Anthony Oberschall

Transaction Publishers
New Brunswick (U.S.A.) and London (U.K.)

Second paperback printing 1997

Copyright © 1993 by Transaction Publishers, New Brunswick, New Jersey 08903.

Library of Congress Catalog Number: 91-47657
ISBN: 1-56000-011-2 (cloth); 1-56000-868-7 (paper)
Printed in the United States of America

Library of Congress Cataloging-in-Publication Data

Oberschall, Anthony
    Social movements : ideologies, interests, and identities / Anthony Oberschall.
        p. cm.
    Includes bibliographical references and index.
    ISBN 1-56000-011-2
    1. Social movements. 2. Social conflict. 3. Social movements—United States—History—20th century. 4. United States—Social conditions—1960–1980. 5. United States—Social conditions—1980– I. Title.
    HN17.5.024 1992
    303.48'4—dc20   91-47657

To Mama, who awakened my concern for public issues and has kept encouraging me all these years.

Contents

Preface

Two decades ago I published *Social Conflict and Social Movements*. Since then, the field of social movements has grown by leaps and bounds, much enriched by a great deal of empirical work using a variety of methods of inquiry. Over the years, I have been influenced by the changes in the field, whose foundations I have contributed to anchoring more firmly in the theory of collective action. I have been engaged in all these years, with the help of my students, in the study of ongoing social movements and contentious public issues. I have learned much from this research, and much about the movements themselves. Together with some previously published articles, I have collected my thinking and research into this volume for specialists, students, and the informed public alike.

My style of research has been principally participant observation, with much help from undergraduate and graduate students. The unit of analysis has been an issue or problem that becomes a matter of public debate and contention. I have tried to steer away from intellectual debates over terminology, labels, and classifications, and concentrate on a strong "story line" that reveals an interesting aspect of our contemporary world. Research provided a chance to add to theory and check it against stubborn reality. The final six chapters of the book follow a rough chronological order and can be read as a commentary on social and cultural changes in the contemporary United States.

I wish to thank several publishers for permission to reprint and/or reproduce the following material in this book: JAI Press, Inc. for "The Decline of the 1960s Social Movements" from volume 1 of *Research in Social Movements, Conflicts and Change*; "Loosely Structured Collective Conflict" from volume 3, and "The 1960 Sit-Ins: Protest Diffusion and Movement Take-Off" from volume 11; the University of California Press for "The Los Angeles-Watts Riot of August 1965" from *Social Problems* 15, 3, (1968); Annual Reviews, Inc. for "Theories of Social Conflict" from *Annual Review of Sociology* 4 (1978); Franc Cass Publishers for "Rising Expectations and Political Turmoil" from the *Journal of Development Studies* 6, 1, (1969); the Law and Society Association for "Group Violence: Some Hypotheses and Empirical Uniformities" from *Law and Society Review* 5, 1, (1970); and Mayer Zald and John McCarthy for "Protracted Conflict" in Mayer Zald and John McCarthy eds. *The Dynamics of Social Movements*, Cambridge, Mass., Winthrop, 1979.

Many individuals, too numerous to list, have helped me in my work on social movements. Here I only single out those I have been most closely associated with: Steven Howell, Bart Dredge, Tim Baylor, Kevin Everett, Julian Groves, Richard Garnett, and Kristin Park. I owe a special thanks to Deborah Tilley who patiently and meticulously prepared the material for publication.

1

Social Movements and Collective Action

Most of the time people pursue their goals or seek relief from hardship on their own, through individual effort. They conform to the inherited institutions without challenging their legitimacy. Yet, on occasion, many people pool their efforts in collective actions to benefit a large category of persons jointly—women, the elderly, blacks, farmers—not just themselves and their families. They find it necessary to challenge and change routines and institutions that others remain attached to. Controversy and conflict follow. What distinguishes *collective* from *individual* action are not the goals sought, nor the personality, motivations, and thought processes of participants. It is the public, nonroutine dimension of collective action, its challenge and threat to established groups, and its potential for being an agent of social change.

Social organization results from adaptations to technological innovations, economic forces, and population changes, and also from purposive, collective efforts to shape and alter existing institutions in order to deal with human needs and aspirations. When reforms are made, it has often been under pressure from social movements, as was the case of the 1930s New Deal administrations responding to the movements of the unemployed, farmers, industrial workers and miners, elderly, populists, and radicals. When privileged groups have resisted demands for change, they have at times been overthrown by popular movements, as King George III's administration was by the American colonists. Even when a social movement remains unsuccessful, its ideals and goals are at times later adopted, as was the case with the abolition of slavery in the nineteenth

1

century. Collective behavior and social movements have molded our contemporary institutions and are likely to keep changing them in the times ahead.

Terms, Concepts, and Questions

Although no satisfactory definitions of social movements and of collective behavior have yet been formulated, it is possible to convey a sense of their meaning by listing instances of both.[1] Collective behavior refers to the spectrum of crowd behavior from strikers manning a picket line, demonstrators attending a rally at the steps of a state capitol, and other collective manifestations of citizens exercising their constitutional rights peacefully to assemble and petition the government; all the way to the potentially destructive actions of a rioting mob. Collective behavior episodes are infrequent and unusual. They attract curiosity and comment. They elicit support and condemnation. They compel a search for their meaning, and call forth contradictory explanations. Social movements are large-scale, collective efforts to bring about or resist changes that bear on the lives of many: the temperance and prohibition movement at the turn of the century, the anti-Vietnam War movement of the late 1960s, the women's movement of the past two decades. Because collective behavior episodes frequently occur within the context of a wider social movement, these two topics have often been studied together.

More to the point, both collective behavior and social movements are forms of collective action. Much of the time, in the routines of everyday life, each of us pursues private goals that benefit us alone and our closest kin and associates. We cook a meal in order to eat it; we watch a television program for enjoyment and relaxation; we work and study in order to earn a living and get ahead. If we do not earn sufficiently, we work overtime or look for another job. If we are bored by television, we turn off the set and read a book. If we cannot afford a steak for dinner, we buy ground beef or chicken, or buy steak less frequently. These are *individual* strategies for dealing with individual needs and problems. We take action independently of what others may be doing.

On occasion, however, some people come to define a condition shared by many as a public issue necessitating *joint action*. They take steps to pursue a collective solution by pooling their efforts and resources, and coordinating their actions. Shoppers organize a boycott of beef at markets in order to force down the price of beef. Employees in the same occupation and industry pressure employers by striking in order to obtain a collective wage hike contract. Viewers form an association to put pressure on the networks and program sponsors in order to "clean up television." These are instances of *collective* action. Whether they succeed or fail will depend on how many join, how determined they are, what sacrifices they are willing to make, and on the resistance of their opponents. Furthermore, bystanders' decisions to join, and participants' decisions to contribute, are in turn much influenced by their perceptions of what others are also doing for the common cause and by their expectations of who else will join and how much they'll contribute. Collective action then, is not simply the sum total of thousands of individual decisions taken in isolation, such as the decision to cut down on beef consumption when beef prices increase. Collective action is the product of interactions, mutual perceptions, and expectations, called strategic interaction. As such, it is more difficult to describe and understand, and hence more challenging and intriguing as a field of study.

Many pertinent questions are raised about collective behavior and social movements: can broad societal conditions be identified that account for the waxing and waning of collective action over a period of time, or account for differences in its prevalence in different societies, localities, and social units? Under what circumstances does an issue or problem, such as temperance or women's rights, become a public controversy and attract supporters? What sorts of people participate in collective actions, both for and against an issue, and what are their reasons and motivations? What is the part played by leaders? How can one explain the character and forms of collective action, which ranges from episodic events to sustained drives, spontaneous to organized, peaceful to violent, from small to large scale? Why do some movements fail and others succeed? What accounts for the stages and phases that many movements go through as they first rise and later decline? What lasting consequences result that wouldn't have otherwise occurred? These and similar questions have preoccupied scholars and the public, as well as participants and onlookers, trying to make sense of social movements and collective behavior.

The study of social movements and collective behavior has been pursued by scholars and researchers from many academic disciplines, and writers and journalists of varied backgrounds. Routine information on these topics is hard to come by, however, because governments and institutional record keepers do not provide it as they do for households, industrial firms, consumer spending, public opinion, and elections. It is simple to look up the distribution of votes for candidates in an election. It is not simple to establish the contradictory claims of numerical support of a movement leader and of the opponents trying to discredit him. Thus theories and explanations are difficult to test and confirm in this field. Particular social movements are the subject of controversy and reinterpretation even among nonpartisan, relatively objective analysts. Still, the subject matter is inherently fascinating, and in recent years progress has been made in providing the field with a broader empirical base, and with a more sophisticated approach to the subject matter. I start with the traditional explanations of collective behavior associated with the crowd theorist Gustave Le Bon, then review difficulties and criticisms of the traditional approach, and end with a competing set of explanations which will be applied to joyous celebrations, the dissolution of a riotous crowd, and the puzzling Jonestown mass suicides. Then I turn to social movements.

Le Bon's Theory of Collective Behavior

At the turn of the century the most widely accepted source for a comprehensive explanation of collective behavior was the French social theorist Gustave Le Bon (1960). Even today, news reporters, police chiefs, legislators, commentators, as well as the public at large, share Le Bon's views, which were much colored by his negative assessment of the French Revolution and by the turn of the century cultural pessimism permeating European intellectual life. In his best-known book, *Psychologie des Foules*,[2] he contended that civilization was in decline in his time because the era of the masses had dawned. According to Le Bon, civilizations are always created by a small intellectual aristocracy that imposes rationality and discipline upon the potentially destructive masses. When the masses take over, "they act like those microbes which hasten the dissolution of enfeebled or dead bodies. . . . It is always the masses that bring out [civilization's] downfall."

Le Bon made a sharp distinction between, on the one hand, *the individual*, the agent of rationality, morality, civilization, high culture and intellectual achievement; and, on the other, *masses and crowds*, harbingers of irrationality, destruction, decadence, the herd instinct, barbarism. In order to make sense of crowd and mass behavior, therefore, principles that differ from those that govern and explain individual everyday behavior must be invoked. His three most important principles were the "law of mental unity of crowds,"[3] the loss of rational faculty and of moral sense, and hero worship and blind submission to a strong leader.

According to the law of mental unity, individual differences in personality and aptitude weaken in a crowd setting, and, correspondingly, a collective state of mind and feeling takes hold: "whoever be the individuals that compose it, however like or unlike be their mode of life, their occupation, their character or their intelligence . . . the fact that they have been transformed into a crowd puts them in possession of a sort of collective mind which makes them feel, think and act in a manner quite different from that in which each individual of them would feel, think and act were he in a state of isolation." Crowds, in Le Bon's view, develop such a collective state through a process of contagion and suggestion that promote uniformity much as the herd instinct does in the animal world. One important consequence of such unity is the great power thus achieved by crowds and masses, for unlike individuals who act at cross purposes, crowds act in unison.

According to the second principle, an individual in a crowd loses his rational faculties and his moral sense. He can be made "to commit acts contrary to his most obvious interests and his best known habits." Men in crowds become akin to barbarians, or to the animals acting out of sheer instinct: "man descends several rungs in the ladder of civilization . . . he possesses the spontaneity, the violence, the ferocity, and also the enthusiasm and heroism of primitive beings." For Le Bon, crowds are not only powerful and of one mind and sentiment, they are dangerous, irrational, and amoral.

According to his third principle, and quite in keeping with the preceding, Le Bon also held that crowds worship strong leaders, are impressed by popular heroes, and submit to and follow these leaders blindly; consequently, they can be manipulated by these leaders to serve evil ends, all the more so because their intellectual and moral faculties are in suspension.

To illustrate and substantiate his principles, Le Bon described several episodes from the French Revolution, such as the killing of six or seven captured defenders of the Bastille on 14 July 1789, after it had been captured by the insurgents, and the September massacres in 1792, when Parisians forced their way into the city's prisons and executed several hundred prisoners, after condemning them in hastily improvised people's tribunals. Beyond these historic examples, well known to every French schoolchild, recent history and daily newscasts abound with examples of collective behavior that appears to fit the Le Bon mold. Consider that the Reverend Jim Jones and 900 of his followers in the People's Temple committed mass suicide together, an act that completely wiped out their isolated religious settlement in the Guyanese jungle. What better example of hero worship, collective irrationality, and uniform mass behavior than that event, and how else explain it but with reference to Le Bon's principles?

Critiques of Le Bon's Conceptions

Contemporary historical scholarship has shown, however, that the crowd episodes chosen by Le Bon to make his case do not fit his principles well and are subject to different interpretations. Nor were Le Bon's examples typical either of crowd behavior in general, or of French Revolution crowds, in particular. For example, the storming of the Bastille was not a spontaneous, unprovoked, destructive attack led by popular heroes with the masses at their heels (Rude 1959). Quite the contrary. It was a planned military operation undertaken by a citizen militia at the request of the provisional government of Paris. The militia was joined by a crowd of a few hundred armed civilians and two detachments of army troops who had recently defected to the side of the Paris insurgents. The purpose of the action was to seize gunpowder, stored in the fortress, which was needed to defend Paris should the king try to stamp out the Paris uprising against his authority. Prolonged and repeated negotiations were undertaken with the Bastille commander for its surrender before any shots were fired. The besiegers lost ninety-three dead and suffered close to one-hundred wounded during the fighting, after the commander opened fire with the Bastille's guns, mistakenly believing that negotiations had broken down and that a frontal attack was imminent. He and his garrison of 109 men eventually surrendered. It is true that he and five or six of his men were killed, as they were being led away into captivity, by some angry participants in the attack. But these actions were perpetrated by only a fraction of the besiegers and were not typical of the fate suffered by the Bastille garrison: the attackers did not act in unison; most of what they had done before, during and after the storming of the Bastille was neither irrational nor immoral; leaders and demagogues played no role in the six killings.

But what about the gruesome September of 1792, when in a week's time nearly half of the 3000 prisoners in Paris jails were massacred? These wretches were executed by hastily constituted people's courts, though most of the victims were common thieves, currency speculators and forgers, and vagrants and prostitutes, and not political prisoners, nobles, and priests. According to Rude (1959, 109), however, "[The September massacres] were by no means a sudden eruption, carried out in a momentary fit of passion or as a result of shortlived panic." It is important to remember that France was at war with an alliance of the great European powers. Many nobles had become exiles at European courts and were plotting to overthrow the revolutionary government. King Louis and his family had tried to flee and join the exiles. In August 1792, he was deposed as a constitutional monarch because it was feared that he was part of a counterrevolutionary plot. The war was going badly. The Prussian army was advancing on French territory. Counterrevolutionaries, nobles, priests, forgers, and speculators in currency believed responsible for inflation and food shortages had been imprisoned. Others' homes had been searched for hidden arms and incriminating papers. As volunteers and conscripts were leaving to join the army, the fear spread in Paris of a counterrevolutionary plot against the vulnerable and defenseless city that would start with the liberation of the enemies of the revolution from prisons and jails. That is the historical context for the massacres.

The authorities knew about the coming invasion of the prisons by Parisians since rumors had circulated and plans of action had been discussed at neighborhood meetings. Yet the authorities did not intervene: some thought it useful for creating greater revolutionary zeal at a time of danger and for eliminating the counterrevolutionaries. Others openly applauded the massacres as necessary and politically desirable acts of popular justice. Though many nonpolitical criminals were executed with the politicals, it should be noted that more prisoners were actually spared than condemned and executed by the people's courts.

Thus even this extreme case of collective fear and the destruction of life does not unambiguously support Le Bon's principles. The September crowds did not do the bidding of leaders and demagogues, but acted on their own. Their actions, precipitated by a real military emergency, cannot be dismissed as simply irrational and amoral. Fears of a counter-revolution may have been exaggerated, but they had a basis in political events of the preceding two years. The people's courts did attempt to discriminate between counterrevolutionary guilt and innocence in qua-sijudicial proceedings. When the authorities did not intervene, and in some cases provided encouragement, it did invest these illegal actions with an aura of legitimacy and of morality.

Similarly, the People's Temple mass suicide in Guyana appears to have been a far more complex event than it first appeared (Naipaul 1981). In California the Reverend Jones had been under mounting scrutiny, pres-sure, and legal action, both from a concerned parents' group charging that their children had been brainwashed by the sect, or held against their will, or both, and from government agencies and legislators looking into these charges. These agencies were also interested in allegations of financial irregularities and fraud: old folks having signed their social security pensions over to the sect leadership.

Here is the sequence of events: In order to escape scrutiny and possible legal action, the Reverend Jim Jones decided to put into effect his plan for a unique religious-communist experiment, and transferred most of his sect into the Jonestown agricultural settlement in the jungle of Guyana. There, a friendly government would hold the outside world at bay, and give him maximum authority to run his own sect without interference and accountability. The jungle would constitute an addi-tional barrier to meddlers, parents, and news reporters.

His strategy and his health were both soon failing. He knew he was dying and was increasingly sustained by and addicted to powerful drugs. He had been unable to stop the investigative visit of California Congress-man Leo Ryan accompanied by news reporters, and as this team was leaving the Jonestown airstrip with incriminating evidence and some defectors, Jones ordered first the murderous attack on them and on the plane's crew, and then, by means of poisoned drink, the mass suicide of his assembled followers and of himself, which he had prepared for.

Because Jones had taped the nightly assemblies at which he preached to and harangued his followers, and because of other information that has come to light about life in Jonestown, we know that the popular version of the event, of willing followers surrendering life at the bidding of their godlike leader, is distorted. To some, Jonestown was a noble utopia and Jones a great leader; to others, however—and we shall probably never know how many wanted to escape but could not—Jonestown had become a prison and Jones himself a lunatic fraud. Some followers had already defected in California, and had come under intimidation and harassment from the People's Temple. In Jonestown itself there were armed guards, fences, and of course the jungle, preventing escape. When visitors or embassy officials came, sect members were not permitted to speak to them in private. The enthusiastic reception given to visiting dignitaries, who later gave favorable reports about life in Jonestown, were carefully staged and rehearsed during the evening sessions. Many sect members were apathetic, suffering from dysentery, weak from hard work and poor food, just struggling to stay alive. And for many there was no alternative; even had they been capable of escaping, they had burned their bridges to the outside world after joining the sect; they had no property and assets left, and had antagonized relatives and friends. Furthermore, to deter opposition and keep the wavering in line, thought control had been instituted; sect members had to confess their doubts publicly and were forced to voice their loyalty to Reverend Jones. In the fatal final act of the Jonestown drama, on 18 November 1978, eighteen months after Jonestown was settled, some—quite possibly most—were forced to drink the poison by Jones' armed guards. The point here is that though to some Jonestown was a utopia to the end, to others it had become a concentration camp. There was a variety of responses by members of the People's Temple, and not the uniform attitudes and behavior posited by Le Bon's group mind. The climactic mass suicide, which superficially supports Le Bon's notions of the irrationality and hero worship of crowds, cannot be accounted for by those principles alone, since it was for many not a matter of voluntary choice at all, but of coercion.

The Controversy over Collective Behavior

In the critique of Le Bon's concepts, what is at issue is not that under some circumstances crowds become angry, hostile, destructive, even murderous; nor that some leaders have dedicated and loyal followers, and that adherents are sometimes willing victims of their master's schemes. What is at issue is whether such behavior is typical of crowds and masses, and whether it distinguishes crowds from other social formations.

In the face of destruction initiated and supervised by the constituted authorities, for example, the anger and destructiveness of crowds pales into insignificance. Again, during the French Revolution, after the September massacres and between March 1793 and August 1794, the terror organized by the government against its enemies led to the execution of nearly 17,000 human beings by revolutionary tribunals and civil and military commissions. Many more were executed by the authorities without trial, or died in prison from disease and epidemics (Greer 1935). More recently, the helpless victims of Stalin's mass purges and labor camps, and of Hitler's concentration camps are counted not in hundreds and thousands, but in millions and tens of millions. Small bands of terrorists have killed and maimed in murderous fashion far in excess of angry crowds. Crowds have no patent on devastation.

At issue as well is whether the supposed sharp contrast between the morality and rationality of individuals and small elites, and the irrationality and amorality of crowds, is useful for making sense of collective behavior. The actions of statesmen, politicians, and their advisors deliberating in the highest councils of government have reflected at times exaggerated fears of conspiracy, emotional stereotyping of their opponents, and willingness to approve monstrous acts against them—acts that they would never have endorsed as universally valid principles of moral conduct and would not think of condoning in their private lives (Janis 1972). Rationality and morality, calm deliberation, calculation, restraint, or their opposites are not the prerogative of particular groups and individuals, nor the distinguishing trait of particular situations and circumstances. On the contrary, it is more accurate and useful to think of all human decisions and situations as containing elements of rationality and nonrationality, morality and amorality, emotion and detachment, enthusiasm and restraint. Nor is it true that emotion and enthusiasm necessarily interfere with rationality and morality, any more than their opposites guarantee clear thinking. A sports team, for example, may well play more effectively and commit fewer infractions when it gets fired up in a close contest with a rival than in a regular humdrum game. The distinctive character of collective action, in contrast to individual action, is not captured by these distinctions and exaggerated contrasts. But if we dismiss Le Bon's three principles of crowd behavior as inadequate, what shall be other, more promising hypotheses and explanations of collective behavior?

Collective Behavior Is Adaptive and Normative

Unlike Le Bon, but like many contemporary students of the subject matter, let us assume that collective behavior is not a unique form of action that needs distinctive concepts and hypotheses. On the contrary, collective behavior can be understood with the same concepts and hypotheses used for explaining everyday routine behavior, whether it be that of isolated individuals, small groups, large, permanently organized social units, or ephemeral crowds. The two most useful hypotheses about behavior is that it is both adaptive and normative.

Behavior can be said to be adaptive when people weigh the benefits and costs of alternative courses of action for reaching a certain goal, and choose the alternative for which net benefit, that is, benefit minus cost, is the greatest. This statement is not to be taken literally. Much of what we do is a result of habit and not of conscious calculation. But habit itself is a product of repeated adjustment during which costly alternatives are eliminated and beneficial choices retained by trial and error. When a new situation arises, we start with proven choices that have worked in the past, make a series of small adjustments, until an acceptable net benefit results, which in turn becomes our new routine or habit. This adaptive process has been called by Lindblom (1968) the "art of muddling through." Not only do we engage in adaptive behavior, but we assume that others do likewise, and by and large it does indeed work out that way. Think only of the regularity of traffic and parking patterns in your locality, how you have found out about them, and the usual steps you take to avoid delay.

Behavior is normative when people limit the goals they seek and the means of obtaining them to conform to law, convention, rules of conduct and other people's notions and expectations about what is right and appropriate. Norms do not always provide unambiguous guidelines and expectations, nor do people always conform to them even when they are clear cut. Nonetheless, without a normative framework that limits adaptive choices, and conformity to it by most people most of the time, life would be chaotic and extremely stressful, or "nasty, brutish, and short" if you prefer Hobbes' characterization of the "state of nature." Imagine what would happen in cafeterias, at checkout counters, and in ticket lines if fairness norms like "first come, first served" and "waiting one's turn" were ignored![4]

Although neither of these hypotheses about behavior is unfamiliar or surprising, what may be novel is their application to collective behavior.[5] Some collective behavior follows a seasonal or institutional rhythm of ritual and celebrations during which a limited range of behaviors is acted out, limited that is by conventions and traditions that are passed down from one generation to another, from one student cohort to another, and is nowadays also learned by watching similar collective events on television.[6] The oddly dressed students performing bizarre and unusual events on campus during fraternity and sorority rushes readily come to mind, as do New York City revelers gathered in one huge mass of humanity at Times Square on New Year's Eve jointly counting down the last minutes and seconds before the stroke of midnight, the celebrating sports fans in big-city downtown areas when their professional team won the Super Bowl, Stanley Cup, or World Series, and similar manifestations in college towns when a rival was beaten or a championship won. These collective events have no purpose beyond the enjoyment that comes from participation itself. Not only does the surge of we-feeling, civic and campus pride create a sense of euphoria, but the temporary suspension of some of the usual prohibitions and conventions about behavior in public places and among strangers—excessive noise making, rocking the vehicles of passing motorists, accosting and fraternizing with strangers, consuming alcoholic beverages in excess and in off-bounds places— heightens enjoyment since they symbolize the extraordinary character of the events celebrated. Though law enforcement officials may be in evidence to prevent the situation from getting out of hand, they turn a blind eye to many minor law infractions for which they would under normal circumstances make arrests for disorderly conduct. Despite such greater license, the majority of participants have a sense of what is appropriate, and of the bounds that ought not be exceeded, and will stop short of destructive, threatening, and offensive behavior, and will even take steps to discourage unruly elements in their midst from exceeding those limits. At times, collective celebrations have gotten out of hand; usually nothing more severe than "morning-after-the-night-before" hangovers and piles of litter for clean-up crews will result.

Much collective behavior is more explicitly purposive, structured and ritualized, and thus also more orderly and predictable, than collective celebrations, whether it be small-town revival meetings or the big-city evangelical crusade in the municipal auditorium, the walking picket line of employees on strike, or the mass march of petitioners in Washington, D.C. come to voice their displeasure at government policy and to demonstrate their political clout. Careful preparations have proceeded these collective actions. A religious crusade is preceded by lengthy planning and fund raising by church groups and business associations. They raise funds, conduct advertising campaigns, ensure transportation for church audiences, recruit and underwrite the expenses of choirs and celebrities, purchase air time on local broadcasting stations, and provide lodging and headquarters for the crusade staff itself. The organizers of large political demonstrations apply for parade permits, negotiate march routes and access to public parks and facilities with local officials and police, train parade marshals, plan and organize a schedule of speakers and performers, arrange for chartered buses and planes, schedule news conferences, and so on.

Participants are seldom a random assemblage of the citizenry. Many come not as isolated individuals, but with family, associates, and neighbors. Participants tend to be self-selected from those who are already in agreement with the goals of the leaders and sponsoring organizations, and thus predisposed to follow the scenario laid down by the organizers. The self-selection and assembly of similarly predisposed participants in collective action—religious-minded crusaders and politically engaged demonstrators—is called convergence. It explains the similarity of behavior and sentiment in many crowds and audiences which Le Bon sought to account to a group mind, contagion, and hero worship. On the contrary, my point of view is that collective action is adaptive and normative because, as these examples demonstrate, it follows from deliberate choice of both goals and means, on the part of organizers and participants alike, based on their experience of what has worked in the past and the expectation of future gain, and it conforms to the expectations of the authorities, the participants, and bystander publics.

Granted that much collective behavior needs no distinctive hypotheses and concepts to understand, as Le Bon maintained, there are nevertheless instances, as in riots, when members of a crowd act in ways quite different from what they would do in isolation or in small groups. The approach espoused here is that if people make different choices in isolation than they do in the crowds, it is because of the operation of two factors, separately or jointly. First, the norms applicable to the crowd situation are not the same as those for isolated individuals in an ordinary situation—recall the wider latitude for permissible, tolerated behavior during collective celebrations that encompass some forms of disorderly conduct.[7] Second, the schedule of benefits and costs of choices for the member of a crowd differ from what it is for isolated individuals making a choice since people in a crowd behave strategically. Le Bon, in contrast, attributes the difference of behavior to the growth of a uniform disposition in a crowd, to the loss of rational faculties and of the moral sense, and to submission to the authority of a leader.

Take a puzzling phenomenon: a riotous crowd dissolves at the onset of rain, even though police may have been trying to disperse it forcefully for some time. If one assumes that crowds acquire uniform dispositions and a group mind, and act irrationally, it is difficult to explain such an outcome merely on the basis of rain. But suppose one assumes the opposite, that a crowd consists of people with different motivations and levels of commitment, ranging from extreme anger and hostility to mere curiosity and a lukewarm desire to be part of and subsequently brag about a neighborhood event. Assume further that regardless of disposition, each participant roughly assesses the expected cost of participation (getting arrested, getting hurt) with the expected benefit (the satisfaction from venting one's anger, perhaps the opportunity for looting, curiosity, being "one of the boys," and so forth). For each person, according to our hypothesis that behavior is adaptive, if benefit exceeds cost, the decision is made to participate in the riot. If not, the decision is to leave.

Two further assumptions are made. First, the determining factor for assessing cost is the size of the crowd, and size is negatively related to cost: the more people present, the lower the chances of arrest and getting hurt. This is the "safety in numbers" hypothesis. Second, benefit is directly proportional to one's level of commitment: greatest for the angry core, least for the curious onlookers at the edge. Because the crowd is large initially, the expected cost is low. For some curious onlookers, the benefit of participation barely exceeds expected cost, for others, especially the angry core, benefit far exceeds cost. When it starts to rain, the extra discomfort of getting wet increases the cost of participation to all, but only slightly. For most, this makes no difference since benefit still exceeds cost. But for some of the curious onlookers, the small added cost of rain tips net benefit—benefit minus cost—in a negative direction. Because cost exceeds benefit, they leave. Since crowd size is diminished, expected cost increases for everyone remaining. Again, for many, the added cost does not change the decision to stay, but for those with only a low commitment, the net benefit becomes negative, and they in turn leave. Thus a chain reaction results. As more and more people leave the crowd, expected costs keep increasing. At each departure, the new, higher cost exceeds benefit for additional members of the crowd, until even the angriest core left to confront the police decide that the risk of arrest is simply not worth the benefit. In the end a simple act of God, rain, accomplishes what the police could not do.

It is not because the rain, in the stock phrase, "cooled tempers": it is because one of the key variables determining participation, expected cost, is a function of the number of participants, and thus of others' decisions to participate. The participation of people in a hostile crowd is thus not simply the sum total of all decisions independently arrived at, but the result of a process of interdependent decisions or strategic interactions. What is distinctive about collective behavior is not that people are angry, fearful, emotional, amoral, and nonrational. What is distinctive is that benefits and costs of their choices in a collective situation are a function of the choices others are making. Thus members of a crowd or audience make choices they would not have made and do not make in isolation or in small groups.

Despite the usefulness of the assumption that collective behavior is adaptive and normative, the folk view draws on elements of Le Bon's ideas and is perpetuated and reinforced by news reports and instant commentary about complex and confusing events that highlight their most dramatic and sensational aspects. Because crowds are supposed to be threatening and destructive, and because it sells copy or attracts viewers in a competitive media marketplace, minor and atypical violent incidents at the fringes of, for example, a large, orderly, peaceful rally routinely receive disproportionate coverage, as may a few hecklers or protesters in an otherwise supportive gathering. Furthermore, one-sided, biased interpretations prevail even after new evidence is uncovered and a new interpretation appears reasonable, simply because there is no longer any interest in publicizing the additional information. As I have written about the Los Angeles riot in chapter 9, the news media and officials were under pressure to provide an instant explanation, before fact has been sifted from rumor, in an atmosphere of recrimination. The tendency is to frame the riot in accordance with the folk view of crowds, familiar to the public, that puts the accent on irrationality and fickleness, amorality and criminality. Some look for conspiracy; others blame criminals and lawless misfits; to others still, poor, unemployed and deprived people are simply a puzzle. The riot is an extraordinary event. Commentators concluded therefore, as Le Bon did, that ideas, concepts and assumptions used in explaining everyday behavior do not apply. With such views I emphatically disagree.

My approach, on the contrary, is that collective behavior—a revival meeting, a political demonstration, a collective celebration, even a de-structive riot—can be understood with the usual concepts and hypotheses of social science: behavior is adaptive and normative. What is different in a riot is that benefits and costs are different from other situations, and consequently different choices are made, and not that benefits and costs are disregarded as criteria for choosing because rioters are emotional, irrational, and angry. What else is different in a riot is that everyday norms become suspended, and different situational and emergent norms receive social support, and not that participants become amoral, unable to tell right from wrong.

The Origin of Social Movements

What occasions social movements? Why do some issues become public and capable of enlisting the support of many when at some earlier or later time proponents of the same causes are largely ignored? No simple answer can be given to these questions.

Many movements start as a reaction to a change or new policy that negatively affects the interests and way of life of many people. Because the authorities were directly or indirectly responsible for the change, activists organize to oppose and reverse it, attract supporters, and build public support for their goals. The antiwar movement was a reaction to growing military participation of the U.S. in the Indochina War. The antiabortion (Pro-Life) movement got under way shortly after the 1973 Supreme Court decision overturned state laws banning most abortions. Similarly we would expect a taxpayers' "revolt" after new taxes are enacted, or existing taxes sharply increased, and parents to oppose busing for public school integration after a court order directs school authorities to implement a busing plan. The situation is clear enough. A precipitating event from outside the group or locality creates grievances and elicits citizen opposition. The point of interest is not that there was opposition, but the scope and strength of it, and the particular actions and strategies adopted.

More difficult to explain is the start or revival of social movements whose goal is to gain new rights or other benefits. An undesirable condition may persist for a long time, and may not even get demonstrably worse, yet without a clear-cut precipitating event a social movement gets under way and builds momentum. Thus it was at the start of the women's movement in the late 1960s, of the civil rights movement a decade earlier, of the environmental and the prohibition movements, and scores of others. In none of them did a dramatic event precipitate collective action, such as increases in race and sex discrimination, environmental degradation, liquor consumption and alcohol-linked social and health problems. Collective action may have been stimulated by new hopes and a more positive sense of opportunity for taking successful steps against an undesirable condition; it may have been stimulated because a condition long endured was increasingly experienced as unjust and inequitable; it may have been stimulated by a group's increasing capacity to act collectively; or, indeed, by all of these factors. To sum it up, four dimensions of collective action need to be examined to account for movement initiation and growth:

1. Changes in the basic conditions of life most likely to produce discontent, and ineffectiveness in the usual ways for providing relief and handling problems. We link up with theories of social change on this dimension.

2. Changes in beliefs and values, aspirations and expectations used to filter, frame, and respond to one's life circumstances. Here we link up with theories of culture and of ideology.

3. Changes in the capacity to act collectively, such as increased group size, more freedom to organize, better communications, greater cohesion among group members, and the like. Here one draws on organization theory.

4. Changes in opportunity for successful action, such as weakness of the opposition, support from powerful allies, and the success of other social movements. On this dimension, collective action theory and political sociology overlap.

Social Change: Breakdown or Solidarity?

Some social movement analysts put the accent on the first dimension, the societal conditions that produce high levels of dissatisfaction and the breakdown of institutions that provide security and stability. In this view, a period of rapid social change—due to industrial growth and economic transformation, urban growth and rural decline, an economic depression, the aftermath of a lost war, rapid population growth, and the like—will weaken and undermine stable groups and communities, such as families, churches, neighborhoods, employers, that normally provide people with stable income and financial security, social fellowship and a sense of belonging, purpose in life and support in time of need, and stable expectations about the future. As social bonds weaken and traditional answers and remedies no longer work, the population will manifest signs of increasing disorganization: crime, mental illness, alcoholism, divorce, suicide, will all increase. Other uprooted and disturbed people will seek relief in a variety of ways, individual and collective. They migrate in search of new ways of making a living; they join religious sects and radical groups that promise a solution and offer refuge; they participate in major social, political, and religious movements that seek to reform and restructure institutions. Eventually, the combined efforts of reformers, elites, and governments restore stability to the social order by creating new institutions, and uprooted and isolated individuals forge new social bonds that restore their identity and sense of well-being. As social stability is restored, participation in social movements, sects, and radical groups decreases, since they no longer serve a useful purpose.

Although breakdown theory encompasses a diversity of points of view, there is agreement on three central propositions:

1. social movements, religions sects, and extremist groups, as well as manifestations of individual disorganization (e.g., crime, suicide, divorce, mental illness, etc.) will flourish in periods of rapid social change and dislocation;

2. the greater the hardship from dislocation, the higher the indices of disorganization, and in turn, the greater the number of movements and sects, and the more numerous their adherents;

3. the most uprooted, isolated, and dissatisfied people are the most likely adherents of movements and sects, as well as the most likely to engage in crime, commit suicide, experience mental breakdown, and the like.

Though these are plausible statements and accord with commonplace views, these propositions have not been confirmed by systematic research. The Tillys' (1975) time series research on fluctuations of the standard of living and economic hardship indices, urbanization and migration rates, disorganization indices, collective violence, and strikes, over a period of more than a century for France found only small correlations between these variables, and some had the opposite sign of what breakdown theory predicts. Studies of adherents of religious sects, converts to religious movements, activists in the civil rights movement, and participants in the Boston antibusing movement, to mention but a few, have failed to establish that participants are isolated and uprooted, come from a deprived social and economic background, and experience personal problems and dislocation any more than nonparticipants (Useem 1980; Stark and Bainbridge 1980). This is not to say that breakdown has not proved useful for accounting for some sects and movements. But as a global theory of the societal conditions particularly favorable to social movement proliferation and of the characteristics of the most likely joiners, it has yet to be confirmed.

Because of the shortcomings of breakdown theory, a rival solidarity theory has sought to explain the origin and success of social movements by putting the accent on the third and fourth dimensions, changes in the capacity to act collectively, and in opportunity for success, that is, mobilization for collective action. Lest there be a misunderstanding, solidarity theorists agree that increases in dissatisfaction and grievances are important for explaining social movement growth, as are the other three sets of conditions. But they hold that even with substantial and widespread dissatisfaction a social movement may not form when the capacity to act collectively is weak and opportunities for success low. Nor do breakdown theorists neglect mobilization; they do not, however, assign it the same importance as solidarity theorists. Because mobilization has become a central topic in the theory of collective action, it is highlighted in the next section.

Obstacles to Mobilization for Collective Action

To adherents and the public, the most important information about a movement are its goals, often inferable from its name (e.g., the prohibition movement sought prohibition of alcoholic beverages; the civil rights movement sought the same civil rights for blacks that white Americans enjoyed).

Movement goals have two properties. They are collective goods, not private goods, and for some they are "bads," not goods. Unlike a private good consumed and enjoyed by a particular person, such as income from work, a collective good benefits all members of a group or social category, regardless of whether they contributed to attaining it (Olson 1968). The benefits of desegregation of public facilities, for example, are enjoyed not only by civil rights workers who may have paid a high personal price during a desegregation drive, but by all blacks regardless of whether they contributed to achieving the goal or not. Noncontributing beneficiaries of a collective good cannot be kept from its enjoyment and are referred to as "free riders." If all potential beneficiaries remain free riders, no collective action would ever be undertaken. How to overcome free rider tendencies and get people to join and contribute to a common cause is a principal obstacle to the formation of a social movement. People free ride because participation entails opportunity costs. That is, the one-hundred dollars one contributes to an organization could have been spent on an evening out, and the afternoon one spends at a rally or stuffing handbills into mailboxes could have been spent at the ball park. Though each in a group may have an interest in obtaining the collective good, each also has an interest in letting the others bear the costs.

Because what is a good or benefit to one group is a "bad" (or negative good) to another, movements will be met by opposition, sometimes by a countermovement. An anti-nuclear power group hoping to stop construction at a reactor site will be opposed by those who fear for their jobs. Countermovements are also subject to free rider tendencies, yet initially the problem is more critical for a challenger because the status quo is protected by law, social norms, and the authorities. The authorities shoulder the burden of protecting the interests of established groups. When demonstrators against a nuclear reactor block the entrances of the plant, it is the police that keep the site open, not a group of volunteer citizens favoring nuclear power—not even the management, employees, and stockholders of the corporation that owns the plant. Thus, if the first major problem for social movements is to overcome the free rider syndrome, a second major problem is to overcome organized opposition, because movement goals will be actively resisted. Often there are direct participation costs beyond opportunity costs for some forms of participation: the risk of arrest and injury, ridicule, condemnation, getting a reputation for being a troublemaker, and the like—costs exacted by the opposition, by the authorities, and by public opinion (McAdam 1986).

Like all voluntary associations, social movements are in a weak position to induce participation. When governments provide collective goods, such as roads, postal service, police and fire protection, and national defense, they rely on compulsory taxation, not on appeals for voluntary financial contributions. Furthermore, negative sanctions (e.g., fines, penalties) are an effective means of discouraging governmental free riders, but social movements have no such power over their constituency.

One way of inducing participation for obtaining a collective good is the provision of an additional private good, called a selective incentive, beyond the collective good itself, to those, and only those who participate. A professional association whose main purpose is to lobby for the profession as a whole induces participation by a whole series of selective incentives restricted to its members, such as cheap subscription rates to professional journals, group health and life insurance plans, annual conventions in attractive places at reduced hotel rates, and the like. Thus the professional association benefits the profession collectively but only participating members selectively. Social movements, however, tend to have very limited resources to provide such tangible, selective benefits to participants. Leaders and activists will try to attract participants by publicizing the justness of their cause through ideological and moral appeals. Beyond that a movement may build a sense of community among kindred souls that will make participation in itself a source of satisfaction referred to as solidarity incentives. Ritual, drama, and entertainment provided by folk and rock bands and celebrities sharing the stage at rallies with movement leaders serve the function of building a close-knit community as well as rewarding those who turned out with an experience that can be gotten only from participation in person. Survey research on participants in many and diverse social movements has shown that moral and ideological appeals and solidarity incentives do overcome free rider tendencies (Useem 1980; Klandermans 1984; Klandermans and Oegema 1987; Opp 1988; Finkel, Muller, and Opp 1989).

But just cause and an attractive message are not enough. One must effectively frame and communicate this message to one's constituency and the larger public in the marketplace of issues, ideas, symbols, and words (Snow and Benford 1988; Gamson 1988). Unless collective action is brief and sporadic, some continuity of organization supported by a core of activists is necessary: funds have to be raised, newsletters written and distributed, a list of names and addresses of members and potential recruits kept and updated, speakers and meetings arranged for and organized, public hearings and bills monitored and statements prepared and read before public bodies and at news conferences, letters to newspapers written and alliances with friendly groups cemented. "Social movement" means "organization," and that means creating and maintaining an organization, and lots of work.

Besides overcoming recruitment problems stemming from free rider tendencies and opportunity costs, and direct participation costs stemming from the opposition, a social movement has got to put together the necessary resources for maintaining organization and undertaking collective actions: activists and organizers, facilities, funds, labor and time donated, means of communication, and the like. It is surprising that social movements ever get underway at all, much less survive and even succeed. The approach to social movements that highlights organization in social movements and the resources needed to maintain it effectively is called resource mobilization theory (Zald and McCarthy 1987). The theory puts the emphasis on the capacity to act collectively and the opportunity for successful action, the last two of the four dimensions for explaining movement start and growth. What makes for such a capacity? What provides that opportunity?

Before these two questions are dealt with, the concept of participation needs sharpening (McCarthy and Zald 1987 appendix). For most adherents, the collective goals of a social movement do not and need not become their most important, overriding concern: family, work, school, and routine activities preoccupy most people most of the time. Social movements make only limited demands on the time, funds, energies, and loyalties of all but their activist core. It is useful, therefore, to distinguish levels of participation and of commitment sustained by a different mix of selective incentives, ideological and moral concern, and psychological rewards from involvement. At the core are leaders and activists who constitute the more or less full-time engines of movement organization and activities, and who embody and represent the movement to the public, the news media, and the movement's targets. Unlike institutional leaders elected or appointed to represent a constituency, movement leaders are open to the charge of being self-appointed spokesmen representing only themselves. They are under pressure to visibly and repeatedly demonstrate substantial backing. Providing such support are episodic participants or part-timers, called transitory teams, who turn out at rallies, stuff mailboxes with pamphlets, gather petitions, and participate in other events that activists organize to influence public opinion, pressure public officials, and sustain the enthusiasm and sense of purpose of movement adherents. Beyond the transitory teams who surround the activist core are adherents making modest financial contributions, signing petitions, and creating a favorable climate of opinion for movement goals among neighbors, friends, and associates in routine interactions and conversations. Such adherents have been called the conscience constituency because they are frequently attracted to a social movement by its justness and worthiness, for reasons of conscience, though they themselves may not be the direct beneficiaries of the movement's goals. At the outer edge of a movement are sympathizers who constitute a passive, but generally sympathetic bystander public. Their presence does perhaps no more than incline the authorities and opponents to exercise some restraint when confronting activists and transitory teams.

The conscience constituency is asked to contribute little, perhaps no more than a small sum of money, and their reward is an easy conscience. Moral incentives motivate these participants. A step closer to the core, transitory teams provide unpaid time and labor. They are likely to be composed of people with flexible schedules and relatively few fixed personal obligations, and their reward is the satisfaction gained from joining with like-minded souls to pursue worthy goals, in addition to satisfying their conscience. Thus for transitory teams, opportunity costs are low, and solidarity incentives high. At the core, full-time leaders and activists must still earn a living somehow, and support their families regardless of how strongly they believe in their cause. In addition to moral and solidarity incentives, what motivates them is the hope that successful movement leadership will serve as a springboard to an institutional leadership position. Because more is demanded of them, their selective incentives must be greater than those of transitory teams and the conscience constituency. Thus to speak of "participation" and "participants" in general terms is to obscure kinds of incentive, level of commitment, amount of contribution, and differences in function.

Obstacles Overcome:
Federation, Networks, Bloc Recruitment, and Solidarity

According to resource mobilization theory, the principal means by which obstacles to mobilization for collective action are overcome are several (Oberschall 1973). Movements for the most part do not start from scratch, but grow out of and federate an already existing set of groups and associations that have leaders, members, meeting places, an activity routine, lines of communication, social bonds, shared beliefs, symbols, and a common language, cemented over a period of years. If they do not already occupy prominent positions in some of these groups and associations, the originators of a new movement will reach out to those who do and try to win them over to their cause. These group and association leaders, if won over, will in turn bring in some of their rank and file members and allocate association resources to the goals and purposes which the social movement is pursuing for the benefit of all its constituent groups. This process is called "bloc" recruitment. Examples abound: The Southern Christian Leadership Conference, the principal Southern civil rights organization, grew out of a federation of black Southern Baptist churches under the leadership of Dr. Martin Luther King, Jr. in the late 1950s. The Free Speech Movement of 1964 on the Berkeley campus of the University of California grew out of a coalition of campus political organizations who were all hit by restrictions on campus political activity unilaterally promulgated by the university administration. The National Organization of Women, the major force behind the women's movement started in the late 1960s, grew out of the National and State Commissions on the Status of Women of the preceding years.

"Federation" of preexisting groups ensures much lower start-up and maintenance costs than a social movement built up from scratch (Olson 1968). Free rider tendencies are also more easily checked; when a viable, ongoing group decides to participate in a wider social movement whose concerns and interests overlap with its own, free riders cannot remain anonymous. Moreover group members make direct appeals to group loyalty, and can successfully shame bystanders. Standing and recognition in the group will come to depend on contributions to the group's goals. Thus both positive incentives and negative social sanctions operate in already constituted and cohesive groups at an interpersonal level, favoring participation. Thus obstacles to collective action are overcome.

The small, tightknit building blocs of a federated social movement have a further stimulating effect on participation because of a "multiplier effect" for grievances. Members not only take offense at injuries and injustices they personally suffer, but will react to the experiences of their peers out of fellow feeling and solidarity. For example, eviction of a tenant by the authorities will become widely known and elicits a collective response. A single injury is "multiplied" by the amount of group cohesion and interpersonal bonds to become a collective grievance. By contrast, in an amorphous population with low cohesion, the mass society of social theorists, what happens to particular individuals becomes little known and is met with indifference. Tilly (1978) summarized these ideas into a concise social structural model. A set of people characterized by sharp social boundaries providing common interests and collective identity (catness) and by dense social networks (netness) will have a high capacity for collective action. Catnet, the joint presence of catness and netness, makes for rapid, low cost mobilization. To make sense of the day-to-day operations and long-term strategies of social movements, and of their success and failures, it helps to analyze more concretely what the social organization of a movement is, i.e. social movement organization, or SMO.

Social Movement Organization (SMO)

If one puts a social movement under a microscope, one discerns a much looser structure than in a formal organization. In a formal organization, for example, a school, authority leads from the Board of Education and school superintendent through the principal and teachers to the pupils. There is a daily schedule of activities which is binding and will, by and large, be followed. The principal's office has a plan and schedule of the entire school such that anyone in the school can be located at any time. The number of students, teachers, and other staff is a known quantity. Absentees will be recorded; strangers will be asked about their business. Members interact with each other on the basis of well-defined roles and expectations. Such an organization has a tight structure.

Not so for social movements. Who precisely are members of a movement and how many there are is uncertain. They are frequently part-timers and adherents at the outer edges who fade into the conscience constituency, and sympathizers who participate only episodically in movement collective action. Leaders themselves have no firm position and are challenged by others who wish to replace them and who compete for the same constituency. Leaders who call a meeting or rally often have no idea how many will attend. Some who do attend may not submit to the plan of activity and discipline of the organizers, and there is not much the organizers can do about it. Anyone who wants to can quit anytime. Looseness of structure is a byproduct of voluntary membership in a social movement and of the origin of many movements as a federation of preexisting groups that maintain their identity and autonomy when they cooperate for a common purpose, and that survive even after the social movement itself has disappeared.

The anti-Vietnam War movement in the late 1960s had such a loose structure. Hundreds of local groups and associations, forming alliances and coalitions with each other in particular areas, took part in many kinds of local collective actions: they gathered signatures for petitions, staged sit-ins at local draft boards, sponsored meetings and produced speakers against the war, staged demonstrations against ROTC and military recruiters on campuses, counseled and helped draft resisters, participated in the election campaigns of political candidates favoring U.S. disengagement from Vietnam, and so on. There were some loose threads linking the local groups nonetheless. Despite differences in ideology and tactics, these groups shared common targets (the Washington administration, military and draft agencies, weapons and munitions manufacturers); responded to the same symbols (the peace sign); followed the pronouncements of the most prominent national figures of the movement; read the underground press; and undertook some supralocal, joint collective actions such as the giant antiwar rallies in New York, Washington, and San Francisco called by the national leadership through the Mobilization Committee to End the War in Vietnam (MOBE). MOBE itself was not a membership organization, but a temporary coalition of leaders, celebrities and organizations covering a wide ideological spectrum united in their opposition to the U.S. war in Indochina: pacifist Quakers, peace activists in churches and denominations, Mothers for Peace, Vietnam Veterans Against the War, The Fifth Avenue Peace Parade Committee, draft resisters, the Students for a Democratic Society, small radical-left groups opposed to U.S. imperialism, and many others—people who in other circumstances might have little in common. MOBE applied for parade permits; organized a program and speakers; publicized the time and place of its rallies through press conferences, newspaper advertising, and news stories in the underground press; and distributed information through its constituent organizations. The bulk of antiwar activity was, however, carried on by local, grassroots groups, who were "doing their own thing," under their own steam, with no directives coming from a national leadership. Even had MOBE wanted to, it could not have orchestrated such local campaigns because it lacked a means of identifying and of communicating with most local groups.

Not all social movements are as loosely structured as was the antiwar movement. In the last two decades of the temperance movement, before national prohibition was enacted by constitutional amendment in 1920, the Anti-Saloon League became the leader and organizer of the movement, superseding and sidelining all other organizations such as the Prohibition Party, the Women's Christian Temperance Union, and dozens of other associations that had long been active and loosely allied (Odegard 1928). Under the leadership of the League, the goals of temperance activity became, simply, the election of legislators and public officials favorable to prohibition legislation, the defeat of "wet" candidates and incumbents, and the passage of prohibition legislation. Professional fundraisers and speakers rode the circuit of cooperating Protestant churches and solicited funds through pledges and donations. Professional lobbyists monitored the votes of legislators on every liquor bill, rated them on their pro-dry record, and let the folks back home know the results through League publications, direct mailings, and distribution of information in churches. The movement became a single issue political machine that raised funds, backed "drys" and opposed "wets," and, on election day, delivered the votes. Participation in the movement for the vast majority of adherents was reduced to financial backing of professional organizers and voting for the dry candidates the professionals were backing. It was a formula that proved successful.

Few social movements, however, have such a narrow legislative agenda as their only goal. Loose structure has advantages as well as disadvantages. For example, many local, autonomous groups can recruit by means of face-to-face appeals, always a powerful process in which trust and social bonds are brought into play. And if such groups of core activists are scattered about in several social strata, geographic locations, occupations, and organizations, the social penetration of a social movement will be quite wide. These are advantages. At the same time, a loose movement will speak in many, often contradictory and confused, voices, and will lack the singular thrust and continuity of purpose that a central leadership can provide. Yet divisions and factions within a social movement may create a competitive dynamism preventing inactivity, settling for partial gains and accommodation to opponents.

Recent social movements in the United States have had a loose rather than a tight structure. No single figure led and inspired them, and no one organization dominated them. What, you may ask, about Dr. King? The prominence of the Reverend Dr. Martin Luther King, Jr. in the civil rights movement may be thought to be an exception, yet the record shows that he was persistently challenged from within the black movement itself, was filled with doubts about his leadership role despite his sense of mission, and was often pressured by other activists to overcome his hesitations. It was the pressure of circumstances, the mass media's practice of highlighting a "star" in the news, the Washington administration's search for a prominent moderate black who commanded a large following, and black activists' recognition of the importance of presenting a united front to the public that led Dr. King to assume the role of leader that he filled so well (Raines 1977). There is a stereotypical view of movement members marching in step, in military formation and uniforms, to a common drummer. This view, which derives from news-films and popular histories of the European fascist movements of the 1920s and 1930s, is accurate only after such a movement has been triumphant, suppressed opposition, and instituted a cult of personality. At any rate, social movement organization is dynamic and changing. It loosens and tightens as it adapts to its constituency, confronts its opponents, and makes alliances.

Research suggests that a certain degree of formal structure in a SMO is associated with success (Gamson 1990). Formal structure consists of an internal hierarchy distinguishing officers, committees, rank and file, and members from outer edge adherents, a written charter or constitution setting down its purpose and goals and legitimating a collective decision-making procedure, and centralization of power along a line of authority. Such a minimum formal structure helps organization maintenance and continuity, checks factionalism, and provides a minimum intake of funds, a collective identity, and selective incentives for members and adherents. Other research (Gerlach and Hine 1970) shows that under some circumstances small grassroots groups with a segmented, reticulated, polycephalous structure, that is, a loose alliance of small, face to face, autonomous, highly cohesive groups with weak ties to each other and lacking an overarching leadership, have a surprising capacity of rooting in new social milieus, recruiting members by interpersonal appeals, providing solidarity incentives, and escaping detection of social control agents. This structure was typical of the 1950s and 60s Pentecostal movement that gained many adherents at that time, and also of the late 1960s black nationalist movement.

These findings are not contradictory. It may well be that a social movement starts with small face-to-face groups, loosely linked, but those that survive eventually develop a minimal formal structure. Evidence on change and adaptation by SMOs is provided in McCarthy's (Zald and McCarthy 1987, chap. 2) study of Pro-Life and Pro-Choice groups contending over abortion in the early 1980s. Pro-Choice had started in the late 1960s with a very active, expanding grassroots constituency, very much like the loose structure described by Gerlach and Hine (1970). After the 1973 Supreme Court victory, resting on its successes, the membership became less active, but remained linked up in a formal organization of state and local chapters run by paid staff very much like a lobby or interest group and kept in touch with its constituency principally through direct mail and annual membership renewals. Such an SMO structure resembles the minimum formal organization described by Gamson (1990).

The Pro-Life countermovement, on the other hand, was in an active expansion phase, determined to challenge Pro-Choice and to overturn court decisions, cut federal and state funding of abortion, and protest and picket at clinics and hospitals providing abortion services. Its SMO structure bore the traits highlighted by Gerlach and Hine (1970) for grassroots activism. A dynamic approach to SMOs will in time allow a more sophisticated organizational analysis of challengers and targets, movements and countermovements.

Social changes in the wider society also present opportunities for would-be movement leaders to innovate. One such innovation, the "professional" social movement, was identified and studied by Zald and McCarthy (1987, appendix). They contrast it to the "classic" social movement, for example, the 1930s labor movement in America, with a well-defined social category or class, with shared identity and common interests (high on catness), and organizers to promote its interests and rights. The leaders and activists are drawn principally from within the social category, which is also the principal beneficiary should success be achieved. The membership provides the manpower, finance, and other resources for collective action. Leaders are in touch with the base and express grassroots sentiments and aspirations accurately and effectively. Such linkages make the movement credible to bystanders, targets, the authorities and public opinion. The movement is member driven: leaders are agents for member demands.

Recent changes in opportunities for third-party funding for issues and causes, in mass media agenda setting in public affairs, and in the technology of organization have made possible, according to Zald and McCarthy, a new form of SMO, the professional social movement, for example, the antipoverty movement of the 1960s, and other social reform and humanitarian movements that differ from classic movements. Leaders and activists are reform entrepreneurs pursuing a professional career in reform causes. They are not from the beneficiary group. Most funding comes from outside third-party sources, from churches, business corporations, government agencies, foundations; for example, VISTA volunteers and young attorneys providing legal services for the poor, funded by government antipoverty budgets and agencies. The leaders do manage to organize a small, vocal group from the beneficiaries who are paraded before the mass media. Moved by dramatic images of babies dying from hunger and the like, a sympathetic public forms and is fertile ground for mobilization as a conscience constituency accessed by direct-mail appeals and newsletters. Thus a supply-side driven professional social movement emerges, headed by moral entrepreneurs divorced from a genuine grassroots constituency.

Illustrations certainly abound, and my students and I have come across the professional social movement syndrome in the course of our research. Yet one should not be cynical about it, nor exaggerate its importance and novelty. It is best to think of many social movements as having some aspects of the professional social movement syndrome. Max Weber (1958) noted it in his studies of religious movements and coined the phrase "routinization of charisma" to capture is essence. Weber's associate Robert Michels (1959) described with great insight the conservative, oligarchic, and bureaucratic tendencies of large scale organizations such as the German socialist trade union and political movement, when leadership became professionalized, undemocratic, and out of touch with the membership. Bear in mind also that liberal humanitarian movements do not have a monopoly on the supply-side driven, professional social movement syndrome. I provide examples of it in this book from my research on the New Christian Right and ultraconservative political entrepreneurs. It is useful to think in dynamic terms of professional social movements and supply-side forces in movement start-up, as Zald and McCarthy pointed out, as well as in movement consolidation and decline when a measure of success and institutionalization have been achieved, as Weber and Michels noted.

Success and Failure

What matters at bottom to challengers and targets, to bystander publics and governments, to movement leaders and rank and file is success or failure. Yet what does "success" mean? How do we recognize it? A short challenge as such is not evidence of success, nor of failure; movements cease to exist because their goals have been realized, or on the contrary because their goals were not attained and their supporters have become discouraged. Success is best thought of as a process of attainment rather than as a clearly defined terminal state. Complex goals such as equality for blacks and for women are not attained when a particular bill is enacted into law. Success is an institutional process whereby established organizations, public opinion and government recognize the social movement as the legitimate voice of a constituency, and assume an ever-greater share of the burden of achieving movement goals. In this process of institutionalization, the social movement itself loses its movement character and becomes a pressure group, absorbed into a political party, and allied to a public agency representing the interests of the social movement's constituency. Gamson (1990) refers to the two dimensions of success as gaining acceptance and gaining new achievements.[8]

The American labor movement has undergone such a transition into labor unions and the overarching federation of the AFL-CIO in the 1930s and 1940s. These have a recognized place in American politics and in industrial relations; they are also institutionally anchored in labor legislation and in government agencies and public bodies such as the Labor Department that routinely promote labor and union interests. Labor's success was achieved as a result of labor unrest, strike waves, and militant unionization drives in the mid 1930s and the political alliances between the labor movement and the Roosevelt administration (Piven and Cloward 1977). To sum it up then, when individuals and groups whose interests are at first ignored organize collectively and force their targets and public decision-makers to recognize their concerns and to commit institutional resources to implement movement goals, the cost of obtaining the collective goods is shifted from movement participants to the polity at large. To the extent that this occurs and movement goals are achieved, the movement can be said to be successful.

Success may not last forever. The decline of the once powerful organized labor in the economy and in U.S. politics is a telling example. Contemporary society changes rapidly, or as Schumpeter put it, capitalism is a process of creative destruction. Structural economic shifts undermine entire industrial sectors and the livelihood of millions. Economic opportunities attract millions of migrants and immigrants into an unfamiliar setting where old timers exclude them from neighborhoods, schools, and public services and facilities. Scientific and technological innovations create entirely new industries, such as nuclear reactors and chemicals with toxic components, byproducts, and waste that threaten the health and life of workers and residents. Better health and nutrition extends the life span of millions and creates new life stages, the retired elderly who still have a life expectancy of some fifteen years, and among them, the very old impaired who have to be cared for. New ideologies and values challenge the conventional wisdom and long standing norms and life-styles. New diseases, like AIDS, raise ethical and moral dilemmas. Established institutions and problem-solving routines are ill prepared to handle new issues and discontent surfacing with such innovations. There exist ample occasions and opportunities for new social movements that take up the cause and problems of those excluded from institutions and mainstream politics. Social movements and collective action will not vanish from public life, not in the foreseeable future at any rate, though they may suffer temporary eclipse.

Unfinished Business and New Directions

Though the study of social movements has grown tremendously in the past twenty-five years, and many empirical studies and theories have enriched the field, there exist some controversies and confusion, and interesting new directions to pursue. In this concluding section I will briefly deal with a few of them.

One controversy goes to the heart of fundamental assumptions in social science. The intellectual tradition that has inspired my work on social movements, social conflict, and collective action is rooted in the Scottish Enlightenment and political economy that developed from it (Oberschall 1973, chap. 1). In recent years, political economy, fortified by neoclassical economics, has burst the bounds of specialized economic analysis to encompass a wide slice of human behavior and social institutions, including social movements. The revived and more sophisticated political economy is known by various names in a number of academic disciplines: the new institutional economics, transaction cost analysis, public choice, rational choice. One of its central assumptions is "methodological individualism," or the notion that thought, action, and choice are anchored in the ultimate reality of individual human beings. From this ultimate reality at the individual (or micro) level, this method seeks to explain not just individual beliefs, behavior, choices, and transactions, but norms, values, property rights, ideologies, markets, organizations, the state, social institutions, that is, systems of social action and belief at a higher level of abstraction referred to as the meso- or group level, and the macro- or societal level of analysis (Coleman 1990).

For some purposes a meso- or macrolevel analysis will be sufficient and yield interesting results, as in international relations where a country or government is usefully assumed to be a unitary actor. Still, and especially in social movement theory, many insights and results cannot be gained from group level and structural analysis: the free rider dilemma and how it can be overcome; the formation and dissolution of hostile crowds; the diffusion of protests, and other topics I deal with in this book. Much headway can be made, however, with methodological individualism.

In sociology, this method has been central in the Weberian tradition of social action. In an important methodological statement, Weber (1964, 110) wrote that

> "Verstehen" [meaningful understanding] is ultimately the reason why . . . sociology [*Verstehende Soziologie*] treats the individual and his actions as its basic building bloc, as its "atom" . . . Concepts like the "state," "association," "feudalism" and the like designate for sociology . . . categories for particular types of human interaction; and it is sociology's task to reduce these concepts to "meaningful" action, which means without exception the actions . . . of the partaking individual human beings.

A common confusion is that this method implies endorsing individualism as the highest value over and above social welfare, public goods, and selfless devotion to a higher ideal. Weber (1956, 12) himself warned against such misunderstanding that he categorically rejected as implying a bias for "individualist values." Commitment to a collective value or good (e.g., a humanitarian cause, patriotism) can be explained by a microlevel analysis of socialization, of action validation of values and beliefs, as I demonstrate in the chapters on the New Christian Right and the European witch-craze.

Another important assumption in the political economy tradition is rationality in decisionmaking, or rational choice (RC). RC assumes that preferences are consistent (if a is preferred to b, and b to c, then a is preferred to c), and that choice maximizes net benefit (benefit minus cost), or at least satisfies some criterion of net benefit, subject to constraints. Because some constraints upon individual choice stem from the norms and institutional environment, I refer to the rationality assumption as the hypothesis that behavior is adaptive and normative.

Several misunderstandings have to be cleared up about the contemporary notion of rationality. It is the rationality of fallible, error-prone human beings, and not that of a mainframe computer. Choices are made despite incomplete and faulty information because information is costly; they are made under uncertainty since nature and other human beings are not fully predictable; and they are made by socialized individuals who are subject to their fellows' influence, not by isolated Robinson Crusoes. One of the intellectual founders of political economy and of RC long ago eloquently described man as a social animal. In the *Theory of Moral Sentiments*, Adam Smith (1809, 169) wrote that

> Were it possible that a human creature could grow up to manhood in some solitary place, without any communication with his own species, he could no more think of his own character, of the propriety or demerit of his sentiments and conduct, of the beauty or deformity of his own face. . . . Bring him into society, and he is immediately provided with the mirror which he wanted before. It is placed in the countenance and behavior of those he lives with . . . it is here that he first views the propriety and impropriety of his own passions, the beauty and deformity of his own mind.

It is this social animal who is the individual of RC and of methodological individualism. A variety of social psychological assumptions, for example, those of reference group theory, are perfectly compatible with this conception of the individual.

Another misunderstanding about RC is that it assumes selfishness and self-interest as the exclusive motivating force of human behavior. The rationality assumption makes no such claim. Rationality refers to means, not ends. The method does, however, assume that the pursuit of altruistic and humanitarian ends can be analyzed with its tools no less than the pursuit of narrow personal advantage in the marketplace and in politics. On this score, once again, Max Weber (1964, 99) was quite explicit about "means-ends" rationality [*zweckrationalität*] as the most useful idealtype for sociological analysis, that is, what one calls a "model" in contemporary terminology.

How does RC and methodological individualism move from the individual to a group and societal analysis, and what difference does it make where one starts? It makes quite a difference, both for theory and for public policy. Rousseau, Marx, and Mao all assumed in their own way that man is essentially cooperative and "good," but has been corrupted by institutions, such as private property and a "feudal mentality." Abolish private property and eradicate the feudal mentality, replace it with a collectivist form of property and mentality, and industry and farming will thrive, the society and people will prosper. They were mistaken, at the cost of millions of lives lost and wasted. One reason for the failure of collectivist institutions is the free rider tendency predicted by RC theory for a large group, and the inevitable resort to coercion to overcome it (Olson 1968). Group and societal institution building that bypass a sound individual level theory are a prescription for disaster.

RC methodology analyzes the conditions under which free rider tendencies are less likely to be important than in the case of large groups, and these turn out to be important in social movement theory, as I have shown in this book in several chapters, especially in "Loosely Structured Collective Action." Olson's (1968) and others' derivation of the free rider tendency makes specific assumptions about the shape of the production function for a collective good. If one assumes an S-shaped production function (which is quite reasonable for activists in a social movement situation), and if one assumes variance of preferences for the collective good, free rider tendencies are not overbearing, though not negligible. Other production functions discussed by Oliver (1984) lead to similar results. Thus a microanalysis using RC provides plausible start-up mechanisms for social movements and identifies the specific conditions under which it becomes problematic.

Methodological individualism can also usefully join the debate on whether particular historic events, such as the outbreak of a revolution, were due to macrolevel structural failure that human intervention could perhaps have delayed but not reverse, or whether such events are due to flawed policy, that is, could have been avoided by wiser leadership. Structural analysis forces a rigid determinism on historic events, whereas methodological individualism confronts the issue of human agency head-on. These two methods lead to very different accounts of historic events, as any reader comparing Schama's (1989) and Skocpol's (1979) account of the causes of the French Revolution will note. For Skocpol (1979, 14), "an adequate understanding of social revolution requires that the analyst take a nonvoluntarist structural perspective on their causes and processes." In application, structuralist theory nevertheless becomes the omniscient writer-theorist with his or her notions about group and class interests of the historic actors and what decisions and choices they had inevitably to make: "I shall not only identify classes and their interests, I shall also investigate the presence or absence . . . of the organizations and resources available to members of classes for waging struggles based upon their interests" (Skocpol 1979: 14).

In contrast a "voluntarist" yields center stage to leaders, activists, and their choices and decisions, constrained as these are by their resources, ideologies, and their opponents' strategies. For Schama (1989, 63):

It needs to be stressed that it was policies—fiscal and political as well as military—that brought the monarchy to its knees . . . historians have been accustomed to tracing the sources of France's financial predicament to the structure of its institutions, rather than to particular decisions taken by government. Heavy emphasis on both institutional and social history at the expense of politics has reinforced the impression of an administration hopelessly trapped inside a system that, some day or other, could be doomed to collapse under the strain of its own contradictions . . . nothing of the sort was true.

Methodological individualism blocks one's temptation to declare what the "true" interests of a group or class are, and whether they are gripped by "false" consciousness. One wonders by what criteria a structuralist decides whether it was in the "interest" of Russian peasants to join or to oppose the Bolsheviks during the Russian revolution. The voluntarist method on the other hand views the peasants' own definitions of their interests and their decisions to join from their own vantage point, at a particular historical moment. That method is what Max Weber called "Verstehen".

In the theory of social movements and collective action, methodological individualism assumes at the microlevel adaptive and normative behavior, participants with varying degrees of commitment (activists, transitory teams, conscience constituents, bystanders . . .), a decision model for participation based on benefits and costs expressed in terms of actor's values, expectation of outcomes, various incentives and costs. At the mesolevel, the method uses concepts like social category, identity, cohesion, networks, SMO, loose structure, factionalism, professional social movement, countermovement, and of course a variety of collective actions. The linkage between micro and meso are dynamic processes such as strategic interaction, free riding, multiplier effect, bloc recruitment, diffusion, production function, coalition formation, and mobilization, discussed in various chapters of this book. At the macrolevel, the method uses concepts like institutionalization, recognition, social control, value system, ideology or thought world, and opportunity for success. The transition from meso- to macrotheory draws on theories of the state, of social conflict, of social change, of culture. A social movement is viewed along the four dimensions of grievance and discontent, values and ideology, capacity to organize (mobilization), and opportunity for success. Each of these dimensions has its three levels of abstraction and analysis. What makes the theory more than just a set of descriptive classifications, conceptual distinctions, and commentary, and gives it a dynamic punch with causal force are the processes and mechanisms linking the micro to the meso, and the meso- to the macrolevel.

An item of unfinished business in the theory is the second dimension, the part played by values, beliefs, expectations, moral sentiments, ideologies, and other elements of culture in an overall explanation. We need to have more sophisticated ideas about the rise and eclipse of public issues, the character of public debate, the motivations of participants, how ideologies confer identity. Here is where the theory of collective action is fortified by and interlinks with theories of culture, of ideology, of communications.

This dimension comes up in many guises. Why do some people dedicate themselves to causes from which they do not personally benefit (Mansbridge 1990)? How do some issues capture public attention and take off while at other times they are ignored or opposed (Downs 1972)? Are there basic value shifts that explain changing motivations and commitment to issues (Inglehart 1990)? Is there an alternating ebb and flow of public participation and cultivating one's private garden (Hirschman 1982)? How are issues contended for in public political arenas and in the social movement sector (Tarrow 1989)? How do moral issues and values get framed for persuasive communication to adherents and bystanders (Snow et al. 1986)? How do the news media, challengers, and targets produce meaningful debate and contention on public issues (Gamson and Modigliani 1989)? Indeed, what is culture, what is a belief system, and how does one encode and decode shared meanings through language, symbols, and ritual (Leach 1976; Geertz 1973)?

In two chapters of this book, on the New Christian Right and on the European witch craze, I describe, argue, and apply my views on some of these important topics. I approach them as I do the other dimensions of collective action theory with the assumptions and insights of methodological individualism. Readers will have to judge for themselves whether the effort was successful.

Notes

1. At the end of this book is a glossary of frequently used terms and concepts.
2. Translated as *The Crowd*. The French word "foules" has the double meaning of "masses" and "crowds."
3. The term *law* was used at that time to suggest an analogy with the laws of the physical sciences. Nowadays social scientists would refer to Le Bon's principles as "hypotheses."
4. When fairness norms break down, for example, in the face of mortal danger in a crowded, confined place, the result is a panic (Brown 1965, 740). When fairness norms do not exist at all, waiting lines at ticket and check-in counters are a pushing and shoving match with much display of ill-temper and aggression.
5. The combination of the adaptive and of the normative behavior hypothesis is what I mean by the term "rational choice," in the contemporary sense of "limited" rationality. Conformity to rules and norms is adaptive behavior and does not contradict limited rationality, as Max Weber (1956, 22) noted,

   > The stability of . . . custom rests essentially on the fact that if one ignores it, one acts in a nonadaptive manner, that is, one has to put up with . . . inconveniences and disadvantages, as long as the majority in one's milieu expects the custom to last and conforms to it.

6. Tilly (1985) term these traditions and conventions "repertoires" of collective action.
7. Turner and Killian (1987) call these "emergent norms."
8. In an earlier book, I referred to gaining acceptance as "recognition" (Oberschall 1973). Tilly (1978) refers to the same process as gaining access to the polity.

2

Theories of Social Conflict

Conflict results from purposeful interaction among two or more parties in a competitive setting. It refers to overt behavior rather than to potential for action and to subjective states. According to Deutsch (1973, 10), "competition implies an opposition in the goals of . . . interdependent parties such that the probability of goal attainment for one decreases as the probability for the other increases." Whereas a competitive situation might exist without any awareness of it by the parties concerned, according to Boulding (1963, 5) conflict "is a situation of competition in which the parties are *aware* of the incompatibility of potential future positions and in which each party *wishes* to occupy a position that is incompatible with the wishes of the other."

"Social" conflict refers to conflict in which the parties are an aggregate of individuals, such as groups, organizations, communities, and crowds, rather than single individuals, as in role conflict. Group conflict is used as a synonym of social conflict in this chapter. Finally, social conflict refers in common usage to interaction in which the means chosen by the parties in pursuit of their goals are likely to inflict damage, harm or injury, but not necessarily in every case. With this small proviso, Coser's definition of social conflict conveys its meaning very well (1967, 232): "social conflict [is] a struggle over values or claims to status, power, and scarce resources, in which the aims of the conflict groups are not only to gain the desired values, but also to neutralize, injure, or eliminate rivals." Social conflict encompasses a broad range of social phenomena: class, racial, religious, and communal conflicts; riots, rebellions, revolutions;

strikes and civil disorders; marches, demonstrations, protest gatherings, and the like.

The Scope of Conflict Theories

Just what do theories of social conflict seek to explain? Any comprehensive theory of social conflict should encompass the following topics:

1. The structural sources of social conflict, in particular structures of domination that make struggles over values and scarce resources likely. At this stage, a theory of social conflict will rely heavily on stratification, social change, and macrosociological theories. These theories will identify the most important explanatory variables in conflict theories.

2. Conflict-group formation and the mobilization for collective action of challenging groups and their targets: for this topic, theories of collective action, recruitment, participation, commitment, and internal structure will be especially useful.

3. The dynamics of conflict: processes of interaction between conflict groups; the forms of conflict; its magnitude, scope, and duration; escalation and de-escalation; conflict regulation and resolution; the consequences of conflict outcomes for the contending groups and the larger society. These are the most important dependent variables of social conflict theories.

This review is mainly concerned with describing and evaluating the two principal approaches to conflict theory: the breakdown-deprivation approach and the solidarity-mobilization approach. The older classics and the well-known theories based on them like Dahrendorf (1959) and Coser (1956) are not reviewed here, because their contributions have become part of the shared fund of sociological knowledge. However, I indicate in a short example how the classics might be more tightly incorporated into current conflict theories.[1]

This review also omits evaluations of the conflict perspective in sociological thinking, because a perspective or orientation is not a theory of conflict defined by the three broad topics. For instance, Randall Collins' *Conflict Sociology: Towards an Explanatory Science* (1975), does not contain the statement of a theory of social conflict. It is rather a work of general sociology written from a conflict perspective. Collins writes little about overt conflict, such as strikes, rebellion, and collective violence. He does not discuss the forms of conflict, the formation of conflict groups, mobilization, recruitment, and leadership, nor outcomes and conflict resolution. And he deals only briefly with major and common group conflicts such as ethnic, racial, and communal conflicts. He seeks instead to explain how structures of domination based on social class, gender, and age differences have come about and how they are maintained. These structures of domination have a potential for conflict, but the link between these structures and overt conflict is not explicitly spelled out.

However, I am concerned with two issues of theory construction that are particularly salient in theorizing about social conflict. The first is levels of analysis. Some theorists treat a conflict group as a single collective actor. Their theories consist of statements about groups and the relations between groups. Other theorists start with individual behavior as the unit of theorizing, and derive group behavior from a summation of individual tendencies and behaviors. Still other theorists handle the problem of level in more complicated ways. Does the mode of theorizing lead to different insights and different kinds of conflict theory?

The second issue is the use of different assumptions about human behavior. Some theorists utilize the rational choice model derived from economic analysis; others incorporate complex psychological and social psychological assumptions into models. Are these approaches mutually exclusive or complementary? Do their conclusions differ?

Theory, Method, and the Classics: A Short Example

Both of these issues in theory construction, as well as the incorporation of knowledge derived from the classics into current theory, are best discussed in the context of a short example.

Two frequently noted empirical generalizations analyzed at length by Coser concern the internal structure of conflict groups: "conflict with another group leads to . . . increased cohesion of the group," and "close-knit groups in which there exists a high frequency of interaction and high personality involvement of members have a tendency to suppress conflict" (Coser 1956, 95, 152). Granted that conflict with outgroups creates cohesion and internal conformity within a group, and granted also that these are common consequences of conflict, how can such knowledge about internal group structure contribute to explanations about the process of conflict and the forms it is likely to take?

One important set of consequences that appears to follow from Coser's propositions was described in Janis' (1972) work on "groupthink." It refers to a concurrence-seeking tendency that results in a deterioration of mental efficiency, reality testing, and moral judgment. Janis' idea can be summarized by his proposition that "the more amiability and esprit de corps among members of a policy-making group, the greater is the danger that independent critical thinking will be replaced by a groupthink, which is likely to result in irrational and dehumanizing actions against outgroups" (1972, 13). Groupthink fosters overoptimism, lack of vigilance, and sloganistic thinking about the immorality of outgroups.

If conflict leads to cohesion and concurrence-seeking tendencies resulting in groupthink within the leadership circle of conflict groups, the leadership will underestimate the cost of further conflict and overestimate the chances of success (overoptimism, risk-taking), and will also be more ready to resort to coercive means (belief in the group's superior morality, taking dehumanizing actions against outgroups, ignoring the moral consequences of actions). If leadership in both conflict groups undertakes such actions, escalation of the conflict will result. Thus, supplementing Coser's proposition with Janis' theory allows one to link changes in the internal structure of conflict groups with the mode of conflict they are likely to choose and the form that conflict is likely to take. Cohesion, under some circumstances, lowers the quality of leadership decision making in such a way that destructive strategies will be chosen by both sides, which in turn will escalate the conflict.

The foregoing example merits two methodological comments. The first concerns the inclusion of social psychological processes into rational choice models in conflict studies. Janis' groupthink proposition specifies the conditions under which rational decision makers collectively arrive at "bad," "irrational" decisions as a result of distortions in their perceptions and their critical faculties. Rational decision makers weigh the benefits and costs of alternative courses of action, and choose the alternative that maximizes expected net benefits, that is, the excess of benefit over cost. Janis' proposition suggests that groupthink results in underestimation of the costs of coercive action and in overoptimism about its chances of success. Thus expected benefits of coercive actions are overestimated.

Rather than sacrifice the rational choice model of decision making in conflict situations, Janis' work suggests the manner in which psychological and social psychological variables might improve it. The framework of the rational choice model can be kept. It is the actors' calculation of costs, benefits, and chances of success and failure that are changed under various circumstances. Decision makers who make "bad" decisions seek to maximize expected net benefits, as others do. It is the information and perceptions utilized in the calculation of costs and benefits that become faulty under groupthink conditions and lead to "unrealistic" decisions.

The second lesson of the groupthink example for conflict analysis concerns the relationship between the individual and the aggregate level of analysis. For Janis, each individual participant in the policymaking leadership group is a rational, moral individual. As individuals they are "the best and the brightest," to use Halberstam's felicitous term. Yet the output of the group is not simply an average of these individual tendencies. Groups have emergent properties, here the concurrence-seeking tendencies of the cohesive group, that fundamentally alter the group's collective output. Theories of group conflict will have to pay special attention to group structure and the emergent properties of group. Group behavior should not simply be assumed to be analogous to individual behavior. Social psychological knowledge will help locate emergent group properties for conflict theorists.

Theory and Method: Does Mobilization Theory Make a Difference?

A further issue in conflict theory is whether it is possible to account for forms of conflict directly from an analysis of structures of domination, without recourse to mobilization and collective action theories. Rather than discussing the issue in the abstract, I evaluate *Agrarian Revolution* (Paige 1975) from this perspective, because it is an ambitious and systematic effort to link structures of domination in agriculture export sectors with forms of conflict. The variables and hypotheses are clearly stated. An empirical test of the theory based on 135 agriculture export factors in seventy underdeveloped countries and colonies in the period 1984–1970 is provided and is supplemented with three case studies. For Paige, conflict is the product of interaction: it is the interaction of two groups, and their characteristics, that determines the forms of conflict. Mobilization and collective action are not treated by Paige as

distinct processes analyzed in their own right. Rather, they deterministically follow from the structures of domination. In his approach to
theorizing, Paige employs a series of dichotomies. Group behavior and
the behavior of the typical member of the group are essentially similar.
This mode of theorizing allows for great clarity of exposition at the price
of overlooking the diversity of rural economies, social classes, and ethnic
groups.

The most fully developed part of Paige's theory is on structures of
domination. The structure of domination in agriculture export economies
is determined, according to Paige, by the conjunction of the principal
sources of income of ordinary cultivators and of rural elites. The commercial hacienda economy is characterized by cultivators and elites both
deriving their incomes from land. Because of low technology and pro-
ductivity, and because of a competitive disadvantage in world markets,
more land must be acquired by either group for increased incomes. Thus
the hacienda economy tends to provoke bitter conflicts over land. The
form such conflict usually takes is the agrarian revolt. When cultivators
derive their income from wages and rural elites from ownership of land,
which is typical of migratory labor estates or of a sharecropping economy, the power of rural elites rests on political control that enables them
to maintain a hold over land, capital and labor. Conflict will then
ultimately center on control of the political system and will take on
revolutionary forms, of either the socialist or nationalist variety.

When rural elites derive their income primarily from the control of
capital (i.e., exports, marketing, machinery, storage, and transportation),
and cultivators derive their income from land, a situation characteristic
of smallholdings export agriculture, Paige hypothesizes that commodity
movements for limiting the power of middlemen will take place. The
plantation economy, the remaining possibility, consists of elites deriving
income from capital, and cultivators earning wages. It gives rise to
conflicts over wage levels within the context of labor movements. In sum
then, when rural elites earn their living from control of land, conflict is
more intense and aims at the overthrow of the structure of domination.
When rural elites derive their living from capital, conflict is over a greater
share of the economic pie and has a reformist rather than a revolutionary
character.

Paige's theory further specifies the variables and processes that lead
from the structure of domination (income sources) to overt conflict by

way of economic behavior and political behavior (1975, 21ff.). For instance, cultivators who derive their income from wages, he argues, will tend to develop cooperative relations among themselves, will be independent of elites, and will accept a risk strategy (e.g., willingness to strike), which in turn will lead to radical, solidary, collective political action. Cultivators dependent on land for their income, on the other hand, will tend to be conservative and low on solidarity, and will engage in individual acts of opposition. Paige shortcircuits a theory of mobilization and collective action when he derives political behavior (ideology, solidarity, collective action) deterministically from the structure of domination and the economic behaviors and outlooks associated with it.

By doing so, Paige's theory creates internal contradictions and inconsistencies that can be overcome only by an ad hoc appeal to variables that are exogenous to his theory. It follows from Paige's own theory that in the commercial hacienda elites will have strong political control, and that the cultivator's opposition will be conservative, individualist, and weak on solidarity, yet "periodic uprisings have been a constant part of manorial economies" (Paige 1975, 42). To explain the inconsistency between theory and data, Paige notes that "peasant rebellions in commercial hacienda systems depend on the weakening of the repressive power of the landed aristocracy, the introduction of organizational strength from outside the peasant community, or both" (1975, 42). These usually result from internal division within the landed elite, loss of military power due to a major war, and organizing drives by urban militants. It is precisely these kinds of variables that theories of mobilization and of collective action incorporate more systematically into an explanatory scheme.

One also suspects that in the revolutionary movements based on socialist and communist ideologies, which Paige finds characteristic of sharecropping systems, mobilizing groups from outside the agriculture export sector typically play an important part, and that the same is true for nationalist opposition movements in colonial-landed estates based on migratory labor. Indeed, Paige recognizes this when he writes that "the explanation of these revolts [in migratory labor systems], like the explanation of revolts in commercial hacienda systems, must depend on the introduction of political organizations from outside the workers' community" (1975, 68).

Structures of domination in the agriculture export sector in many parts of the world existed for a long time prior to the post World War II period

Paige studied. One seriously doubts, however, that for the 1920s and 1930s he would have found, as he did for the 1950s and 1960s, that "most of the events in the study population where revolutionary, socialist, or nationalist, which altogether accounted for 70 percent of the total" (1975, 101). The loosening social control in overseas empires after World War II and the much greater likelihood of outside support, both domestic and international, for rural movements, must have been decisive.

In conclusion, what can be learned from an analysis that relies on structures of domination as the cornerstone of conflict theory? First, it shows the usefulness of macrosociological views of stratification and of social change for understanding the potential for conflict in a social structure, who the likely antagonists will be, and their relative power. Second, it signals to conflict theorists that to pass directly from structures of domination to group conflict, overlooking mobilization and collective action, makes the explanation of many of the dimensions of conflict (e.g., magnitude, duration, timing, forms, outcomes) difficult.

Breakdown and Solidarity

With these preliminary remarks on theory construction completed, a comparison and evaluation of the two principal approaches to conflict theory can be undertaken. What accounts for the production of conflict and the formation of conflict groups? The most common view in sociology has been the "breakdown" theory. Its social psychological foundation rests on grievance-frustration notion.[2]

Briefly stated, breakdown theory points to the dissolution of traditional social formations and communal solidarities as a result of rapid social change. Social disorganization, demographic pressures, and ecological imbalance lead to the accumulation of strains, frustrations, insecurity, and grievances, and the resulting pressure cooker has a tendency to explode in collective violence and civil disorders. After a time, processes of integration take the upper hand. Individuals become incorporated into new social formations and associations. Strain decreases, and grievances are pursued through regular institutional channels.

For breakdown theorists a sharp discontinuity exists between collective violence and more institutionalized forms of social conflict. The two forms of conflict require different conceptualization and theory. Breakdown theorists stress the similarity between the roots of collective violence and other forms of deviant and anomic behavior such as crime, mental illness, and suicide. They emphasize the marginality of participants in collective violence. They expect conflict to locate in growing industrial centers where anomie prevails, or else in weakened, disorganized rural communities. Frequently, they see collective violence as irrational tension release rather than as purposeful collective action to defend or obtain collective goods (Tilly et al. 1975, 4 ff.).

In recent years, breakdown theories have been increasingly criticized on theoretical as well as empirical grounds, and a rival solidarity theory has taken shape (Tilly et al. 1975). Solidarity theorists maintain that uprooted masses do not account for most collective protest. Rather they stress that conditions that lead to violent protest are essentially the same as those that produce other forms of collective action; view all forms of collective action, including violent ones, as essentially purposeful, rational pursuits or defenses of collective interests; and note that violence is most frequently initiated and perpetrated by the agents of social control. Solidarity theorists do not minimize the effects of large-scale social changes upon the incidence and forms of social conflict, but maintain that their impact on social conflict does not derive primarily from the production of tensions and grievances. Grievances and disaffection are a fairly permanent and recurring feature of the historical landscape.[3] Social, economic, and political change act indirectly upon incidence and forms of conflict by changing the mobilization potential of various social formations, by changing the social milieu and ecological locus of conflict, and by changing the social control capabilities of the authorities.

Still another line of criticism of breakdown theories challenges its central assertion that rapid social change destroys traditional social formations and communal solidarities. In a book entitled *Internal Colonialism: The Celtic Fringe in British National Development, 1536–1966*, Hechter (1975) deals with the persistence of ethnic domination and stratification in the British Isles over four centuries despite the alleged leveling and integrating effects of the spread of education and industry, administrative centralization, increased communications, labor mobility, the expansion of citizenship rights, and policies of linguistic and religious assimilation. In contrast to diffusionist and evolutionary views, which maintain that these trends undermine the cultural, political, and economic foundations of ethnic solidarities and identifications, Hechter puts forward the notion of "internal colonialism." In this view, the superordinate core group institutionalizes its original advantages over the peripheral ethnic minority in a stratification system based on a cultural division of labor in which the minority's access to certain roles are denied and their share of societal resources limited. The leveling effects expected by diffusion theory are neutralized, because the economic development of the periphery proceeds in a dependent mode, and because control of political power and of the administrative apparatus of the state remains in core hands. In a stratification system based on the observable cultural differences of religion, language, and life-styles, the disadvantaged group keeps reasserting its own culture and ethnic worth despite considerable costs and pressures for assimilation. Thus a system of ethnic stratification in the internal colonialist setting shows remarkable staying power.

For the specific case of the British Isles, Hechter shows that in comparisons of English, Scottish, Welsh, and Northern Irish counties, economic indices show only slight convergence and indicate that long-term regional economic inequalities persisted. Even though the use of the Celtic language has declined largely as a result of the spread of compulsory public education in the English language, differences in religious affiliation between core and periphery have persisted and served to maintain ethnic solidarity and boundaries. Hechter's analysis of election returns also shows that the institutionalization of class-based politics and voting patterns in the English core took hold only partially in the Celtic periphery where status-group voting persisted and Scottish, Welsh, and Irish separatism and nationalism periodically kept erupting.

The persistence and resurgence of ethnic and nationality conflicts in old states and developed industrial societies are troublesome to explain from the vantage point of theories that associate major social conflicts with the dissolution of traditional social bonds.

Relative Deprivation and Breakdown as a Theory of Conflict

Because it is a well-known statement of the breakdown theory of conflict, I turn to a critical examination of Gurr's causal model of civil strife (1968, 1970). Gurr's central hypothesis is that relative deprivation is the basic precondition of civil strife, and that the greater the deprivation, the greater the magnitude of strife. Relative deprivation in turn is produced by a discrepancy between what people think they are entitled to and what they are actually getting. As deprivation increases, frustration and anger will ensue. These psychological states will produce aggression. At the level of aggregates, many aggressive acts and tendencies will produce civil strife.

The relationship between discontent and strife is mediated, however, by a number of intervening conditions either facilitating or inhibiting overt conflict. Just as punishment, actual or threatened, will inhibit individual aggression, increased size and use of social control agents against regime opponents can be expected to have a deterrent and depressing effect on group conflict. Gurr refers to such inhibiting conditions simply as the "coercive potential" of the regime.

A second inhibiting condition, called "institutionalization" refers to the existence of stable, enduring and strong associations and solidarities beyond the primary group level (Gurr 1968, 1105). For Gurr, such groups provide members with an opportunity to obtain what they think they are entitled to. Their presence will thus lower deprivation, or else provide nonviolent means of voicing discontent. In either case, institutionalization will inhibit civil strife.

Other facilitating conditions identified by Gurr are inaccessibility of regime opponents due to poor transportation in rugged terrain, the strength of subversive groups such as the Communist party, external support for the initiators of civil strife, and past levels of strife, which create a climate of opinion tolerant of violent responses to discontent (Gurr 1968, 1106, 1114, 1115). Finally, legitimacy of the regime is assumed to have an inhibiting effect on civil strife.

Many problems of operationalizing and measuring these variables and processes are admitted by Gurr. There are also difficulties of interpreting the result of multivariate analyses based on crossnational, static comparisons. Here I comment only on the theoretical issues raised by Gurr's model as an example of conflict theory. The most completely spelled-out parts of the model are those concerned with relative deprivation and institutionalization. Both together make Gurr's model a variant of the breakdown-frustration explanation of social conflict. The other inhibiting and facilitating variables in the model come from empirical generalizations in past studies of civil strife, or from widely accepted notions about conflict, rather than from theory.

As used by Gurr, the relative deprivation notion lacks explanatory power. Relative deprivation is the discrepancy between what people think they are entitled to, and what they actually get. Relative deprivation, by definition, involves social comparison. One develops notions about what one is entitled to relative to what some other group is getting, or relative to some norm of equity. Gurr's theory is silent on the choice of the comparison group and equity norms. Robbed of this specificity, the relative deprivation notion reduces to little more than that hardship produces discontent and grievances (Salert 1976, chap. 3). That is plausible enough and agrees with common sense, but is not very useful as a theory of the sources of conflict. Did blacks in the United States in the late 1950s feel deprived relative to the progress being made by Africans toward independence, relative to their own progress immediately after the war, or relative to the growing affluence of nonblacks? Did blacks outside the South in the mid-1960s become relatively deprived as a result of the progress being made by Southern blacks, or were their expectations raised and disappointed by the promises of the war on poverty? Gurr's theory does not provide a means of answering these questions.

Gurr's theory is basically psychological and individualist. Group behavior and tendencies are the result of the sum of individual behaviors and tendencies. The deprivation level of a collectivity is the average level of deprivation in the group. This conceptualization treats individuals as independent, isolated behavioral units. But is this realistic? One might argue that if a frustrated and angry individual (say, as a result of police overuse of force) is released in his immediate social milieu, others in it will also become angered, not because they themselves have experienced directly that frustrating experience, but because they sympathize and identify with the victim. Social interaction may well have such "multiplier" effects. Group or collective behavior cannot be deduced from individual behavioral assumptions alone. It must incorporate effects resulting from the relations of individuals in the group, that is, the effects of group structure.

This observation and criticism is not just a sterile controversy among theorists who have different styles of theorizing. Important consequences for theory do follow from it. This can be clarified in an illustration. It has been observed that though considerable progress was being made by blacks in the 1960s on civil rights, the magnitude and frequency of race riots increased, at least until 1969. An explanation based on individualist psychological assumptions would be that racial progress had increased expectations about further progress even faster. Thus relative deprivation had increased, and hence also the magnitude of collective aggression.

But another interpretation based on social interaction and group structure is also possible. The civil rights movements increased cohesion, pride, communication, and shared symbols among blacks. They became a more solidary group. Though the incidence of grievance-producing events against blacks did not substantially change or might even have decreased, those events did that did occur became more visible to them and created a more intense collective reaction, because group cohesion had increased the shared concerns of group members for each other. I know of no direct evidence to decide between these two views, and I certainly do not suggest that either view is by itself a satisfactory explanation of the growing 1960s riot wave. What the illustration indicates is that neglect of group structure in conflict theory will lead to quite a different perspective on conflict and different explanations of it.

Even some of the policy implications differ. The rising expectation view leads to despair with ever satisfying minorities' aspirations. It might also lead to the view that in order to reduce expectations, racial progress will have to be slowed, which will ultimately reduce expectations more rapidly than accomplishments, and thus also lower relative deprivation. The other model views increased conflict as a likely by product of the greater solidarity, and hence also mobilizing capacity, of the challenging group, and thus as a "normal cost" to pay for racial progress. It does not make sense to slow racial progress in order to decrease overt conflict, nor even to weaken group cohesion, which would increase overt conflict in the short run almost certainly. Raising the costs of rioting by taking firm action against rioters is the only viable policy prescription from this viewpoint, since lower mobilization costs resulting from increased solidarity will have to be counteracted by increasing protest costs.

Critics of the Breakdown-Frustration Approach

Writing from different disciplinary backgrounds and viewpoints, several recent critics of the breakdown-frustration theories of social conflict have shown surprising agreement on what other approach might prove useful. I review three important works in this context.

In *The Rebellious Century, 1930–1930*, the Tillys squarely confront breakdown theories with their findings on civil strife in France, Italy, and

Germany (Tilly et al. 1975). In their view, local, regional, and national struggles for power, and especially state making, account for a high proportion of violent events, rather than immediate responses to misery and economic deprivation. There is no tendency for collective violence to concentrate during or after surges or urban growth. Despite major changes in French social structure, France remained as violent in the twentieth century as it was in the nineteenth. Group violence ordinarily grows out of collective actions that are not necessarily violent, such as festivals, meetings, strikes, and demonstrations. Collective action is not anomic tension release, but purposive and political. Periods of strong repression and firm central government control experience little or no collective violence, because all collective action diminishes and thus also the occasion for collective action becoming violent. Contrary to the breakdown theory, in the short run, rapid social change depresses the level of social conflict, because it weakens many groups' means of mobilization faster than it creates other groups with a high mobilizing capability. A case in point is that of recent urban migrants. They are members of solidary groups in villages and small towns, but remain unorganized for a time in the city milieu.

Urbanization, industrialization, and centralization of government stimulate political conflict, because the authorities make claims on the resources of groups that retain a viable social organization and hence are capable of defense mobilization. Typical collective actions of the earlier nineteenth century in which participants resisted the claims of the state were the food riot, the tax rebellion, and resistance to conscription. The sites of collective action were the natural gathering places of rural folk: markets, church services, festivals. As traditional groups weakened and new solidarities, associations, and trade unions came into being, collective action shifted from the defense of existing rights and resources to a claim for more rights and a greater share of societal resources. The demonstration, strike, and the deliberate assembly in an urban setting became the typical form of collective action.

Other critics of breakdown-frustration theory find it deficient in explaining internal war and rebellion in the contemporary world. Laqueur (1976) is profoundly skeptical of social science theories and generalizations about internal war and collective violence. He is even skeptical of the comparative approach employed in civil strife studies: "The guerilla phenomenon presents endless variety . . . a comparison between China and Vietnam or between Angola and Mozambique, or even between the IRA and Basques may be of value and of interest. Moving further afield in time or space, generalizations can be made only with the greatest of caution" (1976, 386).

Laqueur's *Guerilla: a Historical and Critical Study* (1976) is an exhaustive examination of secondary sources on partisans, guerillas, and wars of national liberation, ranging widely in geography and time. Rich in detail, the book stresses the great diversity of such movements. Laqueur debunks the notion that guerilla war is a recent historical phenomenon, a rare event, and an effective weapon. He holds that recent doctrines of revolutionary warfare are neither original nor able to account for success and failure. According to Laqueur, nationalism, patriotism, and separatist ethnic sentiment have been the most important driving force of guerilla wars. He doubts the usefulness of the breakdown-frustration explanation of popular uprising in traditional societies undergoing rapid change. He questions the assumptions that insurgency is deviant behavior, "as if acceptance of foreign occupations and domestic tyrants is the norm, and the decision to oppose them a deviation" (Laqueur 1976, 386). He notes that a consistent bias of theorists of internal war has been to analyze "the forces which propel societies towards violence rather than those which inhibit it" (1976, 389). He suggests that more attention be paid to incumbents, the targets of the insurgents.

Based on the numerous cases he examines, Laqueur is willing to make some low-key empirical generalizations. The most useful ones for conflict theory are the following:

1. Guerillas tend to locate in inaccessible regions (mountains, jungles, forests, swamps) where they are difficult to find and where their opponent cannot deploy full strength. Moreover, guerilla wars often occur in areas where they have previously occurred, that is, peripheral regions where the hold of governments has been weak. Successful guerillas operate, however, near some centers of population where they are not entirely cut off from the people. These generalizations suggest that the cost of social control for the authorities is an important variable for explaining the likelihood of success.

2. Propaganda and terror have always been essential parts of guerilla warfare. Though a noncombatant fringe has been very helpful to such movements in providing them with money, intelligence, and supplies, the majority of people take a neutral, passive attitude in the struggle between

insurgents and incumbents. Moreover, terror is used to frighten government collaborators. Local people are more often the casualties of guerillas than foreigners and social control agents. In summary, "no guerilla
movement can . . . survive . . . against an overwhelming hostile population. But in the light of historical experience the measure of active
popular support required by guerilla movements need not be exaggerated" (Laqueur 1976, 393-409).

These observations suggest that theories of insurgency inspired by the
imagery of an uprising of large, disaffected masses, as some breakdown-
frustration theories are, provide a mistaken view of participation in and
support for insurgents. Such also is the opinion of Leites and Wolf (1970),
in *Rebellion and Authority* where they contrast the "hearts-and-minds"
approach with a systems approach to insurgency.

The hearts-and-minds approach is a variant of the breakdown-frustration theories of social conflict. In that view deprivation causes rebellion,
and poverty and inequality account for deprivation. Popular attitudes,
sympathies, and support for the rebels then play a decisive role in
ensuring their success or failure. Whichever side will gain the hearts and
minds of the population will win. The hearts and minds approach
represents a demand-pull view of rebellion: the demand for change by
the people is the driving element of rebellion.

Leites and Wolf level several criticisms at the hearts-and-minds approach. Like Laqueur, they do not find evidence in the contemporary
record that rebellion thrives on poverty and inequality of wealth, that a
high proportion of the population is required to sympathize with and
support the rebels, and that the scope of support must be broad and come
from within the rebel region. In contrast, they maintain as Laqueur did,
that only a small proportion of the population need to be active supporters. Nondenunciation to the authorities is the only critical action required
by the majority of people for rebel success. Rebels can create support
and nondenunciation through coercion and the fear of retaliation instead
of conquering people's hearts and minds. The individual caught between
authorities and rebels will engage in short-term, damage-limiting behavior. His expectations about the winning side will largely determine the
side he will collaborate with.

Leites and Wolf state an alternative systems approach to insurgency.
Unlike the heart-and-minds approach, which focuses on the demand for
change on the part of a population, they emphasize the supply side of the

rebellion's growth, that is, the opportunities and costs that determine the supply of rebels and the amount of opposition activity. Rebellion is a system of action. Resource inputs are used to provide output activities by means of a conversion mechanism, the insurgents' organization. Inputs are recruits, information, shelter, and food, usually secured from within the rebel region, and weapons, financing, and publicity, frequently obtained from without. Local inputs are obtained through persuasion and coercion. Caught in the conflict, the population calculates the costs and benefit of different options and chooses a course of action that maximizes short-term gains over losses (Leites and Wolf 1970, chap. 3). For decreasing rebellion, the demand view of insurgency prescribes costly, major reforms that are difficult to implement in a conflict. The authors' cost-push version emphasizes factors that increase the costs of rebel activity: raising rebels' costs of obtaining resources, impeding the conversion of inputs into outputs by reducing the efficiency of rebel organizations, destroying rebel outputs, and blunting the effects of outputs by increasing the capacity to absorb rebel activities.

Leites and Wolf's systems approach and their conceptualization of rebellion as a production process is a promising innovation for conflict theory. Both challenger and target have a resource base from which to mobilize inputs. Assembling resources for inputs in the conflict system are referred to as mobilization in the literature. The output produced by the conversion mechanism is collective action. The mechanism of conversion, the production apparatus of the insurgents, is the organizational structure of the challengers. The conversion process itself will use up resources: organization maintenance is costly. Collective action that results in conflict will itself be destructive of resources. Outcome of the conflict will depend very much on each party's ability to deny or destroy the other's resource base, and to increase the other's cost of mobilization, organization maintenance, and collective action.

The central concern of conflict theory becomes mobilization, organizations, and collective action. Grievances, discontent, and societal breakdown are not ignored insofar as they will affect the resource base of the various parties and their mobilizations, organization and collective action costs. People may harbor intense grievances; yet they may possess few resources and may be vulnerable so that they can provide but negligible inputs to challengers. Others with but mild grievances, yet plentiful resources, might make substantial contributions even if they provide but a fraction of their resources to challengers. Societal breakdown is, to be sure, associated with the generation of discontent, but its main impact on conflict is by way of the costs of mobilization and collective action. Mobilizing the resources of disorganized collectivities is far costlier than doing it within solidary groups, because the latter already possess well-defined leadership and organization that can be enlisted on behalf of the challenger.

Mobilization and Solidarity

What are the salient features of a theory of conflict that thrusts processes of conflict group formation into center stage? As other theories do as well, such a theory starts with an existing structure of domination that identifies the number and type of major collective actors in the system, their collective interests, and the major resources at their command. Mobilization refers to the processes through which individual group members' resources are surrendered, assembled, and committed for obtaining common goals and for defending group interests. Because mobilization is facilitated or impeded by the internal organization and structure of the collectivity, group structure is a major variable in the analysis. The extent and forms of collective action taken in pursuit of collective goals depend on levels of mobilization and on repertoires of collective action.

A widely applicable general model of structures of domination has been put forward by Tilly (1975, 1978). It consists of a government that controls the principal means of coercion in a population, and contending groups that apply their resources for influencing the actions and outputs of government on their behalf. Contenders are of two kinds. Members of the polity, favored in the structure of domination, have routine, low-cost access to the government. Other contenders, called challengers, seek to obtain greater influence and more government outputs, though the costs of challenge are considerable for them. Backed by the government, members of the polity resist the demands of challengers for a greater share of societal resources. A successful challenger modifies the initial structure of domination. When he becomes a member of the polity, the challenger has his interests routinely recognized and shifts some of the costs of obtaining resources onto institutionalized politics. For instance, the civil rights movement in the United States was eventually able to shift the costs of desegregating and integrating public facilities to the Justice Department and other government agencies instead of bearing the cost of direct action itself, as it did in the earlier challenge period.

A major issue in mobilization theory has been identified in Olson's theory of collective action (1968). Challengers frequently seek to obtain a collective good. A collective good is a good that once supplied to one member of the group cannot be withheld from any members of the group, even those who did not contribute to the cost of obtaining it. According to Olson, all members of the collectivity have a common interest in obtaining the collective good, yet they have no common interest in paying for the cost of providing it. This gives rise to the so-called free rider problem in large groups. Each individual knows that his own efforts will have no noticeable effect on the chances of obtaining the collective good; he also knows that he can enjoy the benefits of others' collective efforts even when he has contributed nothing to these efforts himself. The rational individual will thus have a tendency to be a free rider. But if all or most members of the group are free riders, no joint action will be mounted to obtain collective goods in the first place.

Olson suggests that in order to circumvent this dilemma groups seeking collective goods mete out negative sanctions to noncontributors, or else provide selective incentives to contributing members. Selective incentives are individual benefits obtained exclusively by contributing group members. Olson's analysis accords well with the observations of Laqueur and of Leites and Wolf on insurgencies and guerilla movements: only a fraction of the population that might benefit from success of the insurgents' goals will voluntarily support the insurgency; the insurgents typically rely on negative sanctions to secure collaboration of the people. As for the active insurgents themselves, positive selective incentives, for example, future leadership and opportunity for advancement should they be successful, enter this calculation. The notion of selective incentives as a motivating force for leaders and political entrepreneurs who initiate mobilization has been systematically developed within the framework of a rational choice model of collective action (Frohlich et al. 1971). Moreover, insofar as resources are provided to mobilizing groups from without, which frequently occurs, the free rider hurdle is more likely to be overcome (Oberschall 1973, chap. 4).

Nevertheless a mobilization theory based on the utilitarian rational choice model leaves one somewhat unsatisfied, because strong passions, group consciousness, ideological appeal, and appeals to solidarity in group conflict are relegated to secondary place, if they are taken into account at all (Gamson and Fireman 1978). Psychological gratification from participating in a collective effort, or from personal commitment to a cause, must surely have some bearing on recruitment and participation. And one would like to know why certain causes rather than others enlist greater enthusiasm and loyalty, and why some movements are able to provide more satisfaction to joiners than others.

Group structure and solidarity do enter directly into mobilization theory. Mobilization, it will be recalled, refers to the transfer of individual resources to agents or organizations that commit them to group goals. Groups may already be organized in such a way that substantial amounts of individual resources are routinely allocated through existing associations and leadership for group ends (Oberschall 1973, chap. 4). As the opportunity arises, existing leadership and organizations can then rapidly commit mobilized resources to new group goals, and can expand the reach of their mobilizing effort at low costs by making use of existing networks among group members. For groups lacking solidarity, mobilization will cost much more: a mobilizing agency will have to be created; its link to the population will have to be forged; and since organization is not a routine by-product of existing group structure, organization maintenance costs will be considerable.

Tilly (1978 chap. 3) summarized the basic relationship between group structure and mobilization in a particularly useful fashion. Solidary organization is a product of catness and netness, called catnet for short. Catness refers to the strength of a shared identity in a group and to the sharpness of social boundaries that comprise all those who share a common characteristics. Netness refers to the density of networks among group members that link them to each other by means of interpersonal bonds. Solidarity increases with catness. Mobilization in turn can be measured by the amount and kinds of resources in a group multiplied by the probability that these will be delivered for the pursuit of group goals, when needed. The greater the solidarity of the collectivity, the higher the probability of delivery. Collectivities poor in resources may in this view compensate for it by greater catness and solidarity, and may exceed in resources delivered for group goals the mobilized resources of more richly endowed, low solidarity groups.

The notion that solidarity is positively associated with the probability of delivery of individual resources to group ends allows one to enter psychological gratification from group membership into a theory of mobilization based on the rational choice model. In solidary groups, people derive many material and psychological benefits from membership that they cannot provide for themselves individually. Social fellowship, social support, sense of belonging, and other benefits are possible only through the preservation of the solidary group itself. Because there is a visible relationship between individual welfare and group solidarity, people in a high-solidarity group come to value the preservation of their group and of its qualities more than people in low solidarity groups. Consequently, members of high solidarity groups can be expected to allocate more resources for collective ends, including the preservation of its solidary qualities, than members of low-solidarity groups. This would especially be true in situations of conflict where the preservation of the group itself is at stake. And one should not forget that groups high on solidarity, and therefore also on catnet, have a better chance of identifying free riders and pressuring them to conform to group norms. For both these sets of reasons then, the mobilization capability of high-solidarity groups are greater than that of groups low on solidarity.

Though mobilization theory is relatively well developed, much work remains to be done to increase its explanatory power. In particular, it appears useful to differentiate several categories of participants in conflict groups, because their recruitment into a conflict group and their commitment to a collective movement will be generated and sustained by a different mix of selective incentives, psychological gratifications, and ideological appeals. Useful work along these lines has been done by McCarthy and Zald (1973) who distinguish constituents (those who provide resources to a conflict group), adherents (those who value the collective good), bystander publics, and opponents. Constituents may further be divided into a leadership cadre or full-time activists, and transitory teams of part-timers. Finally, all these categories may differ according to the direct benefits they expect to derive from the realization of the conflict group's goals. These distinctions have allowed McCarthy and Zald to identify the important categories of conscience adherents and conscience constituents, that is, participants and supporters who are not direct beneficiaries of the collective good. Strategies of mobilization can then be analyzed from the point of view of the different resources each of these categories contributes to the struggle and the differing selective incentives and appeals necessary to ensure resource delivery. Internal splits and factionalism within conflict groups may also be usefully understood by looking at the internal heterogeneity of conflict groups.

The Forms and Dynamics of Conflict

Mobilization provides a potential for collective action. Conflict however results from collective action, and in particular from the interaction of challenger's and target's collective actions. One party's initial advantage may spur the other party to greater mobilizing efforts and to different strategies and forms of collective action, which in turn may induce changes in the first party's mobilizing efforts, strategies, and collective action. Unfortunately no theory of the dynamics of collective action has yet been formulated in sociological theories of conflict. Recent work by Gamson (1975), however, showed that even a static analysis linking mobilization variables and forms of collective action to outcome variables produces useful empirical generalizations. Much interesting work has also been done on an empirical documentation of the forms and magnitudes of violent conflicts in the contemporary world, on types of conflict, and on linking these to structures of domination and to mobilization variables (Gurr 1969). Tilly's (1978) work on the repertoires of collective action is especially promising for uncovering relationships between mobilization and forms of collective action. Finally there exist fragments of theory on confrontation dynamics (Heirich 1971; Coleman 1957; Deutsch 1973; Oberschall 1978b).

The empirical generalizations in Gamson's *The Strategy of Social Protest* (1975) are based on a sample of fifty-three challenging groups drawn from the American experience between 1800 and 1945. The central dependent variable is the degree of success achieved by challengers. Success is conceptualized along two dimensions: gaining full acceptance, that is, recognition as a member of the polity, and gaining new advantages, that is, achieving the collective goods, objectives, and other goals of the challenge. Among other findings, Gamson shows that challenger's size is positively associated with acceptance but only slightly so with new advantages. Challengers who seek to overthrow a target group have a much lower success rate than challengers who limit themselves to influencing a target. On the other hand, challengers who resort to violence or the threat of it, or to coercive tactics, have somewhat higher success rates than those who use noncoercive means alone. Moreover, there exists a fairly high positive association between success and challenger's use of selective incentives, as opposed to providing members with psychological gratification alone. Finally, variables measuring the internal organization of the challenger are associated in complex, yet systematic ways, with success. Gamson demonstrated that for conflict theory some of the variables identified as important in mobilization theory do indeed have significant observed associations with a focal dependent variable of conflict theory, success of the challenge.

Much quantitative work on collective action is essentially descriptive, classificatory, and crossnational. The crossnational literature on collective violence has grown immense in recent years. Here I only selectively discuss some findings from a representative of this school (Gurr 1969). For a set of countries, over a limited span of years, specific strife events are coded from news sources for number and social categories of participants, their goals and their targets, the human costs of strife, as well as many other variables. Strife events are categorized in various ways along the dimensions of internal organization, popular participation, and objectives. This procedure allows one to distinguish turmoil, conspiracy, and internal war, or some equivalent categories. Finally indices of pervasiveness, duration, and intensity of civil strife are calculated, and a summary index of the magnitude of civil strife is computed. Comparisons are made of these indices and types of conflict with countries grouped by world regions, political regimes, level of economic development and other variables. Such studies often compare and rank nations by magnitude and types of conflict as well. Findings are also used to test models of civil strife.

Aside from differences in quality of data across a variety of countries, a further problem is the particular time period investigated, because many countries experience sharp spurts and declines of collective violence. A study based on the 1950s and early 1960s would certainly draw different conclusions about levels of civil strife in the U.S. than one that included the late 1960s. Whatever time frame one chooses, some countries will have quite different levels of strife in a somewhat different time span.

Nevertheless, cross-national studies provide many insights into conflict. One particularly useful conclusion is expressed in Gurr's statement that "among nations generally, political groups most often mobilize people for strife . . . strife in the more developed and democratic nations is often more organized by political groups than in other nations . . . the implications are that strife is a recurrent facet of the political process and that the effect of economic development and of political democratization is to channel it into the political process rather than to insulate politics from violence" (Gurr 1969, 558). These and similar findings confirm empirically the view of solidarity and mobilization theorists that conflict, whether violent or nonviolent, is firmly embedded in the larger political process.

Specific empirical generalizations from crossnational studies (e.g., the relationship between regime coercive force size and magnitude of civil strife) are sometimes difficult to utilize in conflict theory. The direction of causation may be uncertain. Nations differ on so many variables that even if the direction of causation is obvious, the observed relationship may be spurious. For conflict theory, a study of the magnitude and forms of collective action in relation to the size and utilization of coercive forces within the same polity over an extended period of time would probably yield more interesting information about interaction between challengers and authorities. Indeed, it is the study of collective violence in France over somewhat more than a century that allowed Tilly to uncover the relationships between broad social trends, mobilization variables, social control, and collective action that I described above (Tilly et al. 1975. chap. 2).

In accounting for the forms of collective action, Tilly (1978) introduced the useful concept of repertoires of collective action. Given the range of possible collective action, the observed forms of it are surprisingly limited. For instance

> Most "twentieth century Americans" know how to demonstrate. They know that a group that has a claim to make assembles at a public place, identifies itself and its demands or complaints in a visible way, orients its common action to the persons, property, or symbols of some other group that is seeking to influence. Within those general rules, most Americans know how to carry on several different forms of demonstration: the mass march, the assembly with speech-making, the temporary occupation of premises (Tilly 1978: chap. 5).

Such a repertoire is learned directly in a living political tradition, by participating in such actions or witnessing them in the mass media. Other forms of collective action that were once part of the repertoire of some American groups, such as lynching, have dropped out of it.

Tilly argues that the innovation, diffusion, and incorporation of certain forms of collective action into a group's collective action repertoire can be accounted for by the daily routines of the population, its internal organization, its past experience with prior collective action, patterns of repression, and prevailing standards of right and justice. He shows how the growing acceptance of electoral assemblies and associations in the modern era promoted the demonstration as a form of collective action because the protection enjoyed by electoral assemblies spilled over to other collective actions that were marginally related to elections. Such protection then lowered the mobilization and collective action costs of demonstrations compared to other forms and led to its increased adoption (Tilly 1978, chap. 5).

One of the most promising yet little used ways of studying the dynamics of conflict is the investigation of the diffusion patterns of collective action in physical and social space and over time, for it allows the formulation of fairly precise models subject to empirical testing. A decade of research on urban riots has shown that an atomistic analysis of riots that centers on the characteristics of participants and the character-istics of cities does not have much explanatory power (Spilerman 1970). The surge and decline of collective action occurs within a system that has dynamic properties of its own. Contagion effects, bandwagon effects, strategic interaction among participants, focal points, and pacesetter-fol-lower relationships are important properties of such systems, which merit further study in their own right (Oberschall 1978a, 1978b).

Another area worth more study is escalation and de-escalation. Much collective action is essentially legal and nonviolent, though often threat-ening, to the target. Why is it that in some conflicts there is a convergence on destructive means, whereas in others conciliation is successful? A useful approach to escalation and de-escalation is suggested by Deutsch's social psychological analysis of destructive conflicts (Deutsch 1973).

Destructive conflict becomes independent of its initiating causes and is likely to continue after these have become irrelevant. Expansion of the conflict occurs along the various dimensions of conflict: the number of participants drawn into the conflict; the number of issues at stake; the intensity of hostility towards the other party; the increased reliance on threats and coercion. The tendency to escalate results from the conjunction of three interrelated processes: increased competition, biased perception, and heightened commitment (Deutsch 1973, 52). Communication between the conflicting parties becomes unreliable and impoverished. The competitors become more sensitive to differences and threats than to similarities and conciliatory gestures. Perceptual distortions arise from pressures for self-consistency and social conformity. Heightened group identity and solidarity increase hostility against the competing outgroup. Actions acquire moral connotations such that errors of judgments and mistakes based on lack of information are interpreted as intentional measures designed to harm and as indications of bad faith. As a result the usually accepted norms of conduct and morality that govern one's behavior become suspended. Despite mounting costs, the parties persist in a spiraling effort to destroy each other.

In Coleman's view (1957, 14), an escalating conflict obeys "Gresham's Law of Conflict: the harmful and dangerous elements drive out those which keep the conflict within bounds." This process results from both attitudinal and social polarization, "the division of the community into two socially and attitudinally separate camps, each convinced it is absolutely right" (Coleman 1957, 13). Polarization grows with the formation of new partisan organizations and the emergence of new extremist leaders, while existing leaders and organizations are crosspressured into inaction. The issues under dispute have a tendency to change from specific to general, new issues are added to the original ones, a wider set of people become drawn into the controversies, and disagreements give way to bitter antagonisms. Eventually the conflict may become independent of the initial disagreements and is sustained by the antagonists' goal of winning and of harming each other. Many of these same processes are noted and analyzed in Heirich's (1971) elaborate effort to provide a theory of escalating conflict based on a detailed study of the Free Speech Movement at Berkeley. Although full of insight and very suggestive, the conceptual and theoretical apparatus he develops lacks parsimony and will be difficult to apply.

Can escalation and de-escalation be analyzed from the perspective of rational choice models? A start in this direction has been made by Oberschall (1978b). During confrontation, challenger and target both have three options: abandon the conflict and submit to the other side, make a conciliatory move, or make a coercive move. They choose the alternative that maximizes expected net benefit, that is, benefits minus costs. As in mobilization theory, benefits can be collective goods and selective incentives. Costs are opportunity costs and the costs of collective action itself. This model shows that, under a variety of circumstances, conflict groups persist in continuing highly destructive conflict even in the face of low success chances. Because of the certainty of high penalties, abandoning the conflict can be costly. This conclusion applies to targets as well as to challengers. It suggests that a relatively low cost exit from destructive conflict has to be provided to the protagonist for conflict termination. Frequent demands for amnesty and safe conduct in highly destructive conflicts suggests that the cost-benefit approach to escalation is worth pursuing.

Only a beginning has been made in modeling conflict as a dynamic system. Much work needs to be done to combine the social psychological and rational choice approaches. This task is perhaps even more necessary for a satisfactory theory of conflict dynamics than it is for a theory of mobilization. This difficulty plagues the application of game theory to strategic analysis in realistic settings. Although yielding rich insights, the introduction of psychological concepts, such as trust, commitment, intentions, and promises into game theory leads to a proliferation of variables that hinder precise deductions from formal models, which is their principal advantage (Schelling 1963). Yet these two intellectual traditions will have to be bridged for a realistic theory of conflict dynamics.

Conclusion

The topic of conflict cuts across a range of disciplines, from economics to biology by way of history, political science, sociology, anthropology, and psychology. Conflict has been studied with a number of methodologies and techniques, ranging from detailed case studies to abstract mathematical models. Theories dealing with particular classes of conflict, such as international conflict, strikes, race riots, guerilla war, and ecological competition have received far more attention than a general theory of conflict that might be applicable to all manner of conflict.

Sociological theories of conflict at the present time are a mixture of insights, hypotheses, conceptual analyses, typologies, observed empirical regularities, and some modest attempts at systematic modeling. Social conflict analysis overlaps with existing macrosociological theories about stratification, social change, group formation, and collective action. Insofar as there are clearly formulated and tested theories of the relationship between structures of domination and the origin of conflict, and of the links between group structure, mobilization, and collective action, this knowledge can be and has been readily incorporated into conflict theory.

I have shown above that two competing clusters of sociological thinking and theorizing, referred to as the breakdown-frustration and the mobilization-solidarity approaches, have provided the sociological underpinning for explaining and understanding the forms, incidence, and outcomes of social conflict. Whatever the relative merits of the two approaches, it should be said that neither is yet close to providing a dynamic analysis of conflict as a process. I have also shown in the discussion and in several illustrations that the choice of levels of analysis (group vs. individual) and of fundamental behavior assumptions (rational choice vs. a more complicated psychology of the actor) does make a difference for the interpretation of conflict. At the present time, neither the substantive theoretical controversy nor the two methodological issues are close to being resolved. And that is all to the good, for better theory will probably result from the existence of controversy over conflict theory.

Notes

1. A comprehensive review of the literature on social conflict is provided by Kriesberg (1973). This chapter is primarily concerned with modes of theorizing and theory construction.
2. The social change and modernization literature that incorporates breakdown ideas is immense. Two sophisticated exponents of breakdown views are Huntington (1968) and Smelser (1968).
3. This sentence has been misinterpreted. It most certainly was not intended to mean that grievances are unimportant in the explanation of collective action. My 1973 book *Social Conflict and Social Movements*, has the entire second chapter devoted to the topic. What the context makes clear is that compared to the breakdown theory, the solidarity theory puts less emphasis on grievances as the principal dimension of collective action to be explained (1991 note of the author).

3

Loosely Structured Collective Conflict

Theory

Loosely Structured Collective Action

In this chapter, I present a simple theory of conflict group formation and of loosely structured collective action. In the U.S. during the 1960s, much civil strife and social unrest, as well as nonviolent collective actions, was loosely structured. This was true for the civil rights and black power movement, the student movement and the antiwar movement (Oberschall 1978). Loosely structured collective action refers to collective action that is undertaken by a loose coalition of activists, part timers and sympathizers whose boundaries are ill-defined and shifting, who lack common, central leadership, organization and clear-cut procedures for deciding upon a common course of action.

If one puts broad social movements and revolutions under the microscope, one will often observe a loose structure. Hundreds of groups and organizations—many of them short-lived, spatially scattered and lacking direct communication, a single organization and a common leadership—episodically take part in many different kinds of local collective action: they gather signatures for a petition, stage a sit-in at a local draft board, sponsor meetings and produce speakers in favor of their cause, stage demonstrations against ROTC and military recruiters on campus, counsel and help draft resisters, open coffee houses near military bases and so on. There is some wider common structure nonetheless: despite different ideologies, tactics and commitment to the issues, most adherents to a movement share common targets (the Washington administration and its local agencies), respond to the same symbols (the peace sign), follow the pronouncements of the most prominent national leaders and figures of the movement, and undertake some supralocal, joint collective action, such as the giant antiwar rallies in New York and Washington called by national leaders and coordinating committees (Mobe).

Collective action is often undertaken against the constituted authorities or privileged social strata protected by the authorities. Even if the collective action is legal and nonviolent, it does involve some effort and cost (risk or arrest, injury and perhaps even death) to participants. There is no assurance that collective action will be successful; the authorities may not be persuaded to change, yield to demands, enter into negotiations, or make unilateral concessions.

The goals of collective action are frequently collective goods, such as terminating the draft, stopping an unpopular war, getting legislation passed or repealed, rescinding increased food prices. Thus, free rider tendencies impede collective action (Olson 1968).

The organizations and activists who seek to get collective action underway lack the resources to provide selective incentives to participants—at least tangible, material incentives such as lobbies and associations provide their members. Nor do they have the power to compel participation by coercive means. They may have to induce voluntary participation through moral and ideological appeals and create a sense of fellowship and community (Fireman and Gamson 1979).

The theory assumes a rational view of human action (in the sense of limited rationality). People weigh the benefits and costs of various courses of action and choose the alternative with the highest anticipated benefit. I adopt these assumptions not on philosophic or empirical grounds, but rather for pragmatic reasons. They help develop theories and models that yield useful insights. Models of decision making in a group context, based on benefit and cost of alternative courses of action, help explain some collective behavior episodes that are otherwise puzzling (Brown 1965). It has sometimes been observed that a hostile and riotous crowd that police are unable to disperse melts away when it rains. Assume that members of the crowd have an unequal stake in the collective event: some are merely curious onlookers, others are deeply dedicated to the cause, most are in between. The former are willing to pay only a low price for participation, the latter a high price. Each participant stays as long as anticipated benefit exceeds cost for him or her. Assume further that anticipated cost decreases as a function of the number of participants: people think there is safety in numbers. When it starts to rain, the additional cost of getting wet for those who are experiencing only a small excess of benefit over cost before the rain tips net benefits from slightly positive to negative and they leave to seek shelter. As size diminishes, anticipated costs increase; that, and the additional cost of getting wet, tips net benefits from positive to negative for still other participants. Thus a reverse bandwagon results, until size is so small that even the remaining diehards will quit. The crowd has "melted" away as the result of rain.

A riotous crowd thus scattering does not make sense from the point of view of the conventional wisdom that assumes loss of rational faculties and of moral judgment resulting from the influences of demagogic leaders and of contagion during collective behavior (Le Bon 1960). Critics of the rational view of human action have failed to understand what the assumptions of rationality are and what they imply. The rational view does not deny that most behavior, including collective behavior, is embedded in emotions, sentiments, social norms, conventions and habits, and that the calculations of benefit and cost might be based on faulty and incomplete information, distorted perceptions and erroneous arithmetic. All these, however, do not undermine the usefulness of the method, because rational choice is basically a systematic application of the notion that human behavior tends to be adaptive. One reason that the assumptions of rationality are useful—even when one knows that people do not in their minds perform the calculations assumed in the model—is that habit and normative prescriptions are the cumulative and ever-changing end result of millions of trials and errors, during which the rational-adaptive choices led to higher net benefits than other choices. Nevertheless, much behavior does involve self-conscious calculation of alternative courses of action, and the effect of norms and of social sanctions upon choices can be incorporated into the expression for benefit and cost.

In the theory of loosely structured collective action, two questions need clarification: What accounts for the formation and persistence of small local groups of activists and followers? What accounts for these groups' periodic participation in much larger, supralocal collective action?

At the local level, it is useful to distinguish the more permanent activists from the part time transitory teams they enlist episodically for demonstrations and other collective actions (McCarthy and Zald 1973). The activists usually bear much of the costs of local organization, publicity, and recruitment. Transitory teams contribute mostly to the cost of collective action itself: opportunity cost and the costs associated with arrest and injury. For any participant, assume that the participation decision will be positive if anticipated net benefits from the collective action are greater than zero, as far as he is concerned. Benefits are of two kinds: the value V_i of obtaining the collective good itself, and selective incentives S_i. Costs C_i are organization maintenance costs, other opportunity costs and costs resulting from collective action.[1]

Assume that the value of the collective good, V, is distributed in the population as shown in figure 3.1: there are a small number of individuals who would benefit a great deal from obtaining the collective good; many individuals are indifferent; and there are some for whom it is a collective bad. It is from those with the highest V that the small group of activists is formed. For a small group, Olson (1968) has argued that it will supply itself with at least a certain amount of the collective good. Activists will maintain a rudimentary organization and engage intermittently in some opposition activity. When an opportunity arises for mobilizing a larger following on behalf of an issue or cause, they will step up their organization and recruitment activities. They know that unless they do so, no one else will.

How do activists enlist a larger number of part timers for episodic collective action—for instance, a demonstration? Assume that the probability of success P of the collective action is measured by its public opinion impact, which itself is a function of the number of demonstrators N, as shown in figure 3.2. This production function is assumed S-shaped because a small demonstration is expected to have little impact up to a certain size, and again large numbers beyond a certain size would not make much difference either, whereas in the middle range, additional numbers increase visibility and impact. Further assume that for the i-th participant, the decision to join or not join will depend on whether the anticipated net benefits are greater, equal to, or less than zero; i.e.:

(1) $\Delta P_i V_i + S_i - C_i = 0$ (join)
                                              0 (not join)

where $\Delta P_i = P_i - P_{i-1}$. Though the expected value of the collective action is $P_{i-1} V_i$, a person would benefit to this extent regardless of whether he is a free rider or whether he joins. The marginal contribution a person makes to success, $\Delta P_i V_i$, is what enters his decision to join: it is the difference *his* participation makes to P.

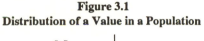

Figure 3.1
Distribution of a Value in a Population

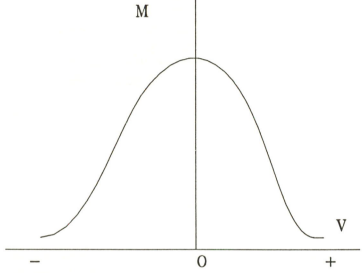

M: number in population
V: value of collective good
N: number of participants
P: probability of success
C: per capita cost of participation
N(i): number of earlier successful collective actions

Finally, assume that the average cost of participation C in the collective action decreases with increasing number of demonstrators, over the range of N here considered, as shown in figure 3.3. Such an assumption is reasonable because all three components of cost decrease with number of participants: organization maintenance benefits with economies of scale; opportunity costs with less effort required per capita with rising numbers; and direct costs with safety in numbers. What then are the dynamics of participation in collective action?

For the activists, who are the first to commit themselves, though ΔP is very small, V is very large, and the high cost C is offset by the high selective incentives S of participation, which include the personal rewards of participating with like-minded others in a cause, the conviction of doing the right thing, the earned esteem of group members. Given a small N, ΔP will increase for each additional recruit, at first slowly, then more rapidly; V will decrease slowly with each new recruit as those with less dedication to the new cause join; C will decrease with N (safety in numbers, ability to withstand ridicule and negative social sanctions, economies of scale); and S also can be expected to decrease somewhat because the more marginal part timers get less social incentives. Thus by expression (1), whether more will join will depend on the net effect of all these functions as they change with N. Under realistic assumptions for the shape of the functions, inequality (1) stays positive over quite a range of N. One can end up with a larger number of participants until eventually both V and ΔP become small, and their product very small, and thus net benefits become zero or negative. A critical mass of protesters is thus formed.

The activists and the authorities try to influence these functions. Activists propagandize in order to raise the average level of V in the population; if they build a cohesive moral community in which new recruits can be readily absorbed, they increase S for joiners; if they get outside support, C is lowered. They also try to convince followers that the authorities and targets will give in to demands (P is high). The authorities, on the other hand, disseminate counterpropaganda about their resolve to hold firm (P is low), and raise the cost curve C by placing restrictions on mobilizing activity and by taking intimidating measures against collective action itself (Kriesberg 1973).

I have no empirical evidence confirming these curves and functions. But we do know that in many collective behavior episodes of the 1960s, a small band of activists triggered collective action by recruiting sizable transitory teams. The process summarized in expression (1) provides a plausible explanation from a rational choice perspective. It can also explain the demobilization of collective action when applied in reverse. The case of protracted conflict is also amenable to a similar analysis (Oberschall 1979; also chapter 4 in this book).

The Diffusion of Collective Action

The second question is what mechanism makes possible much larger collective action on a supralocal, national, or international scale. Many social movements promoting a cause influence public opinion and political leaders by means of mass rallies, huge petitions and demonstrations, for which they need enlist many more than their most active members (Oberschall 1973, 308). For a movement and leaders who do not have access to the usual political channels of interest aggregation, identifying the size of their following by visible means is a necessity if their demands are not to be dismissed. Another purpose of such "identification" moves is to demonstrate to one's supporters one's true strength, sustain their hopes, reinforce their commitment to the cause and provide an occasion for direct communication between top leadership and movement adherents.

Figure 3.2
Success as a Function of Participants:
The Production Function

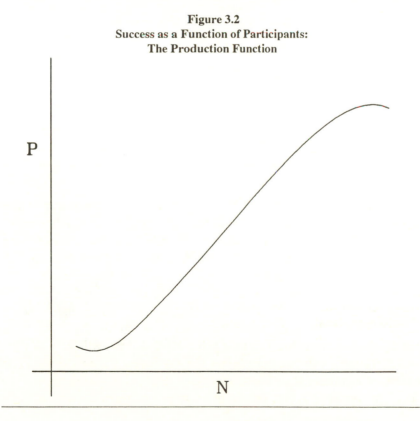

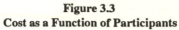

Figure 3.3
Cost as a Function of Participants

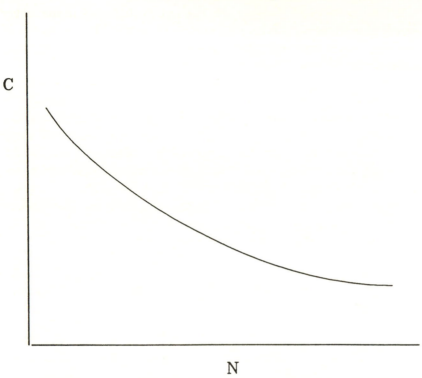

It should not be assumed that large events are the result of the aggregation of large numbers of isolated individuals making independent decisions. Block recruitment tends to be the rule rather than the exception (Oberschall 1973). Olson (1968) pointed out that a federated structure is the surest way of overcoming free rider tendencies in large groups. Large events such as the New York teachers' strike of 1969 is the aggregate result of teachers making collective decisions in particular schools: some schools joined the strike, some remained open. Similarly, in the huge antiwar rallies, many local antiwar groups decided to participate as units and recruited local transitory teams for the larger national event. The existence of intermediate social units in a larger event is not peculiar to social movements. A presidential primary campaign or election is made up of the state campaigns and each state campaign is composed of hundreds of smaller campaigns in given localities.

What incentives do local groups have in participating in the larger event? They know that some collective goods (a Civil Rights Act) will have to be obtained at the federal government level, even though local collective goods (the desegregation of a local public facility) can be gotten with local action. Since obtaining local changes is going to be easier if the national legislation is passed, it is in their interest to participate in national action that will maintain the effectiveness of the national leadership. Highly publicized national events will raise V and P in the local population as well, and make recruitment easier locally. Participation in a large, dramatic event also provides selective incentives. But what else helps overcome free rider tendencies?

The process captured in expression (1) can be applied in this situation as well, with local groups playing the role of building blocks that individuals did earlier. In the literal sense, groups do not have a group mind and do not calculate gains and losses as individuals do. But a cohesive group composed of individuals coordinating their actions may be treated as a single entity like a firm or household. The argument then remains the same. The most dedicated groups (highest on V) will commit themselves to supralocal action even when they anticipate a low turnout. If that is communicated to other somewhat less dedicated groups, they will commit themselves to the national rally; that will increase the expected size of the national demonstration, increase the anticipated probability of success, decrease the per capita cost and put the next groups on a steeper slope of the probability curve, decrease anticipated costs yet further, and so on, until the product of V and Δ P becomes small and no more groups join. Newsletters, traveling speakers, publicity in the news media provide the means for communicating these moods and commitments that are needed to set off the positive bandwagon dynamics according to inequality (1).

These dynamics can also clarify why many collective behavior episodes cluster in space and time: the sit-ins of 1960; the nationwide student strike in the spring of 1970 following the Cambodia invasion and the Kent State shootings; the black riots following the assassination of Dr. Martin Luther King, Jr.; coup d'etat in Asian and Latin American countries in the 1960s; rebellions in Eastern Europe in 1956; and before the age of mass communication, the peasant uprising in 1789 in France and the revolutions of 1848 in Europe. Indeed, the chain reaction of the 1989 democracy movements in Central and Eastern Europe can be explained in this manner. Clustering in space and time can also be observed for skyjackings and some other noncollective actions. No single process can account for the diffusion of such diverse phenomena, though at times the concept of contagion is invoked to explain them. A useful hypothesis is that diffusion occurs partly as a result of reassessment by potential activists and participants and by authorities of the chances of success (P) and the costs of collective action (C), after the outcomes of similar collective action elsewhere becomes known to them.

This is especially true in situations where the initial precipitating event occurs at some focal point in a system, as Paris was in 1848. Since the French Revolution, the eyes of revolutionary and reactionary groups alike were focused on Paris. Ideologies, organizational forms, collective action tactics, the authorities' reaction to opposition there were being discussed and adopted and monitored for cues about what might occur elsewhere. When the Orleanist regime was easily toppled in Paris, revolutions broke out in Vienna, Berlin, Budapest, and many other cities shortly after the news got there. Within Germany itself, Berlin was a secondary focal point. Prussia was the strongest of the German states. When the King of Prussia made concessions and promised reforms after popular disturbances, the other kings and princes in German states followed his lead, even where large disturbances were not taking place. As well, in 1989, when it became clear that the Soviet armies would not intervene, as they did in 1956 and 1968, anticipated C was lowered everywhere in the Central and Eastern European countries.

The mechanism that might explain diffusion is as follows: local collective action is based on expression (1); the P and C curves, which depend in part on the authorities' reaction, are based on the participants' guesses and estimates. When the outcomes of collective action elsewhere similar to what the local activists were considering becomes known, they and the authorities both revise their estimates. If similar actions were successful, the revised curves would look as in figures 3.4 and 3.5 where n (k) is the number of other successful collective actions that have taken place in the system. What makes for diffusion then is that with each additional success, a group of activists for whom expression (1) was slightly negative revises estimates of P upward and of C downward so that expression (1) becomes positive for them and they initiate local collective action. If they, in turn, are successful, and that becomes communicated to other localities where no collective action has yet been undertaken, it will have a stimulating effect by way of further revised P and C curves.

Why do such events often cluster in time and space? Where a focal point exists—that is, a pacesetter country, or group, or campus—collective action there will have a great impact on the P and C curves of all other social units at the same time. Thus, if collective action at the focal point is successful, many activist groups' estimates of net benefits will change to positive at the same time. Successful collective action at successive peripheral points may also set off diffusion, but probably more slowly.

Beyond this, there is an incentive for activists to act quickly. The P and C curve change can have an impact on collective action only if all concerned—activists, potential followers, opponents—recognize the relevance for local events of similar events unfolding elsewhere. Because spatial and temporal proximity is positively correlated with similarity of all sorts, and most people know that, potential followers and opposing authorities frame the local situation in terms of spatial and temporal proximity. Since activists know this, they will act quickly to catch opponents by surprise. Given more time, authorities will take measures to lower P and increase C, such as declaring martial law, or arresting known local activists.

I am not in a position to test systematically the theory of mobilization of loosely structured conflict groups and of the diffusion of collective action described above. Yet the theoretic ideas can be further explicated, and their usefulness and limitations better grasped, by applying them to a real-life conflict. For this purpose, I have chosen the controversies, conflicts and demonstrations on the occasion of the United States-South Africa Davis Cup matches held at Vanderbilt University in Nashville, Tennessee from March 17 to 19, 1978, that my students and I studied in great detail.

Application: The Davis Cup Protests[2]

The Setting

In 1970, Nashville, the capital city of Tennessee, had a metropolitan area population of 700,000 of which about one-fifth was black. As in many southern cities, public facilities were desegregated in the course of the 1960s civil rights struggle, and at the end of the decade the public school system was integrated after a countywide busing plan was ordered by Federal Court. Three well-known black institutions of higher education (Fisk University, Meharry Medical College and Tennessee State University) provide a sizeable black student population and a black middle class of professors and administrators, augmented by teachers and civil servants.

For decades, Vanderbilt University has been an upper middle class white university with a southern reputation, and high standing and influence within Nashville. In the early 1960s, steps were taken to broaden the university's social base, yet the image of Vanderbilt as an elite institution identified with the privileged white upper and upper middle-class has persisted.

In the fall of 1977, the tennis coaches made a persuasive case, based on revenue and prestige, to top administrators for signing a contract with the United States Tennis Association (USTA) for holding the American zone semifinals of the Davis Cup at the university gymnasium. Though South Africa might advance to the semifinals, this was not anticipated as a problem. Late in 1977, South Africa beat Colombia and thus was scheduled to face the United States team in Nashville from March 17 to 19 at Vanderbilt. This fact was not publicized until the Coalition for Human Rights in South Africa, at a New York news conference in late January, demanded that Vanderbilt University and the USTA cancel the tennis matches.

Though the coalition included a number of black groups and committees, the major organization within it was the NAACP. Its executive director, Benjamin Hooks, announced in a national television interview that unless the matches were cancelled, the NAACP would organize the largest U.S. demonstration since the 1960s on the weekend of the Davis Cup play in Nashville. The USTA and Vanderbilt University (VU), however, declined to cancel the matches. Thus a confrontation became inevitable.

In addition to the coalition and the NAACP, a number of Nashville individuals, groups and organizations publicly announced their opposition to this event and sought to persuade the USTA and VU to cancel the matches. The following two months saw a steady stream of meetings, press conferences, television interviews, news releases, out of town speakers, posters, leaflets, pickets and marchers (mainly on the Vanderbilt campus), and numerous other incidents as the major actors in the drama appealed to particular constituencies and to the broader public in support of their various positions.

The stakes were high for all concerned. The Davis Cup issue had the potential of polarizing the city along racial lines. Nashville knew that the Davis Cup controversy would attract national and even some international attention, and wished to maintain the image of a progressive city. For the USTA to withdraw from the matches would eliminate the United States from Davis Cup competition for two years, according to rules the USTA had vigorously sponsored. Given the publicity surrounding Steve Biko's death, the NAACP decided that the Davis Cup would be a favorable occasion for arousing United States public opinion against the inhumanity of the South African apartheid system. The NAACP also aspired to strengthen its leadership position among United States blacks by utilizing an issue that was bound to increase in importance in the coming decade. Finally, Vanderbilt University and its top officers wished to protect their liberal, progressive image without jeopardizing the largest fund-raising drive among alumni and business corporations in the history of the university. Financial backers of the university would be upset if it yielded to organized black pressure on the Davis Cup issue.

Despite appearances, the opposition to the Davis Cup was better served by being staged in Nashville than by its cancellation or by a shift to a small, remote community. Nashville has a large NAACP branch of some 1000 members and three black student bodies that could supply a local mass base for protest. Cancellation might mean momentary victory without, however, the attendant access to virtually free publicity and public education about South African matters. Thus, the controversy had the properties of a mixed motive game, with elements of both conflict and cooperation in the sense that the NAACP was well served by the matches being held in Nashville, and Vanderbilt University and the city of Nashville would project a tolerant, liberal image, at least to much of the public, if they allowed maximum scope for nonviolent, orderly, constitutionally protected opposition.

The Controversy

The boycott of South African team sports and opposition to apartheid are not issues that have an immediate impact on the daily life of Nashville people, whether black or white. They are issues of principle and conscience. Therefore, both sides in the controversy reached out to their constituencies and to public opinion at large by means of moral appeals and philosophic arguments.

The argument of opponents of the Davis Cup matches was that the South African system of apartheid is the most oppressive and inhuman form of domination in the world today, and that only a total isolation of South Africa from the outside world will topple the white regime or create sufficient pressure for change. Thus, any event, activity, or transaction with South Africa that provides relief from increased isolation and mounting outside pressure serves to strengthen and perpetuate the apartheid system.

Two major lines of argument were defended by those who favored keeping the Davis Cup matches. The first, stressed by the USTA, was simply that a tennis match is a sports event and should not be politicized. A second argument for holding the Davis Cup at Vanderbilt was put forward by Chancellor Heard and by university officials. Heard insisted that staging the Davis Cup at Vanderbilt did not mean that he himself, or Vanderbilt as an institution, sympathized or supported in any way the apartheid policies of South Africa. Heard nevertheless maintained that the Davis Cup was covered by the principle of the "open forum" under which Vanderbilt had provided an opportunity for controversial nonconformist and radical groups to present their views before the university community in the context of free and open intellectual debate. The open forum policy had covered speakers ranging from George Wallace to Stokely Carmichael, from the Ku Klux Klan to the Communist Party. The chancellor maintained that artistic and athletic events were also covered by the open forum principle. This line of argument found considerable favor with the Vanderbilt student body, as well as with faculty and alumni, but did not carry much weight with the opposition groups and blacks.

The Events

In February and March a loosely structured opposition movement was slowly taking shape, even though it lacked common leadership and a common purpose, aside from opposition to the South African racial policies. The challenger groups did not agree on the choice of protest targets and tactics, and sometimes worked at cross-purposes with each other. On their part, Vanderbilt University officials, local authorities, and the police were also making extensive preparations for the Davis Cup weekend. In a series of meetings, the leaders of the protest groups, VU administration officials and the Nashville police negotiated the details of the opposition activities that would take place during the Davis Cup weekend. By and large, both sides adhered to the scenario that was thus created.

The first event of the protest demonstration was an afternoon rally on Friday, March 17, by 1200 students drawn mainly from the three black Nashville colleges. The students gathered in a parking lot adjacent to the gym where the cup matches were going to start at 6 P.M. The rally was followed by two spirited picket lines at the gym entrances, conducted under the watchful eyes of the visible, massed, but restrained police. Though the demonstration was by and large orderly, some protesters intimidated spectators, verbally abused them and occasionally physically jostled them as they entered the gym. Police officials and protest leaders and marshals managed to defuse all situations in which an angry protester might physically clash with a spectator or policeman. On Saturday, the NAACP-sponsored three mile march of 1400 people started at noon from Legislative Plaza and ended, incident free, at Centennial Park, located three blocks from the VU gym. Joined by another 200 people in the park, the NAACP marchers listened to a series of speeches by national and local black leaders and notables. Most of them went home at the end of the speeches at 3 P.M. A group of about 200 marchers, composed of militants and radicals and some students, broke away from the NAACP Centennial Park rally to join the picket lines already formed at the gym. The tensest moment of the entire weekend occurred when they arrived at the gym site and some of the radicals sought to provoke an attack on the gym. But the organizers, marshals and police managed to contain the situation. Spectators leaving the march were subject to even more harassment than on Friday night, yet only one arrest was made.

Sunday, the last day of the matches, proved to be an anticlimax, with curious onlookers and police outnumbering pickets at the gym. Despite the massive show of force by police and the mostly peaceful nature of the protests, spectator attendance was much below seating capacity and below even the financial break-even point for the sponsors.[3]

Application of the Theory

In the theory, the role of a small number of activists was stressed. It is they who bear the costs of creating and maintaining an organization, of developing a plan of action and of attracting a larger following of transitory teams to participate in collective action. According to the theory, the strategy for attracting transitory teams consists of raising the awareness of an issue and creating commitment to a cause (V); providing selective incentives (S); keeping costs of participation low (C); and convincing people that the collective action will be effective (P) and their participation will contribute to its success (Δ P).

Raising awareness of an issue is usually done by means of an information and propaganda campaign. In the Davis Cup controversy, the protest organizations had three advantages:

1. No group campaigned in support of the apartheid system.

2. Because of Steve Biko's death, the public's attention had for some time been drawn to white minority rule in South Africa.

3. Vanderbilt University's public commitment to the open forum principle ensured that, at least on the Vanderbilt campus, picketing, meetings, speakouts and fund-raising against apartheid would be permitted maximum scope.

Two factors inhibited translating concern over apartheid into active opposition to the Davis Cup matches:

1. Approval of the open forum principle (a poll of students at Vanderbilt indicated that about 85 percent of the undergraduates supported it)

2. Vanderbilt University was being attacked by outside groups and could therefore count on institutional loyalty from its members at a time of crisis.

Creating selective incentives for participation on moral issues is a function of the social and political milieu. If an issue arises that would profit from liberal collective action in a liberal milieu, it can be expected to be supported by opinion leaders and leading circles. Participation in collective action will then affirm and enhance one's position in a group. There thus exist strong, positive, selective incentives for participation. On the other hand, minority liberal action in an indifferent or conservative milieu will lead to embarrassment, criticism and isolation from peers, all of them negative selective incentives. The noninvolvement of Vanderbilt students and the participation of students on the black campuses was in part due to the entirely different climate of opinion on the black campuses, where student leaders and influentials came to support protest action and thus set in motion an upward spiral of positive incentives.

The cost of participation is low when the costs of organization maintenance, planning, and recruitment have been borne by others. If the collective action is of short duration, does not conflict with other important activities, and involves only low risk to personal safety, collective action costs for transitory teams will be low. In the Davis Cup controversy, activists sought their participation only for a few hours on one weekend.

Finally, convincing people that collective action will be effective and that their participation will make a difference in success depends upon the visibility of collective action and the number of participants. Extensive media coverage for whatever was going to be happening during the Davis Cup weekend was assured ever since the NAACP announcement of massive demonstrations. Elements favorable for collective action were thus present so long as someone initiated the mobilization process.

The Activists

Two small, New Left groups preexisted the Davis Cup controversy. On the Vanderbilt campus, the Progressive Action Coalition (PAC) was headed by John Pike, with a dozen followers. Living in a house not far from the campus, another informal group of six to eight young adults— led by former Vanderbilt campus radical David Huet-Vaughn and his wife, Yolanda, a medical student at Meharry—formed the Tennessee Coalition Against Apartheid (TCAA). TCAA supported the liberation movements in South Africa and the international sports boycott. After TCAA entered the Davis Cup controversy, attendance at weekly meetings was about twenty individuals.

TCAA worked jointly with PAC; they both saw the Davis Cup controversy as an opportunity for building a broader radical base in Nashville by getting people involved in the antiapartheid movement and the Davis Cup protests. When USTA and VU did not back out of the matches, TCAA decided to organize nonviolent protest rallies and demonstrations all three days at the site of the matches. Among other goals, the protest was meant to dissuade spectators from attending the matches. Aside from conducting an information campaign, TCAA hoped to stimulate and coordinate the opposition activities of other groups and organizations. It met with little initial success among church groups and trade unions, and decided instead to concentrate on Nashville campuses. A Student Coordinating Committee (SCC) was created and included members from the black and white universities.

TCAA and PAC, sometimes with the help of other individuals and groups, sometimes on their own, and with no more than about half a dozen of their most active members working thirty to fifty hours a week during the last month before the matches, managed to work out the basic plan of the three days of protests and negotiate arrangements with Vanderbilt University officials and the Nashville authorities down to the last details. These included securing parade permits, permission to use a university parking lot adjacent to the VU gymnasium (the tennis match site) for protest rallies, closing off streets to traffic, erecting a speaker's platform with a sound system, recognition of TCAA marshals as a buffer between demonstrators and the police (as well as anticipated counterdemonstrators), the details of the picket lines and many other matters that provided a predictable and orderly structure to the protest demonstration. To the end, however, TCAA did not know how many people would participate in the protests it had planned.

TCAA and PAC had little success in directly mobilizing transitory teams. TCAA sent out a national call to antiapartheid and radical groups throughout the country. Because it was plugged into this radical network, by Saturday, March 18, as many as 200 out-of-town radicals had shown up from as far away as Boston and Wisconsin. But at Vanderbilt University, the largest and most active protest group, with about fifty students, was based in the Divinity School and called itself Students Protesting Apartheid (SPA). SPA was already a constituted and operating group at the time TCAA became active, and affiliated itself with TCAA. The only part of Vanderbilt University where there was a majority sentiment against the Davis Cup matches was the Divinity School. Its faculty sent a statement to the chancellor and president early in February urging withdrawal of university sponsorship of the matches, and cosponsored the first antiapartheid and anti-Davis Cup speaker on the campus before an enthusiastic audience of about 200, mostly graduate students and faculty. This event received television coverage on all three Nashville channels.

The Black Universities

Through the SCC, the TCAA had been trying to reach the students on the three black campuses (TSU, Fisk, and Meharry), but the blacks' commitment to the TCAA-sponsored protests was late in coming and remained ambivalent. The big event of the weekend, as far as the news media and public opinion were concerned, was the Saturday NAACP march and park rally. These would clearly be black dominated collective events. TCAA was mostly white and to some extent identified with VU. Among activist black students, there was considerable anti-VU and antiwhite sentiment and also a feeling that the South African issue belonged to them. On the other hand, since mid February the NAACP had been moderating its initial call for a huge turnout. It sought to avoid a confrontation with VU by making no plans for marching on the VU campus itself or for joining up with the TCAA picket line after its own rally in Centennial Park. The national leadership of the NAACP de-escalated its collective action to a single three-hour protest against apartheid rather than against Vanderbilt University and the Davis Cup matches. This largely symbolic event would be held at a site some distance from the university. From the point of view of many black students and even some NAACP members, the NAACP action was too limited and cautious.

By the time opinion leaders and activists on the black campuses fully realized the limited character of the NAACP protest, there was little time left for organizing collective action from scratch. It proved expedient to follow the script already prepared by TCAA.

Mobilization on the black campuses, though late, was rapid, but not without difficulties. At Fisk, the head of student government, the editor of the student paper and the head of the Political Science Club had talked about planning some collective action with the other black colleges on the Davis Cup weekend even before the TCAA had reached them with their plan. Since TCAA had parade permits, a full protest scenario, and possessed handbills and other materials it would supply to the black campuses, the Fisk group decided to join the TCAA action.

Meanwhile, another small group of NAACP-affiliated Fisk students was starting to mobilize Fisk students on behalf of the Saturday NAACP march. They received assistance from a few professional organizers sent to Nashville by the national office to assist the local branch in their operations. Because the NAACP was afraid the students would dissipate their energies on Friday afternoon and evening, it urged them to stay away from the TCAA-SCC protest plans. The NAACP may also have feared that cooperating with radicals entailed unnecessary risks, though TCAA had publicly reiterated the nonviolent character of its opposition actions. The NAACP and TCAA rivalry for black student support on black campuses created some confusion and divided loyalties. At Fisk, the issue wasn't resolved until a mass meeting of students voted to support both groups' protest actions.

Because of the week-long spring holiday that started two weeks before the Davis Cup at all area colleges, the Fisk student body wasn't mobilized by activists until the final week in a postspring vacation blitz. Activists contacted the leading members of various student group, athletes, key people in fraternities and sororities, choir groups, the Jubilee Singers, the large Business and Economic Club, the Georgia and Alabama Clubs and every important group and clique. Numerous meetings were held; posters were put up; handbills were pushed under dormitory doors; Julian Bond, an influential black leader with a strong following among black youth, was brought in by the NAACP the day before the Davis Cup started and delivered a rousing speech at Fisk. Fisk's administration was supportive: several deans marched with the Fisk students, as did the Campus Security Chief. TCAA, the NAACP and Fisk security personnel provided training for student marshals. All these activities and meetings created a sense of increasing and large scale participation and commitment at Fisk.

On the TSU campus, much the same mobilization process took place as at Fisk with the head of student government, the "big men" on campus, and leading students in the sororities and fraternities activating channels of influence to existing groups to get a huge student turnout on Friday afternoon. TSU mobilization lasted barely a week and was very effective. TSU, as Fisk, ended up with several hundred black students at the Friday afternoon gym rally. They came carrying signs and chanting slogans, under their own leadership and command structure, with their marshals and campus security personnel. At the peak of the rally, between 1000 and 1200 people had collected, about 80 percent black. After 4:30 P.M., in small groups, the majority of black students drifted back to their campuses, with rally leaders unable to counteract the effects of the cold, snow and boredom. The remaining 400 or so more committed activists, organizers and marshals then formed picket lines at the two gym entrances.

Organization of the NAACP March

NAACP had some 600,000 members nationwide, large local branches in the Southeast region, and a 1000 member local branch in Nashville itself. It also had the backing of the Coalition for Human Rights in South Africa. Therefore, their proclaimed goal of mounting the largest demonstration since the 1960s during the Davis Cup matches was a real possibility. Until the very end, the plans of police and university officials were based on the assumption that thousands of demonstrators might sweep into town, bringing in their wake radical groups not committed to peaceful tactics, and white counterdemonstrators bent on disrupting the NAACP march.

For reasons that are not entirely clear, the top leadership of the NAACP had decided sometime in February to scale down the size of demonstration and to de-emphasize a direct confrontation with Vanderbilt over cancellation of the matches. It was clear, however, that a small turnout would be embarrassing to the NAACP national leadership, because it would undermine its claim of representing the views of American blacks on South Africa and publicly expose weaknesses within the organization itself.

Be that as it may, with out-of-town participation de-emphasized (in the end, about ten buses from big cities like Houston, Memphis, New Orleans, Philadelphia, Louisville, and Atlanta brought in about 300 to 400 NAACP members and sympathizers from outside of Nashville), the local Nashville branch was under pressure to deliver a respectable number of marchers on Saturday, for which it received little help from the national office. The South African issue was not one to which black masses would readily respond. Thus, the local strategy became to activate the black leadership in as many associations, groups and communities as possible, and hope that each group would deliver its most active members. Since the majority of the black leaders in Nashville are NAACP members and some sit on its board, there was no problem of reaching the leadership element itself. A major effort was mounted to pull in the leaders and active members of a number of neighborhood, community, labor, fraternal and civic groups. There was also an effort to mobilize black churches and ministers and their most active members, and the three black college campuses (as I have already described) were the target of an active recruitment campaign. However, many fewer black students participated in the NAACP march than the previous afternoon's march and rally sponsored by the student organizations themselves. Three local NAACP organizers did the lion's share of getting the local march organized.

About one in ten marchers were white, though no effort was made to recruit them. They were largely VU students and faculty, TCAA members and the out-of-town radicals who also participated in the TCAA picket lines. NAACP marshals were recruited from among industrial workers with whom one of the NAACP organizers had personal ties, but the march was heavily weighted in the direction of adult, middle-class Nashville blacks.

Participation in a Loosely Structured Movement:
Activists, Transitory Teams and Diffusion

There can be no doubt that the Davis Cup protests were loosely structured. The most glaring division was between the NAACP and its Saturday march on the one hand, and three days of picketing organized by the TCAA at the VU gym. Its concrete manifestations were the competition for black students, especially during the last week before the matches, the attempt by the National Office of the NAACP to keep TCAA members out of its march, and the refusal of the NAACP leadership to join the TCAA picket lines, even for a short time as a symbolic gesture. As a matter of fact, Executive Director Hooks strongly urged his audience not to join the gym pickets at the end of the NAACP rally, but to head for home. On their part, some 200 of the out-of-town radicals and militant black students broke away from the NAACP Centennial Park rally shortly after its start to join the gym pickets in a visible, public display of their disagreement with the NAACP leadership.

Aside from this division, the TCAA itself was a precariously constructed edifice.[4] The Nashville-based TCAA-PAC-SPA coalition managed to hang together because it was largely composed of white Vanderbilt students or former students, but it had no wide membership base among VU college students or the white population. The black students supplied over 80 percent of the participants at the Friday afternoon rally, and perhaps a little over half at the picket line on Friday and Saturday. They considered the protest largely their own affair, though a measure of unity and common purpose was achieved, especially on the picket line itself. Finally, the TCAA had only a tenuous hold on the out-of-town white radicals that it had summoned, and these radicals themselves were split into half a dozen ideological factions and splinter groups. Without the participation of the black students and the out-of-town radicals, the Friday and Saturday picket line might have been as tame, small, and frail as the Sunday afternoon picket line turned out to be when these two groups did not participate.

Less obvious was the generation gap between the NAACP on the one hand, and the TCAA and some militant black students on the other. Both groups were fundamentally opposed to the apartheid system in South Africa; for both, the Davis Cup match was a symbolic issue around which a more permanent and widely based opposition might coalesce. Yet their styles of protest differed. The TCAA and black students were more willing to take risks and to confront VU by means of militant tactics that would intimidate spectators, and thus create a financial loss for the university.

Loose movement structure results from the class, racial, generational, geographic and institutional divisions within the larger society. Activists are best placed for recruiting within a limited social milieu in which they are already occupying key positions. Thus, the rapid and effective mobilization at Fisk and TSU followed the classic pattern of mobilization for collective action through influential and leading campus personalities using existing networks, groups and associations in a relatively homogeneous social environment (Oberschall 1973). Moreover, the leadership group received help from without, principally the NAACP and TCAA. In such a milieu, then, aside from the heightened commitment to an issue itself resulting from information campaigns (V), strong selective incentives (S) are created as the mood swings in favor of collective action and group members conform to majority sentiment and the leadership. As the mood spreads and information about collective action becomes widespread, anticipated costs (C) decrease: one senses that participation will be massive (safety in numbers) and one learns about a concrete, well organized plan of action that entails few risks. Even though one may lose some sense of being urgently needed to make the collective action effective (Δ P may decrease), free rider tendencies are overshadowed by the magnitude of other terms in expression (1).

Even so, at the Friday rally, after about three and a half hours of assembling, marching, and attending the rally in the face of cold temperatures and a poorly planned program, large numbers of black students drifted back to their campuses before the anticipated climax. Interestingly, their action did not create a runaway reverse bandwagon resulting in a total dissolution of the protest crowd. With diminished size, the sense of being personally needed (Δ P) to make the protest a success sharply increased, and among the remaining active elements of the various protest groups (high V), selective incentives (living up to one's public image and earlier public commitment) operated strongly.[5]

With the same model, it is possible to explain the lack of success TCAA-PAC had on the Vanderbilt campus. Here, the open forum principle achieved such wide acceptance within the student body as well as the faculty that support for protests over the Davis Cup remained weak. Many students were visibly ambivalent, leading students and groups remained on the sidelines over the issue, and protest advocates were clearly in a minority position. A sense of futility in trying to get things going in the face of indifference and ambivalence operated on the VU campus (Δ P was very low). Moreover, TCAA and PAC had nothing to offer students by way of selective incentives. PAC operated as a small clique in which new recruits would not be comfortable at first.

As far as the NAACP march is concerned, only a few remarks will be made. With its large membership in the Southeastern region within half a day's drive from Nashville, NAACP could count on some out-of-towners who would already be highly concerned about the South African issue (V) or who had a strong sense of organizational loyalty (S). The financial cost of travel for these out-of-towners' was borne by the NAACP itself (C). As far as Nashville blacks were concerned, the total participation demanded was no more than four hours on Saturday afternoon. The security arrangement and massive police protection was by then highly publicized and had previously been worked out to the march organizers' satisfaction, so that the risk involved in participation was low.

The theory of participation put forward does not account for the existence of small groups of activists prior to a controversy. However, the theory, as well as the Davis Cup events, point to the small number of activists with a prior commitment to an issue or to similar radical causes who act as catalysts and bear the cost of collective action disproportionately, even in the face of a low probability of success. The small number of activists in the TCAA and PAC had a prior history of engagement in radical causes, including opposition to South Africa. In terms of numbers, as few as five and perhaps no more than a dozen key individuals engineered the organizational framework and the scenario for collective action. The main resource they invested was their time.[6] Up until the very start of the demonstrations, they did not know how successful the protest would be in attracting transitory teams, yet that did not discourage them. Even in the more organized setting of the NAACP, only three local individuals played a key role in making the Saturday march a reality. As for the Fisk campus, one is again struck by the small number of activists who began mobilizing the campus. An application of the theory of participation put forward here assumes the presence of a small number of such activists.

Can these events tell us anything about the theory of diffusion of collective action? TCAA-PAC activists performed a crucial role in lowering mobilization costs for the black student activists when they developed a total protest plan and negotiated its details with the authorities. Such an effect is shown in figure 3.5 in the following manner: the TCAA-PAC actions lowered the entire cost curve on the black campus from n(1) toward n(k). On the other hand, black student mobilization had no reciprocal effect on the TCAA-PAC mobilization effort at white campuses, as figure 3.4 implies: it did not shift the relationship of P to N from the n(1) curve to a higher curve, such as n(2) or n(k). This was partly due to the late mobilization on black campuses and the lack of communication across the black-white divide so that white college students were totally unaware of the buildup of protest sentiment among the black students. Even the TCAA leadership did not fully realize this, so loose was the overall structure of the movement.

Yet had there been advance information about black student mobilization, I doubt that it would have helped TCAA-PAC recruitment on the Vanderbilt campus. If anything, it would have strengthened the sentiment that opposition to the Davis Cup was a black collective event, with some white radicals espousing a black cause. The theory of diffusion postulates a reciprocal positive feedback (shown in figure 3.4). But for it to occur, some sense of shared purpose and community has to exist or be created, and that was missing in the case at hand.

Are the reciprocal effects of the TCAA and the NAACP upon each other illuminated by the diffusion theory? The TCAA would have demonstrated against the Davis Cup matches even if the NAACP had not become involved in the issue. By entering the controversy, the NAACP assured national attention and news media coverage not only for its opposition activities, but for that of other protest groups as well. It certainly encouraged more vigorous opposition activity, since local opposition would contribute to the anticipated, climactic NAACP march and would thus fit into a wider, more visible protest movement. In terms of the theory (as shown in figure 3.4) the relationship between P and N for local opposition activity moved from $n(1)$ into the direction of $n(k)$.

Another positive effect of the NAACP upon local activity was the lower cost of mobilization. Faced with the prospect of a massive demonstration in the full limelight of the national news media, both the VU administration and the Nashville authorities and police bent over backwards to negotiate a highly structured, nonviolent protest scenario that came close to the maximum demands of TCAA-PAC as far as time, site, duration, and permissible protest tactics were concerned, at a time when the protesters were no more than a small group of activists speaking for no visible constituency. Had the shadow of a huge NAACP demonstration not hung over all the dealings between the authorities and the local protest groups, the authorities may well have been less accommodating. In terms of the theory (expressed in figure 3.5), the NAACP action shifted the cost curve for TCAA from $n(1)$ to the lower $n(2)$ and beyond. Thus, even though the NAACP ended up competing with the TCAA for black student support, the net effect was a more vigorous, large scale information and propaganda campaign aimed at black students which probably increased their knowledge about South Africa and created greater commitment to all manner of protest against it.

Figure 3.4
Success as a Function of Participants and Earlier Successes

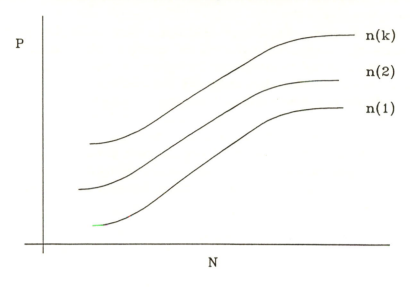

What kind of effect did the local Nashville opposition have on the NAACP? The NAACP statements, press releases, and march would have drawn just as much attention in the national news media with or without the TCAA opposition activity. It is difficult to say what impact the greater local media coverage of the controversy had upon NAACP local mobilization as a result of continuing opposition activity in Nashville itself. The greatest dangers for the NAACP were the possibility of strife and disorder occurring on the weekend of the Davis Cup for which they might be blamed, even though they were in no way responsible for them, and the possibility of having too small a number of participants in the march and rally. The presence of the more militant TCAA represented for the NAACP national office a threat, or at least a question mark, on both these counts. Their actions had a greater chance of leading to incidents, and in return for the small number of participants that TCAA might contribute to the march, it would more likely siphon off some of the black students that the NAACP was counting on. This resulted in the calculated dissociation between the national NAACP and the TCAA, while at the local level a measure of tacit coordination and division of labor was actually achieved. The diffusion theory put forward in this chapter doesnot account for the asymmetrical effect of the NAACP and TCAA upon each other, however.

Other limitations of the theory ought to be mentioned. The theory does not explain the organizational forms that emerged from a combination of cooperation and rivalry among the opponents protesting the Davis Cup, and between them, their targets (VU and USTA) and the authorities. The theory furthermore does not account for the existence of small groups of activists who trigger mobilization, nor does it explain why the value of a particular collective good (V) is distributed as it is. Nevertheless, with all these limitations, I hope to have demonstrated that a parsimonious, rational choice model comprising only five variables (P, C, V, S, N) can help organize vast amounts of data and explain a complex set of events.

Figure 3.5
Cost as a Function of Participants and Earlier Successes

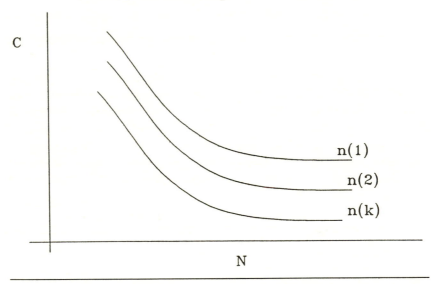

Notes

1. Since this was written, Granovetter (1978) has published a formal analysis of collective behavior that bears many similarities to my thinking. We both recognize the importance of variance in values and dispositions (V in figure 3.1), and changes

in the cost of collective action with number of participants (figure 3.3). Whereas Granovetter investigates thresholds and equilibria for number of participants, I am dealing explicitly with collective, goal-directed behavior, and hence emphasize chances of successful outcome (figure 3.2) in the decisions of would-be participants. Granovetter deals with the paradoxical case of no collective behavior despite an average positive preference for it in the group. In my model, I purposely analyze only the positive cases where a group of activists initiate collective action and bear disproportionate costs of mobilization (in figure 3.1, I assume a normal distribution of V). Both of us recognize the importance of social structure on costs and benefits of joining collective action (cf., my analysis of different outcomes at black colleges and Vanderbilt). Finally, I deal with collective action in which individuals seek to obtain both collective goods (V) and individual goods (S). V and S in my model have to be kept conceptually and substantively distinguished throughout (cf., expression [1]). For Granovetter, this distinction is not crucial. In both cases, however, the achievement of goods, whether collective, individual, or both, depends in part on the number of others also taking action.

2. I was both a close observer and a participant in the controversy. The data and information on which the account is based are varied and numerous: newspaper accounts and other printed sources; research papers written by students in a course I taught while the conflict was in progress; my own observations and interviews with protagonists and key informants. I personally knew, or came to know, most of the Nashville activists, as well as the officials responsible for dealing with the Davis Cup protests. Their willingness to talk to me about their role in the controversy was invaluable as a source of information.

3. Aside from the collective actions that occurred during the Davis Cup weekend itself, February and March witnessed a number of less dramatic actions by both supporters and opponents of the Davis Cup matches which for lack of space I cannot here chronicle. The most important omissions were the Lamb and the Lapchik episodes. Peter Lamb, a nonwhite South African Vanderbilt University sophomore and tennis star, was named to the South African Davis Cup squad as one of the junior players and the first ever nonwhite team members. Proponents of the matches saw it as indication of South African willingness to move away from apartheid in good faith. Opponents saw it as a token gesture and publicity stunt quite in keeping with South African manipulation of public opinion when apartheid faces international criticism. Understandably, the nomination created support for the matches on the Vanderbilt campus.

    The second episode (actually a series of episodes) resulted from the Nashville activities of Dr. Richard Lapchik, Professor of Political Science at Virginia Wesleyan College and Head of ACCESS, The American Coordinating Committee for Equality in Sport and Society, an antiapartheid lobby. Lapchik urged top VU administrators to cancel the Davis Cup matches and spoke to campus audiences and Nashville news media about South Africa and the need for a protest and boycott. In between two of his Nashville appearances, two assailants allegedly attacked him and carved a racial slur on his stomach. The news media sensationalized the ensuing controversy about whether the wounds were self-inflicted. In retrospect, according to activists, the Lapchik episodes had a distracting and negative impact upon the protest. News media highlighted the Lapchik assault instead of apartheid. Lapchik wasn't oriented to building a lasting, radical grass roots organization in Nashville. The controversy delayed the activists' mobilization of support for the protests on the black campuses, which turned out to be the key for their success.

4. A TCAA fund-raising and testimonial dinner, for paying off debts and recognizing those who did the most work, was held two months after the Davis Cup protests. It proved to be the last occasion before TCAA became defunct.
5. I can testify personally to the importance of these selective incentives for me and my friends in the picket line. There was also a sense of drama, excitement, curiosity, and fellowship that kept us marching, chanting and joking as we moved back and forth in front of the gym entrance under the watchful eyes of police, even while spectators kept arriving and sought to get around and through us.
6. Only one protest leader paid a high price (opportunity cost) when he did not graduate after failing to make up course work in time. Yet prior to the controversy, this student had a history of incomplete course work, so that there is some doubt whether he would have in any case.

4

Protracted Conflict

Much intellectual effort has been devoted to understanding the origins of social conflict, to explaining mobilization for collective action, and to describing leaders, participants, and their ideologies. Less attention has been paid to the dynamic aspects of group conflict: its course, duration, intensity, and outcome. In this chapter I will present a useful way of analyzing some dynamic aspects by viewing them as the result of a sequence of interrelated choices made by the contesting parties: choices about means of confrontation, conciliation, escalation and repression, and withdrawal. The benefits and costs of these choices change over time as the parties in the conflict mobilize and use up resources, and as the balance of forces and the chances of success change. Conflict dynamics needs to be linked systematically to mobilization theory. I will link the two as a first step by analyzing the extent to which size of challenger, support from without, and degree of organization of the challenger constrain the choices of both contestants.

Assume that there are two groups, one positively privileged and the other negatively privileged. Some members of the negatively privileged group seek a collective good—equality, independence, religious freedom, political rights, full citizenship—that to members of the positively privileged group is undesirable, that is, a collective bad. The demand for change will therefore be resisted.

Negatively privileged groups, the "challengers," put forward collective goods demands because they cannot increase their well-being through individual effort. Such a situation is common when group membership and boundaries are defined along ascriptive criteria. If blacks cannot become white, Moslems cannot become Christians, and Catholics in Northern Ireland cannot become Protestants, then the only way that blacks, Moslems, and Catholics can obtain the rights, advantages, and goods enjoyed by the privileged groups is by obtaining a collective good. If you can't join them and if you want a better deal for yourself, you've got to obtain a better deal for your entire group. In Hirschman's (1970) terms, if the "exit" option is not available (through emigration, social mobility, changing group membership), the "voice" alternative alone remains. What forms will it take?

There are three ways of inducing others to give up or share something they consider valuable. The first, through exchange, is to provide them with something that is equally or more valuable to them. The second is persuasion. The third is to threaten, pressure, and coerce them into giving it up or sharing it. The challengers make life so unpleasant for the target that the target's welfare is diminished. An entirely new situation has been created. The challenger now is in a position to offer the target something that will increase his welfare: he offers to desist from threats, disruption, and violence in return for the collective good he is seeking (Wilson 1961).

When a negatively privileged challenger faces a positively privileged target, exchange and persuasion are not likely, because the challenger has no positive inducements for the target. The initiative therefore rests with the challenger. His only option is to pressure, threaten, or coerce the target. The prospect of the cessation of disruption becomes the positive inducement for the target to negotiate.

It is therefore likely that a negatively privileged challenger will resort partly to nonconventional means of conflicts for obtaining his desired goals, and that these nonconventional means will have to include at least some elements of harassment, obstruction, coercion, and threatened or actual violence, which lower the welfare of the target. By nonconventional means of waging conflict I mean marches and demonstrations, picketing, strikes, boycotts, civil disobedience, civil disorders, riots, terrorist acts, kidnappings, sabotage, and guerilla warfare. Nonconventional conflict lowers the welfare of the target group, if only through public embarrassment, such as may result from a demonstration, civil disobedience, or a hunger strike; much nonconventional conflict does create damage, injury, and disruption. Conventional means, by contrast, are the exercise of persuasion, influence, and bargaining in negotiations and routine political transactions. Conventional means of conflict are not intended to lower the welfare of the contestants but are undertaken for the purpose of increasing it. I do not mean to draw a sharp boundary between conventional and nonconventional means. In most real world conflicts, both parties pursue their aims with a mixture of means, conventional and nonconventional, at least for a time.

In most situations of interest, the positively privileged target is either protected by the authorities or includes the authorities. Nonconventional means of challenge necessitate a response: demonstrations are tying up traffic, workers are on strike and prevent nonstriking workers from entering work places, students refuse induction into the army, a meeting has been disrupted, a bomb has caused injury and death, and so on. Authorities are under pressure to provide a safe, peaceful environment for the citizenry so that it can go about its daily business without a fear of personal injury, property loss, and inconvenience. And if laws are violated in nonconventional confrontations, the machinery of law enforcement and justice is put into motion. Consequently, whether or not the target or the authorities are inclined to be conciliatory, social control measures will be taken to deal with the immediate problem of law violation and disruption.

Thus, in addition to the original issue at stake in the conflict—the collective good sought by the challenger—the challenger's nonconventional tactics and the authorities' social control response in the confrontation create new issues; that is, derivative issues are added to the original issue. Did the police use rough tactics and unnecessary force against peaceful demonstrators? Were the demonstrators responsible for broken windows? Did the prosecuted lawbreakers get fair trials? Was the speech made by a leader an incitement to violence? And so on. Derivative issues will create conflict over the apportionment of responsibility, blame, penalties, and compensation for wrongs, damage, injuries, and deaths resulting from nonconventional means of waging conflict. Conciliation between the antagonists may now be complicated by the derivative issues piled on top of the original issues.

The target's response of reestablishing law and order and of prosecuting lawbreakers is not the only social control option open to it. The challengers may well have resorted to nonconventional means in order to pressure the target group into negotiating over the original issue. But instead of making unilateral concessions or entering into negotiations, the target group may decide in turn to lower the welfare of the challenger in order to induce the challenger to abandon his challenge or lower his original demands: he may decide to repress the challenger. In return for ending the repression, and thus restoring the welfare of the challenger to its previous level, the target expects the challenger to give up nonconventional means of conflict. If the challenger, however, responds by stepping up nonconventional conflict, which lowers the target's welfare yet further, a spiral of destructive conflict is well on its way. The aim of the antagonists eventually is no longer to induce conciliation or establish a strong bargaining position, but to destroy or permanently weaken the opponent and unilaterally impose an outcome to the conflict. On top of the original issues and the derivative issues, a third and even more fundamental issue has been created by escalation: that of survival.

A simplified version of the sequence of moves and countermoves described here can be presented schematically as a decision tree in figure 4.1. The technique is similar to viewing a system in continuous motion by means of a sequence of still photographs. The sequences *NE - ne, ne - NE,* and *uc - NE* result in conflict resolution, whereas the *TE* choice results in a unilateral imposition of an outcome upon the challenger. These terminal points to the conflict are indicated by a dot with a small circle. The possibility of a unilateral win by the challenger resulting from a disintegration of the target (or vice versa) is omitted from the scheme.

The choice of the amount, type, and mixture of conciliatory and coercive means of challenge and of response will depend on expected gains and losses, of benefits and costs, by both groups. I assume that both antagonists will maximize net benefits, subject to constraints.[1] What are the benefits and costs of conciliation and of confrontation?

Conciliation

By conciliation I mean recognition of and negotiation with representatives of the opposition in order to reach an agreement that will lead to a cessation of nonconventional conflict. Conciliation implies abandoning the goal of weakening or crushing one's opponent, lowering his welfare, and imposing an outcome on him unilaterally. What, then, are benefits and costs to both parties of conciliation during confrontation? How do they change with duration of the conflict?

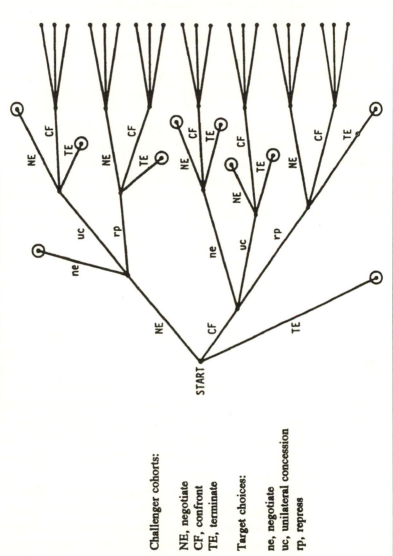

Figure 4.1
A Decision Tree for Moves and Countermoves

Challenger cohorts:

NE, negotiate
CF, confront
TE, terminate

Target choices:

ne, negotiate
uc, unilateral concession
rp, repress

The authorities, or target, seek to reestablish peaceful life, so that citizens and businesses can conduct their routine activities in complete security. At the same time, a termination of hostilities will reduce the cost of social control. Continued coercive social control may also be a source of international and domestic embarrassment for a target whose claim to legitimacy is based on the consent of the governed.

The costs the target will have to bear are those resulting from concessions on the collective goods demand of the challenger and those of settling the derivative issues. Low resistance to challengers' demands and lenient treatment may encourage other potential challengers, however, and may even undermine the legitimacy of the regime in the eyes of its supporters. In an extreme case, vigilante groups may form to protect members of the target and to settle scores with challengers if the authorities are unwilling or unable to do so. Protestant assaults on Catholics revived the IRA and IRA violence produced Protestant execution squads.

It is evident that, to the target, the principal immediate benefit of conciliation is the cessation of hostilities. But to the extent that challengers are not an organized entity, with a leadership capable of enforcing discipline among followers, negotiations do not guarantee the cessation of destructive conflict. The choice of conciliation by negotiations is thus not an attractive one to the target. Moreover, if the target is faced with a factionalized challenger, as is so often the case, the same dilemma exists. It is the more violent and hard-line factions that most influence a target's calculations of benefits and costs from conciliation, because they hold the trump cards for stopping hostilities. If the target appears to yield to the hard-liners' threat of force, it invites the more conciliatory, moderate challengers to resort to coercive tactics, which would increase their bargaining power in an overall settlement. If, on the other hand, the target seeks to isolate the hard-liners by reaching a settlement with the moderates, the cessation of destructive conflict is not assured. There are indications that Ian Smith, the Rhodesian Prime Minister, boxed himself into just such a dilemma at the 1976 Geneva Conference on Rhodesia.

A dynamic view of conflict will have to incorporate some assessment of the impact of prolonged confrontation on the challengers as an entity. Paradoxically, then, if intransigence and repressive social control weaken, factionalize, or destroy the leaders and social movement organizations of the challenger, the likelihood of a subsequent enforceable agreement with the challenger will decrease, and thus also the target's incentive to negotiate a settlement to the conflict.

Unilateral concession made without a negotiated agreement is another possible conciliatory response in conflict. It corresponds to Schelling's (1963) notion of tacit bargaining. The target then faces the dilemma that loosened social control and reform (the conciliatory moves) decrease the challengers' costs of mobilization for collective action and increase their resources as well. Thus, the target may be faced with a more powerful challenger in the near future, should the challenger not reciprocate in turn by curbing coercive means of challenge and by demobilizing (Oberschall 1973, 137–38, 163–64).

Benefits from conciliation expected by challengers include gains on the original collective good issue; personal security; a lower cost of organization maintenance and mobilization, resulting from a greater freedom of action and a lower risk of prosecution; an image of moderation and restraint that will attract third party support; and the establishing of a cooperative relationship with the authorities, leading to low cost, conventional, institutionalized access. The principal cost of conciliation is settling for less of a collective good than originally sought and for paying some of the penalties from settling derivative issues.

The dilemma faced by a conciliatory challenger is very much the same as that of the target when it loosens social control. After personal security and collective goods benefits are promised and partly implemented, the challenger will demobilize in part. The target may then decide to renege on promises or on the terms of the settlement.

Insofar as destructive conflict increases suspicion and mistrust between antagonists, the mutual trust necessary for taking a gamble on conciliation may be lacking on both sides. Prolonged and destructive conflict often brings to prominence hard-liners within the target who will not be trusted by the challenger and extremists in the challenger who will not be trusted by the target. Conditions favorable to conciliation decrease as the duration of coercive conflict increases.

Even if conciliation is initiated by both sides, the chances of bringing it to a successful conclusion amidst a destructive conflict are low. Who to negotiate with is by no means a clear-cut question, for a loosely structured, factionalized challenger speaks with many voices, each claiming to represent its constituency. Thus, the authorities' recognition of some, but not other leaders and factions as legitimate spokesmen of the challenger may itself become an additional issue in the conflict, and sometimes becomes *the* principal issue. This was the case with the seating of the National Liberation Organization of South Vietnam with the North Vietnamese and inclusion of the South Vietnam government with the United States in the Paris peace negotiations, and it is still the principal issue in the inclusion of the Palestine Liberation Front on the Arab side in an overall Middle East peace settlement.

What issues to negotiate (i.e., what to do about nonnegotiable demands and other preconditions set by the two sides); in what sequence to take up issues; under what rules, where, and when to negotiate—these are all potentially divisive issues in nonconventional conflict resolution. Moreover, even if negotiations are undertaken, violence, provocations, arrests, and injuries may continue and keep calling into question the good faith of the parties for honoring future agreements and their capacity for abiding by a negotiated settlement.

Because protracted conflict keeps creating derivative issues, factionalizes opponents, destroys trust, invites outside intervention, and brings to power hard-liners and extremists, the conclusion from my analysis is that the chances of conciliation diminish with the duration of the conflict. Expected net benefits from conciliation tend to decrease for both sides as the conflict escalates and becomes more intense, destructive, and prolonged. Conciliation in destructive conflict will in many cases be undertaken only as a result of third-party interposition based on superior force: for example, NATO pressures and UN interposition in Cyprus.

Benefits and Costs of Nonconventional Challenge

If a conflict is not terminated by conciliation, it can end only with the imposition of an outcome by one party upon the other: the target might cave in, or the challenger could unilaterally abandon nonconventional confrontation. What then determines the choice of confrontation by the challenger in the face of target resistance?

Costs and benefits of nonconventional challenge to a participant in the challenge can be broken down into the following component parts, which will be commented upon later:

$$NB = P(G1 + G1^*) + (1 - P)(G2 + G2^*) - C1 - C2 - G3 - G3^* \text{ where:}$$

NB is the net benefit from participation in the challenge;

P is the probability of obtaining the collective good;

G1 is the gain (or loss) to the challenger from the collective state if the challenge is successful (i.e., if the collective good is obtained);

G2 is the gain (or loss) to the challenger from the collective state if the challenge is not successful (i.e., if the collective good is not obtained);

G3 is the gain (or loss) to the challenger from the collective state if the challenge is abandoned;

G1* is the gain (or loss) to the challenger from his individual status if the challenge is successful;

G2* is the gain (or loss) to the challenger from his individual status if the challenge is not successful;

G3* is the gain (or loss) to the challenger from his individual status if the challenge is abandoned;

C1 is the cost of collective action;

C2 is the opportunity cost of challenge.

The *G* and *G** can be positive or negative quantities.[2] The assumption is that a rational challenger will participate or continue participating in a challenge if his net benefit is greater than zero, but that he will abandon the challenge if his net benefit is zero or negative.[3] I now turn to an explanation of the expression for net benefit.

Benefits will first of all consist of the gain *G1* from the collective good itself, contingent on obtaining the collective good. At a particular point in time during the conflict, benefits of a collective kind will be the gain of the collective good *G1* multiplied by the probability *P* of obtaining it, plus the probability of not obtaining it (*1 - P*) multiplied by the gain from another state of group welfare *G2* (what one expects if the challenge is not going to be "successful" from that point on). The gains have to be assessed relative to the expected state of group welfare without continuing the challenge, *G3*, which may be quite different from the preconflict state.[4]

For instance, during the antiwar movement, after United States ground troops were being withdrawn, net benefits from continued antiwar activity would be derived in this way. Multiply the probability *P* of immediate, total United States disengagement from Indochina (the goal of the movement) by the gain from disengagement *G1*; add *1* minus this probability multiplied by the gain from some other state of troop withdrawal and Vietnamization of the war, *G2*; subtract the gain, *G3*, associated with some other level of American involvement in the Vietnam War that would occur without the antiwar movement.

Looking only at the collective good component of the net benefit, then:

$$NB = PG1 + (1-P) G2 - G3$$

Costs of a collective kind do not have to be introduced separately in this expression because they are already included in the definition of net benefit. Should continued challenge give rise to a repressive regime (a collective bad for challengers), then $G2$ in the above expression would be negative, and unless P is close to 1, net collective benefits are likely to be negative. Negative net collective benefits would deter continued challenge. This is a state of affairs in which active opposition is expected to make things worse, rather than better, for the challenger as a group.

In addition to collective goods and bads, individual incentives and disincentives also enter choice. Some gain $G1^*$ is expected from being part of a successful challenge, such as, for instance, being in a leadership position. Another gain, $G2^*$, is expected if the challenge is not successful, such as spending time in prison or losing one's job (this instance is of course a negative "gain", i.e., a loss). Still a third gain, $G3^*$, is expected if the challenge is abandoned.

$C1$ refers to the costs of collective action, that is, the time and effort of one's contribution to the challenge and the (expected) risk of injury, imprisonment, and even death to which one is exposed in confrontations. Costs will depend on the means of challenge chosen, as well as on the social control response. Another cost is opportunity cost, $C2$: participation in a challenge uses up time and other resources that might have been put to other uses. When peasant bands melt away at harvest time, the opportunity cost of collective action for them has become too high: they know that even if the challenge is successful they simply have got to provide themselves and their kinfolk with food.

Net individual benefits depend on the sign and magnitudes of $G1^*$, $G2^*$, and $G3^*$, as well as P. Consider the kinsmen or close associates of an active challenger who expect a regime to persecute them even if they are not themselves active challengers. For them, $G3^*$ may be less than either $G1^*$ and $G2^*$; that is, there may be a positive incentive for joining the challenge regardless of the probability of success P. Marx argued along these lines when he told the proletariat that it had nothing to lose but its chains. Similarly, if a challenging group can make life miserable for fence sitters, and if the target cannot protect them from challenger coercion, they may have positive incentives for joining the challenger, whether or not they think they would benefit from the hoped for collective good: $PG1^* + (1 - P) G2^*$ in that case would exceed $G3^* + C1 + C2$.

Individual incentives and disincentives ($G*$) are here viewed in terms of the future. If the challenge is continued and successful, an activist may look forward to high status, leadership position, and material rewards (G_1*); if the challenge is not successful ($G2*$), or if it is terminated (G_3*), he may look forward to a life in prison or perhaps to being blacklisted from decent jobs for a long time to come. This is particularly the case with conflict that has become violent, where an accounting for deaths, injuries, and law violation will follow its termination. To be on the losing side in these situations may involve costs greater than those from continued active opposition, $C1$.[5]

Consider the case of a young IRA gunman. Assuming that the probability of British withdrawal from Northern Ireland is quite low, and because many of the Catholic civil rights goals have been achieved, he would expect that the net collective benefits from continued terrorism are low: P is low; thus $P(G_1)$ is small. Though $G2$ and $G3$ do not differ by much, $G3$ exceeds $G2$ because the exercise of civil rights and the reestablishment of a normal peacetime economy are delayed by continued civil strife. Thus, net collective benefits are negative. Individual incentives and disincentives outweigh those benefits in his choice of continued terrorist activity. Whether or not he and the IRA quit, costs are going to be high: ten to twenty years in prison after he is tracked down, unless he can spend a life in exile, which is not likely, as the Republic of Ireland has also outlawed the IRA. If he does not quit, although he has a very low chance of success this low probability is multiplied by a very high benefit term—being a free man, a hero with good patronage prospects and influence. Individual incentives therefore keep him fighting. Other motives also exist: loyalty with his comrades, commitment to a cause.

One can express his dilemma, looking at the net personal benefit terms of the larger expression, as follows:

$$NB = PG_1 + (1 - P) G_2 - G_3$$

where P is probability of success and is very small; G_1 is positive and substantial; $G2$ is negative and substantial (e.g., ten years prison), and $G3$ is almost as negative (e.g., eight years prison) as $G2$. As far as the cost terms (C) are concerned, they have become small. The IRA has been avoiding direct fire fights with British soldiers for some time, preferring to assassinate civilians and bomb nonmilitary targets. The British army in turn has avoided search and confrontation tactics that would lead to shootouts with the IRA. Thus, $C1$ is low. Opportunity cost $C2$ may even have become positive. The typical IRA activist has low skills and low earning potential in the labor force. For some time the IRA has been involved in economic crime, rackets, and extortion that have eluded law enforcement. Thus, the sum of $C1$ and $C2$ is probably close to zero or but slightly negative. For a wide range of realistic values, then, net benefits from choosing continued conflict will be greater than zero (because - $G3$ will actually be positive and exceed the negative $[1 - P]$ $G2$ term).

Indeed, net benefits from continued confrontation may grow larger. It may be more difficult to prosecute crimes as the time lapsed increases, which difficulty would offset the somewhat higher penalties to be expected (i.e., $d [G2 - G3] / dt > O$). Opportunity costs decrease over time as IRA members become specialists in crime (i.e., $dC2 / dt < O$). By the same token, their skill at escaping detection may also increase (i.e., $dC1 / dt > O$). Thus, net personal benefits from continuing may even increase with time. Finally, the IRA believes that time is on its side (i.e., $dP / dt > O$) because British public opinion will tire of the Northern Ireland mess and will force a withdrawal of the British army.

A move available to the British authorities is to declare (or negotiate) an amnesty or partial amnesty (an issue raised by the IRA in the past). $G3$ would then be only slightly negative, perhaps even positive, making net benefits less than zero. Such an amnesty might well lead to unilateral termination of the conflict by the IRA. Whether the British government would negotiate an amnesty depends, however, on *its* calculation of benefits and costs from its various alternatives for ending the fighting.

The target's benefits and costs can be broken down into similar components, which, for the sake of simplicity, I do not present. The target, too, anticipates gains or losses from its way of life and contributes to the costs of a social control apparatus which protects that way of life. The collective good demands of the challenger would lower the net benefit. The confrontations lower it as well because of injury, damage, disruption, insecurity, and so on. If the target group shifts resources from normal institutional uses to social control in order to reduce the collective action of the challenger, the increased cost of social control also lowers the resources available for enjoying the chosen way of life. Members of the target group calculate costs and benefits of resisting the demands of the challenger by various means and of conciliating the challenger. Estimates of the chances of success also enter their calculations. They, too, choose the course of action with the highest expected net benefit.[6]

Conflict as Interaction

The analysis that follows differs from the usual analysis of collective goods production insofar as I do not assume that a production curve for collective goods can be expressed as a function of the challengers' inputs, in the way that it is possible to state a production function for shoes or automobiles. In a conflict, the probability of obtaining the collective good depends not only on the amount and type of collective action mounted by the challenger, but on the social control response of the target. Although it is reasonable to expect probability of success P to be positively related to amount of collective action A, that is, $\partial P / \partial A > O$ and P to be negatively related to the amount of social control S, that is, $\partial P / \partial S > O$ a, there is an interrelation between A and S, because both parties may increase or decrease A and S depending on what the other does. The situation is similar to an arms race, which is a dynamic process (Boulding 1963: chap. 2).

There is a further complication. The probability P of obtaining the collective good depends on the amount of collective action A and of social control S in the confrontation. The individual's net benefit depends on C_1, his personal cost from collective action. Increasing the amount of A will increase the total cost of A. What will be the individual's own contribution, C_1, to this total cost?

In many cases of group conflict there are substantial outside sources of support to defray the cost of A: the white, Northern, liberal conscience constituency that contributed to the civil rights movement; Khadaffi's financial support of Palestinians; the contributions of American citizens to the IRA. How to keep and increase such contributions may weigh heavily on the means of confrontation chosen by the challenger, and how to decrease them on the means of social control chosen by the target.

Despite support originating from allies, substantial costs borne by the challenger will usually remain and will have to be divided up among the challenger's members. I assume that the individual cost of collective action C_1 will be negatively related to the number of challengers, $\partial C_1 / \partial N < O$ for two reasons: mobilization costs per capita will decrease for a given level A, and confrontation costs themselves will also be lower (there is safety in numbers, holding S constant). Thus, the net benefit from challenge will depend on the challenger's estimation of the total number of others who will share the mobilization and confrontation costs of the challenge. Such an estimation gives rise to the problem of strategic interaction in collective action (Frohlich, Oppenheimer and Young 1971). Strategic interaction depends on communication among challengers, on a collective action repertoire, and on bandwagon and reverse bandwagon effects; it will be discussed below.

The target's choices also take into account strategic interaction and outside sources of support for challenger mobilization. An overreaction in social control may well create a negative public opinion reaction and increase conscience constituency contributions to the challenger. On the other hand, if confrontation costs $C1$ are kept low as a result of lenient reactions to the challenger's actions, net benefits from challenge will be positive and anticipated net benefits even more positive, because positive benefits can be expected to increase the number of challengers, which further reduces $C1$, and may set off a positive bandwagon.

Strategic interaction is important also within the target group. An assessment of lower probability of success in resisting the challenger at a reasonable social control cost may well lead to low morale, factionalism, neutrality, defections, or outright emigration (as happened among Rhodesian whites), which further lower the probability of target success and increase social control costs for those remaining in the target, and thus may set off a negative bandwagon effect.

The target has the option of manipulating $G3$ and $G3^*$ to insure that net benefits from challenge will not exceed those from abandoning the challenge. A firm social control response keeps $C1$ high, deters an increase in N, and lowers P, and concessions on the collective good demands decrease the net benefits from challenge by raising $G3$. Nevertheless, such a firm response has the built-in difficulty of lowering $G3^*$ as well, which in turn increases net benefits from continued challenge. A firm social control response, as in the case of the British response to the IRA already discussed, may not leave the challenger an attractive individual exit mechanism, and it thus keeps net benefits from challenge positive, despite high $C1$ and low P. That is why a political settlement in group conflict is important. The challenger may then have a chance to negotiate his own future $G3^*$ level as part of the settlement, that is, to negotiate on derivative issues concerning penalties for injuries and law violations that resulted from confrontation.

Constraints on Social Control

So far, I have examined the benefits and costs of various means of confrontation for both antagonists in the conflict. Choice of means of confrontation is constrained by the resources the challenger and the target have for investing in collective action and in social control, respectively. Because the target is frequently the state itself, or relies for protection upon the authorities, the resources of the target are usually enormous, compared to those of the challenger. But authorities face legal, political, and constitutional constraints in the exercise of social control.

Social control has three dimensions. *Confrontation* control, social control in the narrow sense, refers to means used by social control agents during confrontations, such as crowd control and riot control. The authorities have considerable flexibility in reallocating agents of social control to trouble spots, mobilizing reserves (calling out the national guard), and using emergency measures (curfews) for reestablishing order. A second dimension of social control consists of measures designed for the *prevention* of nonconventional conflict in the first place: regulations governing meetings and marches, laws dealing with possession and use of weapons, prohibition of certain groups and associations, preventive detention and internment, censorship, and so on. Lastly, social control has a *judicial* dimension consisting of prosecution of law violators and the imposition of penalties. Judicial control comes too late to prevent conflict but has a deterrent effect upon future conflict.

Authorities face constraints in the use of confrontation, prevention, and judicial control. In democracies, agents of social control will be held accountable for the use of force, and that will discourage the overuse and indiscriminate use of force. Visibility of social control actions, resulting from access by the news media to confrontation sites, and freedom of the press increase accountability and thus also constrain the means of confrontation control. Preventive and judicial control are constrained by constitutional and legal norms for the protection of individual rights, which are backed by domestic public opinion, interest groups, political opposition, and international opinion. Some restraints will be felt even in authoritarian and totalitarian regimes sensitive to international reactions and pressures. Soviet and Eastern European control of dissident intellectuals was constrained by the reaction of Western governments, international public opinion, and even Western European communist parties. Thus, the far greater resources of the authorities in a conflict are severely restricted in actual use, especially in a democratic state, and the antagonists are more evenly matched than it might at first appear.

The target will have an incentive to be conciliatory if it is restrained from social control that would make confrontation costly to the challenger, and if repression is counterproductive (that is, if it will create sympathy and support for the challenger). Political opposition to preventive control and accountability of agents of social control, news media that increase visibility of social control, and an independent judiciary that refuses to back preventive control—all reduce the effectiveness of social control.[7]

Constraints on the Challenger

As far as the challenger is concerned, choice of means of conflict will be constrained by size, by dependence on outside sources of support (allies), and by the degree of which it is an organized entity. I highlight these three variables because they play a key role in mobilization for collective action.

The size of the challenger N will bear centrally on the cost of collective action C_1 and on the probability of success P, as I have already indicated. Thus, size will be positively related to the amount of collective action A. Much collective action increases the visibility of the challenge, which, as we have just noted, increases the likelihood of restraint in the exercise of social control. Much collective action also increases the bargaining power of the challenger, because disruption and embarrassment from even mildly coercive, nonconventional confrontation is then great. The target has an additional incentive to conciliate, because the social control costs are going to be high when there is a great deal of A.

On the other hand, the cost of providing a collective good to a large number is higher than that of providing the good to a small number. Moreover, if the amount of collective action by the challenger is so large as to represent an overwhelming threat to the target, the target may well decide to repress the challenger once and for all, or at least make an intransigent social control response in order to weaken the challenger and force it to abandon its challenge.[8]

The dilemma of a large challenger, then, is that it might appear too threatening. Large challengers able to mount a great deal of collective action have an incentive not to push the target against the wall with costly collective goods demands and destructive collective action, for fear of drawing a repressive response that might make them worse off collectively ($G2$ would be much below $G1$, and below $G3$ as well). For large challengers, moderation could be expected to increase the probability of conciliatory responses and of their obtaining some of their goals.

The dilemma of a small challenger is that its nuisance power is so low that it may not draw a conciliatory response. Consequently, a small challenger may decide to increase the coercive and destructive component of its collective actions, as the Weathermen chose to do after the failure of its call for mass protests in Chicago in 1969 and of other attempts to radicalize youth.

Under ordinary circumstances, a small challenger will be deterred from this escalation by the great personal risk, $C1$, of doing so. Outside support, such as safe operating bases from another country or a safe escape route with a skyjacked airliner, will decrease $C1$, as has been the case with transnational terrorists. If the outside source of support is only moral, a small challenger, such as the dissidents in the Soviet Union and Eastern Europe, had an incentive to use noncoercive means of challenge, so long as these are highly visible to potential third parties and allies. The leverage of the third party on the target is then expected to increase the probability of a conciliatory response and to moderate social control, despite the small size of the challenger. This is the reason why a firm commitment to human rights by the Western democracies had a positive impact on the treatment of dissidents in Eastern Europe and the Soviet Union increasingly courting Western credits and investments.

To summarize the discussion of the effect of the challenger's size upon nonconventional challenge, I offer some hypotheses. Holding everything else constant:

1. The amount of challenger collective action increases with the size of the challenger.

2. The probability of a conciliatory response by the target to the amount of collective action is curvilinear.

Putting (1) and (2) together:

3. The probability of a conciliatory response to the challenge increases at first with the size of challenger and then decreases.

These relationships are depicted in figure 4.2.

The second constraint variable, support from allies, plays a complex yet important role in conflict. It compensates for resource deficits and the small size of the challenger and is perhaps the principal means by which a weak challenger can overcome the mobilization costs of collective action, $C1$. Outside support can, however, be obtained by the target group as well, and its social control costs can thus be shared. The incentive for conciliation on both sides is much diminished when outsiders share in the costs of confrontation. Since World War II, U.S. and Soviet intervention in domestic conflicts in the Third World has contributed greatly to their destructiveness, their intensification, and their prolongation beyond their "natural" life. Even if third parties decide to withdraw from a conflict that has become destructive, the chances of conciliation are much lower than prior to their intervention, because destructive conflict decreases the likelihood of conciliation, as I have already indicated.

If only the challenger draws outside support, the amount will depend on the means of conflict used by both the challenger and the target. Paradoxically, the target is in a dilemma. To forestall outside support for the challenger, the target may decide to be more conciliatory than would otherwise be the case, given the size and weakness of the challenger. Yet the challenger has little incentive to respond in a conciliatory fashion, because a repressive response by the target will increase outside support, which will further increase the challenger's bargaining power. Maintaining pressure by nonconventional confrontation on even a fairly conciliatory opponent, in order to draw a more repressive response, will be a rational tactic for a weak challenger counting on increased outside support.

To some extent, this was the tactic of the southern civil rights movement. It was too weak to desegregate each city, each separate jurisdiction in the South, in localized confrontations, even with the financial and manpower help of Northern liberals. Despite some conciliatory responses in southern towns and cities, the movement's strategy had to be the national one of getting the Congress and the federal government to enact

Figure 4.2
Challenger Size and Collective Action:
Some Hypotheses

1. Amount of
   challenger
   collective action
   A

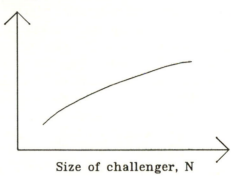

Size of challenger, N

2. Probability of
   conciliatory
   response by
   target P(C)

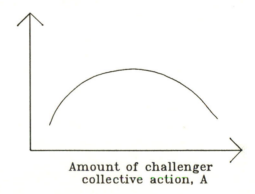

Amount of challenger
collective action, A

3. Probability of
   conciliatory
   response by target
   P(C)

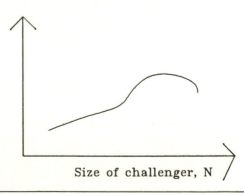

Size of challenger, N

and enforce civil rights legislation that would be applicable across the country. Only confrontations could produce the kinds of beatings and injuries by southern opponents that would outrage public opinion and pressure the federal government to enact such legislation. On their part, many southern politicians advanced their political careers by being nonconciliatory with civil rights groups and by defying the federal government. Thus, both sides in the Southern civil rights confrontations had few incentives to conciliate (Oberschall 1973, chap. 6).

The third constraint on the challenger considered here is the extent to which the challenger is an organized entity. A challenger can be thought of as a social interaction field with zones of varying organizational density (Oberschall 1977). Organization provides a mechanism for resource mobilization to some central group or agency, which then allocates these resources to the pursuit of collective goals and organization maintenance. There are challengers whose entire social interaction field is encompassed by a social movement organization (SMO). Other challengers are much more loosely structured, with most supporters and many activist part timers (transitory teams) only weakly linked to a permanent leadership in the SMO. The SMO of a loosely knit challenger can be thought of as the tip of the iceberg, most of which is under water. The black nationalists of the late 1960s and the antiwar and student movements were loosely organized movements. A few SMOs (SDS, Mobe, Black Panthers, SNCC) and "media" stars performed leadership roles with but limited organizational resources at their disposal. The blacks who rioted in American cities in the 1960s had no organizational links with civil rights and black power organizations, though black SMOs and leaders had some influence on them. Their situations are in sharp contrast to that of organized and disciplined insurgencies, such as the National Liberation Front in South Vietnam and the IRA in Northern Ireland.

Loosely Structured Movements

Since loosely structured movements have received less attention in the social movement literature than SMOs, I will try to clarify some issues in mobilization for collective action and conflict regulation in the case of loosely structured challengers. Consider first the least organized end of the collective action continuum, food price riots, spontaneous demonstrations and wildcat strikes. The situation is that of a large collectivity whose collective welfare has been unilaterally lowered by the authorities. The collectivity is not represented by an existing SMO or political organization with access to the authorities, nor, in the absence of freedom of association and personal liberties, is it possible to create such organization. The first individuals to attempt organization run high personal risks as a result of innovator-loss dynamics; there are free rider tendencies; and the sheer length of time that would pass before SMO efforts might bring relief, even if they could get underway, also make an organized challenge unlikely.

The negatively privileged group does have, however, some important resources at its disposal. It is large in size, and all of its members' welfare has been negatively affected. The potential challengers often live in crowded neighborhoods, so that interpersonal communication and interaction among them is routine and relatively cost free. The negatively privileged collectivity possesses solidarity based on a sense of shared fate and opposition to the privileged classes and the authorities and will frequently possess a repertoire of collective action (Tilly 1975). The collective action repertoire includes knowledge of past collective actions and their degree of success in similar situations, shared norms about the appropriateness of nonconventional protest actions, and a common response to shared symbols.

Participation in collective action will depend on the assessment of personal costs $C1$ from overt opposition, the probability of success P, and the opportunity costs $C2$. Opportunity costs (lost wages for the most part) can be kept low if the collective action is of short duration, such as a massive demonstration (especially on weekends), short-lived riots, and short strikes.[9] Collective action costs $C1$ are negatively related, and probability of success P is positively related, to the number of participants N. For pressuring authorities to rescind food price increases, a massive show of collective action and of solidarity is required, and everybody in the challenger knows it. Participation of any particular individual is, however, contingent on that individual's assessment of the likelihood of others participating, that is, on strategic interaction.

Roger Brown (1965, 755-76) pointed out the importance of milling prior to rioting and of other forms of spontaneous collective action: "Milling . . . is a process of information communication . . . by which members learn that they are of one mind . . . It is a process of acquainting one another with their preferences . . . " During milling potential participants assess how many others will join a collective action.

Aside from the milling of crowds, other processes of strategic interaction during which preferences, moods, and the likelihood of joining in collective action are communicated, take place in neighborhoods, work places, and casual encounters. These meetings also provide occasions for applying social pressures on those who are timid and fearful. In a relatively short time, then, massive collective action can be mounted without prior organization, leadership, and SMOs. Because of the collective action repertoire shared by the challengers, they carry in their minds the "battle plans" to be followed.

The target group is not in a position to negotiate with an unorganized entity and can only resort to well-publicized, unilateral concessions if it decides upon conciliation. Its choices are few in any case: usually a rollback of the announced price increases and the dismissal of some particularly disliked officials, who are made into scapegoats. The challenger will in most cases thereupon stick to its side of this tacit bargain and stop coercive collective action. In many such confrontations, destructive escalation of conflict is avoided by both sides.

An Illustration: The 1960s' Black Riots

An explanation of black rioting in the 1960s in the United States can also be made along these lines, though what marks them off from the food price riots just discussed is their spread over a number of years, from 1963 to 1968, the increase in the frequency and severity of riots during these years, their outbreak in the late spring and summer months, and their higher incidence on weekends than on weekdays. One consistent finding from riot analyses (Spilerman 1970, 1976) is that the two structural variables that explain frequency and severity of rioting in United States cities are the absolute size of the black population and location in the nonSouth, with other variables measuring absolute deprivation, relative deprivation, social disorganization, and political access explaining little or no variance.

During the mid 1960s, lower-class blacks were exposed to frequent and intense stimuli about their negatively privileged condition and the injustice of that state of affairs, communicated through the mass media and proclaimed by civil rights and black power leaders, by white liberal activists, and by elected national political leaders. Thus black political consciousness grew, especially among youth. Yet none of the existing political parties, black organizations, and New Left groups succeeded in penetrating the black ghettos with an effective organizational network.

The situation was more critical outside the South because the two most visible and important reform measures, the Civil Rights Acts of 1964 and 1965, benefited southern blacks collectively but made little difference for the status of blacks elsewhere. Rioting as a means of applying and maintaining pressure on the white political leadership, both national and municipal, became the collective action response (some refer to it as the growth of a riot ideology) for exercising this pressure, in the absence of effective institutional and organized channels of political access.

Rioting occurred precisely where and when the conditions for strategic interaction were present and would lead to massive participation and low collective action costs: large size of black population ($\partial P / \partial N > 0$; $\partial A / \partial N > 0$; $\partial C_1 / \partial N < 0$); ease of informal communication in black neighborhoods in the warm months, when people hang out in the streets; and weekends, when opportunity costs are low. The growth of a riot ideology, that is, of a collective action repertoire of rioting, helps explain the increase in frequency and severity over the years. The probability of others' joining in a riot would increase as this ideology became the norm; strategic interaction would thus set off positive bandwagons in riot participation. The nationwide riots following the assassination of civil rights leader Dr. Martin Luther King, Jr., point also to the political dimension of the black collective action repertoire that had developed during the 1960s. These riots meant that blacks expressed support for Dr. King's civil rights goals and were determined to press ahead to greater equality, even without their most prominent national spokesman.

One may well ask how and why such a riot wave came to a rather abrupt end in 1969, as neither the conditions for strategic interaction, nor the size of the black population, nor the riot ideology, nor indeed the socioeconomic condition of blacks could possibly change so abruptly from one year to another, and indeed did not. If rioting was a calculated means of gaining unilateral concessions from political leaders to whom lower class blacks had no effective means of access and nothing positive to offer by way of exchange, then one has to take seriously the notion that the costs of rioting (fairly substantial when measured in terms of property damage, injuries, deaths, and arrests, borne principally by blacks and some white merchants) might outweigh the expected benefits once the political leadership was no longer responsive to this form of tacit bargaining. Nineteen sixty-eight was an important turning point in the sixties, for in that presidential election year the Wallace candidacy and backlash, the law and order theme stressed by all three candidates, the priority that the Vietnam issue had come to occupy over the black issue for the New Left, and the final Nixon victory were visible signals to blacks that the coercive pressures that appeared to be effective against liberal Democratic administrations in Washington would no longer work and might even be counterproductive.

Thus, it was not more severe and more efficient social control that would account for the cessation of riots (I know of no information that would lead one to believe that such changes in social control occurred in the first place), nor the achievement of important collective goods breakthroughs by blacks between 1968 and 1969 (though evidence of gradual socioeconomic and political gains for blacks throughout the 1960s does exist). It was rather a realistic assessment that the probability P of a favorable response to rioting had considerably decreased between 1968 and 1969, and thus also the net benefits from rioting.[10]

Nonconventional conflict with a loosely organized challenger cannot be resolved by negotiated agreements, for there is no agent or group that can speak for the challenger and enforce compliance with the agreement. Authorities will therefore make unilateral concessions exacted under pressure and rely on social control. The individual incentives from participation in a loosely structured movement made up largely of part-timers with weak affiliation to SMOs and movement leaders are going to be quite modest, compared to the expected benefits from obtaining the collective good itself. Participants cannot be provided with selective incentives by an SMO if they are not formal members (it often happens that the SMOs cannot even identify their supporters individually), and part-time participation provides less "solidarity" benefits than in the case of permanent membership in a group dedicated to a common cause. Nor do participants in a loosely structured movement ever burn their bridges for a safe exit from the movement. They can withdraw from the movement into anonymity without fear of penalty, whereas members of SMOs may not be able to do so, because the social control agencies are most likely to have identified them, to keep track of them, and to harass or prosecute them. Finally, the opportunity costs of part-time participation are going to be quite low compared to those of full-time, dedicated SMO members, who may give up their jobs and professions altogether.

For the case of loosely organized challengers, the differences between $G1^*$, $G2^*$, and $G3^*$ are going to be much smaller than for highly organized movements, and $C2$ less negative. Consequently, the decision to participate and to continue with a loosely organized challenger will depend heavily on $G1$, $G2$, $G3$, P, and $C1$. The three Gi are subject to manipulation by the authorities by means of unilateral concessions. P and C are sensitive to the number of challengers N and to strategic interaction. Thus, the decline of a loosely organized challenge will be very rapid, as a result of the reverse bandwagon set in motion by a decreasing number of challengers if unilateral concessions satisfy and demobilize some of them. The remaining challengers, consisting of more radical and full time activists who wish to pursue the struggle, may then turn to more violent and anonymous means of conflict. For them $G1$ and $G1^*$ are still very much higher than $G3$ and $G3^*$, compensating for the lower probability of success P; and $G2^*$ still remains high, counteracting the more negative $C1$ from loss of membership (only partly compensated by going underground and engaging in unpredictable hit-and-run actions against selected targets).

Unlike the short-lived food riot that ends in tacit bargaining between challenger and authority, the sustained, loosely organized challenge will end with the demobilization of the majority of participants as a result of substantial collective goods gains, even as a small group escalates the conflict by means of violent actions. Eventually, this small group will abandon the challenge unilaterally or will be tracked down by authorities, or, more likely, both.[11]

Conclusion

Though I hope that this application of the rational choice approach and of mobilization theory provides useful insights into conflict dynamics and conflict resolution, much more theoretical work remains, aside from empirical tests of deductions and generalizations. A fully articulated, dynamic analysis of social movements and of social conflict will have to specify the most important resources—material, psychological, and structural—that are assembled for, and used up in, organizational and collective action. It will have to specify how resource stocks constrain the protagonists' choices in conflict. It will have to incorporate analyses of strategies, bargaining, alliances, and coalition formation to explain the changing composition of social movements and of their targets. The goals of participants, their assessment of gains and losses, their perceptions of chances of success, their responses to incentives, both selective and collective, will have to be systematically grounded in socialpsychological theory. Lastly, a complete theory will have to specify the sources of conflict in the larger social and cultural environment, and spell out the impact of social movements upon the larger societal environment.

Notes

1. For simplicity's sake, I assume that both challenger and target are a single entity. In the theory of mobilization and collective action, it has been found useful to think of the challengers as consisting of activists or political entrepreneurs (Frohlich, Oppenheimer, and Young 1971), transitory teams, a conscience constituency, and other sympathizers (McCarthy and Zald 1973).
2. Collective goods and bads enter into G1, G2, and G3. Selective incentives enter into G1*, G2*, and G3*. The point of reference for measuring gain (or loss) is the state of the chooser at the time of choice. If net benefits were to be expressed in utilities, the last terms, C1 and C2, would have to be expressed differently. The analysis that follows would remain the same regardless of the notation used.
3. I have assumed for the sake of simplicity that the probability of obtaining the collective good and the probability of individual success are the same. Though not likely, it is nevertheless possible that a challenging group might be successful in obtaining the collective good, and yet an individual participant in the challenge might not obtain the individual benefits associated with a successful group challenge with the same probability. To allow for this contingency, the expression for net benefit could be rewritten as:

$$NB = PG1 + (1 - P) G2 + QG1^* +$$
$$(1 - Q) G2^* - C1 - C2 - G3 - G3^*$$

where P is the probability of obtaining the collective good, and Q is the probability of obtaining personal benefits from a successful challenge.
4. I have assumed only two outcomes, success and lack of success, associated with gains G1 and G2. The approach can be extended to a number of outcomes, each associated with a probability and a gain (or loss), without changing the conclusions. A second assumption is that net benefits depend on the expected value of the gains and losses. If one were to describe the choices of risk averters or risk takers, a more complicated probability expression would be appropriate.
5. In these benefit and cost calculations, I have not included the cost of providing the collective good, because it is not borne by the challenger, should he be successful. The type of group conflict analyzed here involves situations in which the challenger

undertakes collective action of some kind, which is a cost for him, in order to have the target group supply the collective good, which will be a cost to the target. A movement that is successful in legalizing abortion does not supply the abortion service itself, nor contribute to the costs of these services. It is health insurance, the users of the service, or a national health service that pays for the abortion.

This formulation of the benefits and costs differs from Olson's (1968) and Frohlich, Oppenheimer, and Young's (1971) analysis of collective goods provisions, because the group conflict situation differs from those they dealt with. But insofar as the challenger supplies collective action to obtain the collective good, the collective action itself is a collective good for the beneficiary group. Thus, the Olson and Frohlich, Oppenheimer and Young analyses apply to the question of contributions to collective action by those who would benefit from the collective good.

6. To continue with the IRA example, the best benefit to the British government of a conciliatory policy would depend on the governments assessment of the probability P of success of that policy; G1, gain or loss to the government from a peaceful Britain; G2, gain or loss from the state of Britain should conciliation fail; G3, gain or loss from the state of Britain should the government continue a policy of repression; G1*, the political advantage of successful conciliation; G2*, the political costs of unsuccessful conciliation; G3*, the political gains or losses from taking a hard line; C1, the political cost of social control in lives lost and resources expended; and C2, the political advantage given up had these resources been invested in economic and social programs rather than in conflict.

7. In the late 1960s and the early 1970s in the United States, as I have elsewhere shown (Oberschall 1977), judges, juries, and courts repeatedly refused to convict or else set mild penalties in cases involving antiwar, New Left, and black activists; and university administrators and faculty disciplinary boards did the same for students in campus confrontations. Despite their vast scale, the FBI, military intelligence, and police efforts proved singularly ineffective in curbing dissident groups. Moreover, the legal and illegal social control activities of the authorities did not succeed in intimidating civil liberties groups, such as the ACLU, the news media, and the political opposition to the Johnson and Nixon administrations. Unable to repress the antiwar movement, the Johnson and Nixon administrations were constrained to make conciliatory responses to the antiwar and other protest movements (bombing halts, Paris peace negotiations, Johnson's decision not to run for president, U.S. troop withdrawals, termination of the draft.) My essay has been included in this book as chapter 8.

8. A more complete treatment of the size variable would have to take into account not only absolute size but the relative size of the challenger and of the target and the size of the active, mobilized portion of the challenger.

9. The longer the duration of collective action, the greater the opportunity costs.

10. There exists some evidence of the growth of a similar collective action repertoire in the student and antiwar movements in these years, touched off not by greater organizational mobilization of challengers and the emergence of a central leadership and disciplined cadres, but by conditions favoring strategic interaction and bandwagon effects made possible by costless communication among challengers through the mass media, especially television (Oberschall 1977).

11. This conclusion does not apply to the more complicated case of a highly organized movement emerging out of an initially loosely structured challenge.

5

Rising Expectations and Political Turmoil

What is the importance of rising expectations—or more precisely, the rising frustrations produced by the inability to meet them—in accounting for social unrest and political turmoil in some of the new states of Africa? It has long been a widely shared belief that a revolution of rising expectations is sweeping the poorer nations, and that the inability of their governments to satisfy the desire of their peoples for rapid material betterment produces pressures and strains that contribute to political unrest and turmoil including the breakdown of fragile democratic institutions where they had been established at the time of independence.

In this chapter the arguments and evidence for a revolution of rising expectations will be examined and its links with political turmoil briefly explored, with special reference to two African countries, Nigeria and Uganda, with a recent history of political upheaval. The argument will, however, be that these upheavals are more appropriately traced to the contest for political power and domination in a culturally and socially plural state lacking strong integrative institutions. Furthermore, the processes of national unification and social and economic development tend to accentuate rather than to dampen divisions and cleavages, at least during an initial period.

The Concept of Rising Expectations

The revolution of rising expectations has been defined by Blanksten (1963, 184) as "the process by which people on a lower standard of living

125

become acquainted with the benefits of a higher standard, and in consequent of this 'demonstration effect' come to desire or demand the goods
of the higher level." De Sola Pool (1963, 291) refers to the "sectors of
the world not yet modernized [which] have an image of the modernized
portion of the world," and states (1966, 106) that the "[mass media]
disseminate awareness of aspects of life that are not part of the personal
experience of the reader or listener or viewer himself. Those who fear
this phenomenon call it a demonstration effect or revolution of rising
expectations. The media create knowledge of desirable things faster than
these things themselves can be produced . . . like all revolutionary forces,
they prepare men's minds for new desires more rapidly than those new
desires can be satisfied." In a dramatic statement, Daniel Lerner (1963,
349) writes that:

> the revolution of rising expectations has been a major casualty of the past decade. In
> its place has risen a potential revolution of rising frustrations. This represents a deep
> danger to the growth of democratic polity in the world. People who do not aspire do
> not achieve; people who do not achieve do not prosper. Frustration produces aggres-
> sion or regression. Aggression in today's transitional societies expresses itself through
> violence based on moralistic but often inhumane ideologies. Such doctrines . . .
> authorize fear, greed, and hate to operate as racism, xenophobia, vengeance.

Apart from the role played by the mass media in creating an awareness
of Western life-styles, several other processes that produce rising expectations have been identified. Rapid population increase and shortage of
land in rural areas drive the rural dweller into the towns in search of a
means of livelihood. The uprooted rural migrants supply an ever-growing
urban proletariat who are directly confronted with the Western style of
life of the colonial, expatriate, and foreign business class and more
recently the new indigenous political and civil service strata. The expanded education system discharges a growing number of school leavers
and holders of certificates who no longer consider manual work and
farming appropriate, but who cannot be absorbed into the nonmanual
clerical and civil service sectors of the economy. This leads to the growth
of an educated unemployed or underemployed stratum whose aspirations
have been unfulfilled.

Moreover, the nationalist leaders have themselves contributed to the
rising expectations of the people during the struggle for independence
by stressing how the colonial regime and/or the dominant, conservative
oligarchies have exploited the natural wealth of the country and have

blocked the material prosperity of the masses, and how all this would be changed after independence. Given the limited resources of the new governments, in terms of capital, trained personnel, the social infrastructure, and because of a large number of other adverse factors such as the low or falling prices for raw materials and agricultural products, they are unable to meet the pressures for jobs, increased government services, rural development, and economic progress, while the scarcity of foreign aid and loans and private investment necessitates the imposition of ever higher taxes upon the people to sustain the government administration and some of its ambitious projects. Thus the new states appear to be fighting a losing battle to meet the rising material expectations of their peoples. But, as Karl Deutsch (1961), Lipset (1963), and others have observed, the popular acceptance and legitimacy of these new regimes depends on their responsiveness to the felt needs of the people and their ability to satisfy these needs. Since these governments may be unable to satisfy them, country after country is thrown into a state of political unrest and turmoil.

Now it can certainly not be denied that many of these countries are undergoing a period of political and social upheaval, in which democratically elected governments have given way to authoritarian regimes, in which authoritarian regimes themselves have been toppled by military coups, in which secessionist movements and rural rebellions have occurred. Nor is it necessary to question the fact that most of the rural and urban peoples in the new states desire and seek material betterment, increased educational opportunities for their children and jobs or other sources of cash income for themselves. Finally, it will be granted that most of the political leaders of the poor nations are concerned with raising the standard of life of their peoples and are doing more than merely paying lip service to economic growth, and that at the same time they are experiencing many difficulties in achieving these goals.[1] Yet one may nevertheless be skeptical of the hypothesized rising and high level of material expectations of the masses and the process by which these expectations are generated. Even if high expectations should be found to be present, it still does not automatically follow that the primary, or even a major, cause of political and social unrest can be assigned to this factor. The hypothesized causal link can be questioned on several grounds.

There are several difficulties with the use of the concept "rising expectations." These can be classified under the headings of conceptual confusion and ambiguity; the scarcity of supporting empirical evidence; the plausibility of the social-psychological processes that underlie the theory; and the factual accuracy of the sociological setting in which rising expectations are thought to operate.

The conceptual confusion in the use of "rising expectations" is the failure to distinguish that process from several other related processes such as simply the demand for material betterment or improvement, demand for jobs and employment, for wage or salary increases on the one hand and such processes as "mobilization" or "social mobilization" on the other. There are very few places left in the world where people are unaware of the existence of and undesirous of obtaining such simple consumer goods and services as bicycles, radios, printed fabric for clothes, soft drinks and bottled beer, schooling for their children, a clean water supply, hospitals and dispensaries, and the like, and where there is no demand for employment opportunities or for commercial crops that provide the possibility of making money with which these goods and services can be bought. The revolution of rising expectations has come to refer, however, to an extreme instance of such demands, where presumably the more one knows and gets, the more one wants, where new needs keep being generated ahead of satisfied wants in an ever-mounting spiral, where standards and values from the richer nations are being adopted and internalized by the people in the poorer ones, and where the goods and services coveted by the ordinary man are quite unrealistically out of his reach. The economist who first called attention to the concept of the demonstration effect in the theory of consumer behavior meant by it something more specific and limited. Duesenberry's problem was to account for differences in the proportion of income saved (as opposed to spent on consumption) by families variously located along an income distribution. The sociological translation of his approach consists in assuming that the reference groups of families with respect to consumption are the families located immediately above any given family in the income distribution with whom they are likely to have direct and visible links of social interaction (Duesenberry 1959, 3, 27, 32). His model did not postulate an open-ended spiral of consumption spending.

In using the term "rising expectations," theorists have not sufficiently distinguished between mere desires and hopes on the one hand, and expectations proper. Hopes and desires, in the sense that many individuals would like their sons to become civil servants and win at the national lottery, are desired states in the future one knows have a low probability of occurring and one is not deeply and emotionally committed to reaching. Those hopes and desires one actually takes concrete steps to achieving, like saving money or studying for a diploma, are preferably termed aspirations. Expectations, on the other hand, are future states or objects and individual regards as his by right. It is not known just how desires and hopes become aspirations, and aspirations expectations, yet the social scientist should not assume that exposure to modern consumer goods or even politicians' promises automatically generate expectations, as opposed to hopes and aspirations. To what extent hopes and desires, or even aspirations, represent an effective, short-term demand upon the economy and the government in underdeveloped countries is again something about which very little is known. In using the concept of "rising expectations" uncritically, social scientists implicitly assume, however, that hopes and desires are an effective demand in the same sense as customary food at the usual prices. Unfulfilled hopes and desires probably do not have the explosive social implications that a rise in food prices or a drop in purchasing power have, when expectations are frustrated.

The plausibility of the revolution of rising expectations rests on an exaggerated model of the discontinuities produced by the processes of social change in predominantly agrarian societies. This general line of reasoning loses force if the majority of the people have not been uprooted from their traditional social roots and have not severed their ties to land, village, and kinsmen who provide at least a minimum of social and economic security in the form of food, shelter, social support and fellowship, and a sense of belonging to a group and area which is considered one's home. But this is still a fairly accurate description of the condition of rural people, and applies to some extent to the urban dweller as well, at least so far as much of Africa is concerned. Several investigators have shown that townsmen who have spent most of their adult working lives in towns still maintain considerable ties with their home village, and eventually hope to retire there. The extended family with its system of mutual support against economic hardship has been in many instances adapted to the new circumstances of urban life. Generally speaking, education and urban residence to not lead to a wholesale rejection of traditional beliefs, values and associations (Wallerstein 1966; van den Berghe 1965; Gusfield 1967). It is quite true that even in remote rural areas, the material benefits of modern industry from bicycles and tractors to pots and pans and medical treatment—are appreciated and sought, and that their possession confers social standing in the community. Yet these aspirations for obtaining modern consumer goods do not lead to a desire to adopt indiscriminately Western norms, values, and practices which would require a radical modification of one's entire way of life and thinking.

In particular, the sharp discontinuities implied by an exaggerated version of the rural-urban dichotomy have been increasingly questioned by social scientists who have done extensive research in the field. Gutkind (1962), in a review on African urbanization, writes that "the shortcomings of the rural-urban typology is plainly evident in a large number of African social surveys, particularly those conducted since 1945 . . . which have indicated that the African family and household, be it an elementary (nuclear) or extended unit, is capable of considerable transformation and radical changes in function, yet retains strong internal and external kin ties, even when lifted out of the context of homogeneous tribal life." At the same time it has become increasingly evident that for some time now rural areas themselves have been undergoing social change in terms of increased education, transportation facilities, production for the market, communications, geographic mobility of the rural dwellers, and political participation that by no means lead to an inevitable deterioration or disintegration of rural social structures (Halpern 1967). Other studies have shown that the African cultivators' response to the production of cash crops for the market has been in the main rapid, more voluntary than coerced, and economically rational (Dean 1966). The effect of these processes of social change is that while there are demands, sometimes even very strong ones, even in remote rural areas, for material improvements, for consumer goods, and for jobs, these demands often occur within a still viable traditional context in which provision of a minimum of economic, social, and psychological security dampens whatever frustrations unfulfilled demands generate.

Quite apart from the sociological context in which the phenomenon of rising expectations operates, the social-psychological model underlying it can also be questioned. It is assumed that through the mass media or urban experience people are exposed to a Western standard of life, whether that of foreigners or of an indigenous *elite*, which then becomes internalized as a felt need and whose satisfaction is quite outside the realm of the possible.[2] The view assumes a leap-frogging mechanism in reference group orientation, such that a person from a simple peasant stratum, when he becomes oriented to improving his social status, will not merely desire to acquire the material style of life and status symbols of the social stratum immediately above his own (rich cultivators or rural officials and notables), but rather that of foreign or urban national *elite* with whom he is not in direct social intercourse and who are far removed from him in economic standing and social status. It is however equally, if not more, plausible that instead of a leap-frogging process, social strata or groups that are near rather than far in economic and social status from one's own and with whom one is familiar from personal observation and daily interaction are chosen as reference groups (Friedl 1964; Merton 1957). If this is the case, it would suggest that people desirous of social advancement and economic improvements operate within a gradualist and incremental framework, in which they might of course be disappointed and frustrated, but certainly not inevitably and permanently as the terms "revolution" and "rising" expectations suggest.

Some Empirical Findings

Direct evidence bearing upon the revolution of rising expectations is relatively meagre, nor are there standard instruments for measuring hopes, aspirations, and expectations. One of the earliest studies in this area, Lerner's (1966) six nation Middle Eastern communications survey conducted in 1950, measured none of these dimensions, aside from the satisfactions and dissatisfactions of the respondents.

More recently Hadley Cantril (1965) and his collaborators at the Institute for International Social Research have completed a thirteen-country study specifically concerned with hopes, wishes, fears, aspirations and expectations. Two distinct methods were used by Cantril to measure these. Open-ended questions were used on "wishes and hopes" and "fears and worries" for the future, and what specifically would make the respondent "happy" and "unhappy". This was followed up by the so-called self-anchored striving scale, a ladder with ten rungs on which the respondent was asked to rate where he stands at the present time, where he stood five years ago, and where he expects to be five years from now (Cantril 1965, 23). A similar ladder was added with the respondent's country, rather than the respondent himself, as the object of the rating. It is instructive to provide here a brief summary of the findings from Nigeria, the only African country in the Cantril study.[3]

The Nigeria study was conducted in the fall of 1962 at the time of the first severe postindependence political crisis when the Action Group leaders were tried for treason and the Western Region put under emergency rule, but before the 30 December 1964 election, which is usually considered the starting point of a continuous crisis that eventually resulted in two military coups and the civil war. The leading category of response to the personal hopes question (with 69 percent) was "improved or decent standard of living for self and family; sufficient money to live better or to live decently, relief from poverty," followed by "opportunities for children" (60 percent). The two leading personal fears were "health" and "deterioration of the standard of living" (Free 1964, 25-33). When cross-tabulated with the usual socioeconomic, demographic, and regional-ethnic variables, it was found that "improved or decent standard of living" leads among all categories of respondents, even among rural, low SES, and illiterate groups. The findings indicate a strong concern with material improvements throughout the entire country, yet the statements of the respondents show that they aspire to concrete and immediate improvements in their everyday life and not some utopian and unattainable Western standard of life: "house of our own . . . enough money to educate my children . . . enough money for the maintenance of my dependents . . . save enough money to train my children to do some skilled trade . . . house of my own." and the like are typical statements (Cantril 1965, 207). As Cantril (1965, 311) sums it up in a statement about the findings of the entire study, "It must be emphasized that the standards and expectations by means of which people judge their own development are relative to their experience".

Turning now to national aspirations, Nigerians in 1962 had high hopes and wishes for an improved standard of living, political stability, and development in such areas as education, public health, employment, agrarian reform (Free 1964, 35-42), but political instability (civil war, disunity among the people or the leaders, etc.) leads the list of national fears (with 77 percent), highest in all socioeconomic and demographic categories, fears that in retrospect were quite realistic.[4] The findings on the ladder ratings indicate that nearly all respondents who completed them rated their personal and national present above their past and their future above the present, with all groups and categories optimistic and aware of improvements and no category substantially deviating from the countrywide pattern (Free 1964, 66–71; Cantril 1965, appendix D, table 14). One may well conclude that Nigerians in 1962, even in rural areas and even the illiterates, were very desirous of personal material advancements and hoped for increased government sponsored development, that they were conscious of progress and optimistic about the future, yet realistically apprehensive about national unity and political stability. On the other hand, the notion that Nigerians strove for an unrealistically high standard of life, that they had become frustrated in these hopes and disillusioned with their government's ability to satisfy them, and that the urbanized and better educated Nigerians in particular were most disaffected than their peers who had been less exposed to modern ideas and influences, does not receive support from these data.

In another study constructed under my direction in Uganda, a country of small peasant cultivators that was 95 percent rural, 416 interviews with adult males were completed in twenty-one different locations throughout the country by university students using the local vernacular languages with cultivators, laborers and rural notables such as teachers, chiefs, and African traders in each location about five months after the Buganda secessionist crisis of May 1966. In addition to communications behavior and information about current events, the schedule measured the broad area of satisfactions and aspirations in several different ways. We asked each respondent to state whether he was satisfied or dissatisfied with the way things had turned out for him, the reasons he felt the way he did, what his biggest problem was, and what he thought could be done to solve it. Then we read him a list of twelve items, ranging from a pair of shoes to a car or truck, and inquired each time whether he owned the item; if he did not, he was further asked whether he wanted it, and if he did, whether he thought he would get it. We asked respondents about their evaluation of changes in the village in the last four or five years (since independence), both in general and with reference to six specific items (making a living, condition of the roads, children's education, amount of theft, young man's ability to find work, treatment by officials). From the latter we calculated an index of the number of favorable changes mentioned. Finally, we also tried to establish the demand for development and increased government services through specific items and open-ended questions.

There are several specific hypotheses linked with the revolution of rising expectations which it is possible to test with these data, even though survey findings from one country at one point in time can clearly not settle these matters with any degree of finality. The theory would lead one to believe that it is those who have been most reached by modern influences and have been relatively uprooted from their traditional way of life who should be more dissatisfied with their present condition, more critical of the pace of change in rural areas, more desirous of obtaining modern consumer goods and more demanding and impatient with the government's ability to achieve social and economic development. Thus one would expect those who have been more exposed to an urban environment and the mass media (radio and newspapers in Uganda) to indicate higher levels of discontent and impatience.

With respect to age and education, it is more difficult to formulate specific hypotheses. On the one hand, educated respondents are more likely to have experienced an urban environment, more likely to be frequently exposed to the mass media and knowledgeable about the standard of life in the richer countries. Thus potentially they are more likely to have higher hopes, aspirations, and expectations that might remain unfulfilled and lead to frustration. On the other hand, they are also more likely to have a salaried and relatively well-paid position through which they can satisfy some of these aspirations. Young persons are more likely to be educated and have unrealistic career aspirations and desires for material goods than older persons. Yet, because much of their life is still ahead of them, their aspirations may not yet be disappointed. On the other hand, one would expect the younger and better educated persons who are un- or underemployed to be relatively high on aspirations, expectations, and frustrations.

With over half the respondents classifying themselves as dissatisfied, rather than very or fairly satisfied, Ugandans express high levels of dissatisfaction. The large majority, as in Nigeria, gave some economic or financial reasons for their dissatisfaction, such as lack of money, no job (meaning in this context no means of livelihood in addition to raising cash crops such as cotton, tobacco, and coffee), low crop prices, and the like. A cultivator, for instance, stated that he had financial difficulties, especially in educating his children, and as a solution to this problem suggested the government should raise the prices of crops. Younger respondents (those under twenty-five years) are somewhat more dissatisfied than the middle aged and older ones, and those with primary grade schooling are more dissatisfied than those with either less and no formal education or more than six years of schooling. But these differences are small. The largest differences between categories of respondents are those between the teachers, traders, and chiefs (called "notables" for short) on the one hand, and the other respondents who are mostly cultivators and laborers (called the "rank and file" for short), nor is this very unusual since the notables are better off materially and have a steady source of income outside and often in addition to agricultural pursuits. Because of this difference, type of respondent or education (which is highly correlated with the notable/rank and file distinction) will be controlled.

Contrary to the hypotheses, there are no marked differences in satisfaction level expressed by groups differing on urban experience and frequency of media exposure, whether or not other variables such as education, age, or type of respondent are held constant. These results are illustrated in tables 5.1a and 5.1b. The basic difference in satisfaction level is between notables and the rank and file. Within each category, urban experience or frequency of radio use has no impact upon satisfactions and dissatisfactions. Nor is this finding unusual. A Swedish political scientist who did extensive field work in Northwestern Tanzania (bordering upon Uganda) at about the same time as the present study and using similar methods to get at the effects of mass media exposure and geographic mobility upon satisfactions found similarly negligible correlations as reported above (Hyden 1968, 205).

Table 5.1a
Satisfaction Level, by Type of Respondent and Urban Experience

Satisfaction	Urban experience *		No urban experience *	
	Notables	Rand and File	Notables	Rank and File
Very Satisfied	25%	11%	15%	7%
Fairly Satisfied	37.5%	26.5%	39%	29%
Dissatisfied	37.5%	62%	44%	64%
Number of Respondents	(40)	(102)	(59)	(211)

* Urban experience was dichotomized by whether or not the respondent had ever lived in a town for six months or longer.

Table 5.1b
Satisfaction, by Type of Respondent and Radio Use

Radio Use	Notable			Rank and File		
	Never	Seldom *	Often *	Never	Seldom *	Often *
% Dissatisfied	67%	43%	41%	67%	59%	66%
Number of Respondents	(3)	(14)	(81)	(42)	(136)	(137)

* Seldom: once a week or less; often: more than once a week.

It could, of course, be the case that the most dissatisfied rural inhabitants have already left for the towns and the finding is an artifact of the research method. However, with only 5 percent of the Uganda population living in towns this is not likely to be an important factor. Nevertheless it is possible to contrast the present findings with those of another study conducted in the capital, Kampala, a year and a half earlier, with adults over eighteen years of age who had at least some secondary education, as shown in table 5.2. Considering the different methods used in the two studies, slight differences in the wording of the questions, the year and a half time discrepancy, and the presence of uncontrolled variables, the figures suggest only a small difference in dissatisfaction level in favor of the urban respondents.

Turning now to the evaluation of changes in the village since independence, it will be seen in table 5.3 that while the pattern of findings is complex, increased education and exposure leads in the direction of a more favorable evaluation, contrary to the hypotheses formulated in accordance with the theory of rising expectations. In fact, despite the high volume of personal dissatisfactions expressed earlier, these Ugandans are aware and are appreciative of improvements since independence.

There are larger regional variations on this question than variations between socioeconomic and demographic categories. In particular, three out of four respondents in Buganda, the region in which a secessionist attempt had just recently been put down by armed force, report a worsening of conditions, and they alone gave many political reasons for their dissatisfaction on the earlier questions. No doubt this is related to the pessimistic mood and uncertainty about the future that many Ganda express as a result of the shock of recent political events. Yet these coffee and cotton crops have been particularly poor in Buganda because of drought and other weather problems. By contrast, respondents regional variations are also in broad agreement with some aggregate economic trends since both the 1964/1965 and the estimated 1965/1966 in the North, the region that has been politically ascendant at the national level and which has also shown a steady increase in its cotton and tobacco production, report better (rather than worse) village conditions by a 15 to 1 ratio.

Table 5.2
Satisfaction Level of Urban and Rural Respondents Compared

	Urban Respondents	Rural respondents (with some secondary education)	
		Urban experience	No urban experience
Very Satisfied	4%	13.5%	6.5%
Fairly Satisfied	25%	32.7%	35.5%
Dissatisfied	69%	53.8%	56.5%
D.K. N.A.	2%	—	1.5%
n	(395)	(52)	(62)

* From Gordon Wilson, "The African Elite," in Stanley Diamond and Fred Burke, eds., *The Transformation of East Africa*, New York, Basic Books, 1965, 450.

Table 5.3
Evaluation of Changes in Respondent's Village in the Last 4 or 5 Years, by Education and Radio Exposure

				Education Primary (1-6)			6+ years of schooling		
Radio listening	Never	None Seldom*	Often†	Never	Seldom*	Often†	Never	Seldom*	Often†
% who think life in general has changed for:									
better	32%	33%	61%	45%	58%	56%	—	65%	61%
worse‡	26%	31%	36%	45%	19%	28%	—	5%	17%
% who mention 4-6 (out of 6) favorable changes	23%	26%	32%	27%	47%	27%	—	50%	46%
Number of Respondents	(31)	(57)	(28)	(11)	(72)	(92)	—	(20)	(94)

* Seldom: once a week or less.
†Often: more than once a week.
‡ "Better" and "worse" do not add to 100 percent because "no change" and "no answer" are not shown.

As in Nigeria, the hope of increased development and government services is widespread. We asked a series of questions to ascertain them. On every one of the items, such as increased government aid to farmers, more factories, tractors, improved roads, more police protection against thieves, hospitals and dispensaries, 90 percent or more of the respondents answered that they would like these things to increase.

The answers given to the open-ended questions on what the government should do which it is not now doing in this village confirm the above results about hopes of improvements. If we take answers referring in some way to the maintenance of law and order as expressing the traditional function of governments, we find that only nineteen out of 490 concrete suggestions fall into this category. The most frequent sort of answer, with ninety cases, refers to help from the government in general terms. Next come seventy-two mentions about drilling boreholes, building dams or improving the water supply; fifty-three mentions referring to hospitals, dispensaries, or health services; forty-eight responses about raising the prices of crops and/or decreasing taxes, and thirty-eight mentions about some improvement in education. Other answers are too few to be classified in broad classes but are nonetheless revealing, for many persons or groups with special interests would like the government to introduce a change beneficial to them. Some traders or aspirants to trading would like loans and assistance for Africans to set up or expand their shops. The fishermen near the National Park want the government to ease the park water boundaries for better catches. Tobacco growers in the North would like to obtain more barns for tobacco curing. Just about everyone thinks he can derive some benefit through the government.

We turn now to the findings on material desires and expectations as reflected in questions about twelve specific possessions (questions relating to ownership, desire for and expectations about getting them). The results are summarized in table 5.4. With respect to ownership, there are wide variations by groups, with the notables and those with more education reporting on the average more items than the rank and file and those with no education. Examination of columns (2), (3), and (4) shows that most Ugandans would like to own the items they do not possess (contrast sum of [2] and [3] with [4]), but that for each item those who do not expect to get the item outnumber those who do (contrast [2] with [3]). An analysis of these data will proceed along two complementary lines. We seek to establish whether or not respondents' desires and expectations are realistic: that is to say whether they are more likely to want and expect to get those items which are within the realm of possible attainment. For this purpose, two ratios were computed for each item, the want/does not want ratio (w/w̄ in column [5]) which is the sum of (2) and (3) divided by (4); and the get/will not get ratio (g/ḡ in column 6), which is (2) divided by (3). We also want to establish whether those groups with a greater objective chance of securing ownership desire and expect to get them in greater proportion than groups with a lesser chance.

The two items with the lowest w/w̄ ratio are electricity and a car or truck. These are clearly beyond the reach of these respondents and this fact is realistically acknowledged. The two items with the highest w/w̄ ratio by far are "land" and a "tin roof," precisely the two items which are the most "traditional" on the list, followed by shoes, radios, and blankets. Shoes and blankets are the cheapest items on the list; as for the radio, the answers reflect the increasing chance of obtaining a cheap transistor model and the high desires for it. The g/ḡ ratios, except for blankets (a cheap item) are below 1, indicating fewer of those who want it expect to get it than not get it. There is not much variation between items except for the realistically low ratios for electricity and car and truck already pointed out. These results would suggest that while stated desires are generally high, both desires and expectations operate within a framework of realistic calculation. In fact, if education of respondents is controlled, it is found that for each item the g/ḡ ratio increases with education, that is the more educated the respondents—and they do have an objectively better chance of obtaining the items because many have a source of income outside agriculture—the higher the proportion who expect to obtain an item they want. So far as the w/w̄ ratio is concerned, there are no marked differences with education.

These data can also be looked at in a different way. For each respondent, one is able to calculate the proportion of items he wants of the items he does not own, and the proportion of items he expects to get of those he wants, and use these proportions as indices of individual desires and expectations, as done in table 5.5. The results indicate a generational gap between those under thirty-five desiring and expecting to obtain more of the items they do not own than those over thirty-five years old, and a systematic relation with education confirming the earlier findings on g/ḡ ratios for each item.

Table 5.4
Material Possession, Desires, and Expectations *

Item	(1) % owners †	(2) % Does not own, wants it, expects to get it	(3) % Does not own, wants it, does not expect to get it	(4) % Does not own does not want	(5) w/w̄	(6) g/ḡ
Blankets	92%	3%	3%	1%	5:1	1.1
Land	85	3	8	1	11.7:1	0.38
Bed with mattress	79	5	11	4	4.4:1	0.47
Good pair of shoes	64	11	19	4	8.4:1	0.55
Bicycle	63	10	16	9	2.8:1	0.62
Silverware	56	12	18	10	2.8:1	0.65
Tin or iron roof (rather than thatch)	52	16	26	3	14.5:1	0.62
Radio	46	18	28	6	7.8:1	0.63
Watch	36	17	28	15	3.1:1	0.58
Dark Suit	31	16	37	12	4.3:1	0.43
Electric light	5	13	50	28	2.2:1	0.27
Car or truck	4	9	58	24	2.8:1	0.16

* Rows based on 416 cases; rows do not add to 100 percent because "no answer" not shown; w/w̄ and g/ḡ ratios based on raw members.

†Occasionally a respondent indicated that he owned an item, but wanted another or better one. He was then classified in columns (2) and (3) depending on whether he expected to get it.

Table 5.5
Proportion of the Items Desired and Expected by Population Groups

	Age				Education		
	25 and under	26–35	36–45	45 and over	no formal	Primary 1–6	Beyond Primary
% who desire 4/5 or more of the items they do not have	72%	72%	50%	50%	50%	64%	73%
% who expect to get 1/5 or more of the items they desire	63%	57%	39%	36%	40%	50%	62%
Number of Cases	(65)	(167)	(119)	(62)	(117)	(177)	(115)

The following tentative conclusions can be drawn from these results. On the one hand it is quite true that it is the younger and better-educated groups, precisely those who have been most touched by modern influences and ideas, who articulate stronger desires and expectations for modern consumer goods. Yet, there is no indication in these data that rural Ugandans seek an unrealistically high or Western style of life as distinct from a gradual improvement beyond their present condition that some of their neighbors are already enjoying. Indeed, the positive relationship between increased education and higher desires and expectations can be explained both in terms of objective chances and within a framework of rural reference groups: it is precisely in the relatively prosperous groups that already show a relatively high incidence of ownership of modern consumer goods that a relatively high demand for them exists among those who do not own them.

It is an exaggeration to view the educated respondents as being in some sense uprooted, alienated, or disaffected with their traditional milieu. They are more prosperous, they occupy positions of influence and of higher material reward and prestige, and as has already been shown, they express higher levels of satisfaction and have more favorable evaluations of changes in the village environment than their less privileged neighbors. Moreover, in another set of questions on what should be carefully preserved and what should be changed in Uganda, educated and uneducated respondents, influentials and rank and file, are in essential agreement: the most common answer to what should be preserved does refer to some specific tradition or custom, especially in the North. In West Nile District 11 answers can be classified in this way and range from traditional music, crafts, language, and dress to marriage customs. One man for instance thought that "women should preserve their fashion of dress" and another found "tight dresses" for women objectionable. In Acholi District 6 men specifically want to keep the bridewealth (though two more want to have the amount of bridewealth reduced because it is excessive), and nine others want to preserve such things as traditional dances, music, marriage, costume, land ownership, and native medicines. In Lango District many respondents specifically refer in one way or another to their system of land tenure and communal cultivation. Only in Buganda, the locus of the recent political upheavals, was the question interpreted in a strictly political sense, and a majority of Buganda stated that they wanted the Kabakaship (the traditional kinship) preserved. All in all the impression gained from these questions is anything but a stampede for the abandonment of traditional social and family institutions.

A number of conclusions can be drawn from the Uganda rural survey as well as the Nigeria findings, which are in broad agreement with the Uganda data despite the differences in method and instruments used. The demand for modern consumer goods and economic and social development is strong and pervasive, and governments are expected to play a leading role in satisfying these demands. Personal material advancement is equally strongly sought, especially among the younger and better-educated groups. Yet these are the groups who do have a better chance of reaching the goals they aspire to, and they are neither disaffected nor disillusioned with the amount of progress that has been made, nor pessimistic about the future.

Rural Uganda is already at a stage of development where a majority of the people are exposed to the mass media, are geographically mobile, are aware of the world outside their immediate environment, and are generally dissatisfied with their present economic circumstances and in favor of more opportunities for themselves and of economic and social development for their community. Several decades of growing commercial crops and the past decade that saw the creation of political parties, the rise of a nationalist movement, the introduction of universal suffrage and the achievement of independence, together with the expansion of education and the diffusion of transistor radios in rural areas, have left these legacies and produced these cumulative changes. Nonetheless, with respect to the currently fashionable view of the revolution of rising expectations and the processes which generate it, there is no evidence here that a cultivator is no longer satisfied with a bicycle because he has seen cars in the city or the roads, that he does not want a simple school or dispensary but a fully equipped modern school and hospital that he has seen in the capital or in the cinema, that he does not simply wish to improve his home and standard of life with a few consumer goods within his reach rather than a brick house with modern facilities, and that he is anxious to abandon traditional customs, institutions, and systems of land tenure. Indeed, at least in the case of Uganda (Rothchild and Rogin 1965; Young 1966; Hopkins 1967) and Nigeria (Harris 1965; *Africa Report* 1966), none of the area specialists have assigned the revolution of rising expectations a significant causal force to the recent political upheavals. The central problem of these two countries has to do with forging national unity in a plural social setting.

National Unity

Most newly independent states are faced with the twin problems of forging national unity and advancing material progress. The first of these is the more basic problem, and the pursuit of the second sometimes makes it more difficult to achieve the first. New states enter the contemporary world without having prior cultural unity and a sense of national consciousness among the population. The historical processes that account for the pluralism of the new states are too well known to bear repeating here. It is a fact of life that their populations are divided into religious, ethnic, tribal, communal, linguistic, cultural, and other groups whose sense of identity and loyalty are directed often to these collectivities and not to an overarching citizenship in the newly established state.

Nor is there anything unusual or surprising about the existence of "micro-nationalism" as these sentiments and attitudes have appropriately been called (Geertz 1963). Mair (1963, chap. 4) has aptly stated that "community of language and culture, and association with a common territory, are the sources of the kind of consciousness which is properly called 'national' if the number of people who share it is large, and 'tribal' if the number is small." It is an error to think of these sentiments as an irrational and emotional hangover from the past. Most people in the new states perform the daily rounds of their existence within the context of these collectivities, and derive through them a sense of identity, economic support, and social fellowship. Even villagers who have become more or less permanently settled townsmen derive tangible economic, social and psychic benefits from continued association with their fellows. And this has been the case not only in the new states but for immigrants to the United States and indeed elsewhere as well. Mutual mistrust, hostility, and fear among members of these groups can often be explained by pointing to memories of antagonism and exploitation, broken promises, and violence in the past, and competition for jobs and other scarce resources in the present. Many of the antagonisms do not have roots in precolonial times since these groups did not even know of each other's existence. They were often the unintended consequences of economic and administrative policies designed to make the colonies economically viable and governable. Cash crops were introduced and readily accepted, but the economic benefits accrued to those who lived in areas where the soil, temperature, and rainfall were suitable for cultivation. The accident of early missionary activities in certain areas and the location of colonial administrative and commercial centers favored the surrounding population with educational and employment opportunities that resulted in their subsequent monopolization of civil service and clerical positions, and became later seen as blocked opportunity or dominance by other groups. The location of mines and colonial plantations or settlers left these areas with a more highly developed infrastructure of roads, schools, and other services. Even disparities of physical size between groups might give rise to later divisions, since many colonial governments favored taller soldiers and police, and consequently recruited disproportionately from certain regions where the inhabitants were taller. In sum then, the consequences of European penetration left a legacy of unequally shared opportunities, development, and modernity.

During the period of the independence movement against the colonial power, these particularist identifications and loyalties receded somewhat into the background for the sake of achieving unity and the common goal of independence. After independence and a brief honeymoon period, they reassert themselves with force as the new state is trying to grapple with some fundamental problems of organization and policy. National symbols, such as the flag and holidays, have to be agreed upon (Marriott 1963). The position of traditional chiefs, kinds, princes, and other rulers has to be settled. The boundaries of political subunits have to be defined, and the distribution of power between the central government and these subunits determined. The status of the major religions has to be settled. A national language or languages have to be agreed upon, and the languages of instruction at different levels of the school system. The status of "foreign" minorities who often dominate the business world, and the replacement of European administrators by nationals, come up. The position of the new state on the international scene arises and is intimately connected with the necessity to raise capital for economic development. At the very start, the territorial integrity of the state may be threatened by a secessionist movement and foreign interventions.

The settlements or attempts at settlement of each of these issues may accentuate the identifications with and loyalties to traditional communities and groups and lead to an articulation and aggregation of interests along lines of cleavage threatening to national unity and superimposed on each other so that the same groups face each other as antagonists on all major issues. A secular state may be offensive to the members of the dominant religion, yet the establishment of an official religion unacceptable to other groups, who remember past humiliations and injustices suffered at the hands of the majority. The relegation of traditional rulers to figurehead status may be offensive to a population group who see in him a living embodiment of their cherished values, traditions, and collective identity and pride. Yet the continued privileges and political rule of a traditional ruler may be utterly repulsive and unacceptable to those groups who are committed to a leveling of inequalities based on tradition and to the democratization of the political process. The choice of one over another indigenous language for administration immediately favors some groups' civil service career chances over that of others, yet the retention of a foreign lingua franca may be opposed by many on nationalist or political grounds. The replacement of colonial and expatriate administrators and army officers by indigenous personnel may immediately favor those groups who for historical reasons have become more highly educated and urbanized, and raises fears among the other groups of a government dominated by one particular group. The alternative of staffing posts according to ethnic quotas, rather than according to criteria based on competence and merit, is opposed by the more West-ernized groups who stand to lose by it and for whom it is ideologically distasteful. Indeed as the country initiates programs of social and economic development, the competition for the distribution of scarce goods and advantages leads to clashes of interest between previously mobilized groups and to an increase in hostility between them. The very processes of forging a modern state and of economic development heighten ethnic and regional antagonisms.

It is important to realize that neither the causes for such turmoil nor the consequent breakdown of constitutional government and violent confrontation are peculiar to the new states of Africa. The fear of continued (or threat of permanent) domination between historically hostile and rival peoples, and demands for autonomy or self-government, have played an important part in the turbulent history of Eastern Europe and the Balkans, of Ireland, Spain, Belgium, and Canada, to mention but a few instances. In fact very few countries in the past two centuries have altogether escaped political controversy over ethnic or regional demands for autonomy, and in many instances these have resulted in armed risings and even civil war. In the United States, after eighty years of accommodation, the dominant groups in the Southern states thought that the ascendancy of Northern interest in the Union could be solved only by secession. In both Uganda and Nigeria, rising expectations and frustrations about unfulfilled economic demands played only a secondary and indirect role in the recent political upheavals.

Conclusion

It is not the intention here to carry out a polemic against the importance of economic factors in accounting for political stability, but rather to point out that in some of the new states other problems have an immediacy and a priority which is not usually the case in the older established states. The theorists who have emphasized the factor of rising expectations have developed these views more with reference to Asia and Latin America where the problems of the distribution of land in a highly stratified society and of inequality in growing urban centers are far more pressing than in the African context, except where white settlers are or were present. Even in the African context, the restratification of society and the strains created by it are becoming increasingly politically relevant, and as the fundamental ethnic-regional problems become slowly sorted out, will increasingly shape the internal politics of those countries. Social changes result in complex and shifting relationships between nationalist politicians, the educated stratum, the traditional leaders, the emerging urban working class and the rural social strata. A fully developed theory of social change and nation building in Africa will have to emphasize both the problems of national unity resulting from ethnic cleavages and the problems resulting from an emerging class structure and the restratification of society. These problems interact in complex ways, yet it is a useful working hypothesis to consider the problem of national unity due to ethnic-regional pluralism as the central one in the earliest phase of postindependence history.

Notes

I wish to thank the Yale University Concilium on International Studies, Department of Sociology, Makerere University College and the Milton Obote Foundation in Kampala, Uganda for support in making this research possible, and Professors Wendell Bell and Aidan Southall for critical comments. An earlier version was presented at the tenth annual meeting of the African Studies Association in New York, November 1967.

1. The strongly democratic and equalitarian orientation of top West Indian nationalist leaders is documented in Wendell Bell (ed.) 1967, chapters. 4 and 6.
2. Despite the extensive literature on the communications revolution in the underdeveloped world, no empirical evidence to support this process has been presented in the two most recent and comprehensive volumes on these topics. See Schramm (1964) and Pye (1963).
3. The Nigeria findings are also separately published as a case study in Free (1964).
4. In fact, in the thirteen-country study, it is in Nigeria and the Dominican Republic, precisely the two countries that subsequent to the study experienced violent upheaval and civil war, that the foremost fear of the respondents was political instability, with absolute levels far beyond those reported in other countries.

6

Group Violence

Some Hypotheses and Empirical Uniformities

Definition of Terms and Review of Existing Approaches

Since group violence is but one of several means of conducting conflict, explanation for its occurrence must be embedded in a comprehensive theory of conflict. Yet violent conflict is so topical and important that an effort to reflect on it sociologically is well worth undertaking at this time even in the absence of a comprehensive theory of social conflict. Indeed, Max Weber (1947, 133) has written that "the treatment of conflict involving the use of physical violence as a separate type is justified by the special characteristics of the employment of this means and the corresponding peculiarities of the sociological consequences of its use." In this chapter, I shall avoid definitional and typological exercises and concentrate rather on specific, testable hypotheses and empirical uniformities of group violence that have been put forward and commented upon at various times. I shall also present some data and findings bearing on the hypotheses that, while not "testing" them in rigorous fashion, will do more than simply provide plausible illustrations that can always be found whenever a large body of historical and contemporary cases is carefully searched. The final aim of the chapter is to link up these hypotheses and uniformities in more systematic fashion than is presently available although the chapter does not spell out a systematic theory of group violence. At this stage of theory when a

149

plausible case can be made for a large number of hypotheses, it is important to spell out the specific conditions under which specific hypotheses are thought to be applicable.

There are several aspects of my approach that bear some brief comments. First, I do not start with a typology of conflict (e.g., revolution, rebellion, riot, coup d'etat, guerilla war, and so on) nor do I break up the topic by the social categories of the participants (peasant rebellions, race riots, labor wars). The reason is not that such typologies and distinctions are unimportant, but that a satisfactory theory of group violence ought to have some general applicability. Furthermore, when group violence breaks out, it is seldom clear until after some time has elapsed what type of conflict is actually taking place, and it may indeed change over time. There is also some theoretical gain in being able to explain differences of magnitude in group violence between nationality, religious, labor, and race groups with reference to variables common in all situations.

Second, I do not differentiate between legal and illegal use of physical violence as a basic category of analysis, even though Weber's (1958, 78) and others' definitions of the state rely so centrally on this distinction. The reason is that group violence is the result of interaction between two or more groups in a conflict, one of which may be the state or its agents, and a theory ought to apply the same concepts and variables to all the parties locked in conflict. Moreover, the authorities often initiate violence under circumstances where its use is perceived as illegitimate and uncalled for, and this then becomes a further and often the dominant issue in the conflict. The use of illegitimate violence by the authorities, whether provoked or not, is also a topic of interest in itself and ought to be therefore explained in the theory.

Third, I avoid explanations based on psychological or social-psychological variables implying aggressive drives such as the "disposition to violence" of certain groups or a propensity to violence which is manifested in the national character. The reason is that many explanations based on these alleged dispositions or propensities are spurious insofar as they are no more than a statement of an empirical uniformity (e.g., low levels of group violence in recent British history) rephrased in tautological terms that really beg the questions (e.g., peaceful British national character). Even if measures of aggressive tendencies independent of the occurrence of group violence are developed, the present approach seeks to exhaust the explanatory potential of sociological variables before these dispositional concepts are invoked. It is precisely the facile and exaggerated notions about innate aggression, irrational drives, the herd instinct, and similar formulations, popular especially since the French Revolution in accounts of group violence and crowd behavior, that the present approach is meant to avoid and supplant. These remarks do not apply to other psychological and social-psychological concepts, variables and processes. It is not possible to come to terms with the question of group violence without discussing grievances, hopes, frustrated expectations, relative deprivations, ideologies, legitimacy and a host of other attitudinal, motivational and state of mind concepts.

For purposes of this chapter, Coser's definition of social conflict (1967, 232) as "a struggle over values or claims to status, power and scarce resources, in which the aims of the conflicting parties are not only to gain the desired values but also to neutralize, injure, or eliminate other rivals" is adequate. The hypotheses on group violence developed below, however, are not meant to be applicable to all cases of conflict. Specifically, wars between states are excluded at one end and microconflicts, such as gang wars, at the other. A borderline case would be protracted internal war or guerilla war with foreign intervention. In this situation, the hypotheses are applicable only to the initial stages of conflict. Since the distinction between legal and illegal use of force was rejected earlier, violence here simply means the employment of physical coercion for personal and group ends. By social turmoil, social disturbances, civil disorders, or some equivalent terms, I mean any episode of collective behavior, not necessarily violent, in which a group of people express grievances, voice demands, stage meetings, marches, demonstrations, or sit-ins, draft petitions, try to prevent or block the execution of unpopular actions, destroy property, assault other individuals or groups and the like. The group itself I will refer to as protesters unless they are called by more specific designations such as strikers, demonstrators, squatters, or rioters. By agents of social control I mean the rank and file executors of the orders of the authorities or the government, namely police, troops, militia, national guard, yeomanry, constables and the like, including their immediate commanders in the field.

Violence is a means used to wage conflict, one of several means, and the same conflict can be simultaneously conducted using several means. Dimensions of conflict that readily come to mind are its duration, scale (measured by the number of participants in the confrontation and its geographic spread), intensity and the magnitude of violence. Intensity, as Dahrendorf (1959, 211) points out, refers to the "energy expenditure and degree of involvement of conflicting parties. A particular conflict may be said to be of high intensity if the cost of victory and defeat is high for the parties concerned." Intensity stands for the importance attached to the issues under dispute by the parties to the conflict. Intensity is probably going to be a particularly difficult variable to measure. The magnitude of violence might be measured simply by the total number of casualties, fatalities, and injuries that result from it, although some researchers persuasively argue for the inclusion of property damage as well. The total magnitude of conflict will probably have to be constructed as an index with duration, scale, intensity, and magnitude of violence as its component parts. For a much more comprehensive discussion of the dimensions and measurement of conflict, the reader is referred to the interesting monograph of Tilly and Rule (1965). In any case, these are only meant to be suggestions for measurement, since a rigorous testing of hypotheses will almost always involve variations and improvisations in measurement techniques depending on the availability of data and the specific circumstances of the conflict process. In this chapter I shall concentrate on the magnitude of violence as a key dimension of conflict and as the dependent variable of interest.

Conflict is an everyday, normal, ongoing, institutionalized process most of the time. Conflict theorists ask however, (1) under what conditions conflict will tend to increase and decrease; (2) under what conditions conflict will tend to be violent rather than nonviolent and what accounts for the magnitude of violence; and (3) what consequences violence has for conflict regulation and institutionalization, its consequences for the conflict groups, the individuals in the conflict groups and the social system. This chapter will deal primarily with the second question.

The Likelihood of Violence: Erratic Reformism

Although the same set of conditions that can account for an increase in conflict may well be able to account for an increase in the likelihood of violent conflict and the magnitude of violence, a number of theorists specify intervening variables between these two steps. Just about every theorist points out that increased social change or rapid social change produces dislocations, strain, grievances and an increase in the normal levels of conflict and the likelihood of violence. Some see a direct link between the magnitude of strain, social dislocation, grievances on the one hand and the magnitude of conflict and of violent conflict on the other. Others acknowledge this causal link but emphasize in addition the importance of intervening variables, in particular, social control variables such as the reaction of the authorities or the ruling strata to the grievances and demands of the protesters. One might further note that some stress the importance of long-range intervention and reforms by the ruling groups as a response to increased conflict while others focus more on the immediate tactical response of the agents of social control during the confrontation process, particularly if magnitude of violence is the variable of interest. Here are some representative views expressed by influential social theorists on these matters.

Smelser (1963, 48-49) holds that although "the more severe the strain, the more likely an episode of collective behavior," still "we should not search for specific causal laws such as 'economic deprivation gives rise to hostile outbursts,'" since social strain comes in a bewildering variety of concrete forms and "any kind of strain may be a determinant of any kind of collective behavior." Elsewhere, he has emphasized that the translation into action of a specific combination of social strain and conduciveness depends "above all on the behavior of the agencies of social control" (Smelser 1964, 122). Specifically, he argues that if disturbed groups are provided access to channels that influence social policy, their response will tend to be peaceful and orderly, whereas if access is blocked, the response will tend to be violent and even take on at times bizarre and utopian forms (Smelser 1968, 143). Ted Gurr (1967, 5, 11-12) draws heavily on the frustration-aggression theory and hypothesizes that "the more severe the relative deprivation, the greater the magnitude and likelihood of violence." Yet he too recognizes in a subsequent hypothesis that "the likelihood and magnitude of civil violence varies inversely with available, institutional mechanisms that permit expressions of nonviolent hostility." Writing on urban racial violence in the United States, Grimshaw (1960, 119) holds that

> there is no direct relationship between the level of tension and the eruption of social violence. While assaults in the accommodative structure doubtless lead to an increase in tensions, violence is constrained by the strength and mode of application of external agencies of control, in particular the police.

In the same spirit, Hodgkin (1957, 187) predicted that in Africa

> whether national movements in particular territories employ violent or nonviolent, revolutionary or constitutional methods to gain their objects seems likely to depend primarily upon the attitudes of the colonial regimes, the flexibility of their policies, their willingness to make substantial political concessions, and generally upon tactical considerations.

Dahrendorf (1959, 213) also thinks that when oppressed groups are allowed the right to organize and voice their grievances, the chances of violent conflict are decreased. Coser (1967, 106–107) and Heberle (1951, 385–387) formulate hypotheses and generalizations along the same lines. Turner (1964, 126) emphasizes the importance of the general public as well as the authorities when he writes that "the public . . . observes, interprets and labels the movement. The public definition affects the character of recruitment to the movement, the means which the movement evolves and the kind of opposition it encounters." While one can easily lengthen the list of supporting quotations, Killian (1964, 450) sums it up appropriately: "Whatever the influence of other variables, the influence of the opposition and of the public reaction to a movement cannot be overemphasized."

The great merit of all these views is that they do not look upon the values, goals, ideology, and especially the means of conflict used by a protest group as a fixed, constant quantity. Instead, the means used to pursue conflict are the result of a process of interaction between the conflict groups. In particular, the reception of the protest groups and the reaction of the authorities and agents of social control are singled out as very important. If the authorities are unresponsive, block channels of communication, do not provide the opportunity for peaceful protest, refuse to make concessions and so on, the likelihood of violent conflict increases. While the magnitude of strain, type of strain, and the number of grievances account for the increase of conflict and threaten to overload and break down the existing institutions of conflict regulation, the magnitude and forms of conflict are explained primarily with reference to the interaction between authorities and protesters (or targets and challengers). Still, the above viewpoints must be criticized for their lack of specificity since responsiveness or unresponsiveness, open or blocked channels of communication and influence, access or lack of access to decisionmakers are rather ill-defined, global conceptions that stand for complex social structures and processes. Moreover, the above views assume that if the authorities are responsive and act in good faith, they are able to undertake effective reforms to relieve social strain and meet the grievances of the protest group. But what if reforms are ineffective or only partially effective? It is a commonplace that concessions and reforms can be "too little, too late." Furthermore, repression may under certain circumstances be an effective means of stopping a protest movement at its start, with little violence. But how can one sociologically come to terms with the notion of an effective combination of the carrot and the stick for handling social protests and for defusing a potentially violent or revolutionary situation?

This issue has been discussed most recently by Huntington (1968, 362 ff.), who starts with Tocqueville's observation on these matters, or what I would like to call Tocqueville's paradox. In his discussion of the antecedent of the French Revolution, Tocqueville (1955, 176–177) observes that

> it is not always when things are going from bad to worse that revolutions break out. On the contrary, it oftener happens that when a people which has put up with an oppressive rule over a long period without protest suddenly finds the government relaxing its pressure, it takes up arms against it. Thus the social order overthrown by a revolution is almost always better than the one immediately preceding it and experience teaches us that, generally speaking, the most perilous moment for a bad government is one that seeks to mend its ways. Only consummate statecraft can enable a king to save his throne when after a long spell of oppressive rule he sets out to improve the lot of his subjects.

Tocqueville's paradox has been noted in numerous instances in history and in the contemporary world, for instance in connection with increased social disturbances and urban racial violence in the United States concurrent with and following the most comprehensive social, economic and political legislation and reforms to improve the condition of Negroes since the Reconstruction Era and the East European anti-Soviet, anti-communist upheavals following shortly upon de-Stalinization and a period of relative "liberalization" in the Soviet orbit initiated after Stalin's death. Crane Brinton (1957, 40) long ago pointed out a more specific variant of de Tocqueville's paradox when he observed in his discussion of the antecedents of the English, American, French and Russian revolutions that

> one of the most evident uniformities we can record is the effort made in each of our societies to reform the machinery of government. Nothing can be more erroneous

than the picture of the old regime as an unregenerate tyranny, sweeping to its end in a climax of despotic indifference to the clamor of its abused subjects.

Another student of revolution, Pettee (1938, 94) refers to the process of attempted reforms by an old regime as "erratic reformism":

Erratic reformism is the only policy open to a ruling class divided in its attitudes, or strapped by unwieldy institutions . . . in Russia, the utmost repression and occasional barbarism was accompanied by spasmodic reforms in industry and agriculture and politics. The result of such reforms and reaction mixed might well be called the quickest way to make a revolution. The result is to cramp the privileged classes without relieving the exploited. . . . To the cramped, the reforms have an appearance of being forced concessions and the reactionary measures an appearance of betrayal.

The paradox is, of course, less surprising if one recalls that the reform attempts tend to be half-hearted and ineffective because of institutional weakness and deliberate efforts by certain groups to undermine them. A period of liberalization after a long period of oppression allows the surfacing of long dormant grievances and demands going far beyond those initially voiced and anticipated by the authorities; it allows the mobilization of discontented groups and expectations of reforms that cannot be realistically instituted in a short time. The subsequent, half-hearted attempts to crack down upon the activities of the freshly mobilized groups creates a situation favorable to social protest on a wide scale.

Contemporary students of conflict are well aware of the consequences of erratic reformism. Eckstein (1964, 54) argues that a sudden relaxation of repression and the institution of a liberal policy after a regime has driven its opponents underground and inflamed their enmity creates a favorable context for violent confrontation. Smelser (1968, 114), in a similar vein, writes that "the type of response on the part of authorities that aggravates and intensifies an episode of collective protest is harshness and rigidity that alternates with evident weakness." On the other hand, "an agent of social control who is firm but patient, consistently prohibiting certain types of protest but consistently permitting and giving serious consideration to others . . . tends to contain the protest." It is immediately apparent from these quotations that the question of reform in the face of demands and social disturbances is an exceedingly complex topic, much neglected in contemporary theories of conflict and not adequately captured by concepts such as open or blocked channels of communication, access or lack of access of disturbed groups to the authorities or ruling groups, or their responsiveness or unresponsiveness.

Moreover to introduce qualifying terms such as "effective" and "ineffective" reform, access, or responsiveness into these hypotheses is to beg the question itself.

Economic Factors and the Structural Location of Group Conflict

The relationship between social change, social strain and grievances, the authorities' response and the likelihood of social disturbances is further complicated by another and related set of issues also first raised by Tocqueville (1955, 175-77) when he pointed out that the years preceding the outbreak of the French Revolution witnessed an increase, not a decrease, of economic prosperity:

> In 1780, there could no longer be any talk of France's being on the [economic] downgrade; on the contrary, it seemed that no limit could be set to her advance. . . . Twenty years earlier there had been no hope for the future; in 1780, no anxiety was felt about it. . . . It is a singular fact that this increasing prosperity, far from tranquilizing the population, everywhere promoted a spirit of unrest. The general public became more and more hostile to every ancient institution, more and more discontented. . . . Moreover, those parts of France in which the improvement in the standard of living was most pronounced were the centers of the revolutionary movement.

Even Marx, whose views are usually contrasted with those of Tocqueville and who, in his theoretical works, tended to uphold the misery theory of political upheaval (deepening economic crises, falling profits, lower wages, increased exploitation and misery of the working class linked to increased revolutionary potential) took a much more flexible and varied approach in his brilliant case studies and commentaries on contemporary French and European political upheavals. Yet ever since Marx and Tocqueville, there has been a continuous debate by historians and social scientists on just what are the precise links between economic changes and social conflict—in particular revolutionary outbreaks. There is no need to review this long controversy about the primacy or importance of economic as opposed to other factors. It is sufficient to recognize that economic changes broadly viewed are such a common, perennial and central component of social change that a discussion of social change, social strain and social dislocations, grievances and protest cannot proceed without thorough examination of economic processes. Short- and long-term economic trends, particular sequences of long- and short-term up- and downswings, migration patterns, rural-urban demographic shifts, the effects of the introduction of new technologies and novel modes of production and other structural economic changes, changes in the cost of living, of wages, of the cost of basic foods, and a host of other economic facts and processes have received close scrutiny by students of social conflict. Moreover, not only changes in absolute terms, but relative gains and losses have been discussed and the concepts of relative deprivation, rising expectations, or some other social-psychological concepts such as hope and cramp have been invoked to assess the reactions of various groups and social classes to absolute and relative economic gains and losses. The literature on these topics has grown immense. The conclusion that several diverse patterns of economic change must bear some direct and indirect links to social disturbances, and that these links are mediated by some intervening social-psychological processes is inescapable but not very helpful. I shall briefly review the major points in one of the most valuable papers on this topic by an economist and then list some of the most common patterns of economic change frequently linked to increased protest activity on the part of negatively privileged social strata and social classes.

In an article entitled "Rapid Economic Growth as a Destabilizing Force," Mancur Olson, Jr. (1963) points out that "economic growth . . . can significantly increase the number of [economic] losers," e.g., increase the absolute number of people whose standard of living has fallen, despite an increase in the average per capita income of the entire population. Moreover, in the early phases of economic growth, there is a tendency for increased inequality of incomes to come about as well. Rapid economic growth is frequently associated with changes in methods of production, new technologies, the type of labor and skills demanded and the geographic configuration of production. While some groups may therefore gain—and indeed gain a lot economically—other groups may lose in relative and even absolute terms if they are located in economically declining regions, in firms or industries caught with outdated technologies and with outdated skills. Furthermore, levels of consumption may decline with economic growth when capital accumulation curbs spending through forced savings, taxation, or some other means. Olson also points out that economic growth as a long-term trend is often associated with short-term downswings, and for particular groups wages may rise slower than prices, increased unemployment and other hardships may occur. Although Olson also stresses the potential for political unrest among groups that are economic gainers and the possibility of rising expectations experienced by these groups, a central contribution of his analysis for sociologists is that nothing in economic theory contradicts the possibility of an increase in the number of economic losers during a period of economic growth, and that such growth might be associated with changes in the relative economic position of social strata and other groups. A major conclusion of his paper is that detailed information on the impact of economic changes (both growth and decline) upon specific groups is needed for understanding the potential for social and political upheaval of different groups, strata and classes in the population. Knowledge of aggregate national economic trends alone or comparative analyses of countries based on aggregate figures can lead to misleading inferences. Unfortunately, as Lawrence Stone (1965, 169 ff.) has pointed out, economic data sufficiently disaggregated and complete are difficult to come by even in the present, let alone locating data on state of mind variables such as relative deprivation, expectations and aspirations for the past. As a result some researchers engage in the risky and often tautological business of inferring relative deprivation from the occurrence of social disturbances and then find their hypotheses on the relationship between these two variables confirmed. Here then follows a brief outline of the kinds of economic changes that commonly produce grievances and frequently result in social disturbances and protest among the lower social strata and classes.

Groups that are economically at the margins of subsistence will react at once to a short-term increase in food prices or a diminished food supply. Such shortages and price increases, often localized, occur frequently after a time of crop failures or of war. The protesters' response is typically the food riot, consisting of attacks upon gain hoarders or merchants and bakers who are holding back their grain stocks or selling them at a high price, forced food sales at the preshortage price and the prevention of grain transfers out of a given locality after food supplies have been requisitioned elsewhere (Rude 1964). When such grievances and disturbances coincide with dissatisfaction among other social strata, the lower classes can be mobilized by them beyond the initial limited aims for the provision of cheap food. Writing about the French Revolution at a time when from 25 percent to 90 percent of the daily wages of urban working people were spent on bread (depending on their trade and skill level), Rude (1959, 200) noted,

Perhaps not surprisingly [an inquiry into the causes of social unrest among the *menu peuple*] reveals that the constant motive of popular insurrection during the Revolution, as in the eighteenth century as a whole, was the compelling need of the *menu peuple* for the provision of cheap and plentiful bread and other essentials, and the necessary administrative measures to insure it.

An effective response of the authorities in such a situation is to provide food at the usual price, often by means of price controls. The lack of support by the working people of Paris for Robespierre and the Jacobins at the time of their fall in 1794 was due in large part to the inability to assure a stable cost of living by means of wage and price controls (Rude 1959, chap. 9).

In the case of rural social strata, one should be careful to distinguish between peasants who are only marginally involved in commercial production for the market and farmers who are independent owner-cultivators producing commercial crops, often for export. Such farmers, especially single-crop farmers producing an export crop, are vulnerable to the fluctuations in the world market prices of their crops, and in particular to a drop in prices after a period of boom when they may have become excessively dependent for income on one particular crop. Examples of the processes of mobilization among farmers under such circumstances are the Populist movement in the American West in the 1880s and 1890s (Hicks 1961, chap. 3), the disaffection and susceptibility to right-wing and Nazi appeals of farmers in North Germany in 1928 and later (Heberle 1945), and the positive response of African farmers to nationalist movements in many colonies in the late 1950s and early 1960s after a drop in world-market prices of cotton, coffee, cocoa, and other tropical crops following the World War II and early 1950s boom period.

Peasant disaffection on the other hand occurs most frequently over the issues of land shortage and an attempt by landlords to extract an increased economic surplus that frequently violates traditional norms of equity and distribution (Moore 1966, chap. 9). The occasion for peasant disturbances is provided by demographic pressure and the behavior of the landlords. Landlords may attempt to increase their income from rents and other extractions from the peasantry when they engage in conspicuous consumption and become indebted in cities and the court. Gerschenkron (1964, 184) points to the attempt by the French nobility before the French Revolution to increase the peasant's financial burden and to revive some rights and claims on land that had not been exercised for a long time. Under such circumstances peasants are convinced that their grievances are legitimate. Peasant revolts resulting from these issues are extremely common. For China, for instance, Shu-ching Lee (1951, 512) reports that in a small border region between Kiangsi and Fukien, approximately the size of Iowa, an investigator found from local records seventy-six instances of peasant revolt, led mostly by tenants, over a period of some 180 years between 1448 and 1627. Another occasion for revolt occurs when a landlord class seeks to exploit its estates in a more rational and profitable fashion by consolidating land, evicting tenants and seizing lands traditionally held in common ownership by the peasant community, as occurred at the time of the Mexican Revolution (McNeely 1966). Furthermore, demographic pressures in rural areas often force peasants to become squatters or otherwise seize the uncultivated lands of neighboring landlords. Of course a part of the surplus population may migrate to the cities in search of industrial employment, but this alternative may not always be present or may become unattractive during periods of industrial depression and urban unemployment. For the peasant putting more land or unused land under cultivation using traditional techniques of production in order to increase or maintain his income is a more attractive and realistic alternative than to use more advanced agricultural technology on his existing holding, for which he may lack the skill and the capital. All of these forms of economic and demographic pressures operated on peasants in Russia before 1905 and led to widespread land seizures, illegal grazings, arson of manors, forest destruction, and other forms of peasant disturbances (Gerschenkron 1964, 191).

Land reform is too broad a term to describe an effective response on the part of the authorities to meet peasant land hunger. Tilly (1964, 196) has shown in the case of the Vendee that the sale of church lands during the French Revolution became an occasion for increased disaffection among the peasantry when the prosperous farmers and bourgeois living in small towns managed to outbid the small tenants and farmers and grab most of the desirable land that rural people felt was rightfully theirs. Effective land reform means the transfer of available land (not only marginal land) to the peasants themselves. Land reform is likely to be successful if the landlords are foreign nationals, e.g., German barons in the Baltic area, Polish aristocracy in Lithuania, Hungarian nobility in Yugoslavia and Turkish Bulgars in parts of Rumania, as was the case in the post-World War I period in Eastern Europe (Gerschenkron 1966, 94). The nationalization of land and the impressment of tenants and small landholders into collective farms or state farms will also be highly unpopular solutions and will be resisted, although in these cases the state and its agents of social control may be strong enough to put down resistance, as happened in Soviet Russia. Collectivization of land is more likely to be an acceptable solution in situations where the majority of rural working people had been a propertyless, wage-earning, rural proletariat rather than an independent class of smallholders.

Among the urban working class three major groups have to be distinguished: unskilled recent rural migrants into cities in search of employment, working people in established and growing industries, and the "preindustrial" skilled workers and independent artisans and craftsmen who are losing their economic base because of competition from new methods of production. It is the last named group that has been particularly noted for its participation in social and political strife, at least in the Western European context (Rude 1959, chap. 13). Starting in the late eighteenth century, as a result of the industrial revolution, artisans and craftsmen have been a numerically declining stratum, threatened with being reduced to ordinary wage workers, economically insecure and caught in a spiral of downward social mobility, even while they were trying to maintain their economic grip and social status. Long-term economic growth did not benefit them, since it increased prosperity mainly in the new manufacturing and industrial sectors. Reform legislation regulating hours of work, conditions of work, safety, female and child labor seldom benefited them and more often than not represented a further immediate loss of income because of their reliance on family labor. Many of these groups sought a solution to their economic problems in the revival of preindustrial curbs on competition, price and wage controls, and other measures that were totally counter to the broader social and economic changes taking place and which were therefore not instituted. Because of a tradition of corporate association and collective action, these groups were susceptible to rapid mobilization to defend their interests.

On the other hand wage workers in new and growing industries did benefit directly from long-term economic growth and labor legislation but were hurt by unemployment and wage cuts during depressions. These wage earning groups, however, were subject to strain and grievances, most often manifested in strikes over the reluctance of employers to restore wage levels when prosperity returned, over conditions and hours of work, over the right to form trade unions and engage in collective bargaining (which was itself a result of the workers' conviction that there was no other effective means of protecting their employment security, wage levels and standard of life), and over the issue of job security when employers tried to hire unskilled workers, often recent migrants, to replace them. Especially explosive outbursts occurred when unskilled strike breakers, often drawn from an ethnic or racial minority, were hired after workers had gone on strike against their employer, as was typical of American industrial conflict. An increase in the standard of living of the working class, industrial legislation in the area of hours, child labor, hygiene and safety, the recognition of the right to collective bargaining and other reforms instituted during the nineteenth and twentieth centuries were the appropriate long-term responses that directed labor conflict into increasingly peaceful and institutionalized channels.

As for recent rural migrants with low skills, who are everywhere known to contribute a disproportionate share to all the social problems associated with the growing industrial city, a great deal depended on the opportunities they had for temporarily returning to their families in rural areas who provided them with an economic cushion in difficult times. At any rate, this group has not figured as prominently in large-scale collective disturbances, especially of a political sort, as the previous two groups, and has even at certain times been coopted by the ruling class to fight against other working-class protesters as was the case with the Mobile Guard in Paris during the 1848 revolution (Rude 1959, 173). At other times they have acted as strike breakers for employers. In effect, recent migrants are often so close to the margins of subsistence that they are very vulnerable to economic pressures, react positively to economic opportunities even when it means breaking the rank of working-class solidarity and are reluctant to take the economic risks that protest activity entails.

Noneconomic grievances, often coupled with the presence of economic grievances, also figure in lower-class social disturbances and are important in understanding the protest activities of economically privileged groups such as merchants and professionals and especially students and intellectuals. The last two groups often supply the ideological, organizational and leadership resources that facilitate mobilization among the working class and peasants for protest activity (for more detail, cf. Oberschall 1973).

The preceding paragraphs are not meant to be an exhaustive list of all types of strain and grievances, but only of the more common patterns of economic grievances that affect the lower classes who so frequently make up the bulk of participants in social movements and confrontations and who are likely to make up the majority of victims of group violence.

Hypotheses: Statement and Discussion

Assuming that a situation of conflict or increased conflict exists as a result of economic and other changes—some of which were listed in the preceding section—what hypotheses and empirical generalizations can one make about the probability of violent conflict and the magnitude of violence (measured roughly by the number of casualties)? Hypothesis 1 is that

> the protesters use violent means only after they have attempted other nonviolent means of seeking redress for their grievances.

Alternately (hypothesis 1a),

> the protest group waits for some time for reforms designed to reduce social strain to take effect, and only after these reforms have proved ineffective do they resort to violent means of protest.

Still another variation (hypothesis 1b) is that

> protest groups initiate violent actions only after the authorities or ruling groups break a promise or agreement of reform, and thus provide little or no opportunity for nonviolent means of instituting desired changes.

For instance, Huntington (1962, 25) states that the Huk leaders in the Philippines first attempted to achieve their goals by peaceful means, but when the legislature refused to seat seven elected Huks, their leaders returned to the countryside to spark a revolt. Writing about the Zapata rising in Mexico in 1910–1911, McNeely (1966, 155-57) reports that Zapata's native village had a long record of contentions over its land rights, that the new governor paid little attention to the villagers' petitions despite the fact that their legal claims were upheld as valid, and that legal action by villagers in Mexico City also failed to produce results. Only after these institutional channels were exhausted did the uprising start. Concerning the Luddite outbreaks in England, 1811, Darvall (1934, 47-48, 64) explicitly states that the stockingers and weavers first tried to negotiate their grievances over wages, the rent of frames, the truck system and other matters with the hosiers, but without any positive results. As for the June days in Paris during the 1848 revolution, the working people of Paris did not start erecting barricades until after Louis Blanc's Luxembourg Commission and the national workshops (the two major gains the Paris working people achieved after the overthrow of the July monarchy and one of the main sources of employment and livelihood for them at a time of economic depression) were dissolved and the workers given a choice of enlisting in the army, draining marshes, or remaining in Paris without work or pay (Rude 1964, 172). Examples can be multiplied and in any case are only meant to be illustrative and suggestive.

A second set of hypotheses deals with some circumstances under which the casualties will be many in number rather than few. Hypothesis 2 is that

> in violent confrontations the authorities' actions produce most, or at least more than half, of the casualties.

A subhypothesis (2a) is that

> violence is more often initiated by the authorities and their agents than by the protesters, as when peaceful demonstrations, marchers, petitioners, peaceful assemblies and the like are broken up and attacked.

Of course, protesters often initiate actions that are illegal and coercive, but not destructive of life and property, such as squatting on land or cultivating land illegally, refusing to pay taxes, occupying factories and mines, or refusing to disperse, that represent a challenge to the authorities. I do not mean to imply that the authorities will randomly and lightly initiate violence as a rule. Another subhypothesis (2b) is that

> when the confrontation is not directly between the protesters and the authorities, but between two hostile population groups, such as employers and employees, or whites and blacks, the casualties tend to be higher when the authorities either openly side with one group against the other, or refrain from intervening in the situation and thereby legitimize the actions of the aggressor.

Moreover (hypothesis 2c),

> the magnitude of casualties will be greater if the agents of social control know that they will not be held accountable for the casualties they produce during repression.

This often happens when public opinion favors repression during a period of "Red" scare, of nationalism and jingoism, of religious enthusiasm, or of similar waves of fear and hostility during which the protesters have been identified as "Reds," "traitors," or "infidels" and "heretics," to cite some common examples. In other situations, social disturbances may occur in outlying areas, usually rural, with poor communications, so that little information about casualties and the details of the confrontation filters out other than through government controlled sources. It may also happen in situations where the judiciary is subordinate to the executive branch and in any case is not much influenced by an unorganized public opinion. Another variant on this theme (hypothesis 2d) is that

> if the protesters belong to a negatively privileged or "pariah" social category, such as a religious minority or peasants, who have not enjoyed full citizenship rights and have traditionally been violently repressed, casualties will tend to be high,

again because public opinion supports repression, and because of low accountability for the use of force by the agents of social control. Finally, as Donald J. Black has pointed out to me (hypothesis 2e),

> the probability of violence decreases to the extent that a third impartial party intervenes as buffer or mediator in the conflict.

This is in fact the rationale behind the U.N. peacekeeping force as it was put into operation in Cyprus and elsewhere.

We note, for instance, from the National Advisory Commission (1968, 68–69, 107, 115–66 fn. 20, 164) that in the 1967 urban riots in the United States, of the eighty-three persons who died in the seventy-five disorders studied, only about 10 percent were public officials and that the overwhelming majority of the civilians killed were Negroes, most of these shot by the police or other agents of social control. In Detroit, rioters were responsible for three deaths at most, whereas the police and national guard accounted for between twenty-seven and thirty deaths. In summarizing the detailed casualty figures resulting from popular disturbances between 1730 and 1848 in Western Europe, Rude (1964, 255–56) concludes that "destruction of property, then, is a constant feature of the preindustrial crowd; but not destruction of human lives . . . From this balance sheet of violence and reprisal, it would appear, then, that it was authority rather than the crowd that was conspicuous for its violence to life and limb." During the Paris Commune of 1871, in contrast to the several hundred troops of the Versailles regiment killed and the sixty-three hostages shot by the Communards, at least 20,000 Communards were killed, shot as prisoners, or subsequently executed by the authorities, not counting the number of imprisonments and deportations to penal camps (Postgate 1962, 286).

In going to standard historical sources one can produce similar figures for the discrepancy in magnitude of casualties produced by the authorities on the one hand and the insurgents, rebels, or protesters on the other in confrontations such as the June Days of Paris in 1848, the Russian Revolution of 1905–1906, the Mau Mau uprising, the Nyasaland (Malawi) protests of 1959, and so on. So far as the authorities initiating or escalating violence is concerned, history is filled with such examples. The precipitating event of the February 1848 revolution occurred when fifty to one-hundred demonstrators were killed or wounded by troops as the protesters marched in support of the parliamentary opposition after the authorities had banned a large public banquet planned by the opposition in Paris (Rude 1964, 167). The precipitating event in the Russian revolution of 1905 occurred on Bloody Sunday when an immense procession of unarmed workers in their Sunday clothes, chanting church hymns and led by Father Gapon, sought to present a petition to the Czar and were attacked by the troops and the Cossacks, resulting in a massacre of about 1000 petitioners. It should be pointed out that in conformity with hypothesis 1, Father Gapon had attempted before this event to seek redress of the workers' grievances through bureaucratic channels and had gotten nowhere.

In the Hungarian Revolution of 1956 (United Nations 1957, 81–83) one of the precipitating events occurred when students, on the evening of October 22, demanded that the radio station broadcast their resolutions to the Hungarian people and were fired upon by security police inside the radio building after student representatives had already entered the radio building to negotiate with the officials of the radio. In a subsequent aggravating incident on October 25, a huge crowd of several thousand peaceful people, many of them women and children, were waiting for Prime Minister Nagy to appear when a number of flag-carrying demonstrators appeared in the square and the security police and possibly also Soviet troops opened up on everybody with machine guns, killing anywhere from three-hundred to eight-hundred people.

Police partiality with an aggressor during clashes between two population groups incites the aggressors to further violence, prolongs the disturbances and escalates weaponry. These are all productive of a larger number of casualties than if the authorities had intervened impartially to separate the two sides. For example, Waskow (1967, chap. 10) has pointed out the partiality of police in the 1919 race riots, and Lee and Humphrey (1943, chap. 4) for the Detroit riot of 1943. Furthermore, in communal or religious riots producing a very large number of casualties, the police or military actually join the aggressor group during the clashes, are directly responsible for many casualties, and often make weapons and ammunition available to one side, as happened in the Ibo massacres in Northern Nigeria in 1966 and the anticommunist massacres in Java in 1965. In these instances of communal riots the agents of social control did not play the part of the impartial buffer associated with lower casualties, as stated in hypothesis 2e. In some of the above confrontations the protesters were drawn from negatively privileged groups (hypothesis 2d) and the agents of social control were operating in a tradition of low accountability for the casualties they produced (hypothesis 2c). The perfunctory manner in which inquests are often conducted—as they were in Los Angeles after the 1965 riot—to establish the cause and responsibility in the deaths resulting from police action is well described in Conot (1967, chap. 53).

Aside from these hypotheses that deal with the circumstances of confrontation, the social status of the protest group and the restraints operating on the agents of social control, other related hypotheses might be formulated, some, for instance, dealing with the relative social status overlap between them and past history of hostility and recriminations, and the capacity for repression of the authorities in the sense of their command over resources, their availability to organize an apparatus of social control and the absolute size of this apparatus. Is violence more likely to erupt and casualties likely to be higher when Cossacks face peasants than if troops made up of peasant conscripts face them? Are they higher if black demonstrators or rioters are confronted by a white or a mixed white and black police force and other agents of social control in the United States? Are they likely to be higher if troops drawn from rural areas in France face the Paris working people than if troops are made up of urban recruits and so on? The answers may well be in the affirmative in all these instances, but at this point I have simply not explored these matters in sufficient depth to formulate a set of clear and meaningful hypotheses. The evidence is, in any case, complicated. For instance, it is doubtful that there was less violence in the United States labor conflict when native employers, agents of social control and armed guards were facing native, English-speaking workers than when they were facing immigrant workers of Southern and Eastern European origin.

Another set of hypotheses dealing with the magnitude of violence has to do with the ecological and technological aspects of the confrontation, although these matters have received little attention in the social science literature and are especially difficult to state unambiguously in terms of hypotheses. Still, hypothesis 3 is worth stating:

> when two population groups are locked in conflict, and when a majority group attacks a numerical minority, casualties will be especially high if the minority group does not live in compact settlements but in small clusters dispersed among the hostile majority.

This ecological pattern existed in several instances of large scale communal or tribal warfare productive of very high casualties, such as the Hindu-Moslem clashes on the Indian subcontinent at the time of partition, the clashes between Greek and Turkish Cypriots, the Ibo massacres in Northern Nigeria, the Tutsi-Hutu clashes in Ruanda-Urundi, the anti-communist massacres in Java, and rural violence in Columbia in the 1950s. On the other hand, compact settlement of a population group in a particular geographic area to the exclusion of other groups makes for the possibility of secession and civil war, as in Biafra and Buganda in 1966.

Access to weapons and the disparity of weapons technology also are important and independent factors in the production of casualties. According to hypothesis 4,

> if only one side has access to modern weapons such as firearms, and the other side does not (it has only agricultural tools or hunting weapons) casualties tend to be higher than if there is no weapons disparity.

This occurs often in conjunction with a situation (cf. hypothesis 2b) as in Ruanda-Urundi and Northern Nigeria, where troops armed with modern weapons join one group against the other or make such weapons available to the side they favor. If there is no weapons disparity, access to lethal weapons becomes the crucial technological factor. Modern weapons used in a confrontation in and of themselves are not necessarily more productive of casualties than the use of premodern weapons and agricultural implements. If the groups in the confrontation have premodern weapons within reach in their own homes at a moment's notice and are skilled and accustomed in their use, casualties will tend to be high. Describing the communal riots in India in 1946–1948 that produced close to one million fatalities, Richardson (1960, 43) writes that "communal killing was mostly by sticks, small knives, small axes, swords, spears, with only a few shotguns, rifles, or automatics." Hypothesis 4a then is that

> in the absence of weapons disparity, possession of modern firearms by both sides is not in itself productive of higher casualties than possession of traditional weapons and agricultural implements.

Because access to traditional weapons by a large number of participants in the conflict is more probable in rural than in urban populations, hypothesis 4b is that

> violent clashes in rural areas between two hostile groups will be more productive of casualties than clashes in cities.

Furthermore, as Juan Linz has pointed out, visibility, both social and physical, is higher in rural areas. Group memberships of people in rural areas are well known by all and potential victims will therefore not be able to disappear socially and physically in the anonymous settings of large cities, as is the case with urban violence. It often happens that the rural/urban distinction is correlated with ecological and other factors described in the set of hypotheses 2 and 3, all tending to favor higher casualties in the rural context, so that the test of hypothesis 4c might involve practical difficulties of locating enough cases for which the other factors can be controlled. There are other variables that are logical candidates for inclusion in hypotheses, especially the absolute and relative sizes of the conflict groups, of the protesters and the agents of social control, but little thought has been so far given to "size" variables in the literature and it may be premature to speculate about them at this point. The effects of size or relative size may well turn out to be less important than another set of variables to which I will now turn.

These variables concern the number and magnitude of grievances, the degree of mutually reinforcing, nonoverlapping social cleavages separating the conflict groups, the ideological level of the protesters' demands, the degree of organization of the conflict groups, and, finally, presence or absence of a recognition issue. In each case, we are asking what the relationship of these variables is to the likelihood of violence and its magnitude. For the first three variables, I shall hypothesize no systematic relationship. Hypothesis 5 then states that

> the number of grievances, the magnitude of strain, the magnitude of the frustrations experienced by the protesters, while making conflict more likely and increasing the intensity of that conflict, nevertheless bears no positive (or negative) relationship to the probability of violence and the magnitude of casualties.

In the same vein, if the conflict groups are separated by a number of nonoverlapping divisions—ethnic, religious, class, cultural-linguistic, and the like—rather than just one such division, conflict is more likely to involve more people, last longer and have a higher intensity, but will not necessarily be more violent (cf. Dahrendorf 1959, 213-15, for an extended discussion of this hypothesis). To state this idea as hypothesis 6,

> the number of reinforcing and nonoverlapping social cleavages separating the conflict groups bears no systematic relationship to the likelihood and magnitude of violence.

It may well be true empirically and historically that a number of other factors previously hypothesized as favoring violence is correlated with the last two named variables but I see no direct causal link.

The same lack of relationship is hypothesized here for the ideological level of the demands expressed by the protest group. Demands will have a low ideological level insofar as they are merely specific measures to relieve particular grievances, such as demands for higher wages, shorter work hours, lower food prices, or the dismissal of a corrupt or hated official. They will have a higher ideological level if they address themselves to major structural changes in the polity and the economy (such as the overthrow of the government) changes in the form of government (e.g., republic rather than monarchy), nationalization of industry and expropriation of private property (such as land, backed up by radical philosophic and ideological appeals and justifications). Hypothesis 7 is, then, that

> the ideological level of the demands bears no systematic relationship to the likelihood and magnitude of violence.

Even if hypotheses 5-7 overstate the lack of relationship, the effects of these variables are dwarfed by the effects of the previously named variables and the next two (and last) variables to be considered—organization and recognition—whose importance for conflict theory Dahrendorf (1959, 223–27) has already pointed out. Hypothesis 8, briefly stated, is that

> the lower the level of organization of *both* conflict groups, the higher the likelihood and magnitude of violence.

By level of organization I mean the degree to which there exists an effective, recognized, stable leadership structure exercising direction and control over the actions of the rank and file participants in the conflict, as opposed to the low level of organization of protest groups that more or less spontaneously collect as hostile crowds after precipitating incidents, and where at most temporary and local leaders may emerge. So far as the degree of organization of the agents of social control is concerned, it is higher to the degree to which networks of communication, chain of command and troop discipline are maintained. That is more likely to happen if the force is professional, has been trained, or is experienced in handling confrontations with protest crowds. A confrontation likely to be particularly violent is one in which an unorganized, spontaneously assembled hostile crowd faces a disorganized police force, troops, or another unorganized crowd. A corollary of this hypothesis is that (hypothesis 8a)

> if the protest group is split into rival camps and factions with competing leaders, the likelihood of violence is greater than if it is united.

By recognition I mean that the authorities, regardless of what position they may take on the substantive issues and demands, recognize the right to protest and are willing to listen to, sit down with, talk to, and negotiate in good faith with the leaders, deputies, representatives, or spokesmen of the protesters. Nonrecognition can be inferred from several indicators that signal to the protest group that recognition is not granted or is in the process of being withdrawn: refusal to receive, listen to, debate, discuss, or negotiate with the representatives of the protesters, arrest of their leaders, harassment of their organizing efforts through arrest, blacklists, curbs on the right to free speech and so on. Hypothesis 9 can now be stated:

> if recognition is granted, the likelihood and magnitude of violence tends to be lower than if recognition is not granted or is being withdrawn.

A subhypothesis (9a) is that

> even after violence has already broken out, it is likely to diminish when recognition is granted, but violence is likely to continue if it is not granted.

Some may object to this last hypothesis as self-evident or tautological, since recognition implies that the conflict is on its way to becoming institutionalized and regulated, if not resolved. Indeed, recognition is the major step in institutionalizing conflict. In a broader context than the social movements and episodes of collective behavior here discussed, recognition is analogous to the extension of political and civil rights to previously disenfranchised "new" groups or classes. Yet the above formulation stated in terms of recognition is more precise and measurable than if a hypothesis were worded in terms of the degree of institutionalization of conflict and the likelihood of violence. Although recognition in some sense implies that the authorities have been responsive to the protest group and have opened previously blocked channels of communication and influence, similar hypotheses stated in terms of "greater responsiveness of the authorities" and "acceptance of the legitimacy of protest" are less precise than hypothesis 9. For regardless of the substantive issues and demands, lack of recognition may well and often does become the major issue of the conflict, so that even if the authorities promise or institute reforms and changes and are thus responsive, the conflict will still remain potentially high on likelihood of violence until the recognition issue is also resolved. Concessions extracted under popular pressures without recognition may perhaps be considered a very low or minimal form of recognition, and as such can lower the likelihood or level of existing violence, but it may not always do so. Recognition, in itself, without immediate concessions on substantive issues, or even before reforms can take effect, will have a tendency to defuse a potentially violent confrontation or lower an already existing level of violence. It is nevertheless true, by virtue of hypothesis 1a, that if recognition does not eventually also bring concessions or reforms on substantive matters, the likelihood of violent conflict will again increase.

Two exceptions are worth noting. There are situations in which the authorities might well grant recognition, but the protesters simply do not demand it because they lack literacy and education, because they lack a tradition of organization and leadership, or because curbs on freedom of assembly, association and speech make even a rudimentary organization of the protest group unlikely. Hobsbawm's (1959, 108–25) description of the premodern city mob represents such a case of partly institutionalized conflict in which recognition was not yet an issue. According to the traditional conception of urban lower class people, "if for one reason or another the usual livelihood of the people was jeopardized or broke down, it was the duty of the prince and his aristocracy to provide relief and to keep the cost of living down." The urban mob usually rioted against unemployment or a high cost of living, not for recognition. Immediate concessions on both these demands were therefore adequate and appropriate responses and would stop violence. But as we move into the nineteenth century, the recognition issue assumes more and more importance relative to the substantive demands of the protest group.

The second exception is much more important in the contemporary world. In this situation, a highly organized and ideologically sophisticated group adopts the strategy of protracted violent conflict in order to overthrow the government, as in guerilla insurgency, often with some foreign support. Since recognition is denied to the insurgents, we are led to predict violent conflict; nevertheless, since the insurgents are, or eventually become highly organized, according to hypothesis 8, conflict ought to be less violent than it usually turns out to be. Of course, many insurgencies actually start at a low ideological and organizational level, not much different from other protest movements and only after recognition is withheld and reforms are ineffective or not instituted at all, do they become full blown, highly organized, ideological guerilla movements. One might therefore formulate the following hypothesis 10:

> in a contemporary context, if the protest movement goes unrecognized and if it is not crushed by the agents of social control, the movement will tend to become highly organized and more ideological, and the likelihood of protracted, violent conflict will be high.

In other words, under modern conditions, the recognition issue is more basic for the explanation of violence than the level of organization of the conflict groups, although, given any single confrontation in an ongoing conflict, it is still hypothesized that the more organized both sides are, the lower the magnitude of violence and the number of casualties (hypothesis 8).

Support for Hypotheses 5 to 10

The following historical instances provide a few of many available illustrations, although it is difficult to isolate the operation of one variable at a time. Compare, for instance, the February 1917 overthrow of the Czar with the Bolshevik coup in October 1917. In February, a week-long, unorganized, and spontaneous movement, which started as a protest for bread led by women and gradually developed into a general strike, produced 1,315 casualties (Pettee 1938, 102; Trotsky 1959, 97-173) at a time when almost all revolutionary leaders were in Siberia or abroad, whereas in October, a highly organized and ideological party overthrew the Kerensky government with but a dozen fatalities (Trotsky 1959, 336-436). This paired comparison would support both hypotheses 7 and 8.

Consider in addition the Detroit riot of 1967 and the casualties produced by the disorganized police and National Guard, in contrast with the disciplined and well-led paratroopers (National Advisory Commission on Civil Disorders 1968, 99-102). The paratroopers who followed orders to unload their weapons and remain in evidence on sidewalks and in the street expended only 201 rounds of ammunition, did not suffer any injuries from gunshot and inflicted only one fatality. By contrast, the panicked police and National Guard disobeyed orders to unload their weapons, expended thousands of rounds of ammunition, sometimes at each other, were hiding behind walls and shooting out street lights in order not to be visible and reacted to all conceivable rumors that kept flooding their communications system. Their actions accounted for between twenty-seven and thirty fatalities.

Conot (1967, 218, 229, 234, 278, 325-26, 329, 339, 367) provides further evidence that in the Los Angeles riot of 1965 many fatalities were produced by police when they became disorganized, panicked, and acted on rumor, no matter how incredible those rumors now appear in retrospect. As a matter of fact, the more violent turn of the Negro movement in 1964 and later years can be explained by invoking hypothesis 8. As the Negro movement shifted from the more organized and better-led southern Negroes to the previously unorganized northern urban lower-class Negroes whom Dr. Martin Luther King, Jr. and other civil rights leaders were unable to mobilize into their organizations, violence increased considerably. In the same vein, the relatively nonviolent summer of 1969 can also be explained partly in organizational terms. By 1969 in urban ghettos, radical and militant blacks had managed to create at least a rudimentary organization network and following, and, in addition, many ghetto dwellers themselves had organized into block or neighborhood organizations for pressing their demands or for curbing youth and rioting. It is also possible that the agents of social control were more experienced and organized by the summer of 1969. Thus, unlike those who focus on magnitude of strain and frustration to explain the lower level of violence in 1969, I draw attention to the change in degree of organization of both conflict groups between 1969 and earlier years. There is no evidence that strain and frustration were lower in 1969 than in the previous four summers. Indeed, as formulated in hypothesis 5, these factors do not account for the magnitude of violence in any case.

So far as the recognition issue is concerned, Huntington (1962, 21) has noted that it is a crucial factor in protracted guerilla wars:

> Insurrectionary war is almost always total. Neither side wants to recognize the legitimacy of the other, and negotiations, much less agreements, imply such recognition. Armistices and peace treaties are possible between governments, but rarely between governments and anti-governments.

Perhaps the most promising area to highlight the importance of recognition comes from comparative labor movements. Taft (1966, 127–34) has noted that a leading cause of violence in American labor disputes was the refusal of management to recognize unions: "In cases where the union is recognized, strikes seldom lead to violent encounters. However, in unorganized strikes or in those which have arisen in an effort to gain recognition, the use of violence is more common." A comparison of the labor movements in the United States with those of Western Europe provides an appropriate illustration for several of the hypotheses under review. The American labor movement was less ideological, less organized, yet, more violent than European labor movements. Taft (1966, 127–34) writes that

> it may appear anomalous that the U.S., a country in which class feeling and class ideology are almost entirely absent, has experienced considerable amounts of violence in labor disputes. . . . With the exception of a small minority, American workers have not been attracted to the various branches of anarchism, communism, socialism and syndicalism. Yet American history is dotted with clashes between strikers and strikebreakers and police authorities.

Another historian of labor movements, Val Lorwin (1957, 37–39), writes in this connection that

> American workers had to fight bloodier industrial battles than the French for the right of unions to exist and to function. Their political history knew nothing like the "June Days" or the Commune. But the rail strikes of 1877, the pitched battle of Homestead, the Ludlow massacre, were bloodier than Fourmies and Draveil and Villeneuve-Saint Georges . . . France had nothing like the private armies, factory arsenals and industrial espionage service exposed by the LaFollette Committee . . . American employers came to recognize the unions only under the multiple pressures of public opinion, administration policy, a reversal of Supreme Court interpretations and finally and essentially, worker self-organizations.

In fact, the history of the American labor movement will provide an opportunity to test some of the hypotheses in somewhat more systematic fashion. Suffice it to remark here that it is not likely, as I have expressed in hypotheses 5 and 6, that American workers were under greater or more numerous forms of strain than French workers, or that there were a greater number of nonoverlapping divisions separating labor from management and the agents of social control in this country than abroad. To account for the greater violence in labor relations in this country it is the recognition issue and the level of organization of the conflict groups that are the most promising explanatory variables.

Hypotheses: Summary

Hypothesis 1:

> The protesters use violent means only after they have attempted other nonviolent means of seeking redress for their grievances.

Hypothesis 1a:

> The protest group waits for some time for reforms designed to reduce social strain to take effect, and only after these reforms have proved ineffective do they resort to violent means of protest.

Hypothesis 1b:

> Protest groups initiate violent actions only after the authorities or ruling groups break a promise or agreement of reform and thus provide little or no opportunity for nonviolent means of instituting desired changes.

Hypothesis 2:

In violent confrontation the authorities' actions produce most, or at least more than half, of the casualties.

Hypothesis 2a:

Violence is more often initiated by the authorities and their agents than by the protesters, as when peaceful demonstrations, marchers, petitioners, peaceful assemblies and the like are broken up and attacked.

Hypothesis 2b:

When the confrontation is not directly between the protesters and the authorities, but between two hostile population groups, such as employers and employees, or whites and blacks, the casualties tend to be higher when the authorities either openly side with one group against the other, or refrain from intervening in the situation and thereby legitimize the actions of the aggressor.

Hypothesis 2c:

The magnitude of casualties will be greater if the agents of social control know that they will not be held accountable for the casualties they produce during repression.

Hypothesis 2d:

If the protesters belong to a negatively privileged or "pariah" social category, such as a religious minority or peasants, who have not enjoyed full citizenship rights and have traditionally been violently repressed, casualties will tend to be high.

Hypothesis 2e:

The probability of violence decreases to the extent that a third impartial party intervenes as buffer or mediator in the conflict.

Hypothesis 3:

When two population groups are locked in conflict and when a majority group attacks a numerical minority, casualties will be especially high if the minority group does not live in compact settlements but in small clusters dispersed among the hostile majority.

Hypothesis 4:

If only one side has access to modern weapons such as firearms, and the other side does not (it has only agricultural tools or hunting weapons) casualties tend to be higher than if there is no weapons disparity.

Hypothesis 4a:

In the absence of weapons disparity, possession of modern firearms by both sides is not in itself productive of higher casualties than possession of traditional weapons and agricultural implements.

Hypothesis 4b:

Violent clashes in rural areas between two hostile groups will be more productive of casualties than clashes in cities.

Hypothesis 5:

The number of grievances, the magnitude of strain, the magnitude of the frustrations experienced by the protesters, while making conflict more likely and increasing the intensity of that conflict, nevertheless bears no positive (or negative) relationship to the probability of violence and the magnitude of casualties.

Hypothesis 6:

The number of reinforcing and nonoverlapping social cleavages separating the conflict groups bears no systematic relationship to the likelihood and magnitude of violence.

Hypothesis 7:

The ideological level of the demands bears no systematic relationship to the likelihood and magnitude of violence.

Hypothesis 8:

The lower the level of organization of *both* conflict groups, the higher the likelihood and magnitude of violence.

Hypothesis 8a:

If the protest group is split into rival camps and factions with competing leaders, the likelihood of violence is greater than if it is united.

Hypothesis 9:

If recognition is granted, the likelihood and magnitude of violence tends to be lower than if recognition is not granted or is being withdrawn.

Hypothesis 9a:

Even after violence has already broken out, it is likely to diminish when recognition is granted, but violence is likely to continue if it is not granted.

Hypothesis 10:

> In a contemporary context, if the protest movement goes unrecognized and if it is not crushed by the agents of social control, the movement will tend to become highly organized and more ideological, and the likelihood of protracted, violent conflict will be high.

Violence in American Strikes, 1870s to 1930s

For the purpose of testing some of the above hypotheses, a list of major strikes from the index of Commons (1918, 1935) and other sources for the period 1870 to 1930 in the coal, railroad, iron and steel, mining (other than coal) and cotton and silk (textiles, for short) industries was compiled. Details on each strike for a number of independent variables and violence were ascertained. Commons (1935) is especially thorough in providing information on violence, often listing fatalities, injuries, and property damage in great detail and the circumstances under which these occurred. Because industries differ on so many of the independent variables and other characteristics that are relevant for industrial conflict, it was felt that major strikes in only these five industries would be analyzed so as to exercise some control over spurious variables. At the same time, there is considerable variation on the independent variables between the five industries, as will be discussed below. On an overall level of industrial conflict, we may note that Kerr and Siegel (1954, 211) rate coal as highest on "strike proneness," textiles as medium high, and transportation and iron and steel are rated as medium for the United States.

Measurement presents a real problem. The primary sources, which I did not check, are contemporary newspapers (including those of the unions), labor department reports of the various states and the frequent state or congressional investigating commissions that were appointed after a period of acute labor violence. Commons (1918, 1935) and the other books I have relied upon are based on these primary sources. I have tried to rate strikes on three levels of intensity of violence—the lowest level, where no violence is mentioned; the next level, where reference is made to clashes, injuries, and property damage, but no fatalities; and, finally, the highest level, where one or more fatalities occurred. Since fatalities almost always occurred when clashes, injuries, and property damage also took place, the underlying variable is here treated as ordinal.

It was unfortunately not possible to get sufficient information on the degree of organization of the strikers and the agents of social control, as well as on a number of other variables such as precise ethnic composition of the strikers and social control agents in order to check out degree of overlap of major social categories associated with patterns of group antagonism in the United States. However, since the causes of strikes are always reported, it was possible to check whether a "recognition" issue was present. The issues at stake might simply be wages, hours, conditions of work, or the like, in which case there was no recognition issue. At the other end, the major issue, or an explicitly stated demand of the workers before the strike, might be recognition of the union in the sense that they sought collective bargaining rights or the right to organize. In between, there are instances where the employer sought to weaken or "bust" a union, such as discharging union members, discriminating against them in employment, or otherwise harassing union organizing activities, but where recognition of the union was not explicitly demanded (aside from demands to reinstate discharged workers). I label this in-between category conveniently "union weakening." Since disputes over wages, hours, and conditions were usually present in all the strikes under review, recognition is treated here as an ordinal variable. For reasons stated earlier, I do not control for the number of strikers involved and duration of the strike, although in a more comprehensive investigation it might be desirable to do that at some point.

Table 6.1a
Occurrence of Violence by Issue: Railroad Strikes

	Recognition Issue	Union Weakening	Wages, Hours, etc.	Total
Fatalities	1	1	1	3
Violence, no fatalities	0	1	0	1
No violence	0	1	5	6
Total	1	3	6	10

The findings on the association between presence of the recognition issue and degree of violence are summarized in tables 6.1a through 6.1e separately by industry, and in table 6.2 for the entire set of fifty-four strikes. In table 6.2, it should be noted that gamma equals .52, which is fairly high considering the usual magnitudes of association found in sociological research, and therefore hypothesis 9 is supported, though this modest investigation is only a preliminary one. The major contrast is between the first two columns and the last one—wages and hours. There is not much difference on violence in strikes where recognition was an explicit issue, as opposed to being implicit in the attempts of employers to weaken an existing union or to prevent its establishment in the first place by harassing organizers, discharging union members, discriminatory employment practices directed at union members and the like.

Table 6.1b
Occurrence of Violence by Issue: Coal Mining Strikes

	Recognition Issue	Union Weakening	Wages, Hours, etc.	Total
Fatalities	4	4	1	9
Violence, no fatalities	0	0	2	2
No violence	0	1	6	7
Total	4	5	9	18

Table 6.1c
Occurrence of Violence by Issue: Iron and Steel Strikes

	Recognition Issue	Union Weakening	Wages, Hours, etc.	Total
Fatalities	2	1	0	3
Violence, no fatalities	1	0	0	1
No violence	1	0	0	1
Total	4	1	0	5

It is worth examining the patterns of violence separately by industry, for some impressionistic support for several other hypotheses can be provided in this manner. In railroads, there is a relatively low incidence of violence. Two exceptions should be noted. The railroad upheaval of 1877 produced over one-hundred fatalities, although at this early date, recognition was not an issue, the strike wave being precipitated by a wage cut at a time of depression. The other major violent confrontation, the Pullman strike of 1894, with twenty-five fatalities, did involve as one of its causes union-busting activities by Pullman against the American Railway Union. The low incidence of violence in the railroad industry can be accounted for by the fact that after the Knights of Labor declined in the latter 1880s in the railroads, management adopted a policy of favorable treatment of the four major railway brotherhoods—the engineers, the firemen, the conductors, and the trainmen—with full recognition, a high wage scale and acceptance of union seniority rules (hypothesis 9). Management also tended to accept outside mediation in railroad disputes by governmental bodies (hypothesis 2e), and the brotherhoods did win an eight-hour day in 1917 through national legislation after President Wilson, the Supreme Court, and Congress intervened. Many of the major strikes after the 1880s involved the shop crafts and switchmen, not the four favored brotherhoods (hypothesis 9).

Table 6.1d
Occurrence of Violence by Issue: Mining (other than coal) Strikes

	Recognition Issue	Union Weakening	Wages, Hours, etc.	Total
Fatalities	2	2	6	10
Violence, no fatalities	0	0	1	1
No violence	1	0	0	1
Total	3	2	7	12

In coal mining, strikes were especially numerous and major strikes tended to be violent throughout the period, the most productive of fatalities being the Colorado coal strike of 1913–1914, during which the Ludlow massacre occurred, and the 1922 strike during which the Herrin massacre took place. Most of the strikes took place in the coal fields of Pennsylvania and West Virginia, and the largest strikes involved hundreds of thousands of miners. The United Mine Workers was successful in getting recognition in the late 1910s in many of the Pennsylvania fields but had rather more difficulty in the decentralized bituminous coal industry and especially in the West Virginia fields. However, in the 1920s unionism was again weakened considerably. Apart from recognition, the relatively high incidence of violence can be accounted for by the frequent practice of employers in importing strikebreakers and armed guards, and in evicting strikers from company housing and otherwise harassing the activities of the strikers (hypothesis 2a). Easy access to weapons was a factor in arming miners. Local authorities generally sided with the employers and operated in remote mountain districts, with low account-ability, and against an ethnic, negatively privileged, immigrant work force (hypotheses 2b, 2c, and 2d).

Table 6.1e
Occurrence of Violence by Issue: Textile Strikes

	Recognition Issue	Union Weakening	Wages, Hours, etc.	Total
Fatalities	3	0	2	5
Violence, no fatalities	1	1	1	3
No violence	0	0	1	1
Total	4	1	4	9

Table 6.2
Occurrence of Violence by Issue: All Industries Strikes (in percentages)

	Recognition Issue	Union Weakening	Wages, Hours, etc.
Fatalities	75	67	38
Violence, no fatalities	12.5	16	15
No violence	12.5	16	46
Total	100	100	100
Total number	(16)	(12)	(26)

$\gamma = .52$

In the iron and steel industry there are very few instances of strikes from which to generalize from, but recognition was a key issue in major strikes, as United States Steel set the pace in destroying the Amalgamated Association of Iron and Steel Workers after 1901. It was only in the latter 1930s that recognition was slowly achieved by means of a CIO sponsored drive.

In mining other than coal, mainly in the Rocky Mountain states, the hypothesis linking recognition and violence is least supported, since almost all strikes tended to lead to violence regardless of the issues involved. The key factors here, present even more than in coal mining, were access to weapons and dynamite by the miners, the universal practice of employers in importing strikebreakers and armed guards and the support of local authorities for strikebreaking activities (hypotheses 2b, 2c, and 2d). A frequent source of violence was the attack of armed miners upon trains of strikebreakers and the dynamiting of mines employing scabs, the attack of guards and deputies upon the tent colonies of strikers and their families, mass arrests of strikers, their imprisonment in bullpens and their forced deportations (hypotheses 2 and 2a). In fact, Western labor conflict in the mining area comes closest to continuous open warfare, yet lacks ideological issues (hypothesis 7).

In textiles, a relatively decentralized industry with a high frequency of strikes, unionism was hampered by the lack of skilled workers antedating machine production, the immigrant work force in New England after 1900 and the competition of southern mills with New England. While violence and fatalities occurred frequently in major strikes despite a high proportion of female labor, overall casualties tended to be very low. Textiles is interesting, however, since it is one of the few industries where the IWW and communist-dominated unions were trying to compete with the AFL-affiliated United Textile Workers in organizing the work force and frequently managed to lead the strikes. While not enough cases are available, it is interesting to note that so far as violence is concerned, it was equally likely to occur when the moderate UTW was involved as when the more ideological IWW and other unions were (hypothesis 7). For instance, an appropriately matched comparison is provided during the 1929 drive to organize Southern textile workers. A strike in Gastonia, North Carolina, led by the communist-sponsored National Textile Workers' Union resulted in three fatalities, whereas in neighboring Marion, North Carolina, a strike over similar issues in a factory of roughly the same labor force composition and size led by the UTW (AFL-affiliated) resulted in six fatalities. The Southern employers, authorities and local population tended to perceive unionization drives as Red-inspired and unpatriotic regardless, and the UTW personnel as well as community labor leaders were frequently assaulted and run out of town.

7

Beliefs and Ideologies:
The European Witchcraze

Historians estimate that some 100,000 persons were executed for the crime of witchcraft in Europe between 1450 and 1700 (Russell 1980), and about 100,000 more were indicted for the same crime but were found innocent and released, or found guilty but punished less severely. How can such events be explained? Why and how did the witchcraze get started? How could so many be convinced of a conspiracy between Satan and some of their neighbors, mostly poor, old women, to subvert organized religion, morality, and cause harm to innocent victims? Why were such drastic steps taken to stamp out witches? How and why did the craze come to an end?

In the past thirty years, an impressive outpouring of historical scholarship has provided some answers to these questions. What historians have uncovered ought to be a humbling experience to social scientists for this scholarship fails to confirm our stock theories about ideologies, collective deviance, and social control, be they based on Marxism, psychoanalysis, functionalism, modernization theory, interest theories, and most recently, feminism. I believe that a rational choice explanation employing methodological individualism and focusing on the truth value of beliefs and ideologies from the actors' viewpoint, together with a theory of communication rooted in cognitive psychology and social structure, can do a better job of explaining the witchcraze. And because the witchcraze is a nontrivial and intellectually challenging manifestation

187

of ideology and of collective action, it is a "test case" for a rational choice theory of ideology.

This chapter is organized into five parts. First I will voice some skepticism about current theories of ideology. Then I will provide a summary of the main facts and trends and explanations that historians have come up with. Third, I will show how these facts and explanations create difficulties to some current theories of ideology. Fourth, I will outline a rational choice view of belief and ideology and account for the witchcraze in rational choice terms. Then I draw some conclusions from this application of the theory.

Skepticism About Current Theories of Ideology

The "state of the art" of theories of ideology is still how Geertz (1973, 201) characterized it almost twenty years ago:

> There are currently two main approaches to the study of the social determinants of ideology, the interest theory and the strain theory. For the first, ideology is a mask and a weapon; for the second, a symptom and a remedy. In the interest theory, ideological pronouncements are seen against a background of a universal struggle for advantage; in the strain theory, against a background of a chronic effort to correct sociopsychological disequilibrium. In the one, men pursue power; in the other, they flee anxiety . . . the two theories are not necessarily contradictory.

After a critique of both theories, Geertz adds (1973, 207) that their principal weakness is "the virtual absence . . . of anything more than the most rudimentary conception of the processes of symbolic formulation. . . . Both interest theory and strain theory go directly from source analysis to consequence analysis without ever examining ideologies as systems of interacting symbols, as patterns of interworking meanings." By raising the issue of meaning, Geertz points to the importance of taking the actors' viewpoint: their perceptions, moods, cognitions, beliefs and the symbols, images, texts, rituals, conversations through which their inner ideas and sentiments are communicated to others should be studied. How shared meanings come to be and are persuasively communicated should be the centerpiece of theorizing. Shared meanings and persuasive communication is a topic in the tradition of Weber's *verstehende soziologie*, and so also is rational choice theory. Unlike other theories, rational choice treats the truth value of beliefs and ideologies as perceived by the actors as having real motivating force instead of as epiphenomena that mask the "real," "hidden," and "true" forces based on interest and strain.

My unease with interest and strain theory stems from reading and reflection and from field work with participants and opponents of social movements I have studied over the years, from civil rights and feminism to the New Christian Right, pro-life and pro-choice, and at present the tobacco control movement. In all these movements, it is not uncommon that siblings, classmates, roommates, neighbors, church members, professional peers, from the same social milieu and with similar life experiences, disagree on fundamental political, moral, and cultural issues. They argue over the factual, moral, legal, and social dimensions of these issues, in interpersonal settings, public meetings, in news releases, in pamphlets, and with critics, bystanders, and supporters alike. Although they fling accusations at each other based on "interest" and "strain," for the most part when they do so bystanders and active participants interpret that as a "cop-out" tactic meant to divert from the real debate, which is over the truth value of the various claims and stands advocated. I am persuaded by these research experiences that unless the truth value of beliefs and ideologies as experienced by the actor is made the object of research and theorizing we shall not be able to explain why some issues and arguments catch on and are persuasive to many while others fall on deaf ears and are ignored.

Studies of the citizenry and of movement participants on public issues based on interest and strain variables explain but 10 to 20 percent of the variance after all conceivable variables have been included (Kriesi 1989). Imperfect research instruments, measurement errors, and other shortcomings of surveys do not account for such modest results. An entire dimension of the human experience remains uncaptured by our current exclusion of a theory of ideology and culture that stands on its own.

Socialization theory fills a few gaps (Wood and Hughes 1984), but leaves key questions unanswered. There are times when a smooth transmission of values and ideologies occur; at other times there is rebellion, counterculture, discontinuity. Thought worlds and life-styles that are supposed to have been eroded and discredited by schooling, urbanism, secularization, and other inexorable social processes live on in viable social enclaves and sally forth militantly to challenge dominant orthodoxies with surprising success. We do come up with plausible explanations, of course, but the opposite findings would have been explained just as persuasively. Socialization theory explains continuities in culture and ideology. But how do we account for innovation, change, discontinuity then?

Skepticism about interest and strain theory is warranted also on methodological grounds, for they tend to be tautological and unverifiable. A plausible scenario can be fitted to just about any outcome. If a powerful elite resists reform and defends that status quo, we attribute it to "interest." Should it back reform instead, it is a clever move to defuse more radical change, and thus also an expression of "interest." The elite now has a long-term view of its interest. The most important question is unanswered. Why and how do some, but not other elites, redefine their interest and back reform? Similar examples can be provided for "strain" explanations.

I do not wish to be misunderstood. Interest and strain should not be scrapped from social theory. Used judiciously, in ways that can be disconfirmed, they do have explanatory power. But they do leave huge blind spots on our intellectual map. We are baffled by the married, college-educated working mother who opposes the ERA; by the small-town, white, southern lady who stood by civil rights marchers; by the black sociologist who is against affirmative action; by the general who favors cutbacks in weapons systems; by the Cairo University woman who dons the purdah and joins a fundamentalist Islamic sect. And we shall remain baffled so long as we use reductionist theories for beliefs and ideologies.

Still, if interest and strain are only a part of the story, what else is there? Geertz (1973), Mary Douglas (1986), Boudon (1986) and others have pointed to a theory of culture, meaning, and communication waiting to be integrated with our stock of ideas about interest, strain, socialization, and social structure. Rational choice is especially suited to do this intellectual integration. But first I will demonstrate how this can be done in a particular instance, a disturbing set of events referred to as the European witchcraze.

The European Witchcraze of the Sixteenth and Seventeenth Centuries

In a brief chapter, I can only summarize the vast historical scholarship on this topic in the last twenty years by historians of the Renaissance and Reformation, historians of religion, anthropologists, legal scholars, and many others (Russell 1980; Monter 1976; Midelfort 1972; Macfarlane 1970; Thomas 1971; Cohn 1975; Kieckhefer 1976; Walker 1981; Mandrou 1968; Karsch 1980), nor would I expect them to endorse everything I write. Yet there is surprising agreement on most pieces in the witchcraze puzzle.

Contrary to what some think, there were few prosecutions of witches in the Dark Ages. Most witches were prosecuted and executed in the Renaissance, Reformation, and Counterreformation, from 1450 to 1700, when literacy, printing, humanism, and early modern science were spreading. The witchcraze raged strongest in the most commercialized, urban regions of Europe, whence it spread. The economic and cultural backwaters of Europe, in the East, Scandinavia, southern Italy, the Iberian peninsula, were mostly spared. Accused witches tended to be women, especially older women, living alone, widows, destitute, with a reputation for quarreling. Yet affluent and powerful men and members of the clergy are counted among its victims. Accusations originated with ordinary folk who believed that various ills, natural calamities, accidents, and social relations gone amiss, such things as a miscarriage, infant death, impotence, hailstorm that destroyed crops, a cow that stopped giving milk, barn fire started by lightning, were caused by magical sorcery practiced by people living in their midst.

Attempts by scholars to establish correlations between the prevalence of such events and that of witchcraft accusations and trials have proven unsuccessful. What accounts for variation, rather, are differences in criminal justice organization and procedures pertaining to admissible evidence, the use and intensity of torture, secular or ecclesiastical control, the legal definition of the crime of witchcraft. Some diffusion of witch trials resulted from campaigns by particular prosecutors and inquisitors who were zealous and fanatical. Yet most accusations and trials were of a single or but a few accused in a particular locality at a particular time. Although some rulers stopped prosecutions because they were skeptics or feared disorders, others encouraged them; many were indifferent.

Though confessions were extracted under torture, it wasn't the case everywhere, and some witches confessed voluntarily, convinced of their guilt. There are even instances of women who asked to be punished because they were witches. Witches were burned, strangled, and hanged, though a minority of prosecutions ended in acquittals. The practice of confiscating witches' assets was common, but did not amount to much since witches tended to be poor women. Prosecution of witches was expensive and did not pay for itself. Magistrates, prosecutors, and their staffs expected to be well paid, took their time, and ran up impressive expense accounts at local inns. In fact, some prosecutions ground to a halt when the local people ran out of money.

Interest and strain explanations for the witchcraze have not stood up well against the evidence. For instance, if control of women and of female sexuality were intended, the targets chosen were singularly inappropriate: women who were beyond their sexually active years. Though it is possible to single out authors on demonology and witchcraft and inquisitors who were misogynous and obsessed with sexuality, they were the exception. Most authors, magistrates, and prosecutors were honest men who believed they performed an important public service that was eradicating a dangerous heresy and preventing spiritual, physical, and social harm. In another section below I will review some variants of interest and strain explanations of the witchcraze. They are many and often quite ingenious, but they don't work. One has to look at a different type of explanation altogether, along the lines suggested by Geertz. What was the thought-world of ordinary folk? What was the thought-world of the political authorities, the intellectuals, the judicial elite who controlled culture production and communication and the machinery of the criminal justice system?

For ordinary folk, before, during, and after the witchcraze, magic and sorcery were a taken-for-granted, socially validated reality of their everyday social milieu. And so were preventive measures purchased from "cunning folks" that protected against them: charms, potions, incantations. Divine, supernatural, magical intervention in the causality of ordinary events, though not routine, was thought to be common enough. People recognized natural causes for natural events: miscarriages and infant deaths, illness, natural disaster were after all quite common. But in their thought-world there was a further question. Why does *my* healthy cow no longer give milk, and not my neighbors'? And why did that start on a particular evening, and not the previous week, or the following week? There was no room for chance in their deterministic search for a total explanation. Intentionality entered into the causal analysis of nature, unlike our view of impersonal mechanism. Any event occurring under unusual circumstances that could not be explained was intentionally caused, and the agent was likely to be a sorcerer using magic. Such thinking was backed by the parish clergy who never missed a chance of moralizing from the pulpit on how ills and calamities were the well-deserved punishment for sin and a warning of more to come unless the sinners turned back to God and the church.

The cultural elite of the Middle Ages was steeped in a mixture of Christian and Aristotelian thought that admitted miracles and supernatural agency in nature but viewed folk beliefs and practices associated with magic, sorcery, and witches (such as a woman flying through the night on a broomstick with her devil) as pagan survivals and popular superstitions. Such beliefs were sinful fantasies and delusions, contrary to Christian doctrine, but not crimes. Though heresy was both sin against God and a secular crime, and thus mercilessly eradicated, the sorcery-heresy link, which constituted witchcraft, was not made in theology, philosophy, and law at this time, or but very tenuously.

This changed with the spread of Neoplatonism, humanism, literacy, and early science. In the Neoplatonic thought of the Renaissance that gained ground over Aristotelianism, there were intimate links among all natural, supernatural, and psychic phenomena in the cosmos. Magic practiced by elites became a respectable pursuit, often coupled with humanist learning and scientific investigation. Notions about causality held by elites and common people converged. Also, as the authority of medieval theologians and the church were questioned, the literate public turned directly to the Bible as the final authority on all questions. In the Old and New Testament they read about the physical reality of Satan and devils, and of their frequent, devious and harmful intervention in human affairs and nature. They also read about sorcerers, witches, and divine command to put magicians, sorcerers, and witches to death. Intellectuals did not however believe that ordinary folk could produce these ills unaided. They concluded that witches are obtaining magical powers from the devil, through a pact, by selling their soul and committing other blasphemous, heretical acts. Meanwhile Satan is using them to subvert the true faith, be it Catholic or Protestant. Thus magic and sorcery became defined as a dangerous heresy orchestrated by Satan, and witches were at the center of that subversion. The Bible (Leviticus 22, 18) prescribed death for witches. Prosecutors and judges took note.

Learned books on demonology and witchcraft were published in increasing numbers by the most distinguished and respected scholars, and were rapidly disseminated to an increasingly literate public. Laws making witchcraft a heresy were instituted, and the extraordinary criminal procedures against heresy, including torture, were applied, enabling more incriminating accusations and denunciations without proof, the suspension of legal safeguards for the accused, and thus also more convictions. Prosecutors interrogated the accused relentlessly about witches' Sabbaths, pacts with the devil, nocturnal orgies, ritual cannibalism, and many other un-Christian, heretical practices whose forced admission confirmed the new thought-world of demonology. Thus the sin of sorcery became the heresy and crime of witchcraft, and fueled the witchcraze. Opponents who spoke out against abuses of justice or in the name of Christian compassion themselves admitted the reality of witchcraft and of Satan's powers, and sometimes got accused of being witches themselves. Skeptics avoided trouble by remaining silent.

Why were women, especially older women, the targets? In Europe, many women married late, some never, and others survived their husbands as widows. Some women thus led marginal lives, unsupported and unprotected by kin in what was still a kin-centered society. Some were midwives, other did odd jobs, other still peddled ointments, charms, powders for remedying ills, protecting against harm, and mending social relations like rejected love. Many begged. Many, including these women themselves, believed that they, or at least some of them, had occult powers that could be used for sorcery. These women were frequently in disputes with their neighbors over food and firewood, over services refused, over remedies that hadn't worked, whence arose quarrels, anger, curses. When these were followed by suspicious illness, death, and other harmful events for which witchcraft was a plausible explanation and the woman the most likely source, it became the occasion for witchcraft accusations. That is why older women were disproportionately its victims.

How did the witchcraze then end? Here again interest and strain contribute little. It is the thought-world of the elites that we must examine, for it is their control of culture, political authority, and the machinery of justice that made the witchcraze possible, as well as ended it. Elites gained as little from the witchcraze as they would from its demise. By the latter part of the seventeenth century, in educated circles, a deist, Cartesian conception of nature became dominant. God created an orderly universe and no longer intervened in natural events on a daily basis. The universe was a well-designed clock that ran itself. Neither did Satan or any other supernatural agent intervene in human affairs and nature. Natural events have natural causes; nature is impersonal, not intentional. Though much about nature could not be satisfactorily explained yet (e.g., sudden deaths, miscarriages), still elites became confident that science and the scientific method would eventually do so. This thought-world spread in literary and scientific societies, academies and social circles in the capitals and main centers of learning. High-ranked officials, magistrates, lawyers, belonged to these circles and contributed to the spread of the new climate of opinion. In conformity with the new thinking, the laws on witchcraft were gradually changed to exclude certain kinds of accusations and proof which were no longer credible, and protection of the accused against legal abuses were reintroduced. Higher courts in the capital overruled the decisions of provincial courts that hadn't yet caught up with the new thinking and new judicial procedures. Witchcraft prosecutions, convictions, and executions declined. This took time because thought-worlds change slowly: they are a collective process of reaching a new consensus, not a single event based on a conversion. As important was the gradual retirement and death of the older, respected magistrates and officials who had been the agents and ultimately responsible authority for the witchcraft trials. While they were in office, it was embarrassing and unwise to make them accountable for the cruel deaths of many innocent victims, or to label them as ignorant, superstitious fools. Eventually, the younger members of the elite assumed high judicial offices and gained authority for the total repeal of witchcraft laws. For a time, village folk who were thus bereft of any legal recourse against sorcerers and witches in their midst occasionally lynched them. The authorities put an end to this practice by severely punishing the ringleaders. That ended the witchcraze. Ordinary folk continued believing in magic, sorcery, witches, devils, and the like, but they now had to deal with these bothersome old women in other ways, by other means of social control, which they had done 400 years earlier in the Middle Ages, and have done since the eighteenth century.

Such an account of the witchcraze does not assume thought-worlds divorced from material reality. Power and social control figure centrally in it, especially elite control of the criminal justice system. Anxieties are certainly present: both elites and ordinary people feared Satan's and the witches' malevolent powers. Yet the criminalization of sorcery into the heresy and crime of witchcraft was not a reaction to the strains of life in the sixteenth and seventeenth centuries—if anything, it caused a lot of anxiety for all. Nor did criminalization buttress the Catholic and Protestant elites' authority—they were much of the time destroying each other in costly religious wars. The witchcraze must be understood in terms of a theory of culture and of meaning, and of the truth-value for contemporaries of the beliefs and conceptions of the world upon which witchcraft rested.

Sociological Theories and the Witchcraze

I do not wish to dwell in great detail on the conventional social science wisdom of the witchcraze, because my goal is to put forward a theory which will challenge these competing explanations. It is nonetheless useful to review some other explanations that have struck a chord with nineteenth and twentieth century observers and theorists.

Start with psychoanalytic and social psychological ideas about the relief of stress, anxiety, and frustrations, and displaced aggression upon convenient scapegoats, the witches. Two problems are immediately apparent. First, as Russell wrote (1980, 72), "It is possible to argue that witchcraft was a product of social anxiety and then link its beginnings with the social unrest of the 14th century and its plagues, famines, and wars. But that is too simple. Plagues, famines and wars are endemic in the Middle Ages and early modern period. Every period in human history is troubled, but every period has not produced a witchcraze." Second, the usual conveniently available targets for scapegoating in Europe, Jews and Gypsies, were not accused and victimized (Midelfort 1972, 189). In detailed village studies, it was found that there was little overlap between those accused of theft, sexual misdemeanors, prostitution, and other typical forms of deviance and alleged witches (Macfarlane 1970, 150 ff.). Also, detailed studies of regions, such as of Essex, indicate that prosecutions were at their height in the 1580s and 1590s, a period of relative prosperity (Macfarlane 1970). Other attempts to correlate the incidence of anxiety-generating events, such as illness, plagues, disasters, find no clear pattern of association with incidence of witchcraft accusations and prosecutions (Russell 1980, 111).

A recent theory by Matossian argues that food poisoning associated with eating rye (especially under cold, wet conditions)—called ergot alkaloid poisoning—produced outbreaks of central nervous system

symptoms, such as convulsions, paralysis, spasms, sensations of prick-
ing, feelings of panic, hallucinations, reproduction function disorders,
and the like, in both humans and farm animals, that were blamed on the
malevolent action of witches (Matossian 1989, chap. 5). Matossian then
argues and marshalls evidence showing correlations between climatic
and weather conditions, rye consumption, and witch prosecutions, both
in spatial distribution and with time (long cycles of decades, seasonal
cycles in a year). Aside from the patchiness of empirical evidence, the
difficulties with this explanation is that witches were accused of many
actions beyond the symptoms and disorders she lists, such as hail damage
to crops, crop failure, birth of malformed children and farm animals,
sudden deaths and illnesses, impotence, and so on, some of which cannot
be linked to food poisoning. All these symptoms and behaviors occurred
with high prevalence, yet most by far never led to witchcraft accusations.
As well, both contemporary African ethnography and European historical research indicates that ordinary people made quite sophisticated
behavioral observations and socially validated distinctions between mental retardation, temporary insanity, chronic mental disorders, epilepsy
and other physical illnesses (including those due to poisoning), mind-al-
tering drugs, spirit possession, and behaviors or events attributed to
witchcraft, though there was a certain degree of fuzziness and overlap
(Walker 1981; Thomas 1971). Matossian's evidence can be interpreted
in a different way: where there was already suspicion of witchcraft,
symptoms of an unusual kind were seized upon in accusations against an
alleged witch.

A functionalist explanation of deviance puts the accent on the positive
consequences of crime and punishment in as much as social order, moral
judgment, the legitimacy of authority are restored by social control
through the criminal justice system, and by the reaffirmation of identities,
norms, and social boundaries between the meritorious and the deviants.
Erikson, for instance, writes that "deviant forms of behavior, by marking
the outer edges of group life, give the inner structure its special character
and thus supply the framework within which people of the group develop
an orderly sense of their own cultural identity" (1966, 13, and in chap.
1). The evidence does not support such a view. Witchcraft accusations
and prosecutions split families, neighbors, communities, and cities into
contending and warring factions, led to protracted conflict whose wounds
took a long time to heal, made partisans out of bystanders, raised fears

and anxieties all around, and ruined the reputations of many citizens. Moreover, as Foucault (1979, 62-65) noted, the spectacle of torture and execution of offenders, often carried out in public, were the occasion for popular resistance, riots, and aggression against judges, plaintiffs, executioners, and the authorities rather than for instilling respect for the law, or on the contrary, attempts to seize the condemned prisoner to lynch, execute, or punish him more cruelly than the authorities intended. Little solidarity here stemming from the punishment of deviants!

A somewhat different theory of labeling invoked by some sociologists contends, in the spirit of Durkheim (1981, chap. 2) that the operations and procedures of law enforcement (or of any institution of social control) generate a certain amount of deviant and criminal labeling and prosecutions. This view has difficulty explaining the huge variations by district, region, and in time of the witchcraze. It also makes questionable assumptions of cause and effect, since the prosecution was usually brought in from the outside to deal with prior local accusations of witchcraft. Nevertheless, once a prosecutorial machinery to uncover witchcraft was in place, it did in some instances produce accusations and convictions far beyond the original incidents, and in some cases, in the hands of ambitious and fanatical prosecutors, got completely out of hand. But the opposite also occurred: a prosecutor who was called in by popular demand, refused to prosecute after investigation, and put an end to the local witchcraze by punishing the accusers and those who lynched or otherwise attacked alleged witches (Henningsen 1980).

I have already criticized "interest" theories of all sorts, in as much as there was no financial gain, and often only loss, in bringing witches to justice since the accused were poor and confiscation of their property did not amount to much. If "interest" is expanded to cover all manner of political, social, material, religious advantage, one runs into further difficulties, for the literature shows how impossible it is to define a single "interest" for the Catholic Church and the Protestant Churches in the matter of the prosecution of witches. Within the Catholic Church, to take but that example, there were at all times advocates, skeptics, and opponents; the divisions and factions sometimes were between orders (Dominicans versus Jesuits), sometimes within the same order itself, between the papal curia and various local bishops and archbishops, between the local clergy and the hierarchy, and between the church itself and the secular authorities (Parker 1982). These disagreements and conflicts of interest created a situation where "neither the law nor the theology of witchcraft was firmly enough established to prevent a wide variety of thought on the subject" (Midelfort 1972, 22). Any attempt to impose on the witchcraze a Gramscian notion of "hegemonic" ideology, based on a homogeneous ruling class "interest" is unsupported by the evidence.

What exactly was the position or "interest" of the political rulers in this matter? There are indications that for them, with but a few exceptions (e.g., James I of England), the witchcraze and witches' execution was a minor sideshow in comparison to dynastic alliances, state formation, colonial expansion, state finances, wars against rivals, and other preoccupations of "matters of state." One of the most influential critics of the witchcraze, Friedrich von Spee, wrote his *Cautio Criminalis* (published in 1631) in the form of an appeal to the kings, princes and rulers of Germany (*Obrigkeiten Deutschlands*) to stop their not-so "benign neglect" of the witchcraze and to put and end to the arbitrary, cruel and unjust actions of the officials in charge of these prosecutions in their domain. Spee's foreword reads like a modern-day investigative reporter intending to expose abuses in the government and hoping to bring it to the attention of the highest authorities. Spee reminds them both of their duty to God for ensuring justice in the realm and of their interest in putting an end to the prosecution of witches, which creates social conflict and unrest among their subjects. Marxist analyses of the witchcraze are at bottom variants of interest explanations and fare no better than other interest theories when it comes to the witchcraze.

Feminist theory does poorly as well. I have already pointed out that the targeting of women who are no longer sexually active does not square with the notion of male control of female sexuality. But there is more. It is true that men in the Renaissance and Reformation had negative stereotypes of women that made them particularly susceptible to the Devil's influence (women are weak-willed, temperamental, gullible, etc.), but the same stereotypes were invoked by the critics of the witchcraze to argue that since women are prone to "melancholy fantasies," they "imagine" being witches and participating in a witches' Sabbath with the Devil, but do not actually do it and should thus not be prosecuted.

Also, these female stereotypes were prevalent prior to the witchcraze, during the witchcraze, and following the witchcraze, and cannot explain the changes in incidence in time and space of the prosecution of witches. Although sexual offenses and deviant sexuality is associated with witches—especially in the visual arts (e.g., Albrecht Dürer's and other well known artists' wood cuts and illustrations)—it is nonetheless the case that the prosecution and interrogation of witches did not dwell on sexual deviance and sexuality. The most popular prosecutor's interrogation manual for witches, the *Kelheimer Hexenhammer* (1487) contains but one out of ninety-three questions probing for a sexually deviant action (sexual intercourse with the Devil). As we shall see, the association of female gender with witchcraft prosecution has another explanation.

Finally, though prosecutors were males (by necessity, since there were no females in those positions, as was also true for other court officials, such as torturers and clerks), accusations of witchcraft tended to originate by women against other women over matters that were often socially defined as the preserve of women (death of a baby, infertility, illness of a farm animal cared for by women, etc.). In fact, men living with or associated with alleged witches (e.g., husbands) sometimes became accused of witchcraft themselves (Macfarlane 1970, 160).

Modernization theory misses the boat. The witchcraze peaks in the Renaissance and Reformation, the Age of Discoveries and the start of the Scientific Revolution, and not in the "dark" Middle Ages. Many leading humanists, scientists, philosophers believe in witches and the heresy of witchcraft, see no contradictions and inconsistencies between these beliefs and their scientific investigations, and support vigorous prosecution and punishment. The craze is at its height in the most literate and schooled districts and regions of Europe, whereas little occurs in the rural backwaters of the continent. The idea that education and enlightenment spread in some steady linear fashion through the population and society, and gradually eliminated superstition, ignorance, wasn't any more true for sixteenth- and seventeenth-century Europe as it is true of the modernizing societies in the contemporary world. That the witchcraze had an intimate connection with changes from one world view to another is plain, but this change is better characterized by a major paradigm shift in conceptions of causation and the relationship of the phenomenal with the supernatural world, including those pertaining to witches and witchcraft. The result was an abrupt discontinuity and reversal in viewing the same evidence, instead of a gradual shift of conceptions and behaviors postulated by modernization theory. It is time to turn to an exposition of how a cognitive dimension can be brought into a theory of ideology, and how ideology and beliefs link up with actions such as the prosecution of witches. As Russell (1980, 119) put it, "A sophisticated social history of witchcraft will give full weight to the history of concepts and avoid simplistic correlations between external phenomena and witch beliefs."

Culture, Meaning, and Truth Value: A Rational Choice Approach

Culture, as I use it here, refers to a socially constructed, cognitive, normative, and emotional meaning system that creates the central reality of a people, so that they "inhabit the world they imagine" (D'Andrade 1984, 115). It is a social fact in Durkheim's sense: it is collective, intersubjective, anchored in social units that withstand people turnover. The information system that culture is encoded in and where meanings are assigned is the human brain and its varied extensions: language, books, songs, ritual, rules, roles, stereotypes, mathematical theorems. Culture is vulnerable to the depreciation and destruction of its carriers. To reproduce, diffuse, create, adapt culture requires physical and human capital investment, i.e., socialization in the broadest sense.

Culture has three dimensions, usefully distinguished:

1. A cognitive dimension I will term a *thought-world*. At its core is a system of classifications and distinctions like gender, notions about causality, etc., by means of which information gets framed, stored, and retrieved in organized meaning-bundles for thought and action. Durkheim called the basic structure of a thought-world "collective representations." Other refer to it as a cognitive map, world view, *mentalité collective*, and so on. A thought-world creates a common framework in which communication among fellow humans becomes possible.

2. A moral dimension: convictions about what is just and unjust, right and wrong, important and trivial, etc. These are guides for value judgments, goal setting, choices, evaluations, and action norms.

3. An emotional dimension: sentiments of like and dislike, love, fear, anger, gratitude, loyalty, hate. These define and orient our emotions.

Culture and meaning have the properties of information and communication systems.

Simon (1969) argues that stable complex systems of all kinds have a hierarchic structure. The human brain is such, and has evolved in such a manner that information received in the senses, internally processed in the mind, and organized for choice and action would be a chaotic and useless mass of signals without a structure for entering, screening, sorting, classifying, combining, storing, retrieving, and processing. Simon also argues that complex systems that are hierarchic are more efficient and stable than other complex systems. Anthropological studies of symbol systems and the cognitive psychology of problem solving and decision making indicate that culture can best be understood as a complex hierarchic system (Leach 1976; Tallman and Gray 1990). Indeed, thought-worlds and meanings endure a long time, often many centuries. That is longer than the life span of much social organization, technology, interest groups, classes and social formations, and far, far longer than the even briefer life span of human beings. It is possible to make sense of a Socratic dialogue on the just society written over two millennia ago, and learn from it.

Meaning systems, be they expressed in language, sound, visual images, mathematical logic, dance, dress, have a structure, as Dumont (1966, 1977) has shown. The structure frames; it puts our thinking, judgments, sentiments, and actions on "automatic pilot" (Douglas 1986). The dimensions of structure are hierarchy, symmetry, opposition, complementarity, repetition. Duality is one of the simplest structures. In duality, opposites are complementary, but one is dominant: right and left, male and female, good and evil, lord and peasant, cause and effect, "us" and "them," God and Satan. More complex structures are built from simple structures: "God and Satan" are linked to "good and evil," "church and heretics," "virtue and vice," "reward and punishment." With these dimensions, intellectuals build a thought-world mansion of many stories with many rooms, and fit into it a great deal of information, whereas ordinary folk live in a simple hut. Yet both mansion and hut have a structure organized along the same principles.

Meanings are communicated with metaphor and simile, the stuff of folk tales, proverbs, poems, familiar images. The complementarity of male and female is analogous to that of the right and the left hand. No physical or social body can operate properly without both. The spatially "higher" mind in the head and the "lower" arms and legs come to stand for the rule of the intellect over the passions, of the intellectuals over the laborers. Thus cognitive structure and moral prescription are aligned with metaphor. A complex social unit, such as a religious organization, is described with military metaphors that convey order, power, success, and thus the Church Triumphant is created: the Heavenly Host, the Rock of Ages, Christ the Lord, a Mighty Fortress is Our God, Onward Christian Soldiers. Basic sociological concepts like stratification, mass society, revolution, elites, role, life course, evoke vivid mental images through metaphor and possess moral overtones. When cognitive structure is aligned with values and moral prescriptions, an *ideology* is created.

Douglas (1986) describes how the uncertain, unfamiliar, arbitrary, and abstract is aligned to the structure of the familiar, shared, observable, and reality tested by means of analogy and metaphor. Thought-worlds and meanings thus acquire face validity, persuasiveness, and legitimacy. Communication becomes persuasive. "Common sense" is created.

Meanings, values, judgments, sentiments claim truth value and legitimacy—the validity of social categories, images of society, theories of causation, the legitimacy of norms, the appropriateness of sentiments, such as grief at death. Truth, justice, love are persuasively communicated with metaphor, but they are further validated by means of action: by example, commitment, sacrifice. We cannot convey, argue, and uphold the sanctity of life and remain indifferent to the taking of life; we cannot convince others and ourselves of the truth of our beliefs if we don't stand up for them. Actions speak louder than words. Beliefs, evaluations, and norms that are not validated by metaphor, by action, and by reference to "authority" are no more than idle thoughts, or the fantasies of a madman. They are useless for communication and transacting with others. They "do not matter."

Culture and meaning systems are socially constructed. They are anchored in viable social units, living communities. Parents teach their children, and neighbors, organized groups, public opinion confirm and back up the thought-world with rewards and punishments in an ongoing process of social validation. The thought-world works in everyday life because it is made to work. Much, however, is not, cannot be, reality tested in any simple way, like the hardness of a stone and the coldness of ice. It is accepted, internalized, and persuades because those we trust, admire, and recognize as authorities and experts say it is so. Socialization and persuasive communication utilizes social bonds for authority validation. Social anchoring makes possible social and authority validation of thought-worlds, investing them with truth-value and legitimacy.

In a complex society, thought-worlds and meaning systems at variance with the dominant culture and ruling groups survive in viable social and ecological enclaves and in subcultures, though they may make tactical concessions to the powerful. As Redfield (1953) observed, the "Little" Tradition of the peasants survives within the "Great" Tradition upheld by officials, judges, bishops, elites, and their local agents.

Let me sum up. Culture is an information system conveying meaning among humans essential for communication and for transacting. Meanings are encoded in elements and meaning-bundles that are organized into a complex system possessing a hierarchic structure which frames them into a thought-world. Meanings and thought-worlds are socially constructed and anchored in viable social units, robust to people turnover. They claim legitimacy and truth value. These are confirmed through structural alignment, metaphor and analogy, reality testing, social validation, authority validation, and action validation.

Stability and Change in Beliefs and Thought-Worlds

The conversion of private ideas, feelings, sentiments, moods, judgments into information understood by others, requires communication encoded in shared conventions (language, facial expressions, familiar symbols and color codes, shared notions of causation and of social categorization, etc.). Conventions tend to be stable and change but slowly because they have the property of positive-sum games (Ullman-Margalit 1977). Weber pointed it out long ago when he wrote (1921 [1956], 22) that "the stability of custom rests essentially on the fact that whoever does not align action to it behaves 'nonadaptively', i.e., must suffer small and large inconveniences and costs so long as the majority in the social milieu expects the custom to endure and accordingly conforms to it."

Sense experiences, personal experiences, observation of "facts" do not undermine shared conventions of social categories, evaluation frames, causation, because sense experience and "facts" are processed into one's thought-world and moral judgment with these taken-for-granted and socially supported social categories, evaluation frames, and cognitive classifications. For instance, if I argue with a person who comes from a culture where the earth is thought to be flat that our planet is a three-dimensional sphere (and round), and I show him a photograph of the earth from a spacecraft, he will "see" a flat pancake. Similarly, a Brazilian will look at a person with 80 percent European features and 20 percent African features and assign him to a different social category than the typical U.S.

citizen who makes a dichotomous choice between "white" and "black" (or "Negro," "colored," "Afro-American"). The truth value or validity of our classifications is not inherent in the perceptions of objects themselves, but on conventions we have learned which are socially sanctioned.

Contradictions of "fact" do not alter the conventional system of classification. Here's an example. In 1971 I made interviews among African small businessmen in the shanty towns of Lusaka and hooked up with an African battery salesman who was making deliveries and who knew their location, which helped me a great deal since there were no maps, street names and lists of such businesses. We became very close and discussed a number of topics quite frankly, one of which was witchcraft. Although my salesman-driver friend had secondary education, he believed in witchcraft and provided several examples. I was skeptical and argued my case in several ways, none of which was persuasive to him. How come, I said, that Europeans are not subject to witchcraft, that they don't experience it? How come, when his delivery van does not start up, he himself looks for a mechanical failure, rather than for witchcraft? Simple, he replied. Witchcraft only works among Africans. Trucks are built by Europeans, and are immune to it. Besides, he added, to make it more bewildering yet, you have to believe in witchcraft for it to work, and he himself couldn't help believing in it since he was brought up that way and all his friends also believed in it. Durkheim would have loved his answer!

Our conversation went around in such loops. In my thought-world, the same explanatory principles had to be applied to all human beings and situations. In his thought-world, Europeans and Africans were lodged in different categories, and for some experiences different principles of causality were applicable in each. There was no inconsistency for him, and my "reality tests" were irrelevant. Similarly, although there is general agreement about the obvious and observable physical differences between males and females, there need not be any agreement about "maleness" and "femaleness." For instance, one culture imposes sharp differences of temperament, intellectual faculties, norms on gender, creating sharp gender differences and an impermeable boundary, whereas another may hold that every human being has a mixture of qualities associated with "maleness" and "femaleness," in a continuously varying blend, and that "males" simply tend to have a higher proportion of "maleness" and females a higher proportion of "femaleness." Because each culture socializes its young and organizes its institutions according to its own conventions of gender and gender differences, and backs it up with social control, its gender classification is confirmed and upheld by the day-to-day experience of its members, both male and female.

How can there be any change then in culture, in beliefs, in thought-worlds, in the system of classifications, in moral evaluations? Briefly put, each form of validation can break down: reality testing, whether it be the socially constructed reality of culture and social organization or of physical reality, can produce negative outcomes, and the accumulation and sharing of such negative outcomes can lead to disagreements and controversies that delegitimize beliefs, norms, social categories, models of causation, and eventually produce widespread skepticism, and/or the legitimation of new beliefs, norms, classifications, etc. Although our senses do not change, we invent tools and instruments (microscopes, telescopes) and otherwise make discoveries (as Europeans did when they confronted the Indians of the Americas after Columbus) that do not fit the accepted scheme of beliefs and interpretations. Similarly for social validation. With the migration of peoples, trade, new means of travel and transportation, people discover that what they had experienced and socially defined as an absolute truth, a universal belief, or a norm, is actually but a "convention," since other people manage to live by adhering to other truths, norms, classifications. Similarly authority validation breaks down when the outcomes promised by trusted authorities are not forthcoming and a wide gap between expectation and reality remains unbridged. Action validation breaks down when the sacrifices socially validating a system of values are circumvented, as when an elite that took power in the name of equality creates a new privilege system.

None of these changes are a simple, automatic process, and there is no reason to believe that it takes place in a gradual, incremental fashion, for individuals and for groups and societies. Religious conversion appears to be sudden; elites appear to be vulnerable to sudden, rapid delegitimation that makes history anything but routine and boring. Bearing in mind Simon's hypothesis about the hierarchic structure of information systems, it is not unreasonable to expect that skepticism about and delegitimation of the linchpins of hierarchy, causation and classification, will have far-reaching repercussions on many beliefs, norms, and other less central elements of culture, producing what is usually referred to as a "crisis of consciousness," "scientific revolution," or "paradigm shift," rather than the routine and routinized incremental changes of "normal" culture change (Kuhn 1962; Fleck 1980 [1935]). And that is precisely what happened in the European witchcraze. But this story cannot be told as straightforward intellectual history. The linkage between the Great Tradition of theologians, lawyers, scholars, and the Little Tradition of simple folk plays a crucial part in the drama, as does the action validation of beliefs and thought-worlds about good and evil and crime and punishment, which enmeshed intellectual debate in the horrible business of prosecution, torture and execution of witches, not to mention popular lynching and other forms of victimization.

Throughout the centuries of the witchcraze, the beliefs of simple folk about sorcery, witchcraft, devils, about the harm witches could and did cause, did not change. Until the late fourteenth century, according to Normal Cohn (1975, 224):

> the educated in general, and the higher clergy in particular, were quite clear that the nocturnal journeys of women [on broomsticks to a witches' Sabbath] were purely imaginary happenings. But in the 16th and 17th centuries, this was no longer the case.

Walker (1981) agrees that in the High Middle Ages the intellectual elite denied the physical reality of flying witches and of deviant actions attributed to them, which were believed to be survivals of pagan folk superstition. Such beliefs were fantasies: to the clergy, they were sinful, but not a crime. Elites' beliefs and actions about folk beliefs on these matters would shortly undergo important changes in response to heresies, the Reformation, and the spread of Neoplatonism closely linked to the emergence of the "scientific revolution".

First, late medieval heresies and the Reformation. They rejected the authority of the Catholic Church, and the doctrines promulgated by the Councils, the Pope, and the official theology of the church. Instead the Protestants turned to the Bible as the final source of authoritative religious beliefs and doctrines, and the Bible was inhabited by a real Satan, real devils and fallen angels, and real witches who had and were presumed to be still taking an active part in tempting humans from the way of righteousness, and subverting God's design for human salvation. Even before the Protestant Reformation, in its confrontation with various heresies (Waldensians, Cathars, etc.) that had a systematized demonology growing out of popular culture, the Church itself got to revising, systematizing, and eliminating inconsistencies in its theological and legal approach to Satan, demons, and witches, all of which tended to make a conspiracy theory of satanic subversion of Christianity with the agency of witches more plausible than in the Middle Ages (Russell 1980, chap. 3). This is in keeping with the notion of "rationalization" by intellectual elites emphasized by Weber in his sociology of religion, a basic theme in Weber's writings. The visible manifestations of it is the tremendous growth in books and editions on demonology during this time (Nicholls 1980).

The growth of literacy, the invention and diffusion of printing enter into the explanation because they made possible and accelerated the delegitimation of the church among intellectuals, town burghers, and some aristocratic circles, and speeded the intellectual debates and pressures for consistency in matters of doctrine, ritual, and ecclesiastical organization between Catholics and Protestants, including a consistent thought-world about Satan, demons, and witches. The Protestant challenge in particular had a further and crucial consequence for the witchcraze. The Protestant attack on Catholic ritual destroyed and delegitimized the traditional protection against ills, misfortunes, the devil's temptations, with charms, sacraments, prayer to saints, holding up the Bible, making the sign of the cross (Thomas 1970, 155, 498). Protestantism created a vacuum of protection against all manner of physical, spiritual, and social ills, including witches. As ecclesiastic magic crumbled, people turned to the courts for legal relief against alleged witches. And both Protestant and Catholic elites were more responsive to popular demand because they were in competition with each other for the allegiance of common folk. On the "demand" side, then, conditions were in place for the prosecution of witches. What of the "supply" side?

Criminal justice, then and now, rested on the demonstration to judges (and juries) that the accusations against an offender were true, and not just a product of the imagination of offender, victim, accused, and witnesses. The case against witches in the secular courts demanded proof of heresy such as making a pact with the devil, participating in a witches' Sabbath, performing sacrilegious acts at the Sabbath, and a number of other events and signs that the harm to people inflicted by sorcery was indeed a consequence of the demonic act and of the magical powers acquired from the devil. How could learned judges, prosecutors, interrogators and the public believe in the physical reality of these accusations when in an earlier century they wrote them off as the fantasies of old women?

The surprising answer is that far from being in contradiction with the "new" or "mechanical" philosophy of the scientific revolution that was then under way, demonism and supernatural intervention in natural phenomena was actually consonant with the new philosophy and wasn't discredited until the eighteenth century. According to the historian of science Karsch (1980, 359-68),

> It has now been well documented that the opposition between science and the supernatural was largely a product of 18th century rationalism, and that throughout the Renaissance and early modern era, no such opposition existed. Natural and supernatural were seen as interdependent, with no clear separation between them. Science, even as presented by its most advanced practitioners was laced with mystical ideas.

Lewontin (1989) fully agrees with the view that Neoplatonism-Platonic and Hermetic philosophy undergirded the religions and mystical beliefs of Copernicus, Kepler, Boyle, and Newton and make it impossible to separate them from their "scientific" ideas and activities. Karsch (1980, 360-61) confirms that

> Among the demonologists we find not only theologians and jurists, but also physicians and mathematicians, seventeenth century proponents of the new philosophy and fellows of the Royal Society

among them the mathematicians John Napier and Jerome Cardan; the political philosopher and proponent of religious toleration Jean Bodin; the physician Ambroise Pare; the mathematician and philosopher George Sinclair "whose discussions of demonology were included even in his technical work, *Hydrostatics*," and so on.

> Among explicit believers in the reality of witchcraft we find Johannes Kepler and Robert Boyle. Boyle's interest and belief in demonology was sufficiently strong that he submitted an account of the 'demon of Mascon' . . . for publication . . . which was intended to be an empirical investigation of demonic activity.

Francis Bacon expressed skepticism about the veracity of witchcraft confessions (as did many others, because of the torture used to make the accused confess), yet wanted the topic of witchcraft included in "natural history" since the boundary between natural and supernatural causation was yet undetermined. Though Hobbes denied the reality of possession by "malign spirits," he accepted their physical existence and avoided contradiction with his materialistic philosophy by providing them with corporeal bodies (Karsch 1980).

Thus popular and elite thought-world on the reality of devils, sorcery, witchcraft, and supernatural causation in ordinary events converged in the sixteenth and seventeenth centuries. Authorities, not only religious experts, backed the cognitive assumptions and beliefs enabling the prosecution of witches with plausible physical evidence. To the question as to why the devil needed witches if he had the power to perform all the actions the witches were accused of, the answer was that Satan also sought the perdition of human (the witches') souls in his confrontation with God (Kieckhefer 1976, 85). Because the devil was believed to protect the witches with whom he had signed a pact, thus enabling simple uneducated women to outwit experienced and learned interrogators, the law and the courts allowed for extraordinary torture to extract confessions from the accused (extraordinary, because the devil also had the power to help the accused resist pain and suffering). And because the elite thought-world postulated a satanic conspiracy (group deviance) of witches rather than the folk view of isolated acts of magical sorcery, interrogators used torture to ferret out the names of other witches and participants in the conspiracy. Thus the combination of torture with the idea of conspiracy led to a proliferation of accusations originating in a single incident of alleged witchcraft. Thus also the witchcraze was fueled by the machinery of justice, and confirmed the thought-world of the learned as well as of the uneducated public.

It is true that hegemony or consensus on demonology and the conspiracy theory was never achieved. Yet during the time it became a dominant thought-world, critics and skeptics had to be cautious and guarded lest they be accused in turn, as happened with Wier and Spee and some other opponents of the witchcraze. But even Wier and Spee admitted the reality of Satan and of witches though they blamed the high incidence of witchcraft on the criminal justice machinery put in place to eradicate it. Eventually, as I have already written, a deist, mechanical philosophy gradually spread among the learned and powerful. Both God's and Satan's intervention in natural phenomena was discredited, the Great and the Little Tradition once more diverged, and the laws and criminal justice machinery against witches was gradually dismantled (Mandrou 1968).

Conclusion

Conventional explanations of the witchcraze have flaws. The witchcraze cannot be explained without a cognitive view of culture and thought-worlds whose socially constructed truth value compels action validation, regardless of interest and strain. Thought-worlds have the properties of information systems, and complex thought-worlds have a hierarchic structure. Though the study of thought-worlds as cognitive and symbolic information systems is in its infancy, a rational choice approach is promising for a social constructionist analysis of culture.

8

The 1960 Sit-Ins:
Protest Diffusion and Movement Take-Off

[T]he majority of us who later became participants did not know that this was it, the "thing"—so-called at the beginning for lack of a proper name—which was to activate so many people all over the U.S. in the coming months.

—Black student leaders from Shaw University, Raleigh, North Carolina, recalling their reaction to news about the Greensboro sit-in.

I remember the sit-ins real well. The sit-ins were a college movement. When it hit Greensboro, it was just like a fad. I don't think people really thought it was as serious as it was. If A&T students are tired of discrimination, doggone it, we can do the same thing at North Carolina Central in Durham.

—Ben Ruffin, Governor Hunt's special assistant for minority affairs, who was age eighteen and in high school in Durham.

Introduction

The temporal and spatial clustering of conflict episodes has frequently been observed, but hasn't received the attention it merits, given its importance and prevalence. Temporal spatial clustering was marked during the urban riots of the 1960s in the United States and more recently the collective protests in South Africa; it was observed during the late

213

1960s campus confrontations, the 1848 revolutions in Europe, the sit-down strikes in the auto and rubber industries in 1937 in the United States, the 1980s Polish workers' strikes, and the 1960 sit-ins that will be described. None of these instances of protest diffusion can be attributed to the concerted efforts of a common organization and leadership that activates its constituent local units against a common opponent; indeed what is fascinating about them is that they originated without common leadership, organization, and prior central planning. In fact, just the opposite occurs at times; out of the Polish strike wave grew Solidarity; the United Auto Workers and labor unions in mass production industries became institutionalized on the crest of the 1937 sit-down strike wave; episodic, varied black opposition to segregation burst into the civil rights movement with the 1960 sit-ins. How does one account for the emergence of these historic events?

In accounting for the spread of collective protests, a number of questions have to be raised. Under what circumstances does diffusion take place at all? What are the mechanisms of diffusion itself, how does it actually happen? How is it that the same sorts of events that remained isolated incidents become precipitating incidents for the diffusion of collective protests at some subsequent time? The purpose of this chapter is to present a simple, parsimonious model of protest diffusion that goes some way to answering these questions, and to apply it in accounting for the start of the civil rights movement. Though several analyses of the initial period of civil rights movement and the 1960 sit-ins have been published in the sociological literature (Morris 1981, 1984; McAdam 1982, 1983; Killian 1984), the diffusion model will provide further insight into this historic event and contribute to the theory of collective action that undergirds social movement theory.

Overview

The historic significance of the 1960 sit-ins is undisputed. They mark the start of a continuous drive by blacks in the South against segregation and for equal citizenship by direct action such as sit-ins, marches, picketing, boycotts, demonstrations and other forms of public defiance. The break with the past was not about goals—equal rights for blacks—but with the means of achieving it. Instead of lawsuits brought by the NAACP and Justice Department, instead of waiting for Congress to enact legislation and for the president to issue executive orders, a substantial number of blacks, in many walks of life, in many different localities, on numerous occasions, participated in collective actions against segregation and for equal rights, often at considerable risk and cost. These actions transformed what had been a regional issue for white Americans into a national problem of the first order of magnitude. They pressured the president, the Congress and the Democratic Party to formulate and implement a national policy of equality for blacks. Despite opposition, blacks did not let up until major gains were achieved in the mid-sixties. From the South, the black movement spread into other regions and stimulated other groups to act collectively, using the same techniques and appealing to the same ideals of equality and equal rights. How did it all start? How did localized sit-in protests grow into a social movement?

Much is known about the 1960 sit-ins. Though everyone was taken by surprise, the sit-ins were immediately front page material in local newspapers and the national press. The Southern Regional Council (SRC) monitored their course, state by state, from news sources principally, and published two short summary reports, in 1960 and 1961. The news sources are strong on dates, places, numbers, the pronouncements of governors and prominent personages, arrests, violence, and so forth, but contain little information about motivation, mobilization actions, continuity, or for that matter the counterstrategies and ways of thinking of local law enforcement officials, merchants, and civic leaders. Fortunately some sit-in activists have described their ways of thinking and activities, and others have reconstructed them in interviews with journalists and scholars in later years (Viorst 1979; Raines 1977). Chroniclers and historians of particular organizations, such as CORE (Meier and Rudwick 1973; Zinn 1965), particular cities such as Greensboro (Chafe 1980), particular sit-in drives, such as Knoxville (Proudfoot 1962), allow one to piece together a detailed account of the events. An outstanding study of the early weeks of the North Carolina sit-ins by a University of North Carolina graduate student is especially valuable (Wehr 1960). The single most comprehensive and valuable account and explanation of the sit-in movement remains Oppenheimer's unpublished dissertation (Oppenheimer 1963). In recent years scholarly accounts explaining the sit-in movement in the broader context of the history of black opposition to subordination and from a variety of theoretic vantage points have been published (Orum n.d.; Morris 1981, 1984; McAdam 1982, 1983; Killian

1984). Compared to most social movements the literature on the sit-ins has been abundant and impressive.

What happened? It all started on 1 February 1960 in Greensboro when four Agriculture and Technical (A&T) freshmen remained seated until closing time at the Woolworth lunch counter after they were refused service. In the following days, their action was massively supported by students on the A&T campus. The protest increased in terms of stores and lunch counters targeted, number of participants, and participants from other Greensboro colleges. For a week, nothing visible happened in other cities, then in short order on February 8, 9, and 10 similar sit-ins and demonstrations started in nearby cities with black colleges: Durham, Winston Salem, Charlotte, Fayetteville, Raleigh. On February 11 the first out of state sit-ins occurred in Hampton, Virginia; the first protest by high school students, in High Point; and the next day college students at Rock Hill, South Carolina went into action, followed by further spread of protest in Virginia and South Carolina. Up to mid-February the sit-ins were geographically contiguous; then on February 13 black college students in Nashville acted. The first protests in the Deep South occurred in Tallahassee on February 13, and then at the end of February in Montgomery by Alabama State College students. In March black students in Louisiana and Texas initiated sit-ins; Atlanta students got into the fray in mid-March. Except for Mississippi, by the end of the spring semester in 1960, black college students had become active in every Southern state, and especially in North Carolina, South Carolina, Tennessee and Virginia. In many places high school students joined the college students or went into action on their own.

Thanks to Paul Wehr's research on the sit-ins as they were taking place in the spring of 1960, we possess a first-rate account of the mobilization of collective protest and of the mood of students at the North Carolina black colleges. The demonstrators were sustained by an intense conviction of the rightness of their actions. In the words of a protest leader

> It gives one a tremendous feeling and assurance to know in your heart what you are doing is the right thing.

On each campus, Wehr writes that some organization activity took place after Greensboro and prior to the initiation of a local sit-in. Those who took the initiative were leaders in campus organizations, in student government, the newspaper, the NAACP chapter. Leadership in the sit-in movement became necessary for maintaining campus leadership position (Wehr 1960, chap. 3).

Student leaders would call a mass meeting and put before them a protest plan—a vote would be taken. Those who took the initiative would be elected to serve as leaders in the campus protest organization. Committees for raising money, publicity, transportation to downtown stores, negotiations, and so forth, were formed and coordinated by a steering committee where the most important decisions were taken. The protest organizations were linked to the student body through the student council president. All major decisions such as discontinuing picketing during negotiations were ratified at mass meetings called by the student body president. Some campuses (e.g., Fayetteville) did not create a lasting protest organization (Wehr 1960, 52–54).

The enthusiasm and participation of black students was great. Returns from a questionnaire survey circulated in May on the A&T, Shaw, North Carolina Central, and St. Augustine campuses indicated that all but six percent of the respondents had participated in some manner in the protest movement; 60 percent participated in mass meetings, 57 percent had boycotted stores, 54 percent had demonstrated, 31 percent walked picket lines, others reported making picket placards, distributing leaflets and so forth. Respondents reported overwhelming parental support. When asked about the degree of their agreement with various groups about what "Negroes should do about segregation and discrimination", nearly 90 percent indicated "strong agreement" or "agreement with most of the views" of student protest leaders and the majority of their fellow students. On attitude and opinion items, Wehr found hardly any significant associations with the usual set of background variables, indicating the high consensus one would expect in a fully mobilized collectivity when all individual differences recede in importance (Wehr 1960, chap. 6).

There was little personal contact and liaison between protest groups in different cities in the first few weeks, though personal friendships existed between students enrolled at different colleges. Wehr (1960, 54) was surprised by the "absence of any effective liaison" between individual protest groups on the eight protesting campuses he studied in the early weeks of the sit-in. "Only after nonstudent leaders became active did liaison develop," he writes. The rivalry between black colleges, stimulated by intercollegiate athletics, helped spread the sit-ins. Wehr (1960, 24–25) reports that "one common response to the question 'Why did the movement start at your school?' was 'we wanted to jump into the movement before_____.'" As a result some campuses acted without much preparation. National and especially local press coverage, with full details about the Greensboro protest techniques, was stimulating and a source of information on how to conduct a sit-in.

From the start, the black students were determined to keep the local protests under campus leadership. Commenting on the activities of CORE Field Secretary Carey and Durham Minister Moore, an "unofficial representative of SCLC," both of whom together "rushed back and forth between protest groups, also visiting cities where demonstrations had not be initiated," Wehr (1960, 29) writes:

> The protesters in well organized groups expressed considerable determination to keep the movement a "student movement," and there was often resentment expressed toward Moore and Carey as they traveled about the state. "We are willing to listen to what people like him have to say," said one leader "but we are going to keep control of this thing ourselves."

The targets were at first the lunch counters of downtown department and variety stores—Woolworth, Kress, Rich, McCrory, and local firms— but in time the protests embraced segregated parks, swimming pools, libraries, beaches, cinemas, and restaurants. The character of the confrontations led to further collective actions: when students were arrested and jailed or expelled, others would march or kneel in prayer.

In most places, students or black adults tried to persuade store managers to desegregate eating facilities, but they were turned down or turned away. Instead, managers closed their lunch counters following the initial sit-ins. After the counters were closed the students picketed outside on the sidewalks. From the start hostile whites converged on the protest sites, intimidated and sometimes threatened and assaulted the demonstrators. Police were kept busy and in many places arrested troublemakers and protected nonviolent black demonstrators. City officials vacillated a great deal; eventually in most cities some black protesters were arrested and jailed on charges of disturbing the peace, trespassing, and the like. In Orangeburg, South Carolina students were hosed down by police and jailed en masse. In Chattanooga clashes between black and white youths escalated into a small riot. Yet the 1960 sit-ins were by and large without the fury of white mobs assaulting the Freedom Riders in the spring of 1961—the ambushes and shootings of the Mississippi voter registration campaigns, the police dogs of Bull Connor in Birmingham, the cattle prods of Sheriff Clark's posse at Selma.

The existing black and civil rights organizations (CORE, NAACP, SCLC) grasped the sit-in movement's importance and provided advisors and advice, encouragement and bail money, but the students maintained their own protest organizations and ran their own campaigns in decentralized fashion from a campus base, college by college. In mid-April at a two-day conference of student protest leaders in Raleigh, a coordinating committee was created and in the fall became SNCC, but SNCC wasn't organized until the winter of 1960–1961 and then it became preoccupied with the Mississippi Voter Education Project. By then the student sit-in movement had ebbed.

More important than the actions and pronouncements of these national organizations was the reaction of the local black citizenry and leadership—the local NAACP, churches, black attorneys, parents, and the black middle class. They were proud of the students; their response was by and large supportive and encouraging. They raised bail money and provided attorneys. They would act as go-betweens between the students and the city officials and white businessmen. Early on it became clear that moral appeals to merchants and elected officials were ineffective. The students' actions and self-sacrifice on behalf of collective black goals moved some black communities to organize economic boycotts of downtown stores called "selective buying campaigns" in order to avoid prosecution on conspiracy charges. Together with business losses from white shoppers who stayed away from troubled downtown districts, the boycotts hurt white merchants and pressured them to negotiate in earnest, and to desegregate some lunch counters, and later on some cinemas, restaurants, hotels and motels.

Success was partial and uneven. Again and again in the years between 1960 and the passage and implementation of the 1964 Civil Rights Act, black protesters renewed campaigns to desegregate yet additional facilities in cities and towns where they had earlier achieved limited victories. In 1961 the initiative passed from the black campus organizations to the local branches and national civil rights organizations, partly because students active in the 1960 sit-ins had joined these organizations. The results were much the same as in the spring of 1960: partial victories in Virginia, North Carolina and Tennessee; mostly defeats in the Deep South. Where state officials pressured black college presidents into dismissing student activists and others were promptly arrested and jailed, as at Southern University in Baton Rouge and at Alabama State College in Montgomery, the student protest movement was smashed.

White merchants and store managers in the spring of 1960 everywhere first thought that the sit-ins were a passing fad. When that didn't happen, they prevailed on local officials to have demonstrators arrested. New ordinances were enacted against picketing and boycotting. Some merchants sought a court injunction against pickets. When these moves solidified campus support and brought about a show of solidarity among black adults, white merchants in the upper South settled for negotiations in biracial civic and human relations committees. In return students would agree to a truce. These committees bogged down because merchants would not agree on desegregation and were using the committees for stalling until the end of the spring semester. When negotiations broke down, students would resume sit-ins, picketing and demonstrations, and boycotts would be resumed or initiated. Meanwhile support groups in Northern cities were undertaking picketing and boycott campaigns against the national chain stores. Financial contributions were coming into national and campus protest groups. Civic leaders became concerned with the poor image of their city, should confrontations persist, at a time when many were campaigning to attract Northern business and industry and trying to revive downtown business districts. As local and national pressures mounted, desegregation by negotiated agreement or unilateral action were reached in the late spring in some cities as in Winston Salem and Nashville. Elsewhere desegregation was initiated in the summer when colleges were not in session. This was the pattern in North Carolina, Virginia, Tennessee and Texas, and somewhat latter in Atlanta. "Voluntary" desegregation of eating facilities by the national chains—Woolworth, Kress and Grant—and some local department stores took place in the summer and fall of 1960 even where sit-ins had not occurred when it became clear that desegregation wasn't hurting business. Elsewhere in South Carolina, Georgia, Alabama, Mississippi and Louisiana, there was no change.

The protests did not die down during the summer holiday months of 1960. There were several hot spots: Petersburg, Virginia; Greenville, South Carolina; and Knoxville, Tennessee. Elsewhere in Atlanta students were organizing for a fall campaign. In the late summer and fall, sit-in drives started or resumed in Atlanta, Jacksonville, New Orleans, Nashville and Tallahassee, and in the winter of 1960–1961 in Rock Hill, South Carolina. But the student protest movement was on the decline at this time, having gained its immediate goals in some cities, run into the realities of intransigent social control in other places, and simply run out of steam at other campuses. By this time, however, civil rights organizations had been revived, and the slack from student protest was taken up by them. CORE moved with the Freedom Rides in May 1961.

Let me recapitulate: One can speak of a sit-in movement rather than discrete acts of protest and defiance in the spring of 1960 because there was a similarity and continuity of goals, participants, targets and tactics, despite a lack of common leadership and organization. Of the forty or so protest sites that spring, in any given week, several were in an active phase of sit-ins, picketing and demonstrations, while at others a temporary truce was in effect and negotiations were being held. Yet the next week as protests were called off at some sites, they were initiated or reactivated at other sites following the breakdown of negotiations. Meanwhile a continuous stream of pronouncements—some supportive, others opposed—were issuing from politicians, civic groups, church leaders, ex-President Truman, and so on. Ordinances were enacted and challenged in court, injunctions sought, demonstrators arrested and jailed, sentences pronounced and appealed, public accusations were made; analyses written; and so forth. Events kept occurring and news was being made daily. According to the SRC (1961, 3), by September 1961, one year and a half after the start, sit-ins and direct action protests had taken place in over one-hundred cities in the South and border states; at least 70,000 blacks and some whites in these states had actively and visibly participated—3600 students and supporters had been arrested, and 141 students and fifty faculty members had been dismissed for their part in protest activities. Thus to participants, supporters, opponents, the news media and public opinion a "movement" was unfolding before their very eyes: the whole became greater than the sum of its local parts.

Diffusion of Protest

In this section I describe a model of protest diffusion which will account for the sit-ins. A pivotal variable in the theory of collective action is the degree of prior organization within the collectivity susceptible to protest mobilization on particular issues (Tilly 1978; Oberschall 1973).

The degree of organization can be thought of as a continuum from absence of organization, through loose structure, all the way to tight structure. For sustained collective action against opponents, it is necessary that people in the collectivity surrender resources to a leadership group that invests them in organization and activity for obtaining collective goods. That happens when a common leadership is recognized in the entire collectivity and when it controls a communications link to all, agrees on the same set of goals and strategies, and can count on a routinized supply of resources from the people. This is most likely the case when the collectivity is organized tightly, what one usually refers to as an organization, an association or a community. In Tilly's (1978) terminology, such a collectivity is high on both catness and netness.

People in a loose structure, on the other hand, lack a common leadership, a shared communication network and a routinized mechanism for collecting and allocating resources for a common purpose. There may exist many small clusters or islands of tight organization and a few even large ones, some loosely linked with each other and some only indirectly linked or not at all, yet many people and small groups are isolated and unintegrated into an overarching organization. The collectivity speaks with many voices, lacks a single ideology and strategy of collective action, lacks the capacity of communicating with all potential participants, and cannot count on a dependable flow of resources for collective action.[1]

I have argued elsewhere that a social unit with "loose structure" has the potential for a sustained social movement growing out of an initial period of localized, short-term protest actions (Oberschall 1973). In this social structure the diffusion of collective protests is an important means of social movement formation, but has to be explained since there is no prior, overarching organization for planned and centrally coordinated protest, as would be true for a centrally coordinated insurgency or a strike wave led by an established labor organization.[2] Under what circumstances then will diffusion take place in a collectivity with loose structure?

The model is based on the assumption that potential participants will join in collective protest when expected benefits exceed expected costs, as seen from their vantage point. It further assumes for the sake of parsimony that expected benefits are a function mainly of the expected chance of success, which itself is positively related to the expected size of the protest group. Further, it assumes that the expected costs of participation are negatively related to protest group size.[3] These relationships are depicted in figure 8.1 by the solid lines.

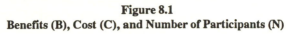

Figure 8.1
Benefits (B), Cost (C), and Number of Participants (N)

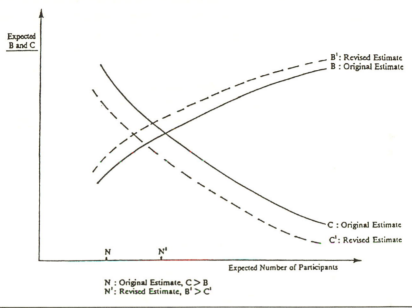

The model assumes that prior to diffusion small groups of activists and many individuals in the collectivity care intensely about some collective goods (e.g., equality, end to segregation) that they seek to obtain. There are nevertheless two principal deterrents for starting a protest. The potential initiators are uncertain about how many others will join in support (N = uncertain), and further, they are uncertain about the benefits and costs they will incur (they are uncertain about the location and precise shape of the B and C curves), because these depend to a large extent on opponents' reaction to a challenge and the positions taken by various third parties (which are unknown prior to any protest). Given these uncertainties, the potential initiators will tend to underestimate potential support (N) and success (B) because of the difficulty in identifying and communicating with potential supporters in a loose structure, and will tend to overestimate repression (*C*) based as it would be on past confrontations that were repressed and common experience of the lack of "give" in the social control system.

There are but two ways of reducing these uncertainties and of arriving at a realistic estimate of support, benefit and cost. The first is to test one's protest environment directly by initiating a protest and getting actual information on these variables. The second way is vicarious. Suppose that in a similar social milieu protest is initiated by people much like oneself, with whom one shares a common identity, and that the outcome and conflict circumstances become widely known. Potential protesters located elsewhere can then make a more accurate, revised estimate of *B*, *C*, and *N* in their own locality. If an original incident or incidents are such that the cost estimate is revised down, and benefit and group support revised up (the dotted lines in figure 8.1), some potential activists who had previously been deterred will relocate themselves on *B* and *C* and *N* in such a way that estimated benefits now exceed estimated costs, and they in turn initiate protest in their locality. If this second protest is successful and becomes widely known, other groups so far inactive and hesitant revise *B* and *N* yet further up, and *C* further down, which tips their action threshold, and they too initiate protest in their locality. Thus a single protest becomes a precipitating incident for other protests, and the diffusion of protests is set in motion.

For an incident to become a precipitating incident in a loose structure, certain conditions must, however, be met. The most obvious is rapid communication of all the relevant information to other potential activists. Because the population in a loose structure does not possess its own autonomous communications system nor an interpersonal network that reaches densely into it, the information will have to be diffused by the news media. Moreover, the outcome from the original incident or incidents must be such that other units revise their estimates for *C*, *B*, and *N* in a favorable direction for protest. What then is likely to be newsworthy and to provide estimates for *B*, *C*, and *N* favorable for protest?

Here we arrive at an interesting paradox. Suppose the first protesters gain an "easy" victory, that is, the target shortly caves in to their demands and they experience no arrests, injuries or other costs. Then the news media will either not pick up the story, or will drop it after a day or two so that the information is not likely to reach other potential activists. Suppose, on the other hand, that the initial protest is brutally repressed and the information is diffused in the media. Then other potential activists are deterred rather than encouraged, that is, they revise B, C, and N in an even more unfavorable direction for protest. But suppose that something of a stalemate is reached after a series of confrontations in which the protesters are resisted, increase their effort, and keep challenging the target, yet they are not repressed. Then the media are likely to pick it up and run it as a developing story, the information gets diffused, C is revised down and N up, because there turns out to be more population and third party support than initially anticipated by activists. This tips anticipated net benefit from negative to positive for activists elsewhere; they initiate protest in turn. Thus diffusion is more likely through stalemate in initial confrontations rather than through easy victory.

For an incident to be an effective signaling device for others, certain additional favorable conditions are likely to be present. The more similar the protest circumstances to the original incident, the more likely are activists to frame the information as relevant for revising their own estimates of B, C, and N. That is, the protest action is the same, if the protesters are similar on important status characteristics, if the targets are similar, if the stated goals of protest are the same, if the protest milieu is similar (for instance opponents are similar, as would be true in proximate geographic locations), the information from the preceding incidents are more likely to be considered appropriate in reducing uncertainty about initial estimates of B, C, and N. From this it follows that the protesters and protest events will exhibit a marked similarity and a spatial and temporal pattern of diffusion from a point of origin, which has often been observed.[4] It further follows then that participants, opponents, and third parties alike will perceive a coherence and unity of action and purpose that was unintended and unplanned. Thus discrete, not explicitly coordinated, local actions become framed and experienced as a "movement." This then increases the chances of similar protest actions elsewhere being reported in the context of the same developing news story about the "movement." Labeling and shared perceptions create a group identity and solidarity among the previously unlinked or weakly linked protest groups, making subsequent purposive linkages among them more likely. Protest diffusion increases both catness and netness. Protesters develop a collective action repertoire (Tilly 1978).

Once such a diffusion process has got going and has become a "movement" in the eyes of both sides and of the public, participation becomes no longer as dependent as in the early phases on information about prior protest events. That is because various groups and organizations come to the support of protesters and even initiate some protests on their own. Thus estimated net benefit and participation size come to be formed from more diverse sources and variables than prior protests. The movement character of the original diffusion process is then sustained by the dynamics of the localized confrontations: at any one time, even if some of the active groups are in a truce or negotiating phase, others are experiencing a revival of activism subsequent to the breakdown of negotiations; still others are just getting started for the first time while trials, appeals, fund raising, organizing and many other mobilization activities characterize the entire set. All this generates a continuous flow of news and information and keeps the movement in the public limelight regardless of the outcome at any particular protest site. A social movement has been created.

Applications of the Model

The model sheds light on the absence of diffusion following upon seemingly similar "precipitating" events in an otherwise similar loose social structure. Take the case of several reported incidents of sit-ins in the late 1950s, as in Durham, North Carolina and Nashville, Tennessee (Morris 1981, 748–49). Small groups of activists undertook these with the idea of getting a better reading on the benefit and cost variables (i.e., Will we get arrested? Will the management meet with us?), but because they were conducted as test sit-ins for the benefit of the activists themselves and not to gauge potential black support outside the narrow activist circle, no estimate on the crucial support variable N was gotten. Thus uncertainty about location on B, C, and N was not much reduced. Moreover, test sit-ins were brief and small scale, and thus not likely to generate a sustained news story.

The Oklahoma-Kansas sit-ins in 1958 (McAdam 1983, 742) suffered from victories too easily won, and from border state location that southern blacks might not consider appropriate signaling devices for accurate estimates for B, C, and N in their own hometowns. A successful precipitating incident in the Deep South would also be unlikely because activists would be firmly repressed at the first incident. It would thus generate information unfavorable for diffusion.

As far as the limited diffusion of the bus boycott movement is concerned, two reasons appear important. The tremendous effort and cost put into the Montgomery boycott could not fail to attract notice, nor the rather modest (though highly symbolic) victory limited to segregation on municipal buses.[5] Moreover, in a technical sense, the victory resulted from the successful NAACP lawsuit in the federal courts at a time when the authorities were about to smash the Montgomery movement with a mass arrest of its leaders. Also, following the Supreme Court municipal bus decision, many southern cities such as Nashville desegregated their buses with as little publicity as possible, often by simply not enforcing segregation ordinances. Thus the target itself was removed.

The first week's sit-ins in Greensboro on the other hand, possessed several features favoring diffusion. The activists kept going back on succeeding days with a rapidly growing number of supporters that signaled a favorable reading on the N variable and made the confrontations newsworthy. The activists were not repressed by the authorities and white counterdemonstrators were held in check by the Greensboro police. Thus C was low, probably lower than expected.[6] Further, the North Carolina-Southern Virginia Piedmont region has an unusually large number of black colleges, which facilitates a geographic diffusion pattern through direct links between the students at different campuses and a proximity effect in diffusion. One would expect little variation on B, C, and N in proximate social milieus, making information from the first sit-in site especially relevant for estimates in nearby college towns.[7]

Also facilitating and speeding diffusion would be links among colleges. In the case of the black Piedmont colleges, such direct links existed through the intense basketball rivalries in the CIAA conference to which all the colleges belonged. Basketball is *the* intercollegiate sport of these colleges. February is the peak of the basketball season.[8] We know from Wehr's interviews that competition and rivalry were important motivations for activists in the decision to undertake sit-ins. Lastly, the protesters' college student status is also of some importance. Early in a semester, as in February, opportunity costs for extracurricular activities are lower than in the other months because final exams, and even midterms, are some time away. Further, campus residence and existing student organizations make for low cost information and mobilization costs at the typical small college.

Might the sit-in movement have occurred some years earlier in 1957 or 1958, or perhaps even prior to the late 1950s? Difficult as this question is, I suggest the following reasons for a negative answer. An opposition movement by a negatively privileged group is likely to be undertaken only after "reform from above" has failed (Oberschall 1973). Such failure disillusions the group and disposes it to seek its own solution. For southern blacks such was indeed the case with school desegregation. It became obvious in 1955 and 1956 that southern whites would go to great lengths in resisting the 1954 Supreme Court decision. Also the white defiance movement, as evidenced by the activities of the White Citizen Councils, gave powerful signals to blacks about the likely high costs that opponents of segregation might be expected to bear[9] (cf. Martin 1957). By 1958 and 1959, however, visible white repression had abated, not because opposition to school desegregation had declined, but because elected officials and school boards had been quite successful in delaying implementation and in putting the NAACP on the defensive. Finally, as Morris (1984) has shown, a great deal of mobilization activity by black activists and SMOs were taking place in the South. Insofar as this created islands of tight social structure with some extralocal linkages, it ensured that once protests were underway, they would get much needed help from these mobilized social units. Thus blacks in the late 1950s were more ready and willing to challenge segregation on their own than in the early and midfifties.

Contrasts

The diffusion model should be compared with both "classical collective behavior" theory (Killian 1984) and other recent accounts of the origin of the civil rights movement designated by their authors as "political process" theories (Morris 1981, 1984; McAdam 1982, 1983).[10] Killian recently lamented the fact that too much emphasis has been placed on organization and rationality in theories of collective action, and that spontaneity and emergent processes have been downgraded in these explanations. I, for one, do not see any crucial differences of either theory or fact between my model and account of the sit-in movement and those of Killian, although there are some differences in emphasis and in terminology. With its emphasis on the three pivotal variables B, C, and N that actors are uncertain about initially and that get revised in a more realistic fashion only in the course of protest, my theory of collective action and model of diffusion can be looked on as a way of handling and operationalizing spontaneity. The contemporary concept of rationality incorporates the fact that information is costly to obtain and thus often inaccurate and incomplete, that decisions are made in finite time before all relevant information is collected and processed, that actors make errors of judgment even when they possess accurate information, and, most important, that a confrontation decision involving two or more parties is by its very essence fraught with uncertainty because the actions of each party are contingent on others' actions. I do, however, express these ideas in the terminology of rationality and uncertainty because it is parsimonious and links directly to a great deal of other social science theorizing.

By doing so, I do not mean to imply that protest actions lack an emotional dimension. That they do is so obvious to participants and observers alike that it goes without saying. My analysis, as a matter of fact, has referred to intercollegiate rivalry, enthusiasm on black campuses and parental encouragement and pride. The model is compatible with a whole range of social psychological processes that emphasize the emotional components of action. I reject the notion, however, that enthusiasm and emotion blocks the simple rationality here assumed, any more than a ball team fired up by a wildly cheering home crowd in a game with an arch rival loses its ability to execute plays. The artificial dichotomy between rationality and emotion has for too long obfuscated a theory of collective behavior, as Turner and Killian (1957, 16–17) long ago pointed out.[11]

Neither does the diffusion model overlook the importance of emergent norms in collective behavior. In fact, not until clear-cut norms about confrontation and social support have merged can all parties make accurate estimates of B, C, and N. In the case of the 1960 sit-ins, there was a great deal of learning by both sides about just what the appropriate conflict norms were, especially on the part of southern law enforcement authorities and agencies, because the protesters adopted nonviolent confrontation tactics. Southern police and authorities were simply not familiar with such tactics. The typical reaction to a sit-in the first two weeks in North Carolina was to close down the lunch counters, and for the police to keep the peace and prevent trouble from counterdemonstrators rather than arresting the black protesters. Not until February 10 when sit-ins had taken place in five additional cities, did the North Carolina attorney general express an opinion on antitrespass laws that might be applied by municipal authorities and store managers. The first arrests of protesters occurred only on February 12 in Raleigh, and the first sizeable fight between blacks and whites not until February 15 at High Point. The first statement by white segregationists (the WCC) was made even later on February 18 (cf. Wehr 1960, 34–38). The point is that the same behaviors in the early stages of confrontation can be described in the language of emergent norms or in that of a learning process about B, C, and N. In both cases, it is assumed that it takes some time for expectations about each party's responses to the other to become firm, with a concomitant routinization of confrontation.[12]

McAdam and Morris' "Political Process" theory is similar to my mobilization theory (Oberschall 1973). On the sit-in movement and the origins of civil rights movement, our differences are a matter of emphasis, with some disagreements on facts. McAdam and Morris stress the forging of a southwide, black protest infrastructure in the 1950s, with local movement centers gradually linking up and preparing for an assault on segregation. Like a "Whig History" that interprets events in the light of subsequent developments that no one could foresee, they write about a civil rights movement when there was yet only sporadic and disjointed challenge to segregation. As the two quotations at the head of this chapter indicate, black leaders and participants in the 1960 sit-ins were not yet conscious of forming a civil rights movement, nor creating one according to some well-thought-out master plan.[13] After an uncertain tentative start in Montgomery, a Southern civil rights movement grew out of the sit-ins by trial and error. The sit-ins were not simply a tactical innovation by a civil rights movement already formed in the preceding decade of organization activity and sporadic protests. To call all black actions "insurgency," from NAACP lawsuits and black parents' petitions for transferring their children out of segregated schools, to lunch counter sit-ins, downtown picketing, and economic boycotts, is to ignore an important discontinuity in the black challenge to segregation in 1960 when their center of gravity shifted from a predominantly legal approach to nonviolent direct action, and when their incidence skyrocketed (McAdam 1983, 739, fig. 1).

I disagree with Morris (1984, 200) that "[The] sit-ins were largely organized at the movement churches rather than on the campuses. To understand the sit-in movement, one must abandon the assumption that it was a college phenomenon," and further, that the diffusion of the sit-ins can be accounted for mainly with reference to the movement centers and linkages built up in the mid to late 1950s. It is worth examining the case of Nashville that Morris highlights in this connection. It is of course true that a small group of activists inspired by the Reverend James Lawson and supported by the Reverend Kelly Miller Smith and the local SCLC affiliate, the Nashville Christian Leadership Council, had for some time been preparing for nonviolent protests, and had even conducted a few test sit-ins. But they were caught unprepared by the Greensboro sit-ins. Morris (1981) himself writes that "the adults [mostly ministers] of the NCLC met with students at movement headquarters and tried to convince them to postpone the demonstrations for a couple of days until money could be raised. . . . Then, according to the Reverend Smith, James Bevel, then a student at American Baptist Seminary said: "I am sick and tired of waiting! . . . If you asked us to wait until next week, then next week something would come up and you'd say wait until next week and maybe we never will get our freedom!" (760). This quotation is an excellent illustration of how the college students in Nashville and elsewhere were taking matters in their own hands, despite cautious adults.

About Nashville, there is the well-documented precipitating telephone call from the Durham activists to the Lawson group, urging the Nashville group to start sit-ins. But I believe the Nashville students would have started sit-ins in any case. John Lewis, one of the students in the Lawson group who participated in the 1959 test sit-ins at Nashville, later recalled,

> It just so happened that at this particular time that apparently different people, student groups, were studying the whole idea of nonviolent direct action, and so the call from North Carolina really didn't find a vacuum in Nashville, because we were ready.

Yet, there was an important difference this time:

> a group of us, about 500, met on campus, went in to sit-in at a lunch counter. And it was not like the "test sit-in" we had in the fall of 1959. We stayed there. (Raines 1977, 101).

Despite the preparations of the Lawson group, Lewis recalled to journalist Viorst (1979, 107) that "about 90 or 95 percent of the people who showed up at the church (in Nashville on the first day of the sit-in) had no training in nonviolence."

Nashville was the most active sit-in site in the spring of 1960 because it had three major black colleges (Fisk, Meharry, Tennessee A and I), and not only because Nashville had become a "movement center" in the late 1950s, as Morris contends.

Many sit-ins started the way Julian Bond and Lonnie King recalled what happened in Atlanta (Raines 1977, 83-87):

JULIAN BOND: [Lonnie] came up to me and he showed me a copy of the Atlanta Daily World . . . the headline said "Greensboro Student Sit-In, Third Day" . . . [he] said, "Don't you think it ought to happen here?" And I said, "It probably will." And he said, "let's make it happen."

LONNIE KING: [M]y position was that the situation in Greensboro would again be another isolated incident in black history, if others didn't join to make it become something that the kids ought to be doing . . . the only people in the black community at the time who were free to take on the Establishment were college kids.

JULIAN BOND: Our original plan was to hit all of the five-and-dimes . . . and we went to the Atlanta University Center presidents . . . and they suggested . . . a delaying move . . . and [Dr. Clement] did succeed in having us delay it until the fifteenth of March.

The students found out about the sit-ins from the news, took the initiative, and black adult leaders, as in Nashville, tried to stall them, mostly without success, and occasionally for some time as in Atlanta.

A key activist's account from Shaw University in Raleigh confirms the same pattern of initiation, which corresponds to the assumptions of the diffusion model:

On February 9, I was sitting at my desk in the Shaw Journal office, William Peace hurried into the office. "Mitch, what are we going to do?" he asked. "The damned thing is spreading all over the place and we haven't made a move yet!" I told him to find Albert Hockaday, the president of the student council. Hockaday . . . had heard that students at St. Augustine's College, also in Raleigh, were considering some action. He thought we should talk with them about the possibility of doing something together. . . . That night we called a meeting on campus which was attended by representatives from St. Augustine's. Our purpose was to feel the pulse of the students as a whole. The pulse beat was anxious. The students wanted to move right away. . . . [T]wo local Negro clergymen . . . requested that we hold off any action until they got a chance to meet with the store managers the following day . . . As it happened, we did not wait. (Mitchell and Peace 1962, 75-76)

Morris (1981) contends that "[the sit-ins] spread despite the swinging billy clubs of policemen, despite Ku Klux Klansmen, white mobs, murderers, tear gas, and economic reprisals" (758). But the early stages of the sit-ins were not characterized by such repression.[14] Rather, repression tended to occur in the later phases of diffusion in the Deep South at a time when the sit-in tactic had widely diffused and a broad social movement was already taking shape. Just as important, Morris (1981) believes that "the preexisting communication networks overcame the problems imposed by the news blackouts" (765). But there was no news blackout. Wehr (1960) checked the news coverage in four major North Carolina dailies and found that "usually four or five articles concerning the demonstrations were to be found in each edition during the first month and a half" (59–60). Moreover, the editorials of three of the four papers were "generally sympathetic." These errors of fact lead Morris to overestimate the role of existing nonstudent centers and linkages in diffusion of the sit-in movement. If Morris had been correct on the magnitude of repression and the news blackout, then the diffusion process I describe could not have taken place.[15] Despite this disagreement, I fully agree with Morris and others, as indeed with my earlier account (Oberschall 1973, chap. 6) and above, of the crucial importance of black churches and civil rights organizations for helping students sustain the sit-ins and bring them to an often successful conclusion in the upper South.

Conclusion

There was an unplanned, unanticipated dimension to the first sit-in and their spread in the first few weeks, which I explain by means of a diffusion model grounded in the theory of collective action. Yes, there was a curious blend of seriousness of purpose and faddishness in the spread of the student sit-ins. Here is where the Montgomery bus boycott movement, King's reputation as a new style protest leader, and the mobilized clusters within the Southern black population came to play a crucial role. Because of Montgomery, King and the islands of tight organization, there had come to be defined the role of "black protester" against segregation. When they challenged segregation, the students were perceived and framed in terms of that role, and as a result of that social definition, came to assume that role. Consequently the fad component in the sit-ins was attenuated, which might not have been the case otherwise.

What then is the interrelationship between the student sit-in movement, the black churches, SCLC, NAACP, CORE and the emerging civil rights movement? These organizations were some distance from constituting a social movement in 1960. The direct actions of the mid 1950s had sputtered to a near halt. Even SCLC had adopted the legalistic strategy of the NAACP of testing the voting sections of the 1957 Civil Rights Act by small scale actions that would generate favorable evidence for litigation in the federal courts.[16] The lack of direct action challenges to segregation in the late 1950s was not a tactical retreat by black leaders in order to build organizations for the next planned direct action assault. It was rather the result of indecision about a long term strategy of challenging segregation which looked more formidable than it had in 1956. The student sit-ins gave the NAACP, SCLC, and CORE a much needed shot in the arm by forcing them into active support for the students, into increasing and expanding their mobilization efforts, and into initiating protests on their own. By doing so, in a partly competitive and partly cooperative manner, and with the help of newly enlisted white supporters, a loose alliance of black protest was created which came to be recognized as, and called the civil rights movement, and was the civil rights movement.

Notes

1. It is my contention that southern blacks in the 1950s had reached a degree of organization described here as "loose structure" rather than "tight structure." On this point I disagree with Morris (1981, 1984).
2. Diffusion of collective action in a loose structure has been very important in the history of opposition movements. A successful wave of sit-down strikes in the rubber and auto industries in 1936–1937 played a key role in the formation of the UAW and the CIO. More recently in Poland in 1980–1981, Solidarity was forged through protest diffusion in a similar context. Protest diffusion in a loose structure is most interesting for theory because uncoordinated, improvised local protests may grow into a social movement, which in time increases the density of organization in the protest population from a loose to a tighter structure.
3. A more fully spelled out model is described and justified in Oberschall (1980). The model does not assume that detailed, precise calculations are made by participants, as one would count one's change or engage in comparison shopping. Rather, and more likely, participants get persuaded after talking it over with each other and others, that if "they did it at X, we too can pull it off here at Y." This entails some knowledge of what happened at X, a rough assessment of the extent to which X and Y are similar, and a sense that number of participants is positively associated with expected benefit and negatively with expected cost. See also a fuller discussion in Oliver et al. (n.d.).
4. The correlation between distance from Greensboro and days elapsed since the first sit-in there, for the sixty-nine towns and cities for which date of first sit-in is available, is .501.

5. In a bus boycott, as McAdam points out (1982, 1983), the participation of almost all riders, often thousands of people, is needed for successful financial squeeze on a reluctant municipality. This requires a huge and costly mobilization campaign.

6. On 27 January 1985 the Greensboro *News and Record* ran several articles commemorating the sit-ins that make the following points about the police in Greensboro (A7):

   [Police Chief] Calhoun told [Woolworth Store Manager] Harris no arrests would be made unless he swore out a trespassing warrant. Harris . . . did not seek a warrant . . . Sit-in participants today praise Greensboro police for fairness during sit-ins. Demonstrators were not abused. Whites with Confederate flags were hustled away when they tried to start trouble . . . Ku Klux Klansmen and white hecklers, some carrying signs with racist taunts, often were present. A white youth torched some newspapers and tossed them under seats occupied by blacks. He was arrested.

   In other cities in North Carolina in the first few weeks, it was the same story. Patrick (1960, 8) writes that "there was very little violence or confrontation (in Winston Salem) . . . at no time was there any extremely vocal or organized effort directed against the movement for lunch counter desegregation." In Charlotte, students kept close check with Police Chief Jesse James to ascertain when they were on shaky legal ground. James told students he would protect them and merchants from any violence.

7. Orum's study of the campus and city variables correlated with protest outbreak based on 34 black colleges and college towns found that "the single most important variables is the distance of the college from Greensboro" (Orum n.d., 67). Here are the distances from Greensboro to the towns and cities where sit-ins were reported in the first two weeks:

Date of First Protests	Town or City	College	Miles to Greensboro
February 8	Durham, N.C.	North Carolina College	50
February 8	Winston-Salem, N.C.	Teacher's College	25
February 9	Charlotte, N.C.	Johnson-Smith	83
February 9	Fayetteville, N.C.	Fayetteville State	91
February 10	Raleigh, N.C.	St. Augustine & Shaw	73
February 11	Hampton, V.A.	Hampton Institute	251
February 11	Elizabeth City, N.C.	N.C. State Teachers	231
February 11	High Point, N.C.	High school students	12
February 12	Rock Hill, S.C.	Clinton & Friendship	109
February 12	Concord, N.C.	Barber Scotia	85
February 12	Norfolk, V.A.	none	230
February 12	Portsmouth, V.A.	none	220

8. With the exception of the South Carolina colleges and Barber Scotia, all the colleges in note 7 were members of the Central Intercollegiate Athletic Association. Note also the striking similarity of the sequence of sit-ins listed in Note 7 and the

Greensboro A&T basketball schedule in the first two weeks of February 1960 (*The New York Times*):

February 4	A&T vs. North Carolina College
February 8	A&T vs. Winston Salem
February 10	A&T vs. Shaw
February 12	A&T vs. St. Augustine
February 15	A&T vs. Johnson-Smith

9. This was not just the case in Alabama and Mississippi but in small town and rural North Carolina as well. Here are some germane excerpts from an interview with the Reverend Gilchrist, a long-time NAACP leader in Roanoke Rapids, North Carolina (*The People's Voice*, 5–18 October 1983):

INTERVIEWER: Reverend Gilchrist, when did you first join the NAACP?

GILCHRIST: I first joined the NAACP in '59 and it was in '62 that I was elected president. . . . Most people were afraid of the NAACP at the time.

INTERVIEWER: When you say most people, do you mean most of the minorities?

GILCHRIST: All the teachers were afraid to join, and some men who were active with me lost their farms . . . I had received any number of threats.

INTERVIEWER: What was the nature of the threats?

GILCHRIST: For example, I was getting mail . . . it would be a postal card with a big oak tree and a black hanging from the limb with a rope tied around his neck and all the card would say was "You will be next!"

10. I deplore that these and other labels have become widely used to characterize (and caricature) various sociologists. I have long held that there is but a single theory of collective action that encompasses the entire range of collective actions, from most institutionalized to most spontaneous, and from deliberate, calculated, detached to emotional behaviors.

11. Another common misconception is that collective behavior in which emotion, impulses, contagion, and like sentiments are manifest cannot be usefully analyzed with the methodology of rationality. Roger Brown (1965, chap. 14) has demonstrated how many useful insights are gained when panics, crazes, hostile crowds, fashions and fads are viewed in game theory terms.

12. Both theories hide an important substantive question. Just how does one account for the difference between Albany Sheriff Pritchet's successful learning of the new emergent national norm about dealing with nonviolent black protesters against segregation, and the opposite response of Bull Connor in Birmingham and Jim Clark at Selma?

13. The term "civil rights movement" does not appear in Dr. Martin Luther King, Jr.'s (1964) account of the Montgomery movement, *Stride Toward Freedom*, copyrighted in 1958. Instead, Dr. King uses a variety of terms such as "Negro resistance," "protest," and "nonviolent struggle." Even Louis Lomax's (1963) *The Negro Revolt* (completed in January 1962) does not have "civil rights movement" in its index. Wehr, writing in the midst of the 1960 sit-ins, does not use that term either. He does use "equal rights" movement, but it refers to the activities of the NAACP which he sharply contrasts with the students' "sit-down movement," "sit-down protests," and "protest movement."

14. The count of arrests and convictions in the first two weeks, based on Oppenheimer (1963, 63) and various newspapers, indicates that at thirteen of the first fourteen

protest sites, no arrests of blacks were made, and that only in Raleigh were there arrests made on February 12, forty-three of them, but none resulted in subsequent convictions. See also note 6.

15. However, the matter cannot be conclusively settled until someone systematically researches the black college campus records on the sit-ins, especially the student newspapers, and we have information on many more black campuses than the handful of well-publicized, leading sit-in sites.

16. Morris (1984, 108) writes, "it was decided that the SCLC would 'carefully and vigorously utilize the Federal Civil Rights Act of 1957,' which gave the Justice Department limited powers to intervene in voting cases when local whites interfered with the rights of blacks to vote. The SCLC was to provide trained personnel to assist local people in filing complaints with the Justice Department."

9

The Los Angeles Riot of August 1965

Although the Watts-Los Angeles[1] riot is now more than two decades past, it has not yet received the scholarly attention it deserves. Most newspapers and national magazines reported it at some length since it was an eminently newsworthy event. Four months after the riot, the commission that Governor Brown appointed to make an objective and dispassionate study of the riot handed in the report of its findings.[2] The McCone Report was a mere eighty-eight pages in length, and in it the actual description of riot events received no more than fifteen pages of space. The Report concentrated mainly on cataloging the social, economic, and psychological conditions that prevailed in the South Los Angeles area prior to the riot (which were well known to students of black poverty and of urban problems), and on suggesting changes designed to prevent a future riot. No attempt was made to provide anything but a superficial explanation of the motivation of the rioters and the patterns of their actions. In this chapter, an attempt will be made to use existing social science knowledge on collective behavior and riots to provide a fuller explanation for the riot. Because the socioeconomic conditions which acted as a backdrop to the riot are generally well known they will receive only limited attention in this chapter. An account of the natural history of the riot and other statistics on the duration, number of victims, extent of the property damage, and magnitude of the law enforcement effort will not be provided here since they have been widely publicized and are readily available.[3]

The sociological analysis of the riot undertaken below relies on Smelser's analytic framework in accounting for the causes of collective behavior and the forms which it takes.[4] The strength of this approach consists in the emphasis on a number of determinants of social action which must all be present at the same time for a riot to occur. In addition to socioeconomic factors, such as high unemployment, low income, well-defined racial cleavages, and authorities inaccessible and unsympathetic to grievances, this approach emphasizes the importance of a generalized belief in the population as a necessary determinant of collective action. It refers to a state of mind, formed over a period of time, that provides a shared explanation for the undesirable state of affairs and pinpoints blame upon specific agents or groups who become the targets of hostility. Incidents such as the police arrest or shooting of a suspect that normally receive but passing attention and are considered the private business of the parties involved can become the precipitant of a riot when that state of mind is present and when it provides a symbolic interpretation of the incident in terms of shared cleavages, grievances, and hostilities. Another useful feature of the scheme is the emphasis on the operation of social control as a crucial variable in explaining the magnitude and course that the collective outburst takes.

A methodological difficulty in applying the scheme should, however, be pointed out and is indeed typical of many instances where the social scientist is confronted with an event whose causes have to be reconstructed after it has already occurred. Evidence for the amount of deprivation in the population and for the presence of a generalized belief prior to the collective outbreak is usually hard to come by. There is the temptation to take the outbreak itself as an indication of the prior presence of a state of mind conducive to the outbreak. Yet if this is done, there does not exist the possibility of disproving the view that an outbreak might have occurred even in the absence of such a state of mind. Evidence for the existence and extent of the generalized belief has to be established independently of the subsequent events upon which it is meant to shed some light. Fortunately, in the case of the Los Angeles riot, there exists some information on the state of police-black relations and black grievances prior to the riot itself. But before a sociological explanation of the riot is presented, it will be useful to review briefly the views about the riot which have been propagated in the press and by official circles.

Popular and Official Views of the Riot and the Evidence

Important questions about the riot need to be answered before one can explain what the riot was all about. How many individuals actually participated in the looting, the burning, fighting the police, obstructing the firemen? Who were they? Was the riot spontaneous or planned, and if spontaneous, did certain groups subsequently provide the riot with leadership and organization? To what extent were youth gangs and adult criminal groups involved in the riot and the looting? Just what did the rioters and inhabitants do during the riot week? What levels of participation were there, and by whom? How widespread was the use of firearms and where did these weapons come from? How did the ecology of the area and the riot events themselves establish covert or tacit communication links among the rioters? Did the news media coverage of the riots contribute to its intensity and duration? Was the aggression of the rioters directed at the police and the white absentee owners as such, or were they conveniently available targets symbolizing the white man and white domination in general? Was the riot an irrational outburst directed against all authority, stemming from the lifelong accumulation of frustrations that found release in generalized aggression and violence? Is there evidence for norms operating among the rioters? Were specific targets selected and bounds to action recognized? Because of lack of information, or inaccurate and biased information, definitive answers cannot be given to all of these questions. Nevertheless, enough information is now available from many sources to rule out some characterizations of the riot, and to permit a plausible reconstruction of the character of the 1965 Los Angeles riot.

Immediate public reaction was a mixture of shock, fear, and belief that the riots were organized and led by some radical and disaffected groups in league with gangs and hoodlums; that quite possibly a conspiracy was at work; that it was a typical manifestation of irrational crowd behavior, unpredictable and similar to an animal stampede; that the rioters were well armed after they had systematically looted gun stores, hardware stores and pawn shops; and that the riot consequently was an armed uprising by blacks against the police, the political authorities, and the white man in general.

This initial climate of opinion was a result of the news coverage and the pronouncements of officials. They focused selective attention upon those events that did in fact fit the above loose conception of what the riot was all about. The irrational aspect of the riot was highlighted in Police Chief Parker's widely quoted phrase describing the rioters as behaving like "monkeys in the zoo." The insurrectionary aspect was stressed by *Time* and by the *Los Angeles Times* coverage, both of which reported extensively on the weapons allegedly used by the rioters and seized from them.[5] The conspiratorial and organized aspects of the riot, after its start, were stressed by Mayor Yorty[6] and other officials such as Police Chief Parker in his testimony on the use of bullhorns during the riot and the "expertly made" Molotov cocktails used by the rioters.[7] Indirect evidence for police belief in riot organization is the August 18th police siege, storming and subsequent destructive search of a Black Muslim temple that was "deliberately provoked by false telephone calls to police that Negroes were carrying guns into the building."[8] The police did not question the veracity of the anonymous callers because the information fitted their belief of some formal riot leadership and organization. The reaction of fear by the white population of Los Angeles is illustrated by the run on gun stores, which took place far beyond the residential areas adjoining the curfew area.[9]

While the conspiracy theory was popular with some officials and could be used as a political alibi, the McCone Commission found no evidence for a conspiracy in setting off the Los Angeles riot. The Commission wrote that "there is no reliable evidence of outside or preestablished plans for rioting," although it pointed to some evidence of the promotion of the riot by gangs and other groups within the curfew area after the riot had started, such as the "sudden appearance of Molotov cocktails in quantity" and of "inflammatory handbills."[10] The Commission did not elaborate a comprehensive theory of its own, yet it nevertheless hinted at another theory that has often been invoked in the explanation of violent collective outbursts, namely the "criminal riffraff" theory of rioting. According to this view, every large urban ghetto contains a disproportionate number of criminals, delinquents, unemployed, school dropouts, and other social misfits who on the slightest pretext are ready to riot, loot, and exploit an explosive social situation for their private gain and for satisfying their aggressive antisocial instincts.[11] Thus the Commission emphasized that many blacks were caught in a frustrating "spiral of failure," that they had been encouraged "to take the worst extreme and even illegal remedies to right a wide variety of wrongs, real and supposed," that nonetheless only a small minority of blacks were involved in the disorder, and that a majority of those arrested had a prior criminal record.[12]

But as Blauner has pointed out in a perceptive analysis, the report is in the main silent about who the participants were and what their motivations were. It did not attempt to explain how in the absence of planning and formal leadership a collective action on the scale and duration of the riot could be sustained in the face of a major show of force by over 1000 police and eventually 13,000 National Guardsmen.[13] Indeed, if the Commission's figure of a maximum of 10,000 blacks taking to the streets is accepted,[14] this represents about 10 percent of the age cohorts fifteen to forty-four, male and female, of the Negro population living in the South Los Angeles area, which roughly corresponds to the curfew area. Moreover, one should distinguish between several levels or degrees of participation. There are some who participated to the extent of physically fighting the police, of obstructing the firemen, of beating white motorists, and of breaking into stores and setting them on fire, in short, the activists. There are others who helped themselves to the merchandise in the stores already broken into. Still others, far more numerous, simply milled about in the streets, jeered at police, and openly encouraged the activists. Finally there were those who were not involved beyond being curious observers, or just went about the business of survival at a time of disaster. Among active participants in a riot, adolescents and young adult males can be expected to predominate. But if a substantial proportion of the remaining population overtly manifests sympathy and support for the active participants, the riot can only be interpreted as a broad group response to shared grievances, and not as the expression of an unrepresentative, lawless minority. An examination of the characteristics of the those arrested during the riot can bring us a step closer to resolving this controversy.

Almost 4,000 people were arrested on riot related charges during the Los Angeles riot, and a considerable amount of information about many of them has been collected and tabulated in two separate studies conducted by government agencies. The first of these, entitled *Riot Participation Study*,[15] concerns juvenile arrests only and rests ultimately on information assembled by deputy probation officers from questioning the arrested youths and other family members, and consulting the police and other official records, for the purpose of presenting the Juvenile

Court with a "social report" on each youth. The second of these reports, entitled *Watts Riot Arrests*,[16] is ultimately based on police and court records, and for a large subset, on data secured by the Los Angeles Probation Department during a presentence investigation demanded by the courts. These data should therefore be treated with caution, but in my opinion can lead to fairly definite conclusions on whether the riot participants were disproportionately composed of criminals, school dropouts, hoodlums, youths from broken homes, the unemployed, recent migrants, in short the rootless and drifting element which according to some is a characteristics of all the large urban ghettos in the United States.

A question that has to be answered first, however, is whether those arrested can reasonably be considered a typical cross section of the unknown total of persons who participated in some way in the riot. It could well be that those arrested are more likely to be representative of the groups that were milling about or looting than of the activists.

Several facts suggest that this may indeed be the case. Available eyewitness reports indicate that on the first three days and nights, Wednesday to Saturday morning before the National Guard was fully deployed, police officers were seldom in a position to make arrests among the rioters who were physically fighting them, assaulting white motorists, preventing the effective operation of firemen, and breaking into stores and looting. Many arrests were of course made, but the bulk of them took place after the curfew had been declared, and the police and National Guard had begun to control the riot. For the juveniles, 30 percent were arrested on Wednesday, Thursday, and Friday, and the rest on Saturday and later.[17] The figures for adults probably do not differ much but are unfortunately not available. Thus the bulk of those arrested were arrested at a time when the pattern of rioting had shifted from mass confrontation to small-scale looting and more isolated incidents of confrontation with the authorities. Furthermore, since roughly 8 percent of the adults arrested were later released by the police, and another 32 percent not convicted by the courts, it is evident that a substantial proportion of the arrests were in fact of people who were not riot participants in the legal sense. It remains therefore an open question whether the activists of the first three nights differed significantly from those arrested for whom data are available.

A total of 3371 adults and 556 juveniles were arrested, of whom about 60 percent were convicted. The most common booking offense for adults was for burglary, yet the most common conviction was for trespassing. It would seem that many individuals who happened to be in or near stores that were broken into were arrested without positive proof that they had stolen any merchandise. The booking offenses in most cases are more serious than the final dispositions, which resulted primarily in misdemeanors, ranging from simple assault and petty theft to trespassing, curfew violation, disturbing the peace, drunkenness and drunk driving, and the like. All in all, only sixty-three cases, or less than three percent of those arrested, received sentences of six months or more.[18]

Examining the prior criminal record of adults arrested—and the distribution is the same for those not convicted and those convicted—one finds that 26 percent had no prior record whatsoever, 29 percent had an arrest record but no conviction, seven percent had convictions of less than ninety days, 18 percent had one or two convictions of ninety days and over, four percent had three or more convictions of 90 days and over, and 11 percent had a prior prison record, with no information available on the remaining five percent.[19] These facts about convictions and prior criminal record prompted the following concluding comment by the compilers of these statistics:

> The relatively minor types of offense for which the great majority of riot participants were convicted would seem to indicate that this group of individuals was not the same type of persons usually booked on similar felony charges. A review of their prior criminal history fails to show a record as serious as that generally present in many of the nonriot felony bookings usually handled in urban areas by the police and courts.[20]

The criminal riffraff and hoodlum theory of riot participation does not receive any support from these data.

It is difficult to establish to what extent those arrested were representative of the South Los Angeles population, because census categories and breaking points often differ from those reported in the riot statistics and the potential reservoir for riot participants is mainly the male 14- to 50-year old group. Nevertheless, since 41 percent of those arrested were in the 25- to 39-age category, and a further 17 percent forty years old and over, it is inaccurate to describe the rioters as mainly composed of irresponsible youth and young hoodlums. Unlike gang incidents and other outbursts that are confined to a particular age cohort, the Los Angeles riot drew its participants from young and old alike.

Socioeconomic information about adults arrested is available for the 1057 convicted cases that were referred to the Los Angeles Probation

Department for a presentence investigation and report. This figure is 31 percent of all adults originally arrested in the riot, and 52 percent of the adults convicted. These cases therefore represent slightly over a half of those arrested against whom proof of criminal participation was sustained in the courts. Of these, 75 percent have lived in Los Angeles County five or more years and only 6 percent less than a year. The rioters were therefore not "recent migrants" to Los Angeles. Furthermore their educational achievements compare favorably with that of the population. The median years of education of the 1057 convicted adult participants is slightly over ten completed years, which is about the same as that of the South Los Angeles area. The information on labor force characteristics of the rioters is unfortunately not comparable to the census breakdowns for Watts and the South Los Angeles area. Among the arrested rioters, only about 10 percent were in the nonmanual category, and of the remaining proportion only 9.4 percent are classified as skilled workers. Moreover, 22.6 percent of the arrested rioters were unemployed, compared with 13.2 percent for the Watts labor force in November 1965, and 10.1 percent for South Los Angeles.[21] The lower class character of riot participation clearly emerges from these figures.

The detailed information on the juveniles arrested during the riot, incomplete as it is, confirms the picture that emerges from the adult data. There were 556 juvenile arrests, resulting in 338 cases referred to formal probation supervision. The vast majority of them were placed under probation supervision in their own home. 82.5 percent of the youths were in school, as opposed to 14.8 percent who were dropouts, not a high figure in an area where two-thirds of the students do not finish high school. The youths arrested cannot be accurately called "dropouts." They appear to have come in disproportionate numbers from the poor and broken homes of the ghetto, but were not typical "delinquents." Thus 81 percent of the cases are described as having "acceptable" to "good" relations with their families, 57 percent have never been on probation before, and a further 26 percent only once. On the other hand, 34 percent of their families were currently receiving their major economic contribution from the Bureau of Public Assistance (compared to 24 percent for the Watts population), only 26 percent were living in homes with both parents present (compared to 53 percent of persons under eighteen years old in Watts living with both parents, and 62 percent for the South Los Angeles area), and a little over 50 percent lived in families classified as having a "major family problem" by the Probation Department, the most frequent one being a major economic problem such as unemployment and poverty.[22]

All in all, piecing together the above information for adults and juveniles, what strikes one is the extent to which the riot drew participants from all social strata within the predominantly lower-class black area in which it took place. The riot cannot be attributed to the lawless and the rootless minority that inhabits the ghetto, though, no doubt, these were active in it as well. The riot is best seen as a large scale collective action, with a wide, representative base in the lower-class black communities, which, however much it gained the sympathy of the more economically well-off blacks, remained a violent lower class outburst throughout. If there were numerous jobless among the participants and many youths from families with problems, it is precisely because such cases abound in the neighborhoods in which the riot occurred.

Police-Black Relations

The conspiracy and criminal riffraff theories of the riot are not supported by the evidence on arrests. The key to a sociological explanation is the state of police-black relations before the riot, for it was a major source of black frustrations and accounts for the presence of a generalized belief that is a necessary ingredient in producing collective action. The objective factors producing strain among blacks in the South Los Angeles area, such as a high unemployment rate and stationary (even declining) incomes at a time of increasing prosperity in the rest of Los Angeles and the country at large, have been well documented and noted.[23] The increases in racial tensions due to other than economic factors have also received the attention they deserve. In the November 1964 election, California voters repealed the Rumford Fair Housing Act in a constitutional referendum by a two to one margin. Repeal was particularly high in Southern California and even higher among the white population surrounding the black neighborhoods in Los Angeles County. White areas there were in favor of the repeal in the 80 percent to the 90 percent range, whereas black precincts voted against it in the 90 percent range. The vote was widely interpreted as a hardening of white public opinion with respect to integrated housing. While most major U.S. cities had come up with acceptable organizational structures within the War on

Poverty Program by the summer of 1965, events took a different turn in Los Angeles:

> Advance billing with respect to federal programs had created the false impression that more job opportunities would be available than actually developed. The endless bickering between city, state and federal government officials over the administration of the authorized programs—most particularly the poverty program—has disappointed many.[24]

There were no compensating factors in Los Angeles such that blacks would be conscious of progress in some matters directly affecting them. The civil rights movement had not been very active in Los Angeles, and its crowning achievement, the passage of the Civil Rights Act of 1964, had not had any impact on the city's black population since segregation did not exist in Los Angeles, and California has had, for many years, laws against discrimination in employment, political participation, and other activities.

The charge of police malpractice and of police "brutality" was of course not confined to Los Angeles, but had been a problem in most large American cities and a precipitant in the 1964 and later riots in the United States. The situation in Los Angeles had been the subject of hearings held in Los Angeles in September 1962, by the California Advisory Committee of the U.S. Commission on Civil Rights, headed by Bishop Pike of San Francisco. The purpose of the hearings was to ascertain the state of police-minority group relations after an April 1962 incident involving Los Angeles police officers and Black Muslims became a focal point of organized black protests against alleged discriminatory treatment by Los Angeles police.[25] According to the Committee,

> Most of the blacks and civil rights organization spokesmen who testified believe that there is discriminatory law enforcement in Los Angeles. The types of discrimination most referred to was excessive violence at the time of the arrest, greater surveillance and arrest in areas of minority group concentration, the arrest of Negroes and Mexican-Americans for conduct for which Caucasians are not arrested, discourteous and uncivil police language, conduct and other behavior directed against Negroes and the Mexican-Americans, unjustified harassment of Negroes and Mexican-Americans, and an unwillingness and inability to distinguish between law-abiding and potentially lawbreaking minority group members. These charges, with one exception, were directed against the Los Angeles Police Department (as opposed to the Sheriff's Department).[26]

Police Chief Parker's testimony stated however that,

He did not think that the Police Department had a "bad image among the black community, the majority of them," and that "basically I do not believe that there is any difficult problem existing in the relationship between the Los Angeles Police Department and the black community." The Chief did allude however to elements who are trying to inflame the black community with false charges of police brutality.[27]

Already in 1962, therefore, the lines of cleavage were sharply drawn. On the one side a generalized belief in police brutality and discriminatory law enforcement was widespread and gaining strength within the black community. On the other side there was a denial of these charges by the police and the elected city officials, with the added insinuation that the belief itself was being spread by agitators who were trying to exploit certain racial tensions for their own political ends.[28]

There can be little doubt that the cleavage itself contributed to bring about the very situation both parties were trying to avoid. In the words of John Buggs, chairman of the Los Angeles County Human Relations Commission, who testified before the Committee:

A situation is being created in which the claim by minority group persons of police brutality and the counterclaim by police of minority group resistance to police authority are beginning to be a self-fulfilling prophecy.[29]

In concrete terms, a belief on the part of a black about to be arrested that the arrest is going to involve the use of force has the consequence of an attempt to avoid or resist arrest, thus increasing the probability that force will in fact have to be used to implement the arrest; whereas a belief on the part of police that an arrest is going to be resisted might produce a behavior in which force is in fact used. Thus the ground is prepared for the fulfillment of the prophecy.

One of the most controversial issues was and still is the existing procedure for handling citizen complaints against police conduct. The Police Department has an Internal Affairs Division (IAD) which has the responsibility of investigating and evaluating serious charges of misconduct made against police officers by citizens and by other police or public officials. Other charges are investigated by the operating divisions themselves, subject to review through the IAD.

The minority groups contended that the existing machinery for registering complaints and disciplining police was such that the Police Department was able to and in fact did whitewash police conduct, and by pressures and intimidations even prevented many complaints from being filed in the first place. Consequently, blacks demanded a civilian police review board, independent of the Police Department. Chief Parker opposed a civilian police review board on the ground that the wrong kind of people would get on it, and that police discipline and morale would be harmed.[30]

The whole matter of police-black relations in Los Angeles was and is a complicated one. Police brutality refers to more than the excessive use of physical force during an arrest, the manhandling of suspects in the police station and in jail, and other physical acts usually associated with the term brutality. It means arrests, questionings and searches of blacks by police without apparent provocation, the use of abusive and derogatory language in addressing blacks, such as the word "nigger," and a general attitude toward the minority groups that represents an affront to their sense of dignity.[31] Police brutality in this sense is a reality to be reckoned with in the black ghetto, no matter how exaggerated some incidents turn out to be and regardless of whether political or criminal groups try to exploit the issue. The presence of the police in the South Los Angeles area was a constant source of irritation and left behind a legacy of bitterness and hostility. Two years before the riot, a study conducted by the Youth Opportunities Board with 220 people in Watts, Avalon, and Willowbrook on their attitudes toward several agencies operating in the community found that a majority of both adults and children felt that "the behavior of the police aggravated the problems of growing up in the black community rather than contributed to their solution" in marked contrast to the respondents attitudes towards schools, probation officers, and health agencies.[32] It is important to note, however, that the tension-filled relations between police and blacks have a structural and situational, as well as a personal, origin. The police as the daily visible representative of a white dominated world bears the full brunt of the accumulated frustrations and hostility of the ghetto. Black attitudes towards the police are not merely a reaction to police behavior and attitudes, but to their total situation in the society. The role of the police in this situation is as unrewarding as it is dangerous.

One reason for the deterioration of police-black relations in Watts can be attributed to Parker's "reforms." Whereas before Parker, policemen patrolled city blocks on foot, thereby getting to know personally the people living in an area, and therefore able to use selective judgment in making an arrest (i.e., they would be able to tell a professional gambling game from an improvised neighborhood crap game, or know which drunks were troublemakers, which ones cared for by family and friends), Parker took the police off the beat and put them into police cars. In a matter of months, police lost the special knowledge and contacts with neighborhoods that alone makes law enforcement bearable especially in lower-class neighborhoods. When police enforced the law strictly and without exception, it was violating previous practices that had become part of the social structure, and hence caused hostility and resentment. These, in turn, led to resistance to arrests, with local groups helping the suspect evade arrest, which in turn led the police to intensify its law enforcement practices in this "lawless" community. Thus, a dangerous spiral of suspicion and antagonism was allowed to develop.

Black objections to the pro-police bias in the existing system of reviewing citizen complaints against police malpractice are borne out by the record. In 1961, 540 complaints were filed against police officials, 64 percent of these by ordinary citizens. Of 121 citizen complaints alleging the excessive use of force, only five were sustained, as opposed to 243 complaints sustained of the remaining 419 complaints (mainly drunkenness on duty, bad debts, etc.).[33] In 1964, of 412 complaints alleging police misconduct received from citizens, forty-two complaints were sustained, a higher proportion than in 1961, but still only slightly above ten percent.[34] These figures strongly suggest that in the overwhelming majority of cases of alleged police misconduct in dealing with citizens, the existing review machinery ruled in favor of the police. Moreover, the recommendations of the Pike Commission with respect to a civilian police review board, a police community program, and increase in the proportion of black police, have still not been acted upon.[35] Furthermore, neither the Pike nor the McCone Commission did anything beyond looking at dozens of case histories of police malpractice on file with various civil rights and black organizations. Both commissions felt that any action based on these complaints was outside their jurisdiction.

The Precipitating Incident and Mobilization for Action

Prior to the start of the riot, therefore, blacks in South Los Angeles were subjected to considerable strain due to unemployment, low income, poor police-black relations, frustrated hopes about the war on poverty, and similar factors. The normal channels for voicing black grievances had been ineffective in bringing about a change in the conditions producing these strains. A widespread belief in police brutality had existed for some time and was coupled with deep hostility against police. The Frye arrest on the evening of August 11, provided the spark that ignited the accumulated frustrations of the South Los Angeles population. In order to explain how a simple traffic arrest could escalate in a short time into a full-fledged riot of the magnitude and duration of the subsequent events, one has to examine the characteristics of the precipitating incident, the communications processes within the riot prone population, the ecology of the South Los Angeles area, and the nature of the police effort to control it.

Marquette Frye, a 21-year-old black, driving his mother's car, with his brother as a passenger, was stopped by a California highway patrolman after he failed to stop at a red light, about 7:00 P.M. near, but not in Watts. Marquette Frye had been drinking and was unable to produce a driver's license. The officer, soon joined by two more, was getting ready to arrest him. The evening this occurred was the hottest one so far of the summer, a lot of people were simply hanging about on the sidewalks outside their homes. A small crowd quickly gathered to observe the arrest. Everything went without incident until Frye's mother, living nearby, arrived on the scene. What happened after that is still not clear since the police, the Fryes, and witnesses have sworn to contradictory testimony.[36] Apparently, while at first Mrs. Frye turned against her son to discipline him, eventually the three Fryes, with encouragement from the onlookers, turned upon the policemen and had to be forcefully subdued and arrested. Meanwhile the highway patrolmen had radioed for reinforcements, and Los Angeles police officers arrived for help. By 7:25 P.M. the patrol car with the Fryes under arrest and a tow truck pulling the Frye car left the scene.[37] As the patrolmen were about to leave, a woman in the menacing crowd spat on one of them, and an officer did go into the hostile crowd to arrest her. She was wearing a shirt outside her skirt. The rumor immediately spread that the police were beating and arresting a "pregnant" woman—which she was not—just as the crowd had earlier "seen" the policemen use excessive force to subdue the Fryes. By the time the last police car left the arrest location, it was stoned by the crowd and the riot had begun.[38]

Regardless of what actually happened, the events surrounding the arrest fitted in with preconceptions and expectations about police brutality. In a confusing context such as an arrest in the evening with lots of people milling about and a high noise level it is plausible that apart from a few blacks who actually eyewitnessed most of the arrest events, many others pieced out an incomplete perceptual record of these events according to their preconceptions and predispositions.[39] It is particularly important to note the belief and the rumors about the police beating of a pregnant woman, for such action is one of the clearest violations of a basic norm of human conduct and arouses condemnation and revulsion. Person to person communication in a neighborhood on a hot night, with many individuals hanging around in the streets or in their houses but with windows open, can spread a message rapidly over a large area, and subsequent movement of people reinforced by the sound of police sirens further revealed where the focal point of the action was.[40] It seems plausible then that the original "witnesses" to the Frye arrest interpreted what they perceived as an act of police brutality, which fitted in with a long prior history of similar behavior that was expected from the police. Later arrivals had no particular reason to question this interpretation of the precipitating event and, sharing the beliefs and emotions of those already present, reacted to it similarly.

The original incident was widely reported in the news media, and in all probability a majority of the entire Los Angeles population knew the next day that a riot had taken place in a particular location in Watts during the previous evening and night. This piece of information in turn acted as a significant clue for the collection of crowds in the vicinity of the original arrest location the following day in the absence of any explicit coordination. Anybody, whether merely curious or wishing to settle an old score with the police, had but the same piece of information to go on, namely the location of the incident of the night before, and knew that everybody else, too, had the same clue to act upon. Hence, the original location acted as a magnet and as the focal point for the collection of similarly disposed crowds on Thursday evening and Friday morning before the riot eventually spread throughout the South Los Angeles area.

During the entire riot a common thread was the aggression against the police. Yet from the start the riot was more than just a police riot. The Los Angeles riot did not exhibit the character of the classic race riot in which crowds of one race systematically seek out and assault isolated individuals and smaller groups of another race. Nevertheless, the first two nights witnessed many incidents that fit the classic pattern as unsuspecting (and later curious) white motorists driving through the riot area were pelted with bricks and bottles, pulled out of their cars and beaten up, and news reporters and television crews were assaulted. It is difficult to document how the subsequent major pattern of breaking into stores, looting, and burning them down became established. The fickleness of hostile crowds as they move from one object to another has been well established in other instances of rioting and collective behavior. People with frustrations and grievances other than the specific grievance against the police witness and join in the riot. The situation becomes defined as one in which a broad class of race related grievances can be translated into direct aggressive behavior, and targets other than the one involved in the precipitating incident become the objects of aggression.[41] The pattern of store-breaking and arson was not totally devoid of some leadership, apparently provided by gangs, though it is impossible to establish the magnitude of this factor.

One of my informants stated that the big time, professional criminals in anticipation of a police dragnet took the first opportunity after the riot started to get out of the riot area and even out of Los Angeles. Many petty thieves and other small time professional crooks came individually or in small groups into the riot area to seize this opportunity of breaking into stores while the police were busy with the rioters. These groups were not, however, interested in leading the riot crowds to loot and destroy the white-owned stores since that would have interfered with the efficiency of their operations. Another informant who has been close to some of the gangs in the South Los Angeles area reported, however, that gang members, in an effort to prove their claims upon leadership in a certain territory and in competition with each other, were vying for leadership over the crowds during the riot, and this meant among other things actively participating in the skirmishes against the police, breaking into the stores, and setting them on fire.

The success of the store breakers, arsonists, and looters in eluding the police can in part be put down to the role of the mass media during the riot week. The Los Angeles riot was the first one in which rioters were able to watch their actions on television. The concentration and movements of the police in the area were well reported on the air, better than that of the rioters themselves. By listening to the continuous radio and TV coverage, it was possible to deduce that the police were moving towards or away from a particular neighborhood. Those who were active in raiding stores could choose when and where to strike, and still have ample time for retreat. The entire curfew area is a very extended one. It was not possible to seal off several blocks and trap rioters, as could be down in cities where apartment houses are built side to side. People could move from street to street through gardens, driveways, and alleys.

The magnitude of the riot measured in terms of its duration, the area affected, and the casualties and injuries sustained, can in part be accounted for by the measures taken to bring it under control. Officials at all levels underestimated the riot at the start. Deputy Police Chief Murdock stated on Thursday morning that "Wednesday was just a night to throw rocks at policemen."[42] Friday at dawn the police department felt that they had the situation under control, and Mayor Yorty flew to San Francisco later in the morning to keep a speaking engagement before the Commonwealth Club under the impression that the riot had mostly spent itself.[43] Police Chief Parker requested formally on Friday at 10:50 A.M. that National Guardsmen be brought into South Los Angeles, yet because of the conflicting reports he received about the seriousness of the situation, Lieutenant Governor Anderson, who was acting in the absence of Governor Brown vacationing in Greece, did not sign the papers until 5:00 P.M. on Friday. While some Guardsmen were deployed in the riot area by Friday night, it was not until after three nights of rioting had taken place that the 8:00 P.M. curfew was imposed on Saturday and the National Guard fully deployed.[44]

The police were of course outnumbered and undermanned, given the size of the riot area and the number of riot participants. Its efforts to disperse rock throwing crowds proved singularly ineffective. Motorcycle officers who penetrated through the thick of the crowd in an effort to disperse it and arrest the rock throwers were vulnerable to physical assault. The crowds afforded a convenient shield for hit-and-run tactics.[45] Much of the police effort on the first two nights of the rioting consisted of protecting itself, motorists, firemen, and news reporters from physical assault. Realizing that it often acted as a stimulant and focal point for the rioting, the police periodically withdrew from physical proximity to the rioters. In retrospect it would appear that the proposal of John Buggs of the Los Angeles County Human Relations Commission and of Reverend Brooking on Thursday afternoon to Deputy Police Chief Murdock to withdraw white uniformed police, and let community leaders control the crowds with the help of black officers in civilian clothes, which was turned down, might have been a more effective way of limiting the riot.[46]

As it turned out, the partial show of force happened to be a demonstration of vulnerability and weakness, and acted more as an incitement than a deterrent to the riot.

Riot Behavior and Motivation

No one would deny the extensive property damage perpetrated by the rioters in looting and burning the stores, the physical assault upon police, white motorists, firemen, and others. One can however question whether this behavior is essentially an irrational stampede and orgy of destruction, and hence void of collective social significance and personal meaning. Nothing is gained by defining riot behavior as irrational a priori. There is considerable evidence that the rioters observed certain *bounds*, that they directed their aggression at *specific targets*, and that they selected *appropriate means* for the ends they intended to obtain.

The fact that no deaths resulted from the direct action of the rioters is evidence that they observed certain bounds and limits. The first two nights when white motorists were dragged out of their cars and beaten, and when newsmen were severely roughed up, none were beaten to death or killed as might easily have happened since the police were unable to offer protection at the time. Furthermore, the sniper fire directed at police and firemen did not result in any fatalities either, despite reports that it was widespread and lasted throughout the riot week and the fact that police and firemen were easy targets. It seems that sniping was aimed toward obstructing law enforcement and fire fighting and not towards killing officials.

The riot crowds gave evidence of being able to pick specific targets for their aggression. Black business establishments, many of them carrying signs such as "Blood Brother" or "Soul Brother" were for the most part spared. Private houses, post offices, churches, schools, libraries, and other public buildings in the riot area were not broken into and burned down, vandalized, or otherwise purposely damaged. Some white-owned stores also were spared. While the McCone Commission states that "Our study of the patterns of burning and looting does not indicate any significant correlation between alleged consumer exploitation and the destruction [of stores]"[47] insufficient evidence is cited to back up this conclusion that would require a careful and controlled study of all stores and their practices in the riot area. Some informed observers have disagreed with the Commission's conclusions on this point. Moreover, the Los Angeles Police, the main target of preriot hostility, was also the main target of riot aggression. Only ten National Guardsmen out of a maximum of 13,900 were reported injured, as compared to 90 Los Angeles policemen out of a combined total of 1653 police at the time of maximum deployment.[48] The evidence, meager as it is, supports the view that there was a systematic relationship between the specific targets of aggression and the sources of the rioters' grievances.

The destructive and violent behavior of the rioters was confined to specific kinds of events within the riot situation. Eyewitnesses reported that rioters and looters in cars were observing traffic laws in the riot area—stopping for red lights, stopping for pedestrians at crosswalks— even when carrying away stolen goods. Firemen were obstructed in putting out fires set to business establishments, yet one incident is reported where "people beseeched firemen to save a house which had caught fire when embers skipped to it from a torched commercial building,"[49] and during which firemen were not hindered in any way from carrying out their job. These and similar incidents testify to the ability of riot participants to choose appropriate means for their ends. While riot behavior cannot be called "rational" in the everyday common meaning of that term, it did contain normative and rational elements and was much more situationally determined than the popular view would have it.

Looting is furthermore quite common in disaster situations other than riots and need not be interpreted as expressions of specifically racial hostility. Its attraction to people lacking the consumer goods others take for granted needs no complex explanation beyond the simple desire to obtain them when the opportunity to do so involves a low risk of apprehension by the police. Such action if facilitated by low commitment to the norms of private property expressed in the propensity of "the poor to seek a degree of elementary social justice at the expense of the rich,"[50] the fact that others were doing the same thing, and the fact that the stores sacked in this case belonged to "whitey." These observations can be illustrated by an eyewitness account of one such incident:

> One booty-laden youth said defiantly: "That don't look like stealing to me. That's just picking up what you need and going." Gesturing at a fashionable hilltop area where many well-to-do Negroes live, he said: "Them living up in View Park don't need it. But we down here, we do need it."[51]

Looting was a predominantly neighborhood activity, often uncoordinated, and carried out by small groups. Between 50 and 65 percent of the minors were arrested less than a mile from their home, and a little over 63 percent were arrested in the company of others, mainly for "burglary," that is they were apprehended in or near stores broken into.[52] The casual process through which individuals would get involved in looting, and the group and neighborhood aspects of it, are illustrated in the following statement of an arrested minor to a probation officer:

> [Minor] states that he was at home when his brother came home and said there was a riot going on in the streets. Minor states that he went out on the streets to watch and met a friend who said that people were going into a store on Broadway and "taking stuff out." Minor states that he and the companion went to observe and after arriving there and seeing everyone taking stuff from the store, he decided that he would take something also. . . . The only reason Minor offers for his behavior is that "everybody else was taking stuff, so I decided to take some too."[53]

While the actions of some looters were described in some accounts as that of a savage mob bent on plunder and fighting each other for the spoils, other descriptions and material, such as a photograph showing two women and one man rolling a fully loaded shopping cart past firemen, suggest a much more relaxed and calm mood.

Looting as well as other riot activity were essentially group activities during which participants and onlookers experienced a sense of solidarity, pride, and exhilaration. They were bound together by shared emotions, symbols, and experiences that a black man inevitably acquires in white America and that makes him address another one as "Brother."[54] They were also bound together by the common enemy, "whitey," and struck out against "whitey's" representatives in the flesh—the police, the firemen, the merchants, the news reporters, the motorists—and they felt good about striking out. Bystanders were swept along in the tide of we-feeling. One such black who was attracted out of curiosity into the riot area on Thursday night and immediately afterwards recorded his impressions and feelings into a tape recorder, described what he experienced in the following words:

> A brick came out of nowhere and smashed through the window of a hot dog stand across the street. Someone yelled: "That's whitey's, tear it down." A number of people from both sides of the street converged on the stand and began breaking all the windows. Several men climbed into this stand and began passing out Cokes and other beverages to the people outside. . . . As they passed a small gas station, several people wanted to set it afire. One of the people standing nearby the station told them: "Let it

stand. Blood owns it." A liquor store and a grocery store were the next targets. . . .
Next to the liquor store was a meat market. These windows were also smashed and
people in cars drove up and began loading meat into the trucks of their cars. Two
young boys . . . came running out of the store . . . carrying a side of beef. The crowd
roared its approval and greeted the boys with laughter and cheers. Several men came
walking towards me laden down with liquor. One of them paused in front of me and
asked: "What do you drink, Brother?" He and the other stopped right here on the street
to have a drink. My reply was: "Whiskey." They opened a bottle of whiskey and
handed it to me. I drank a large swallow and handed it back. Twice around and the
bottle was empty. We laughed and they continued down the street. . . . A cry went up
the street: "One-Oh-Three. Hit the Third!" It referred to 103rd Street, the business
center of Watts (a mile to the east and the north). The people piled into cars and headed
for 103rd Street. Others followed on foot. As I was getting back into my car to drive
to "One-Oh-Three," several men jumped into my car and said: "Let's make it,
baby."[55]

The narrator adds at the end of his impressions: "I did not feel like an
outsider at any time during the night. While my involvement was passive
and some of the sights I witnessed appalling and saddening, I felt a strong
bond with these people."

The rioters did not form an amorphous mass, a collection of individuals acting out private frustrations and hostility. Rioting was a group
activity in the course of which strangers were bound together by common
sentiments, activities, and goals, and supported each other in the manner
typical of primary groups. The riot was a collective celebration like a
carnival, during which about forty liquor stores were broken into and
much liquor consumed. It was also a collective contest similar to that
between two high school or college athletic teams, with the supporters
cheering and egging on the contestants. One could settle old scores with
the police, show them who really controlled the territory, humiliate them,
and teach them a lesson. Just as a rioting youth was quoted by two black
newsmen as saying, "This is what the police wanted—always messin'
with niggers. We'll show them. I'm ready to die if I have to,"[56] Police
Chief Parker mistakenly boasted, "We are on top and they are on the
bottom."[57] Both sides in this tragic and deadly contest had a high
emotional stake in the outcome. While the riot was put down eventually,
many blacks saw it as a victory for their side and derived a sense of pride
and accomplishment from this public demonstration of their collective
power.

In assaulting the police and breaking into business establishments,
some rioters were not only responding to the long-standing frustrations
and humiliations suffered at the hands of the police and the exploitative

practices of merchants, but were reacting along racial lines that can only be understood in the wider social context of the black in America. Rioters were pelting motorists and the firemen with rocks while shouting: "This is for Bogalusa! This is for Selma!" The riot situation became defined in global, dichotomous, we-they terms, where we and they stood for the two races and the long history of conflict associated with them. In such a situation, when one status (racial membership) becomes predominant and one's other statuses and role obligations irrelevant, mediation becomes impossible because one cannot remain sitting on a fence. When black Assemblyman Marvin Dymally tried to calm some rioters a boy asked him: "Who you with?" Dymally answered: "I'm with you, man," to which the boy retorted: "Then here's a rock, baby, throw it!"[58] Those who bridge the dichotomy by siding with the opponent are perceived as traitors, and will be singled out for special abuse as was the case with a black National Guardsman who was called a "white nigger" by the crowd.[59]

Conclusion

These considerations about the actions and motivations of the rioters enable one to come closer to a characterization of the Watts riot. Was it a police riot, a race riot, an insurrection, a revolt, a rebellion, a nationalist uprising, or a revolution? A lot depends upon how these terms are defined, and they are often used loosely and interchangeably. There is no point in engaging a definitional exercise with which many will take issue. It can however be pointed out that in all of the above manifestations of collective behavior, common grievances, sentiments, emotions, and we-feeling bind the actors together, common targets become the object of aggression, and violent physical means are used by the participants. These cannot therefore be used to distinguish a riot from a revolt or a rebellion. One must examine what collective goals and demands are voiced by the actors. If their actions are directed at overthrowing the constituted authorities, if political demands are voiced such as the resignation of certain leaders and officials, if an attempt is made to achieve physical control in an area of territory by forcing out the existing authorities and substituting for them other authorities, then one is dealing with a revolt, rebellion, insurrection, or uprising. If, on the other hand, the main purpose of the action is to inflict damage and/or injury upon certain groups or a category of persons, such as police, merchants, or whites in general, then one is dealing with a riot.[60] The Los Angeles events therefore constituted a riot rather than anything else.

The riot was remarkable for the lack of any leadership and organized effort to express collective demands of the rioters and the black population in South Los Angeles. However many persons in that area may have wished to see the resignation of Police Chief Parker, or the establishment of a civilian police review board, no banners proclaiming these demands were raised.[61] No attempts were made to address the crowds to spell out collective aims. No spokesmen emerged from the ranks of the rioters to make a statement to the authorities or the press.[62] No effort was made to hold an area after the police were forced out of it and to coordinate action designed to prevent its comeback. No barricades were thrown up. Single individuals sniped at police and firemen from different locations and on numerous occasions, but there was no attempt to create a more organized form of armed resistance. While the precipitating incident touched off a police riot, which soon thereafter widened into a riot during which the targets of aggression became other whites besides police, subsequent days and nights produced a repetition of the same sort of behavior over an ever-wider area and involving greater numbers of participants, but did not produce a change towards a more insurrectionary or revolutionary pattern of action.

It is the magnitude of the Los Angeles riot, both in duration, participation, amount of damage and casualties, and the forces needed to control it, which led many to characterize it as more than just a riot. But aside from magnitude, the Los Angeles riot was structurally and behaviorally similar to the black riots in other cities during the summers of 1964, 1965 and 1966. The collective significance of these events, however, is that the civil rights gains made by the black movement in the last few years, which have benefited the southern blacks and middle-class blacks, have not altered the situation of the lower-class urban blacks outside of the South and have not removed the fundamental sources of grievances of a large proportion of the black population in the United States.

Notes

I wish to thank Mr. Borden Olive for helpful comments and assistance in locating some of the data on which this account is based.

1. While the riot engulfed a far wider area of South Los Angeles than the Watts District, it has come to be known as the Los Angeles or the Watts riot, and I use both these terms interchangeably. The question of whether the events that took place are best characterized as a "riot" or something else will be dealt with below.

2. Governor's Commission on the Los Angeles Riots, *Violence in the City—An End or a Beginning*, 2 December 1965, popularly known as the McCone Report after the Commission Chairman's name.

3. For the relevant statistics, see the *McCone Report*, pp. 1, 23-25; for a natural history of events, see Jerry Cohen and William S. Murphy, *Burn, Baby, Burn*, New York: Dutton, 1966; and McCone Report, 10-23.

4. Neil J. Smelser, *Theory of Collective Behavior*, New York: Free Press, 1962, chap. 8.

5. Time, 20 August 1965, 16: "After looting pawn shops, hardware and war supply stores for weapons, the Negroes brandished thousands of rifles, shotguns, pistols, and machetes." See also the *Los Angeles Times*, 17-18 August 1965.

6. Los Angeles Times, 15 August 1965.

7. Ibid., 20 September 1965.

8. Ibid., 16 September 1965.

9. While the immediate reaction about what the riot was all about is to my mind distorted, the news media, statements by many officials, especially Negroes, as well as the later McCone Report, did reveal at least a moderate amount of sophistication and acceptance of ideas current in social science when it came to a description of the broader social and economic conditions that made the riot possible and even likely.

10. McCone Report, 22-23.

11. On how both the conspiracy and criminal riffraff explanations have been traditionally invoked by contemporaries to explain riots and rebellions in the eighteenth and nineteenth centuries, see Georges Rude, *The Crowd in History*, New York: Wiley, 1964, especially chap. 14.

12. McCone Report, 1, 4-6, 24.

13. Robert Blauner, "Whitewash over Watts," *Transaction*, 3 (March/April 1966). Blauner himself concluded from published statements of black leaders and the reports of his informants that the McCone Commission had underestimated the widespread support for and participation in the riot, and explicitly rejects the view that the riot was primarily a rising of the lawless.

14. McCone Report, 1: "perhaps as many as 10,000 Negroes took to the streets in marauding bands."

15. Los Angeles County Probation Department, *Riot Participation Study*, Research Report No. 26 (November 1965), hereafter referred to as *RPS*.

16. Bureau of Criminal Records, Department of Justice, State of California, *Watts Riot Arrests* (June 1966), Sacramento, California, hereafter referred to as *WRA*.

17. RPS, 21.

18. WRA, tables 2 and 25.

19. WRA, table 6.

20. WRA, 37.

21. Figures above taken from or recalculated from *WRA*, *RPS*, McCone Report, and "Special Census Survey of the South and East Los Angeles Areas: November 1965." *Current Population Report*, Technical Studies, Series P-23, 17 (23 March 1967).

22. Figures cited above were taken from or recalculated from *WRA*, *RPS*, and "Special Census Survey . . . " op. cit., and the McCone Report.

23. See "Special Census Survey . . . " op. cit., which contains up-to-date figures and allows a comparison to be made between the separate districts making up the South Los Angeles area. Other pertinent information is contained in the McCone Report.
24. McCone Report, 40.
25. U.S. Commission on Civil Rights, California Advisory Committee, *Police Minority Group Relations in Los Angeles and the San Francisco Bay Area* (August 1963), 1, hereafter referred to as the *Pike Report*.
26. Pike Report, 9.
27. Ibid., 8.
28. Mayor Yorty's campaign flyer (*Mayor Yorty Reports*) distributed in March 1966, at the start of the 1966 democratic gubernatorial primary contest linked the Communist Party and other left-wing organizations with the antipolice campaign. *The Los Angeles Times*, 18 August 1965, 3, quotes Yorty as saying that "for some time now there has existed a worldwide campaign to stigmatize all police as brutal. . . . The cry of 'police brutality' has been shouted in cities all over the world by the Communists, dupes, and demagogues irrespective of the facts. Such a campaign has been pushed here in Los Angeles."
29. Pike Report, 8.
30. Pike Report, 14–15.
31. On these points, see Ray Murphy and Howard Elinson (eds.), *Problems and Prospects of the Negro Movement*, 1966: 232. Belmont, Cal.: Wadsworth Company; Robert Blauner, "Whitewash over Watts." *Transaction*, 3 (March/April 1966), 8; and Jerry Cohen and William S. Murphy, *Burn, Baby, Burn*, 1966: New York: Dutton, 210.
32. Blauner, "Whitewash on Watts," 6.
33. Pike Report, 12.
34. McCone Report, p. 32.
35. In 1962 the Los Angeles Police Department had apparently about 150 Negro police officers out of a total force of 4700. The reason given by police officials for the law proportion of Negroes on the force was their inability to meet eligibility standards and the scarcity of applicants (Pike Report, 34).
36. The most plausible reconstruction of the incident is presented in great detail in chaps. 2 and 4 of Jerry Cohen and William S. Murphy's *Burn, Baby, Burn*.
37. McCone Report, 11.
38. Ibid., 12.
39. Evidence for these psychological processes can be found in Bernard Berelson and Gary Steiner, *Human Behavior*, 1964: New York: Harcourt, Brace and World, 101, 115.
40. The fact that August 11 was one of the hottest days in the entire summer has been regarded by some as the precipitating factor. Actually it was important insofar as more people than usual do hang around on the streets near their homes in the slums on hot nights, so that an incident immediately attracts a larger number of spectators than usual and new of events travels faster and uninterruptedly by word of mouth. To the extent that people tend to be more irritable and "on edge" at the end of a day with high levels of heat, smog, and humidity, these factors in themselves were also contributory causes after the precipitating incident had occurred.
41. On these processes, see Neil Smelser, Theory, 258–60.
42. Cohen and Murphy, *Burn* 74.
43. Cohen and Murphy, *Burn* 121, 126.
44. McCone Report, 17–19.

45. Cohen and Murphy, *Burn*, 69-70.
46. Cohen and Murphy, *Burn*, 88.
47. McCone Report, 62.
48. Ibid., 20.
49. Cohen and Murphy, *Burn*, 157.
50. See Rude, *Crowd*, 244, and passim for historical instances of this.
51. Time, 20 August 1965, 17.
52. RPS, 16, 18. Comparable data on adults arrested are not available.
53. RPS, 19.
54. A black student recalls driving his run-down automobile during the riot outside of the curfew area, and stopping at a red light next to a late model car driven by a middle-aged, prosperous-looking black. The other driver, a total stranger and probably mistaking the student for one of the active rioters, smiled broadly and told him before driving off: "Where are you going to strike next, Brother?"
55. Quoted in Cohen and Murphy, *Burn*, 111-12.
56. Time, 20 August 1965, 17.
57. Time, 27 August 1965, 11.
58. Cohen and Murphy, *Burn*, 119.
59. Ibid., 195.
60. "A riot is an outbreak of temporary but violent mass disorder. It may be directed at a particular individual as well as against public authorities. But it involves no intention to overthrow the government itself. In this respect riot stops short of insurrection or rebellion, although it may often be only a preliminary to the latter" is the definition of Smellie in the *Encyclopedia of the Social Sciences*.
61. Although some handbills from an unidentified source denouncing Parker were passed out during the riot.
62. Black leaders and influentials did of course speak out during the riot on television and through other means. They expressed black demands such as Assemblyman Dymally's call for Parker's removal. But the leaders were reiterating views that they had long held and publicly voiced. They were not asked by the rioters to be spokesmen for riot goals or terms of negotiation with the authorities.

10

The Decline of the 1960s
Social Movements

Introduction

The decline of the 1960s movements in the United States—the civil rights, black power, antiwar, and student movements sometimes collectively referred to as The Movement—in the late 1960s and early 1970s has not been satisfactorily explained. In 1967 and 1968, many commentators thought the United States in the throes of a revolution. Five years later few people remained apprehensive. Yet the decline of The Movement was one of the most important and dramatic developments of the post-World War II cultural and political scene. Surely why and how it happened ought to tell us something important about American society, politics, and culture.

A second goal of this chapter is scholarly and theoretical. Much of the social science literature on social movements has dealt with particular movements, and with theories brought to bear on the causes and the rise of movements. Rather less attention has been given to the simultaneous unfolding of several linked social movements and to their decline. I believe that a particular set of theoretic ideas that my colleagues and I pioneered, and that we have referred to as the resource mobilization approach, can be successfully applied to complex movements and movement decline. Moreover, important new theoretic insights, hypotheses, and a sharper focus for existing theory can be gained by confronting such a theory with recent history.[1]

Because the movements are recent history, there are problems about sources and information. There is an overabundance of data, much of it still unexploited, undigested, and unassessed for validity and accuracy, yet some important pieces in the puzzle are still missing. Nonetheless, I believe that my attempt at understanding and explanation, however tentative, is timely, and will motivate others to dig, sift, and analyze further than I have been able to do. My purpose, as well, is not to describe and criticize others' interpretations of the 1960s movements, but to present my views in a concise and reasoned manner.

I will analyze the organizational structure, resource base, leadership and membership, ideology, tactics, and important activities of the major and vanguard social movement organizations such as the Student Non-violent Coordinating Committee (SNCC), the Black Panther Party (BPP), Students for a Democratic Society (SDS) and its Weatherman offshoot, and the New Mobilization Committee to End the War in Vietnam (Mobe). I will also analyze the organization tactics, and effectiveness of the social control agencies that were opposed to the movements (FBI, CIA, Justice Department). I will assess the part that the mass media, in particular television, played in the movements' rise and decline, as well as the complex links between the movements and the counterculture or youth culture of the middle and late sixties and early seventies. All these materials will be brought to bear on four central questions addressed in this chapter:

1. To what extent were internal weaknesses responsible for movements' decline?

2. To what extent was repression responsible for the movements' decline?

3. To what extent was success responsible for the movements' decline?

4. To what extent were some important changes in the U.S. due to the 1960s movement?

The Major Organizations in the 1960s Movements

The Student Non-violent Coordinating Committee

Starting in 1961, SNCC[2] promoted voter registration drives, literacy campaigns, freedom schools, and community organization in the rural black belt of the Deep South. Its organizers lived and worked in the community itself. Its ranks were periodically swelled by northern student civil rights workers during the summer months. SNCC's original goal was the overthrow of the caste system in the Deep South. In 1963, SNCC's budget was a quarter of a million dollars. Its staff consisted of 150 full-time paid workers. In 1965 it was reported to have over 200 paid field secretaries and 250 fulltime volunteers in rural communities (mostly blacks), and an $800,000 budget provided by churches, foundations, friends of SNCC groups, and direct mail appeals.

SNCC had a loose organization structure from the start. According to Foster and Long (1970, 216),

> SNCC was not at its beginning, and never has been a membership organization. Members are simply those people who share its sympathies and objectives, who by their own individual work and actions define its activities, and who attend its meetings . . . there is no structure of local chapters; and until 1967, participation in SNCC's annual summer conference was entirely self-selective.

SNCC field workers tended to be college graduates or college dropouts from a working-class, southern black background. SNCC's drive ran into the realities of southern resistance and violence when its staffers and supporters were harassed, shot, beaten, and jailed. These experiences proved to be radicalizing. The turning point was the failure of the Mississippi Freedom Democratic Party delegates to get seated in full at the 1964 Democratic Party Convention that nominated President Johnson in Atlantic City. After working within the system only to be checked by its "liberal" allies, SNCC abandoned integration and turned to black nationalism and black power under the leadership of Stokely Carmichael.

Two developments led to SNCC's abandonment of its southern drive. After a year and a half of dangerous grassroots organization in Lowndes County, Alabama, the slate of the SNCC-sponsored Lowndes County Freedom Organization was defeated in 1965 at the polls in a county that was 81 percent black. At the same time, the United States had entered its third year of northern black ghetto riots. SNCC leadership concluded that the urban lower-class blacks were more ready for black power and community organization than the rural Deep South and shifted its energies to the North.

Despite some successes, SNCC's black ghetto organizing efforts failed (Jacobs and Landau 1966). By the end of 1968, SNCC scarcely existed anymore. SNCC had pioneered the black power ideology, the Black Panther symbol, the clenched fist salute, the blue jeans and jackets that became the uniform of the New Left and the counterculture, as well as the language and "style" of subsequent youth-oriented social movement organizations (SMOs).

SNCC was also the first major movement organization to experience the tensions and divisions besetting the SMOs. There were the internal tensions between the white liberals and radicals and black SNCC members that eventually were resolved when SNCC opted to become all black. There was the generation gap and conflict with the adult civil rights organizations such as NAACP and SCLC who advocated less militant tactics and a more moderate integrationist ideology that appealed to a broad spectrum of the American citizenry, the liberal establishment, and potential financial backers. As SNCC become more radical, the search for new means of funding and support centered on media publicity, speaker's fees, books and publications, and left wing and Third World sources.

The Black Panther Party[3]

As SNCC declined, the Black Panther Party for Self Defense (as it was originally called) emerged as the vanguard of the black power movement. The party was founded October 1966, in Oakland by Huey Newton and Bobby Seale. The key to their early appeal was the demand for an end to the police brutality and the murder of black people, and a call for "armed self-defense" based on the constitutional right to bear arms. The Panthers instituted a police alert patrol in Oakland in November 1966.

The forty-member BPP was at first only one of two dozen black nationalist groups in the Bay area. Recruits were drilled in technical skills and the law regarding gun ownership and gun handling. They wore black berets, boots, and shirts, and had a quasimilitary organization. Inspired by Franz Fanon, Panther leaders proclaimed that blacks in the United

States were an oppressed people in need of liberation, and that the police were an occupation army practicing genocide on black people. They advocated black community control, an improvement of the status of blacks, and quoted Mao Tse-tung's slogan that "power also grows out of the barrel of a gun."

Growing friction with Oakland police led to the October 28 shootout in which one officer was killed, and Newton was wounded and charged with murder. The BPP then set a high priority on the defense of Newton. It made an alliance in late 1967 with the white People and Freedom Party (PFP). PFP allowed its nationwide organization to be used for the Newton defense campaign. Eldridge Cleaver eventually became the party's 1968 presidential candidate.

Throughout 1968 the police and the Panthers engaged in a series of increasingly violent confrontations resulting in casualties on both sides. Law enforcement agencies were engaged in a successful campaign of harassing, arresting, and prosecuting BPP members on weapons, drug traffic, and other charges, while the Panthers pressed forward with a hate campaign against police in the pages of their weekly, the *Black Panther*, and in their public pronouncements. By late 1968 the campaign to check the BPP was taking its toll.

The BPP had more formal organization than SNCC, SDS, and many of the other SMOs of this period. It was led by a central committee consisting of national officers, which chartered local and regional Panther organizations over which the Oakland headquarters achieved but limited control.[4] Membership peaked in late 1968 with about 1500 to 2000 members and twenty-five chapters.

Panther headquarters often served as living quarters for officers and trusted members, making police surveillance easy. Members were meant to follow a code of conduct on narcotics, alcohol, guns, and petty crime, and faced expulsion for hard drug use and crimes committed against black people. Members tended to be ghetto youth and young adults, including some women, and were meant to contribute labor in Panther community programs and street sales of the *Black Panther*, which reached a peak circulation of about 100,000 weekly copies. Activists received no more than subsistence wages. Income for Panther activities came from sales of their paper and of Mao's *Red Book*, from sympathetic donors, from Legal Defense Committees, and the campus speakers' circuit.

In late 1968, the Panthers closed several chapters and purged about half of their membership. Internal tension was high because Panther leadership defense absorbed most of their funds leaving no bail and defense money for the rank and file. They dropped their military uniform and started a number of community programs of which the free breakfast for welfare recipients' school children was the most successful one. They joined the United Front Against Fascism and established Third World contacts at the U.N. and abroad through Eldridge Cleaver, who had become a fugitive in Algeria. Nevertheless, confrontations with police, arrests, prosecutions, and jailings of Panthers continued in 1969 and 1970.

Panther alliances and relations with black nationalist and white radical groups tended to be strained and short-lived. Eventually dissension split the Panthers themselves into the Newton-Hilliard and the Cleaver factions in early 1971.

Mobe

Mobe,[5] as the successive Mobilization Committees to End the War in Vietnam were called, was in the late sixties the major organizer of antiwar demonstrations, marches and protests, as well as of the 1968 Chicago protests against the Democratic Party's National Convention. Mobe was not a membership organization, but a coalition of leaders, personages, and organizations covering a wide ideological spectrum united in their opposition to the American war in Indochina. It ranged from pacifist Quakers, church people, and mothers, through Vietnam Veterans Against the War, the Fifth Avenue Peace Parade Committee, draft resisters and SDS, all the way to small radical groups hoping for a victory of the National Liberation Front and of North Vietnam.

Mobe's role in the antiwar movement was largely one of coordinating the antiwar activities of numerous groups for a concerted thrust. It applied for permits and publicized the time and place of demonstrations, raised funds through newspaper advertising and mailings, held press conferences, pressured members of the political elite who were increasingly disenchanted with American war policies, and staged mass rallies and demonstrations that would have a national and international impact. Mobe did it most successfully between the October 1967 antidraft week that brought 100,000 protesters to Washington and culminated in the siege of the Pentagon and 700 arrests, and the ten days of the People's Lobby in Washington, D.C. in the spring of 1971 during which 13,000 were arrested.

Mobe, and indeed the antiwar movement in general, engaged primarily in a reactive strategy. It matched the government's escalation of the war, attempts at suppressing opposition, and disclosures about war policy and conduct with spurts of protest activity (Skolnick 1969, 31). The bulk of organized peace movement activity was nonviolent and based on the constitutional right to free speech.

The antiwar movement had a low level of formal structure and limited collective decision-making capabilities. According to Skolnick (1969, 30–31),

> From within, the movement seems disorganized to the point of chaos, with literally hundreds of ad hoc groups springing up in response to specific issues, with endless formation and disbanding of coalitions . . . the peace movement does have some broad continuities and tendencies well understood by the most prominent leaders, but . . . its loosely participating, unstructured aspect can scarcely be overestimated.

The antiwar movement and Mobe became factionalized, as was true also of the other major social movement organizations here described.

SDS

SDS[6] was the largest pacesetting social movement organization of the middle and late sixties. During its brief and stormy career, alone or in coalition with other radical and reform groups, it pioneered or latched on to the central issues and activities of The Movement: support for the southern sit-ins, community organization among the poor, campus movement against the draft and against university complicity in the military-industrial-war complex, student power and university reform, opposition to the Vietnam War, and other causes. Between 1960 and 1971 its changing activist core ran the gamut from reform to resistance and to revolution. Starting as a small and dedicated band of no more than a few hundred members in 1960 and 1961, it experienced an accelerated takeoff in the spring of 1966 when the Johnson administration decided to draft college students. Its estimated membership peaked in 1968 and 1969 at about 100,000. SDS had a much larger student following that never bothered to enroll formally.

Although SDS had a formal organization structure with a national council and office, regional organization and local chapters (mostly on campuses), after its period of explosive growth was underway, in the words of one of its leaders,

> SDS cannot be understood in terms of traditional political organization. Neither ideological clarity . . . nor organization stability are fundamentally important to SDSers. What counts is that which creates *movement*. What counts is that SDS be where the action is.(Sale 1973, 316)

The most successful SDS actions were improvised and reactive, in the sense of quick reactions to government war escalation policies, university rigidity, and a new turn of events.

Before the break with its adult sponsor organization, the League for Industrial Democracy (LID), over the issue of exclusion of communists, the fledgling SDS got small financial contributions from LID as well as trade unions and foundations which barely kept it and its programs alive. During its rapid growth and antiwar phase, "fat cat" liberal donors, small contributions, membership dues, and the sale of its literature were its primary sources of financing. Nevertheless, SDS always teetered on the brink of insolvency despite the fact that it had very low overhead costs. Most of its revenue was spent in programs, publications, and propaganda. Members' dues after initial entry were only sporadically paid, and the administrative breakdown at the national office meant that at its height SDS had incomplete and out-of-date membership and chapter lists. Ironically and unintentionally, this proved to be an insurance policy against effective FBI infiltration and surveillance.

Nevertheless, the lack of central direction and organization also had negative consequences for SDS. The practice of yearly turnover of the national leadership meant that able leadership was lost and inexperienced leaders put in charge of running the organization. The basic political ideas of SDS failed to be transmitted to the larger, more recent cohorts. The participatory style of collective decision making meant that important decisions were delayed too long or never taken. In the words of an SDS leader, the consequences were that

> once (SDS) stopped passing programs . . . (it) lost the ability to set any course for the student movement, and then the course was set by the New York Times and the TV station, so that whatever was most dramatic was then emulated, whether it was good or not. (Sale 1973, 528)

SDS's open membership and participatory style made it vulnerable to infiltration and takeover by a disciplined, uncompromising bloc such as the Progressive Labor Party (PL), which culminated in the Weatherman-PL split at the June 1969 national convention. The organization was not able to check the behavior of the "crazies," freaks, hell raisers, and infiltrators who had flocked into its ranks and who were responsible for some of the most objectionable confrontation tactics that resulted in adverse publicity and scared away adult donors.

Factionalism created ideological rigidity. It diverted energy away from antiwar and other activity into organizational infighting and manipulation of the rank and file by competing leadership groups, which was resented. By 1969 the leadership group had progressed through a radicalization process from resistance to revolution which the rank and file and mass of student supporters was simply not ready for. The activist ideological cadre had lost faith in relying on a student base for pursuing campus reform, student power, and stopping the war. By the spring of 1969, however, the student movement in the United States had developed a momentum of its own without a New Left organizational core.

Weathermen

Weathermen[7] was one of the factions that lost out in the fight for control within SDS at its June 1969 national convention. Weatherpeople lived in collectives whence they made sorties (known as "jailbreaks") into school classrooms where they forcefully detained teachers and harangued bewildered students on the evils of American capitalism. For this they occasionally got arrested.

Weatherpeople organized the spectacular "Four Days of Rage" in early October 1969, in Chicago. Expecting thousands of "street kids" who failed to materialize, Weatherman nevertheless went ahead with its several hundred college youth and staged two short-lived rampages in the Gold Coast and Loop. The police smashed them easily. Given the prospect of lengthy court appearances and jail sentences, and with no hope of building a working-class following, Weatherman went underground.

Weatherpeople split up in small bands of "firing" squads. Among their most publicized accomplishments were LSD guru Timothy Leary's escape from a California prison to Algeria, and the bombings of the central headquarters of New York police and of the home of the judge in the Panther Twenty-One trial.

Weatherpeople targets were symbolic and aimed at property. Warnings were given so that no loss of human life would result. Three Weatherpeople did get killed in New York on 6 March 1970, when they accidentally blew up the Greenwich Village town house in which they were manufacturing bombs. In 1971, calling terror an elitist, counterrevolutionary activity, they halted their bombing campaign.

Movement Structure and Mobilization

Though they were its most important pacesetting elements, the SMOs were but the most organized and visible manifestations of the participatory explosion, popular unrest, protest activity, and civil disorders of the 1960s. The movements themselves were embedded in a complex cultural revolution (usually referred to as the counterculture and the black revolution) that they at once shaped and were shaped by, whose most political and politicized embodiment they became, but that to some extent ran its own autonomous course, propelled by its own inner logic. The social movements of the 1960s also ran parallel with, and interacted in complex ways with, institutionalized politics, presidential and congressional politics, electoral and pressure group politics. By no means did all incumbent and challenger elites see the social movements only as opponents.

Social movement growth and decline can be understood from a resource mobilization perspective. At the core of the 1960s American social movements was a relatively small number of full-time *activists* (sometimes referred to as cadres or political entrepreneurs), including fifty or so leaders that the mass media and political elite singled out for special attention, more so for ability to innovate in symbol production and manipulation than for organization skills. Their actions and pronouncements became especially newsworthy and were interpreted as reflecting the grievances and aspirations of a large constituency whose voice they became but with which they had but tenuous organizational ties.

Many collective actions, from marches and demonstrations to campus building occupations and ghetto riots, were composed of *transitory teams* in which activists were but a small minority (McCarthy and Zald 1973). Transitory teams were strategically placed for contributing their own time and labor, at their own expense, in brief, but repeated spurts of activity. They swelled the numbers of petitioners, marchers, demonstrators, and rioters into the hundreds of thousands during major events.

The frequent resort to mass rallies, petitions, marches and other forms of visible aggregation—what I have called identification moves (Oberschall 1973, 308-10)—are an important part in the overall strategy of social movements. Movement leaders often are not able to demonstrate their strength by means of the electoral process geared to party politics and the quadrennial cycle of presidential elections. They need proof that their views and demands have widespread support and thus merit recognition by the target group (usually the authorities). They have to instill confidence, hope of success, and a sense of safety resulting from large numbers among their followers and sympathizers. And in the absence of strong organization, collective events are shapers of a collective identity and are a means of political and ideological education and of pulse taking.

Lastly, the 1960s movement had many sympathizers who, although not contributing their labor and their bodies, sent financial contributions to movement organizations, provided broad public opinion support, and often also important skills for legal defense and organization. In addition to scattered individuals, sympathizers included organized entities such as civic associations, churches and foundations, and leaders who had the means to commit association funds and programs in support of movement activity. These social units and association leaders have been referred to as the *conscience constituency* (McCarthy and Zald 1973). It should be noted that movement participants—activists, transitory teams, and the conscience constituency—were not necessarily members of groups who were the principal intended beneficiaries of movement goals. This was also true in the civil rights movement where white liberal backing played a key role in overcoming southern resistance and federal government inertia. In a broader sense, participants do anticipate some personal benefits, which might include relief from guilt, moral outrage, career advancement, and making the United States a "better" country, in terms of their preferences.

The three components of the 1960s movement played specialized roles in overall movement organization. Activists supplied ideologies, symbols, organization, and leadership; transitory teams supplied much of the "labor"; and the conscience constituency provided financial support. But some mechanism had to exist or had to be created to maintain these often very diverse sets of people in a collaborative working relationship for supplying their contributions jointly to some collective goal. The most common means of doing so relies on organizations and a shared political culture.

A social movement can be thought of as a social interaction field with zones of varying organizational density. Organization provides a mechanism for resource commitment to some central group or agency that then allocates these resources to the pursuit of collective goals and organization maintenance. For instance, the NAACP can be thought of as a densely organized interaction field. It had a relatively stable membership, a clear-cut organization structure with a professional staff, mechanisms for dues raising and fund raising, a central decision-making apparatus for the commitment of resources and for communicating to members. Moreover, shared ideology, goals, and commitment to tactics pervaded the organization. Few resources had to be expended upon building or maintaining a shared political culture because it already existed. Thus of the total resources in labor and money committed by NAACP members and sympathizers to the black movement, a high proportion actually passed through the central decision-making group for reallocation to NAACP programs and activities.

This was much less the case for the 1960s movement organizations that became pacesetters. Created hastily and expanding rapidly, SMOs controlled but a small part of their total social interaction field. Only a small fraction of the total resources expended upon movement activity by transitory teams and the wider circles of sympathizers actually passed directly through a central leadership group with a resource allocation capacity. The communications network between the leadership and rank and file was rudimentary, and relied heavily on the mass media over which SMOs had little direct control.

A relatively high proportion of resources committed to movement activity was voluntary labor. Many contribute to movements not because of narrow, anticipated gains for themselves, but because of deeply felt moral concerns and ideals. When constituent groups of a movement share a common social class and ethnic background and have gone through the same historic experiences and battles, they are also likely to share a common political culture and traditions of collective action that leaders can activate by means of symbolic appeals. When the common background and historic experiences are lacking, the mobilization of voluntary labor on behalf of a movement is more problematic.

It is precisely such a shared culture and collective action repertoire that the 1960s movements lacked and failed to develop fully in the course of movement activity. This was especially true of the latter 1960s and early 1970s. In the United States a shared political culture of popular opposition to the authorities and powerful groups has been weaker than in other countries where socialist parties or strong nationalist and ethnic separatist sentiment based on deep-seated cleavages and historic traditions exist, and where such a popular culture is quite immune to confusion and manipulation. Opposition movements can then, at practically no cost in political education and without central initiative and subsequent direction, count on a predictable, substantial popular response along the lines of past scenarios of collective action.[8]

In the United States only the southern civil rights movement with its symbolism of Christian brotherhood came close to this model. In the black power movement, common culture and shared interests became more problematic. Even greater ideological diversity and contradictions marked the movement against the Indochina War. Church people saw it primarily as a moral issue; leading opposition political figures opposed it on constitutional grounds and on the basis of the decline in the American leadership role in the noncommunist world; many citizens opposed it because it was a wasteful use of the country's resources; many students opposed it because they would be drafted to fight it; and some New Left leaders hoped to forge a broad-based, permanent socialist movement that would undermine capitalism and imperialism by means of it.

Although middle-class and upper-middle-class youth participation in the counterculture (characterized by rejection of adult authority, of consumerism, of the rat race, and by adherence to nonconformity and peer-group solidarity) did make them susceptible to protest action and to political radicalization, other central elements of the youth culture (experimentation with mysticism and drugs in a quest for personal fulfillment, rejection of discipline, and long-term commitments in favor of "doing your own thing," a stress on sensual gratification, and the rejection of rationality) were inimical for the creation of a lasting political culture.

The 1960s movements never achieved an overarching ideological, organizational, or tactical unity. Dave Dellinger (1975, 8) remarked that when Dr. Martin Luther King, Jr. was moving toward a close alliance of the civil rights movement with the antiwar movement shortly before his assassination, "For a brief time it seemed that everything might come together in one powerful movement: the struggle for civil rights, the struggle against the war, and the struggle for economic justice."

But this was not to be. The movement actually never became one, but instead remained a loose congeries of parts broadly in agreement on their condemnation of social evils and in their opposition to the "system." Groups coalesced for particular goals but frequently competed for the same limited resource base and jockeyed to achieve a dominant position for their ideological and tactical agenda.

Issues, goals, and strategies did not remain frozen in the period under consideration. The black issue went through a succession of redefinitions: desegregation, full citizenship rights, integration, black power, black community control, black separatism, and compensatory reparations. Some of the earlier concerns survived as movement goals and strategies even as vanguard groups had already moved to new goals and strategies. And the same was true for movement tactics and more spontaneous collective action, encompassing as they did for the black movement civil disobedience, electoral politics, pressure group tactics, rioting, peaceful demonstrations, coercive threats and confrontations, bombing and assassination plots, and so on. The contradictory ideals, ideologies, symbols, rhetoric, tactics, and interest appeals reaching the American citizenry from the 1960s movements had a confusing rather than unifying effect.

It is by no means certain, of course, that a more united, overarching movement would have had greater success than the 1960s movement did. Competing groups provided drive and innovation that were emulated when they worked and prevented the conservative tendencies of large scale organizations from gaining the upper hand. By presenting a diversified and specialized ideological and tactical package to potential supporters, a much wider segment of the overall population could be effectively reached. Nevertheless, on balance, it must be concluded that internal weaknesses due to deficiencies in organization structure and to a lack of shared political culture were important factors in movement decline.

One may well ask how the 1960s movements ever got off the ground and gained momentum in the face of opposition, weaknesses, and handicaps: they had rudimentary organizations and low organizational capabilities, they relied for financial survival on the outermost circle of supporters, and they frequently worked at cross purposes with each other. Their major means of mass communication with supporters and the public was controlled by outsiders. They became factionalized, they were unable to recruit in a population with a shared political culture and action repertoire, and when they were at last in a position to dominate the political agenda, they ended up doing so in an ideologically confusing manner.

Movements seek to prevail against an opposition. The actions and reactions of both parties to the conflict must be examined for an understanding of movement growth and decline. In the case of the 1960s movement, it was important that in the crucial period between 1964 and 1968, the executive branch of the federal government became the common target of all three major movements—of the blacks, of war opponents, of the students. In a book on the black movement, Killian (1975, 81) entitled an entire chapter "The Federal Government: The New Enemy." In it he writes that

> the more the federal government, by piling up civil rights laws and executive pronouncements, committed itself to a policy of intervention on local power struggles, the more it made itself a target of the new strategy of power.

The enemy of the antiwar and student movements was even more explicitly the federal government. A common target gave these loosely coordinated movements a central thrust otherwise lacking.

It is furthermore important that in this period the executive branch and many large cities were in the hands of the Democrats, the party which a short time earlier had counted many of those in opposition among its usual supporters, and which had contributed strong backing to the southern civil rights movement out of which the black power movement had grown. Many Democratic leaders were still counting upon the votes and support of the very same groups that the more radical movement leaders were turning with some success against the Democratic administration. A Democratic president and administration was not in a position to move forcefully against mounting opposition of its erstwhile backers, certainly not as forcefully as a Republican president and administration might (and would).

By the time the Nixon administration took office in early 1969, the movements had gained a strong momentum. The opposition's reactive response style got firmly established and became a collective protest action repertoire triggered through the mass media primarily. The novel role of the media in the 1960s bears more detailed analysis, for it is the media that compensated to a larger extent for the organizational weaknesses of the SMOs.

Substitutes for Structure: The Mass Media

The content of the news media was not purposely biased against the administration, as Vice President Agnew repeatedly charged. Content analysis of television news coverage of the student movement and of race issues between September 1968 and April 1970, found no systematic "denigration of political authority."[9]

Both the government and its opponents managed to manipulate the news media quite successfully on occasion. Since they had no other means of influencing their potential constituency and frequently also of communicating with their supporters, it is not surprising that movement leaders were trying to manipulate the media and gear movement strategy to the media. They sought attention through newsworthy innovative tactics and ideological pronouncements and through confrontations designed to draw a repressive response in the full glare of publicity. In this connection, Jerry Rubin (1970, 107, 137) wrote that

> The media is not neutral. The presence of a camera transforms a demonstration. We take more chances when the press is there because we know whatever happens will be known to the entire world. Television keeps us escalating our tactics: a tactic becomes ineffective when it stops generating gossip. . . . Our goal was to create crises which would grab everybody's attention.

And Dave Dellinger certainly recognized the significance of the "whole world is watching" phenomenon at the 1968 Chicago Democratic National Convention (1975, 99ff.) and at the subsequent Chicago conspiracy trial. Beyond intentional movement building through media visibility, a massive collective action capability by opposition groups was helped by a media created "star system," by media-disseminated focal symbols and stimuli, and by a media-provided instant communications system which stimulated bandwagon effects and a pacesetter-follower dynamic. These effects were neither intended nor anticipated. They followed from media organizational constraints and imperatives. And they provided, for a time, an effective substitute for movement organization structure. The 1960s movements caught the government, the citizenry, the media, opinion shapers, and the academic establishment intellectually and organizationally unprepared. This was particularly constraining on the news media. Under pressure for providing instant coverage, analysis, and commentary in the context of the highly competitive communications industry, news reporters, columnists, and anchormen turned to police chiefs, district attorneys, politicians, and law enforcement and administration officials on the one hand, and the movement leaders and political entrepreneurs on the other.

Both these groups used the media to make essentially self-serving statements and interpretations. Law enforcement officials stressed conspiracy, small numbers, and movement violence. Opposition activists stressed grievances, large size, police brutality, and their own importance and role as legitimate spokesmen of the oppressed and of the protesters. These interpretations were to some extent consistent, for both stressed more planning and central leadership than were in fact the case.

On balance, the media response accrued to the advantage of opposition activists. Law enforcement leaders spoke legitimately for their organizations, and accurately revealed the frame of mind of those in authority who would make the important social control decisions. Leaders and activists, however, in the loosely structured movements of the 1960s, had more tenuous links to movement participants and beneficiaries. By investing them with more influence and importance than they actually had, and providing them a costless communications facility, the media contributed in making leaders out of some who otherwise might not have been, and created more structure in the movements than they typically possessed. Ultimately, the media created "media stars," and the star system helped build the movements.

It is important to realize that the authorities themselves became victims of the media image and reinforced it. For by singling out the media stars for harassment and prosecution, they ended up adding to their stature and provided a rallying point for the opposition. Or else, by making concessions to the media stars, they made them successful in the eyes of their following, and thus helped to make them into genuine movement leaders.

Media coverage of a loosely structured movement is expensive in time and staff. The action is in a number of places, breaks out with little advance warning, speaks through many voices and presents a confusing picture on the scene. For the sake of cost cutting, convenience, simplicity, and rapidly, a few leaders and a few major "trouble spots" received the lion's share of coverage and their true role in the movements was magnified out of proportion.[10]

Emphasis on stars and focal point coverage had effects not unlike those of self-fulfilling prophecies. Because media exposure was a rapid and cheap way of mobilizing a following and of drawing a response from target groups, leaders, activists, and political entrepreneurs of all stripes and colors flocked to the focal points and trouble spots. Aside from some events staged entirely for the benefit of the media, the competitive struggle for coverage put a premium on novelty, inflated rhetoric, and defiant posturing.

It was not only movement activists who engaged in issue definition and ideology production. The administration, other target groups, and members of the political and intellectual elites joined in the fray. Because the lineup of support and opposition on the issues depended on the rhetoric and symbols that were dominating the political agenda and the mass media, the United States in the 1960s became a veritable battleground for achieving dominance of the "symbolic turf" (McCarthy 1974).

All this resulted in a distorted picture and account of overall movement activity, especially so in the decline phase after 1970 when the leadership struggle for a disintegrating following became intense. The rapid leftward ideological drift, and the tactical drift condoning coercion and violence by competing vanguard groups, outpaced the political comprehension and level of radicalization attained by transitory teams and the conscience constituency.[11]

For a time, however, movement building through the media rather than through grassroots organizing worked effectively. Leaders used the media to communicate with transitory teams needed for backing up their pronouncements with action. Television especially provided a learning opportunity on how to organize and stage events, how to phrase "nonnegotiable" demands addressed to the authorities, and what roles to assume in confrontations with various target groups. Much information to movement participants and sympathizers about the movement (leader's ideologies, symbols, programs of action, etc.) and about the targets (the Pentagon, the CIA, university administrations, etc.) was disseminated free of cost to social movement organizations.

Yet neglect of grassroots organization and of an internally controlled communications system for information transfers and political education left the 1960s movements in a vulnerable position when media attention shifted to other issues (women's liberation, environment-ecology-energy, Watergate, etc.) when stars for various reasons became deactivated (Dr. Martin Luther King, Jr. was assassinated, Mark Rudd went underground, Rap Brown was incarcerated, etc.), and when focal points of media coverage became depoliticized (Berkeley's Free Speech Movement gave way to the Filthy Speech Movement). The "generals" were left without a means of communicating with their "soldiers," and the directionless "soldiers" drifted off.

The movement building impact of media coverage and activist's strategic adaptation to it had two important aspects. Surge and decline of participation in movements is determined by changing costs and benefits that are heavily a function of size. The larger the size of the protesters and the stronger the image of the movement, the greater the anticipated benefits because the probability of success is higher. The larger the size, the lower are the anticipated costs from repression (safety in numbers) and the costs of movement activity (economies of scale).[12] Decreasing costs and increasing benefits result in a bandwagon effect that increases size and thus decreases costs and increases benefits yet further. Had movement leaders sought to attach these new recruits firmly to social movement organizations, the maintenance costs of larger organization would have increased. Since their strategy consisted in incorporating the new cohorts loosely as transitory teams and conscience constituencies by means of the mass media, maintenance costs did not increase with size. The bandwagon worked effectively as long as size increased. By the same dynamics, a reverse bandwagon effect was precipitated once size decreased, and could not be dampened through a largely nonexistent organizational structure.

The second media-induced effect was the emergence of a nationwide collective action repertoire that needed little central planning and direction because it was based on "contagion." The contemporary meaning of contagion is void of the connotations of epidemics, herd instinct, imitation, irrationality, and other mechanisms postulated by early collective behavior theorists. Behavioral contagion simply refers to

> a social interaction in which a "recipient's" behavior changes to become more like that of another person, and where this change has occurred in a social interaction in which the 'initiator' has not communicated intent to influence the behavior of the recipient. (DeNardo 1972, 5)

Initiators and recipients might be leaders, organized groups, ad hoc groups or simply crowds. Contagion may apply with equal force to social movements and to their targets, for instance, police.

A decade of research on civil disorders and riots has shown that an atomic analysis of collective events that centers on the characteristics of participants and the characteristics of cities and other social units in which they take place does not have much explanatory power. In a thoughtful paper on racial disturbances, Spilerman (1970, 645–46) concludes that television played a leading role in bringing the activities of the federal government into black homes and in stimulating the development of racial consciousness.[13]

A paper by DeNardo (1972) on campus unrest based on extensive data and probability models provides further clues about how unrest diffused rapidly from trouble spots that became focal points for media coverage, that is, "pace-setters" for an ever larger pool of campuses. Contagion effects decreased reaction time between pace-setter initiative and follower response, and increased magnitude of response on "follower" campuses in the 1968–1970 period.

The precipitous decline of the collective action response might also be explained along these lines. The deactivation of "pacesetter" campuses and shifts in media emphasis would weaken the nationwide communications network needed for diffusion of protest.

Historic precedents of the diffusion of collective protest action and of the contagion process abound (Oberschall 1973, 138–40). What was novel in the 1960s in the United States was its rapidity and geographical scope, a consequence of the rapidity and nationwide reach of the mass media. Though movement leaders like Dellinger (1975, 60) knew about the importance of concentrating protest at focal points with maximum media coverage, and were somewhat aware of the activation of pacesetter-follower contagion, they were unable to make use of this strategy once media attention was shifting away from the Vietnam War. The collective action repertoire that had become established was much more reactive and diverse (lower-class blacks rioted, middle-class whites marched) than in other historic contexts when it was based on a shared political culture or fostered by a strong, central organization. The 1960s media-induced collective action repertoire in the United States proved fragile and short-lived.

Social Control

As a result of the Watergate affair and the reassertion of the Congress' role in making the executive branch accountable, volumes of information on the government's social control activities in the 1960s and 1970s have been released from numerous government sources and supplement the enormous material already published in newspapers and magazines. A preliminary examination of these documents provides as little cheer to civil libertarians as it does to taxpayers concerned with efficient spending of their tax dollars.

At first sight the magnitude and comprehensive nature of the social control effort is mind-boggling.[14] The amounts of money spent, the size of the staffs involved, the number of agencies activated, the number of different programs and operations mounted, the number of investigations conducted, the number of files kept, the pieces of mail opened and telegrams examined, the paid informers, the agents provocateurs, the illegal break-ins, the scrutiny of federal income tax returns, the dirty tricks and harassment, the red squads of local police departments, the illegal wiretaps, the deliberate encouragement of violence by passing explosives to opposition groups, media manipulation, the centrally computerized information systems and technologically sophisticated surveillance techniques, the systematic evasion of the occasional and unsystematic attempts to limit and control these activities, and much else as well, must surely warm the hearts of citizens fearful of revolution. If one looks at output rather than input, a different picture emerges altogether. The summary of the Church committee report on domestic intelligence activities states among other things that

> Between 1960 and 1974, the FBI conducted over 500,000 separate investigations of persons and groups under the "subversive" category, predicated on the possibility that they might be likely to overthrow the Government of the United States. Yet not a single individual or group has been prosecuted since 1957 under the laws which prohibit planning or advocating action to overthrow the Government and which are

the main alleged statutory basis for such FBI investigations/ (*New York Times*, April 29, 1976)

Turning to specific cases, one learns that while the FBI conducted an all-out campaign to discredit Dr. Martin Luther King, Jr., he received the Nobel Prize, had an audience with the Pope, and remained by far the most respected black leader in the United States, according to all public opinion polls (U.S. Senate 1976, 219–23). One also learns that in 1970 the FBI ordered investigations of every member of the Students for a Democratic Society (U.S. Senate 1976, 8), and yet according to Sale (1973, 6353) not a single arrest has ever been made in connection with the most publicized Weatherman bombings. One further learns that during the time the CIA financed the National Student Association, far from being a conservative or reactionary student group, the NSA was actively engaged in the antiwar and student movements (Foster and Long 1970, 27, 206, 465).

Elected on a law and order platform, the Nixon administration vastly expanded surveillance and crackdowns on all manner of protest over that of the Johnson administration. The FBI assigned more than 2000 full-time agents to the New Left investigations, and twenty federal agencies were stepping up surveillance, infiltration, disruption, and harassment of New Left and antiwar opposition. Congressional committees got into the act with hearings, followed shortly by state legislatures. University authorities were increasingly ready to call in police and other social control agencies to check campus disorders.

Nevertheless, the Civil Disorder Digest (September 1969) reported that "disorders of both racial and political nature occurred at hundreds of high schools and universities (in 1968–1969)." The Lemberg Center for the Study of Violence recorded over 260 racial disorders in American schools during the first five months of 1969. Shootouts, plots, and bombings, were on the increase. Attacks on police increased dramatically, and so did threats against public officials. Political and racial bombings rose from an average of 1.6 per day in 1969 to 3.1 per day in the first six months of 1970. Eight hundred and twelve explosions occurred between July 1970, and March 1971. By another count, bombings attributed to white radicals rose from ten on-campus bombing incidents in the spring of 1968 to an estimated 174 major bombings and attempts on campus and seventy-one off campus, with ROTC buildings, selective service offices, banks, and corporate offices as the prime targets.

Instead of giving further examples of the social control agencies' ineffectiveness, it is more instructive to analyze the reasons for it. The FBI had developed a trained incapacity in coming to grips with the 1960s social movements whose structures and strategies it never came to understand. The FBI had developed bureaucratic machinery and routines for dealing effectively with equally bureaucratically run and predictable organizations, such as the Communist Party (CP). The FBI managed to monitor the CP, the Socialist Workers Party (SWP) and its youth affiliate (YSA), the NAACP, and similarly organized entities. The SWP and YSA in particular were the objects of government spying, break-ins, wire taps, and other surveillance measures on a vast scale. All of this busywork turned out to be of little value since the SWP and the YSA were but a small factor in the confrontations between the government and the 1960s movement. Much of the information-gathering effort ended up netting routine and trivial material on the lawful activities of citizens, such as on the Social Welfare Program of the United Church of Christ (U.S. Senate 1976, 76).

The dirty tricks and provocations and informers probably had some weakening effect on the 1960s movement, but hardly as much as factionalism and organizational weaknesses. As with intelligence operations, dirty tricks were probably more effective in disrupting routinized enterprises such as the 1972 Muskie campaign than student and antiwar activities. More important was the exaggerated picture which the authorities formed of the power and threat of the 1960s movements. Having created a vast enterprise for infiltration and surveillance of what they feared was a highly organized and coordinated opposition about to seize power by revolutionary means, the authorities not surprisingly had their fears confirmed by much that was fed to them. When the information did not fit the image, they pressured the social control agencies to expand their activities yet further, and leave no stone unturned (U.S. Senate 1976, 19).

Ineffectiveness of the concealed and illegal activities of the social control agencies also resulted from the rivalries and competition between the FBI, CIA, Army Intelligence and various sections within them (U.S. Senate 1976, 111-13), the inability to cope organizationally with the rapid expansion and proliferation of intelligence activities, and the scarcity of suitably trained personnel. With only forty black FBI agents of a total of about 6300 (U.S. Senate 1976, 84), it is no small wonder that the FBI could not track down the Symbionese Liberation Army in the black slums of San Francisco. The presence of a vast network of paid informants in black ghettos proved to be of little use in this case (U.S. Senate 1976, 75).

The prosecutions of movement leaders by the Justice Department might have had more of a weakening impact on the 1960s social movements. The government's strategy appeared to be to tie down leaders in costly and time consuming legal battles that would impede their activities and put a tremendous drain on financial resources regardless of whether the government would be successful in court. Dave Dellinger (1975, 278) and other movement leaders were aware of this strategy but could develop no effective counterstrategy, for going underground and escaping abroad would automatically remove them from their principal means of mobilization by way of the media.

The two legal instruments of Justice Department prosecution of movement activists were the Federal Anti-Riot Act of 1968, and indictments on conspiracy to commit a crime (e.g., counseling violation of draft laws and selective service regulations, or some other offense). Under the act it was not easy to secure convictions since the prosecution had to prove both criminal intent and advocacy of violence in a context which propels action. Conspiracy charges are difficult to prove. The record of Justice Department prosecution of radicals bears this out.[15]

The New York Panther Twenty-One trial resulted in a jury acquittal of all defendants on all counts (*New York Times*, 14 May 1971). Bobby Seale's trial in New Haven ended in a hung jury and was followed by the judge's dismissal of the case (*New York Times*, 26 May 1971). The case against Daniel Ellsberg and Anthony Russo ended in a mistrial and the dismissal of the case in May 1973. In the Chicago Eight trial, defendants were either acquitted or their convictions were reversed in a higher court. Only thirteen of the original 175 contempt citations were later sustained, and none ended in imprisonment. In the Boston Five trial, convictions in the original trial were either reversed, or else the prosecution was dropped by the government. In the Harrisburg Seven trial, the government was forced to drop the original conspiracy charges, but did secure convictions against Father Philip Berrigan and Sister Elizabeth McAlister for smuggling contraband out of prison. During the period these trials were taking place, the antiwar movement was in full swing. It is unlikely that prosecutions of radical leaders did much by way of intimidating antiwar protesters.

The relative lack of success of the government in its prosecution of top opposition leaders resulted from juries' and higher courts' reluctance to support the government's policy of suppressing the opposition.[16] And it must be emphasized that the extensive surveillance, infiltration, and illegal activities of the FBI and other social control agencies provided no help in Justice Department prosecutions and occasionally backfired as in the Harrisburg Seven and Ellsberg trials. Repression of dissent is not possible in the United States without executive control of the judiciary branch and greater complicity by the legislative branch, at all levels of government. Repression takes far greater intimidation of the citizenry, of voluntary associations concerned with the protection of civil liberties and humanitarian values, and of the counter elites themselves, than the Johnson and Nixon administrations ever achieved.

The record indicates that far from knuckling under, many of these groups even managed to increase their efforts on behalf of individuals and groups targeted by the authorities. Membership dues and contributions of the American Civil Liberties Union steadily increased in the critical period of the first Nixon administration from 1.9 million dollars in 1968 to 2 million in 1969, 2.5 million in 1970, 2.8 million in 1971, and stood at 3.6 million dollars in 1973. The number of contributing member and joint member units increased by 22,000 between 1966 and 1969, and so did the average dollar contribution. Much of the ACLU's activities were directed to the legal defense of draft resisters and other dissenters.[17]

Just as the 1960s movement engaged in rhetorical overkill, so did the opponents of dissent in the Congress and in the White House. Here again the gap between words and actions proved to be wide. Did the federal government and the Congress in fact use federal higher education appropriations for stifling campus dissent?

The record does not indicate it.[18] Total federal funds for education and related activities as a percent of the GNP increased from 0.8 percent in 1960 to 1.1 percent in 1965 and leveled off between 1.3 percent and 1.4 percent in the years 1970 to 1973. Grants and loans to higher education, representing about one-third of total federal education funds throughout this period, stood at 0.4 percent of GNP in 1965 and edged up to 0.49 percent, 0.47 percent, and 0.48 percent in 1971 to 1973.

One can also approach the issue of government crackdown by looking at the income of higher education institutions and checking whether the federal and other governments contributed a decreased share of it. This was not the case. The share of current fund income of higher education institutions derived from federal, state, and local government sources showed a steady increase from 47.3 percent in 1963–1964, to 48.9 percent in 1968–1969 and to 51.3 percent in 1972–1973.

Punishment can of course be direct rather than financial. According to Sale (1973, 324, 500–1, 550–51), the Justice Department prosecuted 663 draft cases in 1966, 1335 in the first six months of 1967, and 1500 in 1968. Police and national guardsmen were called in on at least 127 campuses in 1968–1969 and about 4000 campus arrests were made. In the first six months of 1969, approximately 1000 students were expelled from colleges and universities. Though these are high figures, it should be borne in mind that in 1968 there were 4.8 million undergraduates enrolled in four year institutions, of whom 3.8 million were full-time students, and an additional 800,000 were graduate students. If we take the conservative estimate of ten percent of the student population involved in campus and off-campus activism, the number of prosecutions, arrests, and expulsions amounts to about one percent of the activist students.

Other studies confirm the low risk of drawing a penalty in campus disorders. According to an NSA survey of 221 major campus demonstrations in 1969, less than two percent of the participants appear to have been punished through university disciplinary action (Foster and Long 1970, 434). It should also be remembered that many professors at this time were giving inflated grades for student performance. That kept many from flunking out and hence from being eligible for the draft. Courses of dubious educational value were also instituted at many institutions, and class rankings were abolished. Thus it became easier for students to engage in protest activity by devoting less time to their studies without fear of lowering their grade point average. The point worth stressing here is that repression works effectively only if all social control agencies, target groups, disciplinary bodies, and authorities support and reinforce each other's actions. This was certainly not the case in the United States in the late 1960s and early 1970s.

It might be argued nevertheless that the less visible prosecutions of antiwar activists and black militants in local and state courts, and of student activists at less prominent colleges, was more effective, operated on a vast scale, and ended up intimidating movement activists and rank and file. Only further research can clarify this issue. I suspect, however, that the overall impact of government prosecution, harassment, surveillance, and dirty tricks was less important than generally thought. It was after all not dirty tricks and illegal campaign activity that reelected President Nixon in 1972, but the disarray of the Democratic party, the shooting of Governor Wallace which removed him from the presidential contest, and the mistakes of the McGovern campaign.

Success and Decline

Repression of the 1960s movements was only marginally effective in precipitating movement decline. Internal weaknesses were quite important. In this section, the relationship between success of the 1960s movement and their decline will be examined. It is my contention that this relationship was quite strong and that their successes are considerable and lasting.

The survival of social movements and of social movement organizations is evidence of neither success nor failure.[19] Movements might cease to exist because their goals have been successfully accomplished, or on the contrary because they have failed and their adherents became discouraged or intimidated. Social movements may also become institutionalized as pressure groups, political parties, and public agencies with a stable constituency and a routinized resource base.

Few human enterprises are completely successful or unsuccessful, and the same holds true for social movements. It makes more sense to discuss degrees of success and failure. In the case of the 1960s movement that mobilized a heterogeneous set of adherents participating for a variety of reasons, success and failure will be defined by different individuals and groups quite differently. Nevertheless, it is possible to set some criteria for success and failure that avoid the speculations of counterfactual history and the superficiality of reducing important questions to an exercise in public opinion polling.

Success can be measured by the extent to which the publicly proclaimed goals of social movements have been realized. Success and failure also have other aspects. When individuals and groups whose concerns have been ignored force public decision makers to recognize their needs and to commit institutional resources to implementing them, social movements can be said to be successful.[20] Concretely, this means that the costs of pursuing the goals sought by the movement are shifted from movement adherents to the polity at large. This does not mean that movement goals will be promptly and effectively realized. It means that the interests and preferences of ignored groups has become a routinized input into the political process and will be dealt with by those in authority positions in the same manner as the concerns of other recognized groups and constituencies.[21] Lastly, assessment of success and failure also depends on whether the social movements generate a novel realignment of political forces (coalitions, backlashes) making it easier or more difficult to implement concerns and goals similar to those advocated by the movements.

The principal goals of the antiwar movement was termination of American involvement in the Indochina War. The principal goals of the civil rights and black power movements were full citizenship rights and equality for blacks. The student movement subscribed to these goals as well, and beyond them sought the termination of the draft, more democratic governance for universities and colleges, and greater responsiveness to student needs. All three movements were partially successful in achieving their stated goals, in mobilizing powerful allies, in obtaining institutional recognition, and in avoiding a backlash that would in the longer run undermine their gains. Having said this, it is still true that the combined power of the three movements and the counterculture did not result in a major redistribution of power in the United States as was hoped by some activists.

The antiwar movement was a partial success. The Indochina War did end. American involvement in the war did not end as rapidly and as completely as the movement sought, but it did progressively scale down, from over a half million ground combat troops at the end of 1968 to virtually zero by the time the Ford administration was put into office. And although the bombing campaign in Indochina expanded under the Nixon administration, the pressures for signing a peace agreement and for ending the bombing were so powerful that by the 1972 election campaign the Nixon-Kissinger policy on Indochina had shifted from winning to face-saving exit.

Both the troop reduction and the exit policy resulted from forces generated by the antiwar movement. It succeeded in mobilizing public opinion and Congressional (especially Senate) opposition to the war. The Congress then forced the administration into reverse gear through the institutional political process.[22]

It is difficult to assign causal priority to one or another set of factors for the crucial reversals of American Vietnam policy. Without the antiwar movement, the realization that the United States was boxing itself into a no-win strategy, with costs in lives, material resources, and domestic unrest far exceeding any possible benefits from victory, would not have penetrated so deeply into the Congress and powerful establishment groups.[23] These the President of the United States could not in the end ignore.[24] As the burden of maintaining pressure for war de-escalation and extrication from Vietnam shifted from antiwar movement to the Congress and other groups, the movement itself demobilized.

Together with Watergate and the forces it mobilized, the antiwar movement succeeded for the first time since World War II in checking the "imperial presidency" and the national security bureaucracy in the area of the president's war-making powers, executive privilege, secrecy, and lack of the accountability in foreign affairs. That was no mean feat.[25] No backlash, domestic or international, has materialized as a result of the Indochina fiasco.

The success of the civil rights and black power movements in the area of full citizenship rights and of black political power have been impressive and well documented. In the domain of economic advance, the results so far have been more problematic (Brimmer 1974). Nevertheless, as a result of the black movements of the 1950s and 1960s, race relations and race policies in the United States have dramatically shifted from an essentially "South African" pattern to one that shows promise of absorbing blacks into the mainstream of American life.

The civil rights and black power movement have become successfully institutionalized as the politics of black ethnicity.[26] Much of the burden for enforcing equality of opportunity and for promoting equality in fact have been shifted from the movements to the courts, to executive departments of the federal and state governments, and to routine politics. No backlash of substantial proportions has resulted from black gains.

As for the student movement, it had some success in giving students greater rights and more voice in university governance, at least in many institutions of higher education.[27] The draft was terminated. More importantly, the three movements under review have enabled other minorities and exploited groups—from Indians and Chicanos to women and homosexuals—to obtain a hearing for their concerns and provide a legitimate input into public decisions on matters of interest to them. The movements have fostered an intense examination and critical look at American society which produced new concerns for the environment, quality of life and rights of all minorities. Dave Dellinger wrote (1975, 16) that "gradually other issues won new adherents from the several million people who were energized and activated by the anti-war struggle." The very existence of these new concerns and movements has siphoned off some of the activists and financial contributors of the original social movements, thereby contributing to their decline. Yet in a broader sense the decline from these losses can be seen as more victory than failure, for it helped those forces that favor changes in the United States consonant with the kinds of changes championed by the 1960s social movements.

Conclusion

The 1960s movements declined then for a number of reasons. Increased radicalism scared off the conscience constituency. The Democratic administration's erratic reformism that fueled the civil rights and black power movements gave way to the Nixon administration's consistent opposition to all dissent. Although repression was only mildly effective, it terminated the direct sponsorship by the government of opposition to itself. A weakening national economy forced transitory teams to worry about jobs and careers, to shift from attacking authority to coming to terms with it. The size of the movements could not be sustained after factionalism, partial success, and progressive disillusionment curtailed the steady recruitment stream needed to replenish the high turnover membership base. Internal weaknesses stemming from the absence of a grassroots organization structure and from reliance on the media for recruitment, communication, and political education destroyed the mobilizing capabilities of the pacesetter leaders and movement organizations when media attention shifted away from movement concerns and coverage. Activists drifted away into new movements, into nonpolitical countercultural pursuits, into jobs, and into institutional politics and reform.

Exit from movement activism into attractive alternative careers was possible for even the top movement leaders and media stars. Because the United States lacks an organized left and the 1960s movements failed to create one, the activists and leaders scattered into a wide spectrum of institutions and positions from which a concerted radical thrust is not possible. Yet the 1960s movements turned out surprisingly successful, in large part because institutional elites and organizations pressured and challenged by them took up the burden of implementing some of their goals just as the movements were disintegrating.

Why did the 1960s movements generate so much overt and rancorous conflict? The answer must in part hinge on the character of the issues at contention and the institutional mechanisms for conflict regulation. The 1960s conflicts were over highly charged moral principles, over trust in authority and its legitimacy, over loyalty and dissent, over citizenship rights and a voice for the negatively privileged, and in a broader sense over a collective redefinition of what America as a country and people is all about.

Elsewhere I have analyzed the reasons why these conflicts arouse greater enmity, more hostility, are fought harder, and are more difficult to resolve and to compromise than conflicts over material resources (Oberschall 1973, 50–64). This analysis applies with equal force to the 1960s conflicts. The genius of American politics has been the institutionalization and regulation of material conflicts. The solution has always been to create a bigger pie and to dish up bigger slices to everyone, with no one the loser. Many of the 1960s conflicts were not amenable to American-style conflict resolution.

This was especially true of the Vietnam War. The more the government's policy resulted in the loss of American lives and the expenditure of resources, the more difficult it became for it to admit its errors and to change its policies. But just as Lyndon Johnson, his advisors, and the Congress could not afford to admit that these sacrifices were wasteful mistakes and still remain a credible leadership team, so also the antiwar leaders could not settle for compromise without destroying their credibility before their supporters and destroying the very basis of their influence. In any case, the antiwar leaders could not guarantee the quiescence of their constituents by compromising with the authorities since they had no organizational capability and institutional authority for enforcing it among the rank and file. The incentive for compromise was thus lacking on both sides. It wasn't until powerful groups in the Senate, in the media, in business, and even within the administration realized the necessity for cutting losses and avoiding lasting damage to the United States that administration intransigence was slowly overpowered. But these groups did not move decisively until the Nixon administration sought to "do them in," as it had tried to do in the 1960s social movements.

Were we close to revolution? Not really. There were, of course, some signs of it in addition to mounting social unrest. Elites became divided, the economy was experiencing difficulty, law and order was breaking down, a war was being lost, radical ideologies were gaining adherents, class differences and race antagonisms were deep. None of these conditions were, however, as accentuated as in the great revolutions of the past. And besides, one needs a revolutionary movement for making a revolution. Only a small proportion of dissidents sought it. Their confrontations antagonized the very police and hard hats they would need on their side for success. They were ideologically confused. They pursued the chimera of a worker-student alliance, and when that did not materialize, they proclaimed the students as the exploited class from which revolution was to be expected, hoping to change reality by word magic. Instead of analyzing the American social system on its own terms, they adopted "Marxist" formulas tailor-made for underdeveloped countries and a nineteenth-century capitalism that no longer existed. They were unable to overcome the internal contradictions of the society at large even within their own ranks. Many of them knew less about working people and blacks than the average cop on the beat. And their resource base depended on the liberal conscience constituency and other groups and institutions opposed to revolution.

For all its analyses, the left has consistently misunderstood why the American system does in the end allow for reform, up to a point. American society is a mass society only when it comes to consumption and life-styles. It is a class and race-divided society when it comes to social interaction, community, association, life chances, and thought. It is nevertheless remarkably open for talent up to the near top. It ends up coopting dissidents and critics, and provides them with comfortable and rewarding positions, at least if they have the "right" background, as most of them do. Those who are well-bred, articulate, talented, controversial, entertaining, or just plain visible inherit the largest and most affluent mass market and bureaucracies in the history of mankind. Indeed, English-writing dissenting intellectuals, like the multinational corporations, have the whole world as an audience.

For the chosen, circulation is not only from the Pentagon to Lockheed, but from the Nixon White House to *Rolling Stone*. Those who have made it pay few penalties, if any, for bad judgment, costly mistakes, crime, and political nonconformity. If you are the President's Special Assistant for National Security Affairs and give your boss consistently bad advice, you will be promoted to head the Ford Foundation. If you happen to be Secretary of Defense and make costly mistakes, the World Bank is yours. President Nixon was pardoned and is going to make more money denying his crimes in his autobiography than if he had served out his second term without precipitating a constitutional crisis. Watergate superstar John Dean paid the penalty of four months in prison for, as he put it, "trying to steal part of the Constitution." Tom Hayden and Jane Fonda got each other, and Noam Chomsky is still professor at MIT, though Walt Rostow had to settle for a professorship at the University of Texas. Only the assassins' bullets struck down black and white alike, and patrician and redneck as well.

Reform works because those influential groups who engineer it manage to pass its costs down to other social classes and groups, as they have indeed managed to do consistently with the tax burden. The liberal, white upper middle class who in the end swung the balance of forces around to desegregation and integration do not live in integrated neighborhoods and do not send their children to integrated schools. Reform expands the bureaucracies and industries that the most talented individuals from less privileged groups end up using as their mobility escalator. And thus the system is strengthened.

The 1960s movements did not succeed in changing the system, though they did make it more responsive and more open to new faces. Nor will the 1960s movements recur in a novel guise, at least not in my lifetime. The demographic surge and counterculture explosion on which they fed, and the coincidence of the black revolution with the Vietnam War are likely to remain a unique conjunction of events. The last quarter of the century ushers in a period of tinkering with bureaucracy and the economy in a world of greater scarcity which is not likely to rouse deep moral concerns and strong passions. Though America's continuing strengths and achievements will be admired and thought worthy of emulation, its shortcomings and problems will remain a lesson for others to avoid, if they can.

Notes

I wish to thank the Guggenheim Foundation for awarding me a fellowship that made this work possible. I also wish to thank Mayer Zald, Louis Kriesberg, Maren Carden, and Alan Mazur for helpful suggestions and comments, and Severine Brocki for research assistance. The views expressed here are entirely my responsibility.

1. I do not present a full history of the movements, nor is it my intention to do so. A huge literature and documentary films on them are available. At the time I wrote this chapter in 1977, that wasn't yet the case.
2. Date on SNCC is derived from Zinn (1964), Jacobs and Landau (1966), Laue (1965), Foster and Long (1970, chap 6), and news sources.
3. Data on the BPP is derived from Heath (1976), Major (1971), and news sources.
4. An excellent account of a Panther-affiliated black nationalist group is provided in Helmreich (1973). Based on participant observation and other sources, the book describes the Black Crusaders' ideology, organization, members, activities, and confrontation with authorities. The manner in which the Crusaders were infiltrated and smashed by police, their incessant financial and legal problems, and their inability to create effective black ghetto support parallels the story of the BPP on the national scene.
5. Data on Mobe from Skolnick (1969), Dellinger (1975), and news sources.
6. Data on SDS from Sale (1973), Jacobs and Landau (1966), Newfield (1966), Skolnick (1969), Peterson (1968), Foster and Long (1970), and news sources.
7. Data on Weatherman from Sale (1973), Daniels (1974), and news sources.
8. On the concept of a repertoire of collective action, see Tilly (1975). For an application in a revolutionary situation, see Oberschall (1973, 312-20).
9. For documentation of this point and on media coverage of civil rights disorders and the authorities' response, see Pride and Clarke (1973) and Pride and Richards (1974).
10. Dave Dellinger recognized this point explicitly when he described the Montgomery bus boycott and Southern civil rights movement in the following terms (1975, 6): "The media, in their customary manner, built King into a national figure whose vision and leadership were largely responsible for the dramatic turn of events."
11. Groups like the Panthers who tried to make the transition from a militant radical to a moderate stance suffered from an image lag. It was probably the result of a combination of factors: primacy and recency effects in communication, the BPP's own ambivalence toward moderation, and the authorities' anti-Panther propaganda.
12. I cannot here present a more rigorous treatment of the cost-benefit approach to participation which is an important element of the resource management approach. An early effort was made in Oberschall (1973, chap 5). Much more work needs to be done.
13. See also McPhail (1971).
14. Data from news sources and U.S. Senate (1976), primarily.

15. Information on Justice Department prosecutions of movement leaders, trials, and trial outcomes is based on news sources and in particular, on the Federal Anti-Riot Act, see Title 18, U.S. Code (1970, 2101-2), and Annotation, *American Law Report*, (1975, 22, 256ff.); on the Chicago Eight, see the United States vs. Dellinger, 472 F2d 340 cert den 410 US 970, 35 L Ed 2d 706, 93 S Ct 1443 (7th Cir, 1972); on the Boston Five, Nathaniel J. Nathanson, *Northwestern Law Review* (1970, 65, 153ff.), and *Tulane Law Review* (1970, 44, 587ff.); on the Harrison Seven, *New York Times Book Review* (1972, 2318-22).

16. The government also lost its case against publication of the Pentagon Papers leaked to the *New York Times*, the *Boston Globe*, and the *Washington Post*. The Supreme Court upheld the *Times'* publication of documents based on them on June 30, 1971, after the government had tried to block publication in the courts.

17. ACLU information based on various issues of its journal, *Civil Liberties*.

18. Data from the *Digest of Educational Statistics* of the U.S. Office of Education and from the *Statistical Abstract of the United States*, various years.

19. For a discussion of social movement success and on ways of measuring it, see Gamson (1975, chap 3).

20. For an analysis of the recognition issue in conflict, see Oberschall (1973, 342-43).

21. For an elaboration of Tilly's "contention of power" model which incorporates and refines this perspective, see Tilly (1975).

22. Increasing Congressional votes against the war in these years can be readily documented.

23. On the opposition to the war by the corporate elite, see Barnet (1973, 225-26).

24. On the "revolt of the barons," see Halberstram (1969, 794-95).

25. For greater detail and a historical perspective, see Schlesinger (1973).

26. Kilson (1971).

27. Foster and Long (1970), part 4 and part 5.

11

1968 in Comparative Perspective

Nineteen sixty-eight was a remarkable year. In the United States, civil rights leader Dr. Martin Luther King was assassinated in April and blacks in over one-hundred cities responded by rioting in their neighborhoods. Radical students at Columbia University in New York seized several campus buildings on April 23rd and precipitated a dramatic month of confrontations with the university administration and trustees, the faculty, the moderate students, and eventually the New York City police. Some 35 other college campuses followed suit in brief order with building occupations over the same issues. In the election campaign of that same year, Democratic presidential contender Robert Kennedy was shot dead, the Democratic Convention in Chicago was disrupted by massive antiwar demonstrations and battles between the Chicago police and protesters, watched by the whole country on television (Viorst 1979). In France, students fought the police in the Latin Quarter and millions of French workers joined in a nationwide month long strike that almost toppled the DeGaulle government. In Czechoslovakia the reform wing of the Communist Party under Dubcek ousted the hard-liners, only to be crushed by the Soviet military intervention. There were widespread strikes in Poland and Italy, and student protests and rebellions in Japan, Germany, Mexico, Spain and many other places (Lipset and Altbach 1969). In the third year of the Cultural Revolution, the People's Republic of China was verging on civil war as Mao was reasserting his power with the help of the People's Liberation Army. Millions of Red Guard youth were expelled from cities to languish in village exile for the next few years, where they were "reeducated" by the peasants and hard farm labor.

One may well wonder whether these worldwide events were coincidental, or whether there were some common causes, direct links, lines of influence, unintended but real contagion due to global mass communications that in some yet poorly understood fashion synchronized mass protests on a global scale. In the post-World War II era, international relations became organized on a global scale by the Cold War rivalry of the United States and the Soviet Union which enmeshed many countries in competing alliances. A truly global economy had also emerged. Migration, travel, trade, and mass communications had created a swift if not instant diffusion of life-styles, popular culture, especially among youth. Rapid population growth and environmental degradation were recognized as truly global in scope. Could it be that the events of 1968 were a precursor of the coming globalization of social movements, protests, and mass political participation? If that were the case, an understanding of the interdependence and diffusion of collective action in 1968 would tell us a great deal about the causes and the course of collective action everywhere and would be an explanatory key to a new transnational dimension of social conflicts and of social change.

Before one jumps to hasty conclusions about the novelty of 1968, it should be noted that transnational convergence of collective action has occurred from time to time. In 1848, revolutions broke out in many European capitals and cities. Following the Bolshevik revolution of 1917 in Russia, communist revolutions and uprisings took place in several European countries in the next two years. The anticolonial nationalist movements peaked in the year 1960 when many colonies, especially in Africa, achieved independence (Oberschall 1973, 138-40). The causes that synchronized mass movements and revolts in 1848-1849, in 1917-1919, and in the late fifties to 1960 are no mystery. In all these instances, there were direct activist and organizational links between a central node or metropole where the precipitating or key events took place, and the peripheral locations that later experienced similar collective actions. Early and unexpected success at the focal node or nodes emboldened challengers elsewhere to rise up against similar targets, and thus a favorable opportunity climate of opinion helped diffuse opposition movements. As I shall argue below, the events of 1968 do not have an obvious common cause nor a nodal diffusion mechanism. Before I provide an explanation of the more concealed common dimension for so much collective opposition peaking in 1968, I will describe and account for the four major national crises of authority and surges of political participation in that year: the Prague Spring in Czechoslovakia; the Cultural Revolution in China, underway since 1966; the May–June rebellion against the DeGaulle government in France; and in the United States, black nationalism, the antiwar movement, the student movement on campuses and in high schools, all against the backdrop of a youth counterculture intensifying since the mid 1960s. In what sense were these complex events similar? Were there links between them? Were the issues raised by challengers against those in authority similar? Were the ideologies of opponents similar, and the participants and the unconventional tactics they used? Further, was there a similarity in the dialectic of collective actions and reactions employed by the principal contenders for power? Were outcomes similar?

Despite some common threads (the most obvious was the surge of political activism of people not normally participant in politics), the four crises of authority differed fundamentally. The fact that they all took place in 1968 was not due to any direct links between them, which were at best nonexistent or tenuous. Nineteen sixty-eight was quite different from 1848 and from 1918 and 1919 when there were common precipitating events, common issues, ideologies, participants, and targets; and a diffusion process linking events, victories, and defeats, in one country to those in other countries. This said, I will point to some similarities of underlying causes, of the division in society that fueled the confrontations and of the organizational imperatives that structured the course of collective actions.

China

Start with the Great Proletarian Cultural Revolution in China, underway since May 1966 (Liu 1976; White 1989; Liu 1986, 1987; Liang and Shapiro 1984; Chan et al. 1980). Its mass participation phase was coming to an end in the fall of 1968 when millions of adolescents, many of them former Red Guard, were sent to villages to be reeducated through labor for the next several years, together with thousands of party cadres and government officials and their families. The Cultural Revolution (CR) was an old fashioned showdown between two factions in a successful revolution, similar to Stalin purging his rivals in the 1930s. The obvious difference was that Stalin was by then well entrenched in the Soviet Communist party, whereas Mao and his supporters were losing control of the Chinese Communist party and government to his rivals led by Liu Shao Qi and Deng Xiao Ping. Mao was losing power because his forced industrialization drive of the Great Leap Forward and his agricultural communes had both ended in abject failures and the great famine of 1960–1961. In consequence a more moderate economic line—under his rivals—had dismantled the communes (though not collective agriculture) and slowed the pace of industrialization in 1962–1966 and had achieved some success. Mao's personal drive to regain a monopoly of power became at this point enmeshed with his ideological vision and political goal of continued class struggle to prevent a premature restoration of officialdom, technocrats, and intellectuals, a real possibility given the centuries' old tradition of government by officials based on expertise and the imperial examination system (Balazs 1964). Since Mao was losing his grip on the party and government, he and his followers mobilized and manipulated a mass campaign of youth, workers and millions of other ordinary people to dislodge his powerful rivals. Though at times he lost control over the popular movement he unleashed, he never did for long, and kept restoring his power by means of the People's Liberation Army (PLA). Mao was able to do this because of his great personal prestige as a revolutionary leader and founder of the People's Republic, and the cult of personality that for years conditioned ordinary Chinese to trust and obey him blindly.

In order to understand the chaotic events of the CR, it must be stressed that a communist state is dense with organizations that reach into every neighborhood, village, and work organization, and from the center in the capital to remotest localities, with authority running from the top down (Walder 1986). Mao and his supporters never lost control of the four highest and most powerful bodies of this huge organizational pyramid: the Central Committee of the Party, the State Council (highest body of the state), the Central Military Commission (of the PLA), and the specially created Central Cultural Revolution Group that was to orchestrate the cultural revolution itself. The CR itself was a series of campaigns initiated and legitimized by these four top bodies jointly, with their orders, proclamations, and directives transmitted nationwide by the most important news media also controlled by Mao's faction. Their proclamations introduced new campaigns and slogans, designated who was to conduct them and who were the targets, what methods of conflict were to be used, what punishment was appropriate for the defeated, and who would be rehabilitated or restored to their former positions. As important, these four bodies legitimated the seizure of authority by various groups at the lower organizational levels of the province, municipality, and work unit, which gave the Mao-backed factions important resources to conduct campaigns: means of communication, from wall posters to the mass media, means of transportation, often weapons, free food and wages for activists. As well, the top-level directives deprived their opponents of these important means of waging conflict.

In the 1966–1968 period the Maoist leadership of the CR reversed itself several times, backing its former grassroots opponents and targeting its former supporters, only to reverse themselves at a later time, occasionally switching sides several times. This created a great deal of confusion. All factions initially were mobilized by Mao in his name to eradicate the "four olds"—old ideas, culture, customs, and habits—and to humiliate the "five bads"—landlords, rich peasants, counter-revolutionaries, bad elements, and rightists. The loyal Red Guards and other activists were obviously puzzled when Mao turned on them. Chaos resulted when a faction didn't believe that Mao had really deserted them and was backing their opponents. Thus confrontations continued until the army was called on, and at times the struggle continued beyond. Mao in his supporters acted in such a seemingly bizarre manner because they were anything but anarchists. Though they needed a popular movement to oust Mao's top rivals and to dislodge Liu and Deng supporters all the way down the chain of organization hierarchies, they also wanted to restore authority and the organizational structures after they had been weakened by the CR. Many of the lower- and middle-level cadres with political and organizational experience, loyal communists all and needed to rule China, had been early victims of the CR only because they happened to be in the organizational pyramid headed by one of Mao's principal rivals. Once the top had been purged, these cadres had to be restored to power, against the opposition of their earlier Maoist tormentors. Restoration would then make these cadres Mao's grateful and loyal followers once more.

Nevertheless, once factions had been created by Maoist manipulation and defensive counterintrigue, they often continued to have a life of their own because they were based on very real conflicts of interest that existed in China (as everywhere else) between the haves and the have-nots, or as the Chinese put it, between those who "had it good" and those "who had it bad." In schools and higher education institutions, the earliest Red Guards were the sons and daughters of the five "Red" classes: high party and government officials, military officers, revolutionary war heroes and preliberation communist industrial workers and poor and middle peasants. They looked forward to privileged positions in universities and in jobs because of their "Red" class background rather than their scholastic achievements. Ironically the CR was directed at many of their parents. When the Liu and Deng faction diverted the Red Guards' energies against teachers, administrators, former "rightists," and "counterrevolutionaries" who had been targets in earlier antirightist campaigns, Mao started a "Bombard Headquarters" campaign that targeted "power holders in the party who follow the capitalist road." The Maoists mobilized a new layer of youth—the children of the former intelligentsia, lower officials, the former middle classes, and ordinary workers and peasants—who became the "rebel" Red Guards—and moved these "rebels" against party cadres who were pursuing a "bourgeois reactionary line."

Because of the economic slowdown after the Great Leap Forward, the expansion of secondary education and the huge birth cohorts of the 1950s, there was tremendous competition for scarce university entrance and urban jobs between the youth from the "Red" classes and those of other origins. The factional fighting between the original and the rebel Red Guards coincided with very real conflicts over youth's life chances in a setting of diminishing opportunities. The losers were going to suffer for life and they knew it. In factories, government agencies and commercial enterprises as well, there were those who had "higher political qualifications": higher positions and wages and all sorts of privileges, who had been the model workers, the leading activists in the earlier campaigns held up as models of the new society. They had benefited most from the revolution, and as expected, defended their privileges. They also happened to occupy the organizational infrastructure of the Liu and Deng pyramid of power. Those who "had it bad" and didn't have these "positive" political qualifications were needed by Mao to dislodge his top opponents, and became the "rebels" in their work units, turning against the previously mobilized "had it good" groups against whom they bore many deep seated resentments, having been the victims of the privilege system run by the latter (White 1989). Since each faction would assign some of its supporters from work units and schools to city- and province-wide revolutionary committees and organizations, the two factions at the grassroots easily organized up to the municipal and provincial levels. In effect dual SMO structures fought with each other in all institutions and at every hierarchic level, in factories, universities, hospitals, government agencies, collective farms, neighborhoods.

The outcome ultimately was determined by backing from the very top Maoist groups in Beijing who throughout these events controlled the PLA. Nevertheless, as is typical of social conflict everywhere, the original issues were often superseded by derivative issues stemming from the conflict itself, for example, the harsh treatment of one's supporters detained by one's opponents, which often called for a cycle of escalated retaliations that even the PLA had difficulty repressing (Oberschall 1973, chaps. 7 and 8). The terminal stages of the mass-participatory phase of the CR in the fall of 1967 and winter of 1968 (before the great suppression of 1968) were especially chaotic because many rebel groups, which the Maoist center ordered to demobilize and to turn their weapons in, knew that surrender meant paying a high price for themselves and their families. And that is exactly what happened.

Although millions were active in the CR, many were only occasional participants, preferring to escape to a more quiet home life, playing chess, cards, making furniture, and so on. Many others could not avoid taking sides. In sheer size, the 1966–1968 events in the People's Republic of China (PRC) dwarf the events in the United States, France, and Czechoslovakia, not just because China is more populous, but because a high proportion of the population got mobilized everywhere although more so in cities than in villages. It was also a great deal more violent, if loss of life is an indication. Youth played a central role in the conflict, but they were pawns of those in authority, acting in the name of Mao, even as they were overturning and seizing lower levels of authority. Intellectuals were on the defensive, mostly victims of the CR. And as in Czechoslovakia, the whole drama originated within the Communist party, in fact initiated at its very peak by Mao and his supporters. The collective actions of the conflict followed the organizational structure of the Chinese communist party-state. The grassroots antagonists divided along the great fault line of society pitting the "privileged" against the "underprivileged." The CR was a totally self-contained Chinese event because China had cut itself off completely from the outside world after the break with the Soviet Union. As news of the CR filtered out of China, some Western radicals started aping the ideology and collective actions of the Red Guards, quoting from Mao's *Little Red Book*. But the influence was one-way, and unintended by the Chinese.

The great winners were Mao and his supporters, and the PLA; the principal victims, the youth who had backed him, Mao's rivals in the top levels of the Communist party and their middle-level cadre supporters in the party and the government, and countless intellectuals, teachers, the former middle classes and other innocents who had already been targets of earlier campaigns and purges. In the end, at the expense of untold suffering, Mao and his supporters managed to gain ten more years of power, but the goal of an egalitarian society in which bureaucracy and privilege would be curbed eluded them entirely. The Cultural Revolution is actually misnamed: the conflict was over who would enjoy power and privilege at all levels and in all institutions of Chinese society. In the process, thousands of temples, historical relics, scrolls and books, monuments, both public and privately owned, were defaced or destroyed. Industrial production and the standard of living declined. Millions of human lives were ruined or maimed by death, injury, interrupted schooling and careers, and disillusionment. Tens of million youth, in Mao's name, acted out vicariously the revolution their parents' generation had fought.

Czechoslovakia

The Prague Spring of 1968 bears more resemblance to the Central European 1848 revolutions than to the other 1968 events: the demand for constitutional government and civil liberties against an autocratic ruler, complicated by the nationality question in a multiethnic state, with the intellectuals in the forefront of activism; even the Soviet suppression has some 1848 parallels (Journalist M. 1970; Zeman 1969). To be sure, all this is clothed in the twentieth-century garb of a communist party-state. Thus, as in China, mobilization and collective action follow the organizational structure and events cycle of a contemporary communist state. And as in China, we start with an autocratic regime and leader whose economic policies based on rigid central planning and management (of an already highly industrial country) have been failing and is thus on the defensive and vulnerable. The party bureaucrats needed the help of intellectuals and economists such as Professor Sik and the Institute of Economics of the Academy of Sciences to set the economy right, but proceeded to slow and undermine the implementation of decentralization, price reform, more autonomy and responsibility to managers and enterprises, the restoration of economic incentives for performance, the introduction of competition and of market principles (measures similar to the later Gorbachev reforms and the post-Mao economic reforms in China). Equally troublesome was the slow pace of de-Stalinization, which lagged behind the Soviet Union and some of its Eastern European neighbors. The Novotny regime reluctantly and slowly proceeded with the rehabilitation. The living victims of the massive Stalinist show trials and purges of the 1950s were released from prison, but kept from resuming their former positions and their party membership. Many of the victims had been Slovak patriots. This further exacerbated the nationality question, for the Slovaks never got their promised federal state and had been resenting Czech domination. The regime admitted some errors, talked reform, and stalled in the worst tradition of erratic reformism (Pettee 1938; Oberschall 1973, 74–84).

As in other Central European countries, the intellectuals and especially the writers and artists have historically been the conscience of the nation. In Czechoslovakia, which had the only Eastern European communist party with genuine mass support before the communist seizure of power in the late 1940s, the writers had been communists or left wing with a patriotic record of opposition to Nazi rule. They seethed with resentment at the heavy hand of the censors, who, in keeping with Soviet de-Stalinization trends, nevertheless made more and more concessions. In turn, film directors, writers, and essayists became bolder. At the June 1967 Writers Union Congress, the party ideologues cracked down, expelled three writers from the party, and took over the writer's weekly literary magazine. Later in the winter the students at Charles University protested in the streets against the chronic lack of heat and light in their dorms, got their heads bashed and their dorms invaded by the security police. Students and intelligentsia had been resenting the extreme leveling of wages and the low prestige of nonmanual, creative work. Many able students had been dropping out of higher education into manual work that promised an easier, financially more rewarding life.

So far, the mass of the people had been apathetic, and all conflicts had been hidden behind the veil of silence shrouding all internal party matters. In the fall of 1967, the inner party tensions erupted at the highest Central Committee level, where resentment was building at Novotny's one-man rule and "cult of personality" (without a personality, as the Czechs added), and the inability to solve the country's mounting economic crisis and other problems. The reformist faction believed that the economic reforms were not going to work unless politics were liberalized, socialism was democratized, and the people's support was enlisted. For this Novotny's personal power had to be curbed. On January 6 he was stripped of the first secretaryship of the party, though he remained president. Dubcek, a Slovak, became the new first secretary. The Prague Spring was about to begin.

At this point, the Communist reformers around Dubcek realized that without popular support, from outside the party, the entrenched Novotny party cadres were not going to yield. The reformers decided to mobilize the intellectuals, youth, and the citizenry. The literary weekly was restored to the writers, the end of censorship was promised, which discouraged the censors who without higher backing now let everything pass. More important, the reformers went before the people in mass forums provided by party organs, such as the Youth Organization, where party leaders of the reform faction and rehabilitated communists exposed the show trials of the 1950s, the Novotny police state, and explained the economic reforms. Questions from the audience were answered on the spot. All this before huge audiences in large auditoriums, covered by the radio, television, and the press. This was a revolution through words, a dialogue of the rulers with the ruled. Dailies and weeklies that were only read for the sports news acquired huge circulations and every word was devoured by readers famished by two decades of banalities. The reformers then brought their program before local, district, and regional party conferences and the many congresses and meetings of party dependent bodies, such as women's, professional, youth, and other associations, which came alive for the first time were open to the news media. There the reformers confronted the conservatives, who stood to lose their privileges and their secure positions should the reformers prevail. Mobilization followed the organizational structure and event cycle of the Communist party, as in China; but there were no campaigns in the streets yet, nor popular protests.

What did the reformers want? The Action Program of April 1968 spelled it out: government and party deliberations and decisions must be open to the public and news media; censorship is to be lifted; scientific and artistic freedom is to be guaranteed; new liberal rules for travel abroad; full rehabilitation of those unjustly purged; state security police to be restricted to antiespionage activities and not to spying on citizens' legitimate activities; greater freedom of association, even of some non-party associations; the rights of nationality groups to be restored; the economic reforms to be pursued vigorously; more national sovereignty in foreign policy. Yet the Action Program stood behind the Warsaw Pact, socialism, and the Communist party's leadership in politics and government. In short, the reformers wanted communism with a human face, not quite Democratic socialism (because a multiparty system with free elections was not included), but as close to it as any communist regime had ever come, and without any outside popular pressures forcing its hand. Such a program is the contemporary equivalent in a communist state of the civil liberties and constitutional government demanded of autocracy in 1848.

Though the April program was adopted, the lines became sharply drawn between a conservative party bloc that had opposed Novotny, but didn't want to go this far, the Dubcek centrists standing squarely behind the Action Program, and a small radical wing that wanted more, faster. More important, overt Soviet opposition and intimidation mounted from this time on. Except for Novotny's ouster from the presidency and his suspension from the Communist party, Novotny appointees remained in their jobs. But new elections in the party for an Extraordinary Congress planned for September 9 threatened to oust many of the conservatives. It is likely that the Soviet military intervention of late August was timed to forestall this occurrence.

It is arguable that in the period of May to July, Dubcek and the reformers started losing their grip on the so far totally peaceful and party led popular movement they had created. Some anticommunist manifestations occurred on May Day, workers strikes broke out, a "Two Thousand Word" proclamation issued by prominent intellectuals in late June and eventually signed by hundreds of thousands (when later attacked by the conservatives) called for an evolution towards democracy and a purging of Stalinists from enterprises, organizations and lower party organs, though not through "rough, unlawful" methods. All these events were seized upon by the Soviets and their Warsaw Pact allies as a pretext for the military intervention that suppressed the Prague Spring (Littell 1969). It took months before a collaborationist regime was finally placed in power and the reformers of the Prague Spring purged.

Compared to the other 1968 events, the Czechoslovakia crisis was, until the Soviet invasion, the most gentle and nonviolent, with most collective actions taking place in conferences, congresses, meeting halls, and not in the streets, nor by means of unconventional tactics. Youth was less in evidence, but then there hadn't been a baby boom either twenty years earlier. Workers as an organized body played a minor part. Intellectuals, writers, news media people, scientists, professionals, as in 1848, and the Communist party reformers were in the forefront and had the most to gain from civil liberties and economic reforms. Their opponents, the conservative party cadres, had the most to lose, for as elsewhere and always, political officials in the social control business have no useful functions to perform once social controls are abolished. One gets a sense that had the Soviets not intervened, or done so months later, there would have occurred a far more conflict-ridden showdown between reformers and conservatives in which both sides would have enlisted broad popular participation and used unconventional confrontation tactics, as was true elsewhere.

The timing and pace of events in Czechoslovakia was not influenced by the other events of 1968. Rather they followed the Eastern European communist pattern of erratic reformism in the de-Stalinization period when the conservative hard-liners lost their sure touch on social control (Oberschall 1973, 127–29). The ensuring intraparty conflict of two factions of roughly equal power led to mobilization of the citizenry by the advocates of change by means of the organization apparatus of a communist party-state. When the party of change threatened the communist monopoly of power and Soviet domination of foreign policy, the Soviets intervened. There is an interesting parallel with China nonetheless. Because competitive elections don't determine the top leadership of the party and country, and the incumbents don't yield power, only a prolonged intraparty fight is available for the outs to dislodge the ins. The best opportunity comes when the incumbents are vulnerable because of failed economic policies. In the ensuing contest the weaker side mobilizes support outside the narrow inner party circles in which the usual struggle over policies and power is played out. Until the 1980s, the

Soviets in the end determined the outcome. Gorbachev's new policies changed that and made possible the 1989-1990 rout of communism in East and Central Europe.

France

In France, the Communist party was a central actor in 1968, though not an initiator. Students, intellectuals, and professionals were in the forefront of activism. And as in Czechoslovakia and China, there was a tremendous outpouring of words and print, the graffiti being equivalent to the big character posters in China. There are other parallels to China. In Western Europe, France's social structure is the most similar to that of China, both a legacy of centuries of highly centralized governments run by an elite officialdom, with those in top authority positions enjoying great powers in their fiefdoms. That was true for professors in higher education, senior physicians in hospitals, bosses and "patrons" in enterprises, and in government the elite Grand Corps recruited from elite, small, select education institutions, the Grandes Ecoles. It was true also in the family, and in the Communist party and trade unions as well. Tocqueville had already commented on it, and noted that the French Revolution had actually solidified the traditional pillars of authority (Tocqueville 1955; Crozier 1973). In France, the politicians fought each other, the people participated in insurrections, and the central government ruled through it all, often very successfully, as in the economic modernization of France in the 1950s and 1960s (Suleiman 1978). The French have had a love-hate relationship with authority and strong rulers. On the one hand, France needed a strong executive to get things done in a highly divided and individualist society; on the other, it feared Bonapartism, which had threatened its liberties, and buttressed the authoritarian tendencies in all institutions. President DeGaulle, in power for a decade, was admired for his wartime patriotism and his successful liquidation of the Algerian War, yet feared and resented for his paternalist presidential rule in the Fifth Republic.

The events of 1968 started with the university students' revolt in Nanterre, then the Sorbonne, and pretty soon in all universities (Seale and McConville 1968; Caute 1986; Kravetz 1968). That revolt had demographic roots in the baby boom of the 50s, the recent enormous expansion of higher education, the new universities' and campuses' shoddy education and the lack of decent job outlets for the thousands of liberal arts and social science graduates. As in the United States, a new life stage had been created between adolescence and adulthood for middle class and affluent youth. It was filled with a highly politicized, intellectual proletariat of university youth and young faculty under the strict authority of senior professors, deans, and the Ministry of Education. And as in the United States, the affluent youth had become critical of the affluent society, of their parents' lifestyles, of the continuing inequalities in a complex capitalist society, of the meaninglessness of the rat race, which they labeled "metro, boulot, dodo"—commute, work, sleep (Tchou 1968). They had become alienated. The most radical left- and right-wing group (the "enrages") fought it out at the university, disrupted classes, insulted the university authorities, and were arbitrarily disciplined, which then rallied most of their peers, and triggered the confrontations with the police, university authorities, and the government necessarily, since the police and university authorities are agents of the central government in a centralized polity.

The police used rough methods against the student protesters. The students employed the well-known, historic ritualized collective action repertoire of French protesters: mass demonstrations in the streets, running battles with police, barricades, sympathy strikes (Tilly et al. 1975). Injuries mounted as participants and bystanders were teargassed and clubbed. The public was outraged, not because it sympathized with the goals of student radicals, but because the authorities' repression and stand symbolized the DeGaulle government's authoritarian rule. As in the United States then, the middle-of-the-road mass of students and the public supported the protesters on the derivative issues stemming from the conflict: the police's excessive use of force, the punishment of those arrested, the reasonableness of many demands for university reform that now surfaced, the Minister of Education's refusal to negotiate with student leaders. This was the story of May 3 to May 11, and ended at the Night of the Barricades.

When Prime Minister Pompidou returned from abroad on May 11, he took matters in hand and was conciliatory: he removed the police from the Sorbonne and the Latin Quarter, but it was too late. The students reoccupied the buildings, stayed, and formed a Student Soviet (much as the Columbia University radicals had occupied campus buildings in New York City) and upped their demands to fundamental university reforms and a restructuring of the French government itself. For some, the goal became toppling the DeGaulle government. In the next few days, the occupations spread to other Paris faculties, other universities, and shortly to newspaper offices, the government broadcasting organizations, the National Theater, government offices, and from Paris to the provinces. More important, the occupations spread to factories, especially in the government-owned industries. In short order, two million workers engaged in sit-down strikes, as in the 1930s, and locked out their managers. That was the start of the Great Strike of mid-May to mid-June, involving, at its peak, ten million participants.

In every institution seized, action committees formed (500 in Paris alone) and a huge experiment in participatory democracy got under way, with the bosses, "grands patrons," and organization leaders ousted from office, or forced to engage in a running debate with their underlings. Most participants will remember these days until the end of their lives. It was like living in a momentary utopia, when the moral constraints on interpersonal relations and face to face communication were lifted, and every topic became legitimate for debate, in an endless outpouring of one's inner soul, so typical of revolutionary crises (Reed 1967, 39).

> The political parties and trade unions were caught napping. They feared that striking workers would back into an insurrection under radical student prodding, and decided to take over the workers' strike. The Communist Party and its trade union, the CGT, denounced left wing adventurism, and their cadres saw to it that students would be locked out of the striking factories. They redirected the strike to economic goals: wages, pensions, hours of work, other economic concessions. The government engaged the unions in round table talks on these issues, as it had in 1936 when sit-down strikers had gained unprecedented economic benefits from the Leon Blum popular front government. (Reed 1967, 39)

Still popular demonstrations and huge marches continued at a furious pace, calls for DeGaulle's resignation mounted, red and black flags (communism and anarchism) came into evidence, the possibility of insurrection increased, especially when the striking workers in the contentious meetings with union leaders voted down the generous economic package trade union leaders had obtained in the negotiations, which had the backing of the government, the Communist party, and the unions. The strike had turned political. A huge rally demanded the resignation of Seguy, the communist head of the CGT. The heat was on Communist party leaders to take a more open political stand, lest it lose control of its own rank and file. In fact, party leaders counted on the collapse of the

DeGaulle government, in which case a successor Popular Front government would be dominated by communists.

At the end of May, DeGaulle regained the initiative. He secretly toured French army bases to ensure military support. On May 30, he addressed the nation on television with one of his great fighting speeches. He refused to resign, and called for new elections on June 23 and 30. He dissolved the National Assembly, called on citizens to rally to the defense of their country against the threat of communist dictatorship, and promised to restore law and order, by force if necessary. By the end of his speech, thousands had converged on the Champs Elysees, singing the Marseillaise and carrying French flags and other patriotic symbols (in contrast to the Internationale and the red and black flags of the previous days). This patriotic mass demonstration of the silent majority, of bourgeois and Catholic France, close to a million participants, turned out to be the largest crowd event of the May–June "Revolution" of 1968. DeGaulle had managed to deflect the issue from his authoritarian rule to law and order and the legitimate constitutional transfer of political power by means of elections (rather than an old-style French insurrection).

In the three weeks to the elections, the government regained the upper hand. The labor agreements were ratified by a secret ballot in contrast to the earlier rejection in open meetings where the radicals had prevailed. A back-to-work movement spread. Soldiers and police slowly reoccupied state property and buildings and seized factories from strikers. Street demonstrations were banned until the elections, and continued small-scale violence by radicals, if anything, irritated the public. In the two election rounds of June 23 and 30, DeGaulle rolled up one of the greatest parliamentary majorities in French history. All opposition parties suffered major losses. The Revolution was over.

How is France in 1968 similar and different from China and Czechoslovakia? It was a society-wide, country-wide event, with the principal scenes of the drama acted out in the capital, as is befitting a highly centralized state (in politics and culture). It was a great deal more violent than the Prague Spring prior to the Soviet intervention, but violence had limits: property loss and injuries aplenty, yet loss of life was negligible (possibly three deaths altogether, in demonstrations and confrontations measured on the scale of millions of people hours). It was from start to finish a French event, with little influence and borrowing from abroad except for the links between the French and the other European student movements. To be sure, many of the opposition ideas that surfaced France shares with other Western countries. France has a rich political culture of citizen collective action against government, which was freely drawn upon, from sit-down strikes to building seizures, from mass marches up broad boulevards to the manning of barricades, the formation of revolutionary committees and committees of public safety that seized authority in organization and associations. Student radicalism of the left and right was nothing new. Alienation, cultural malaise, and an intellectual stance critical of bourgeois materialism and institutions originated in European romanticism of the mid-nineteenth century and was also prominent in "fin de siecle" cultural pessimism. The low risk, non-revolutionary bent of mass parties and trade unions of the left in Western Europe had been commented on every since Michels. The deep-seated ambivalence with France's style of authority, from family to the state, had a long history. If anything, May–June in France exemplifies the staying power of a national political culture. What was novel was the sheer magnitude of mobilization and participation and their convergence at one historical moment: numbers far beyond critical masses had been reached for making collective opposition from below a real threat to the authorities in many institutions, rather than being confined to small circles of intellectuals, artists, and political dissenters. The critical mass phenomenon was the result of the twenty years earlier baby boom, the expansion of higher education in an affluent society, and the shift from an industrial economy to a more diversified consumer goods, high-tech and service-oriented economy, with many more intellectual, scientific, media/communications, and professional workers in evidence than in earlier decades. Their challenge to authority consisted most concretely in demands for co-management and authority sharing with mandarin elders in all institutions. For a decisive breakthrough they needed the alliance of blue collar workers and lower-level white collar employees demanding an equally fundamental restructuring of management and labor relations in industrial enterprises and government administration. That did not happen for two reasons. Because of the wide gap between intellectuals and workers, the educated and the uneducated, bourgeois culture and working-class culture, there hadn't been any ideological and organizational preparation for building such an alliance. And just as important, was the opposition of the Communist party to such a change that would threaten its hold on the blue collar workers and lower-level white collar employees. In the absence of such an alliance, DeGaulle managed to redefine and redirect the crisis along the conventional fault line of French politics between the Left and Right. His trump card was the communist and anarchist threat, and the legitimacy of electoral change for deciding regime change in Western democracies. Bourgeois and Catholic France rallied behind him, and the army's position in the showdown was never in doubt.

The United States

In the "Decline of the 1960s Movements" reprinted in Chapter 10 of this book, I have provided a brief narrative and analysis of the main activists, SMOs, goals, confrontations, successes and failures of the social movements in the United States in the late 1960s. In this section I will make only comparisons with the events in China, Czechoslovakia, and France with an eye to detecting similarity of underlying causes and evidence for any direct or indirect lines of influence which bear on the hypothesis of a globalization of social conflicts and mass participation in opposition movements peaking in 1968. I will provide fewer details on 1968 in the United States since we are all more familiar with our own recent history.

Compared to the other three crises, events in the United States lacked a central focus, on issues, on a geographic center, on a political institution whose control by an opposition was decisive, though control of the Democratic party and the Chicago convention were a watered down focal point. There are good reasons for this. The United States is a country of continental size and more important, a country with decentralized and geographically dispersed political institutions and division of powers. Power at one level does not guarantee society-wide power. With France the United States shared the baby boom, the huge youth cohort, the rapid expansion of higher education, the new life stage phenomenon and the generation gap, the countercultural stance of youth and young adults. Thus there existed the critical masses of easily mobilized political actors. We lacked however the widely shared political culture of the French, and as important, lacked an organized political left that brought the French crisis to an abrupt halt. The New Left in the United States was able to advance its agenda unimpeded by an Old Left.

The American crisis started earlier, some would put it at 1960 with the resurgence of the civil rights movement, others at 1964 with the Free Speech Movement at Berkeley, still others at 1965 when the antiwar movement picked up steam. And it meandered on to the early 1970s without a clean end; the closest candidate is perhaps the McGovern-Democratic rout in 1972. Unlike the other three crises, the American events had a major foreign policy issue that kept feeding both the antiwar movement and the other reform movements as well. The dynamics of the 60s movements were partly determined by the military and diplomatic fortunes of the war, such as the invasion of Cambodia, and not just domestic developments.

In the 1960s, in the U.S., there were several parallel social movements that but for brief temporary alliances never achieved a political, ideological and organizational unity. The crisis was more diffuse than in the other three countries. The civil rights movement had declined by 1968, and was becoming institutionalized in the South where its greatest gains were achieved. Black nationalism hadn't peaked yet, was divided into many competing factions, and ensured lack of unity between black and white campus protests. No one successfully mobilized the rioting ghetto blacks, not even the Black Panthers. The student movement on campuses had been successfully redirected to antiwar aims by SDS in 1965 to 1968, but SDS itself was about to fall apart. The antiwar movement itself hadn't yet peaked either (because the war hadn't ended)—the 1970 Cambodia-Kent State crisis and the resulting nationwide collective protests and campus shutdowns exceeded anything that happened in 1968. The women's movement was just starting; the Chicanos and American Indians barely stirring, the gays yet invisible. There was a momentary hookup of the counterculture youth and dropouts (The Yippies) with the politically articulate student radicals and antiwar activists in 1967 and 1968, but by and large the counterculture and political wings of The Movement did their own thing, separately. And very decisive for the final outcome was the unbridged gap between the white ethnics and blue collar workers and The Movement. Governor Wallace, President Nixon, and still later the New Christian Right and the Republicans successfully mobilized this opposition and organized a series of political and cultural countermovements that left the national Democratic party in a shambles for more than a decade.

Nineteen sixty-eight was thus just one of several peak confrontation years in the 1960–1974 "long" decade. It wasn't without importance or significance. An incumbent president, Lyndon B. Johnson, was forced out of political life; the Democratic party proved incapable of successfully absorbing the opposition groups and coming up with a credible program for social change. The successor Nixon administration was, however, pressured for the first time in American history to acknowledge the possibility of military defeat in a foreign war, and The Movement forced part of the congressional and corporate elite to clamp limits on the Imperial Presidency, with some limited success. Many concrete, limited reforms benefiting all the opposition groups of the decade were achieved—I shall not review them here—but a fundamental restructuring of the American economy, government and especially a Cold War-based foreign policy with its world-wide military commitments did not happen. As a result, the unenviable decline of the American economy and of its international position in the world economy started and later accelerated throughout the Reagan years.

Conclusion

Although no direct links have been demonstrated among the four national crises to sustain a globalization hypothesis, it is nonetheless likely that some similar causes operated in all four instances, and thus the synchronization of collective action in 1968, or at least in the late 1960s, is no mere historical accident. The common causal thread is a consequence of World War II, a global war, which had set off a similar set of events two decades earlier, and which, together with other more immediate causes and triggering events already described, precipitated the crises of 1968. Going back to Mosca and Pareto's ideas about the circulation of elites, which, if interrupted, sets off challenges and popular unrest by counterelites, one may hypothesize that if a particular set of incumbents become entrenched in power for a long time and blocks the routinized process of elite recruitment, tenure, and turnover, several likely consequences follow. Opportunities for younger, talented, and ambitious challengers decline. Innovation, new ideas, and creative responses to social problems and new issues are shelved as the entrenched aging elite sticks by the proven policies, institutions, and political philosophy it successfully rode to power on and governed with. Also, interest groups and small distributional coalitions become entrenched during a period of social stability and slow down economic growth (Olson 1982). The result is a blocked society that will invite challenges from more youthful counterelites provided favorable conditions exist for mobilization of opposition groups against the elites and the government.

The end of World War II and its aftermath in our four countries and elsewhere as well created conditions for a slowdown or cessation of the circulation of elites and of innovation in a rapidly changing world. The victory of the Allies discredited the collaborationist political and business elites in France and brought to power a new elite of young politicians and technocrats who successfully modernized the French economy (Kindleberger 1963). In Czechoslovakia and China, the successful communist seizure of power in the late 1940s ousted the previous elite and entrenched a relatively young ruling group that created a new social system based on the party-state that concentrated enormous power in their hands. In the United States the circulation of elites was not so visibly slowed, but there were similar developments that kept challengers with innovative ideas on the sidelines. The Cold War froze American foreign policy and international relations into a rigid anticommunist mold, with bipartisan backing, and militarized the economy into what became known as the military-industrial complex. All problems, domestic and international, were analyzed and processed by elites primarily in terms of the global communist threat. Many issues and problems, for example, racial equality and poverty and economic justice, became backlogged as reform advocates were discredited as leftists and were on the defensive (Oberschall 1973, chap. 6). In international affairs, Third World nationalism was responded to primarily in terms of anticommunism and the domino theory, and led to the American backing of military regimes and right-wing elites who were openly undemocratic, suppressed human rights, and were corrupt.

Consequently, in the late 1960s, twenty years after becoming successfully entrenched as new elites, the same political actors and their chosen loyal lieutenants were still wielding the reins of power, still basking in the successes they had achieved, and responding to the issues and problems of a new age with the same political ideas and policies. And their handling of these issues and problems was increasingly ineffective. This then set the stage for a crisis of authority and a challenge by a more youthful, excluded counterelite with new ideas and a disposition to innovate.

At the same time, on the supply side of collective action, World War II everywhere had meant loss of life, postponed marriages, and low fertility. When normalcy was restored, the population's response was a baby boom, started somewhat earlier in the victorious United States. Twenty years later a huge adolescent and youth cohort weakly socialized into the traditional culture, crowded the education institutions and economy, and became increasingly critical and cynical of the entrenched elites' goals and ideals, and of the institutions that cramped and blocked them. This huge youth cohort provided the mass base and shock troops backing the political activists who mobilized opposition movements. The challenges started somewhat earlier in the United States with its accumulated racial and social problems that hadn't received proper attention in the Cold War climate, and with its active military interventions, covert and overt, throughout the contested terrain of the Third World countries. In China, the mobilization was started by Mao and his followers against his rivals who were allegedly betraying the Maoist principles of a revolutionary society and vision of the future. In Czechoslovakia, a reform counterelite weakened the power base of the old guard Stalinists and initiated popular mobilization of hitherto conformist bystanders whose support was needed to topple the entrenched elites decisively. Thus conditions and events traceable to common consequences of World War II and its aftermath, and not direct lines of influence and mass media diffusion, explain the synchronization of opposition movements and mass protests in 1968.

Despite the notion of a global village and of a world-wide communications revolution, and the realities of a global economy, the four crises of 1968 were largely national events following their own historical and structural logic. Nineteen sixty-eight does not spell out a global message. On the surface, there were crises of authority and an explosion of participation in all four countries. Millions of citizens usually bystanders in public affairs collectively challenged the authority of those whom they would normally obey, and challenged as well the rules and culturally defined norms of appropriate conduct. Beyond that, the issues were different, the ideologies of opposition differed, the organizational structures enabling mobilization and countermobilization differed. Everywhere the incumbents or their successors and the system of authority prevailed, though some reforms and changes were made, at least in France and the United States.

The radicalism and spirit of participatory democracy survived in Western countries among the German Greens and several other social movements targeting environmental degradation, the nuclear arms race, and culture issues. In the United States, though it had an impact on the women's movement and several other rights movement of disenfranchised and marginal groups (American Indians, Hispanics, gays, and of course the black nationalists), the turbulence and mass protests of the late 1960s and early 1970s stimulated the mobilization of conservative countermovements ranging from the New Christian Right to Pro-Life, anti-ERA, Pro-Family and other movements loosely linked and sponsored by the conservative wing of the Republican party. The conservative countermovement greatly helped the Reagan electoral victories and the successful resurgence of political, economic and cultural conservatism in the United States.

12

The Women's Movement

In this brief chapter I cannot present a comprehensive account of a large, complex social movement, such as the women's movement of the mid-1960s to the 1980s, nor provide the appropriate historical dimension for assessing the status of women these past two centuries. The contemporary women's movement has had important historical antecedents—for example, the suffragette movement—and other social movements in which women played prominent roles and promoted women's issues under the cover of other social issues such as social and religious reform, temperance, the abolition of slaves, to mention but a few. For historical and comparative depth, these earlier social movements and the transnational diffusion of the contemporary movement should be examined. Fortunately, others have written and written competently about antecedents (Buechler 1990), and about the past condition of women (Goldin 1990). What I can do is apply some key ideas from the theory of collective action and of social movements to make sense of important questions about the contemporary women's movement: What accounts for its origin and takeoff at a particular time? What accounts for the goals it is espousing? Why did particular groups and categories of Americans become participants, and why were others bystanders or opponents? Why did the movement engage in particular forms of collective action? What measure of success did it achieve?

The overall goals of the women's movement was and still is equality and nondiscriminatory treatment of women in American society. Inevitably, in such a loosely structured social movement of diverse groups and points of view, many particular goals surfaced that had varying priorities for various groups, yet the core demands were plain enough: equal pay for equal work, nondiscriminatory hiring and promotion by all employers, equal opportunities in education, elimination of disadvantages and discrimination in marriage and divorce laws, and changes in legal and institutional practices ranging from banking and credit to health insurance and pension plans that were operating on the premise that women's access to these services should be through their husbands (Bird 1979).

A further goal of many groups within the women's movement was and is a redefinition of the traditional woman's role of wife, mother, and homemaker in American culture since this role, they alleged, was the foundation for the discriminatory laws and practices in the economy and in other institutions. In the traditional view, a woman's sense of womanhood, sense of personal identity, and sense of accomplishment in life derived from the satisfactory fulfillment of her domestic and familial responsibilities. The nonmarried status was a temporary condition preceding marriage, an unfortunate consequence of marital disruption, or an inevitable and regrettable condition arising from the death of a spouse and the longevity of women. The women's movement sought to redefine and broaden this traditional role by creating a climate of opinion and institutional practices that would enable some women to continue in the traditional role, others to go it alone independently of a male protector, and still others to combine family and work outside the home without penalty, and indeed with support, from employers, husbands, children, and society at large. This meant opposing the stereotypes of women in the mass media, in the school curricula, in advertising, and in the arts; opening male-dominated institutions such as the military, sports, and the ministry to women; insisting on control over one's body and of reproduction as these are manifested in the right to contraception and abortion; demanding greater sexual freedom for women and attacking the prevailing double standard of sexual conduct; and pushing for humane and dignified treatment of women in their families, by the medical profession, by law enforcement authorities, and by others in such matters as rape and assault, abuse by husbands, and the like (Carden 1974).

Those are the goals. To answer questions about the origin and rise of the women's movement, or for that matter of any social movement, we need to inquire into four sets of causes, two on the demand side, and two on the supply side:

1. What changes in life conditions are likely to produce dissatisfactions and public controversies, and why the usual ways of providing relief and of handling problems are not working?

2. What are the beliefs, values, expectations, and thought-worlds for filtering, interpreting, communicating and responding to these dissatisfactions, problems, and public controversies?

3. What is the capacity to act collectively, such as freedom of association, communications, solidarity, size of challengers, and the like?

4. What are the opportunities for success, such as weakness of the opposition, support from public opinion and allies, success of other challengers, a favorable international situation, and the like?

Translated into specific questions about the contemporary women's movement, we have to ask: Did women's life condition change for the worse, making them more dissatisfied? Did values and attitudes spread that made women's condition more inequitable and intolerable? Did women's capacity to act collectively increase? Were opportunities for success growing? Recall that for breakdown theory the principal, though not sole, cause of movement rise would be, in this case, a deterioration in women's condition due to rapid social change, and manifested in social dislocation and hardship for women. Recall also that for solidarity theory, the principal, but again not sole, cause would be greater capacity to act collectively, such as a growing number of women in nontraditional roles, stronger social bonds among them, and access to an organization base.

If one inquires into the condition of women in the late 1960s, when the women's movement emerged, for obvious signs of deterioration, one will not find them (Freeman 1975). Ever since the 1940s, year by year and gradually, more women were participating in the labor force. There was a rise in married women's work, as many of the children born in the baby boom decade after World War II were now in school, and their mothers were helping make ends meet. Women were getting jobs in the expanding clerical, sales, and service sectors, and in the teaching, nursing, and social service professions, much as their predecessors had. Full-time, year-round female workers were getting about 60 percent of the wages that men were getting; this figure had not changed. No evidence exists that men were any more or less helpful in sharing domestic tasks with their wives than they had been, or that women were experiencing life as more stressful, if one were to measure such a thing by increase in mental illness and alcoholism. It is true that divorce was rising, but not at an alarming rate, and this rising rate need not have reflected the deterioration of marriage so much as modification in the law making divorce easier.

So the overall condition of women was changing but slowly. Contrary to breakdown theory, women were not victims of social dislocation. It is nonetheless true, however, that year after year, ever so slowly, the proportion of women who carried the double burden of responsibility for homemaking and children and working outside the home was edging up. At the same time, the smaller number of children per couple, the lower marriage rate among young adults, the greater longevity of women making for the increased likelihood of widowhood, and increasing divorce were all shrinking the proportion of an adult woman's life span spent in the traditional role of wife and mother in an intact family, for which the inherited culture had prepared her. This trend went unnoticed however until after the women's movement got under way and all aspects of the women's question were scrutinized at length. Still the growing number of women in nontraditional roles was a factor in the rise of the women's movement, and such a movement would readily recruit adherents when it addressed itself explicitly to this cultural contradiction that millions of women were experiencing in some fashion on the personal level. Breakdown and solidarity theory both agree on the importance of this trend.

The situation of young women in the 1960s bears special examination. There were many more of them than ever before, as the baby boom children were becoming young adults. They were getting into, and staying to complete college. They were faced with a marriage squeeze: because men tend to marry women two or three years younger on the average, and because births had been increasing twenty years earlier, every cohort of young women in the 1960s was faced with a smaller cohort of eligible young men, and young women's marriage rate was indeed decreasing. As some women made more serious plans for a career because early marriage was less available, they discovered that despite their college degrees they were facing the same career prospects and salaries as older women with less commitment to full-time work and fewer qualifications. Thus a pool of young women was being created who were particularly likely to join a movement that assigned high priority to the concerns and aspirations of young, single, independent women.

It is difficult to document a visible increase in premovement feminist ideology, though a best-seller like Betty Friedan's *The Feminine Mystique* publicized the dependent condition of women and the limitations of the traditional role. Many women kept their thoughts and dissatisfactions private, and perhaps these were too diffuse to be articulated in the absence of public debate. Betty Friedan (1963, 10, 27) put it this way:

> The problem lay buried, unspoken, for many years in the minds of American women. It was a strange stirring, a sense of dissatisfaction, a yearning that some suffered in the middle of the 20th century in the United States. Each suburban wife struggled with it alone. As she made the beds, shopped for groceries, matched slip cover material, ate peanut butter sandwiches with her children, chauffeured Cub Scouts and Brownies, lay beside her husband at night—she was afraid to ask even herself the silent question —'Is this all?' . . . The problem that has no name stirring in the minds of so many American women today is not a loss of femininity or too much education, or the demands of domesticity. It is far more important than anyone recognizes. It is the key to these and other new and old problems which have been torturing women and their husbands, and puzzling their doctors and educators for years. . . . We can no longer ignore that voice within women that says "I want something more than my husband and my children and my home."

Women must have thought that if they were cramped in the traditional role, it was their fault for not adjusting to it, and saw no alternative. Still, the 1960s were a likely time for surfacing of questions and analyses about one's life condition, because the civil rights movement and the radical students in the New Left had put the issues of equality, freedom, and first class citizenship for minorities squarely on the public agenda. Blacks, Hispanics, American Indians, homosexuals, youth, the poor, the aged, even the handicapped put their concerns before the public and demanded that government act. A spirit of questioning and criticizing inherited truths and institutions was abroad. There was a permissive attitude towards challenging authority by public, vocal demands. Any group that presented itself as victim would receive a sympathetic hearing. It became legitimate, even expected, to voice grievances. Both the liberal temper of the 1960s, and the visible successes of the civil rights movements encouraged all other minorities and dissatisfied groups to organize and press their demands. That was true for women as well. The black movement served as a model and a hope for the others, including women. Thus on two of the four sets of conditions for social movement growth, a conducive value climate and opportunities for success, the mid- to late-1960s registered positive readings. But, as was our conclusion for life conditions making for dissatisfaction, the trends were only mildly favorable. That leaves the changing capacity of women for collective action, the last of the four sets of conditions, as the key to the explanation. We now turn to this factor.

Any social movement based on female participants is going to be handicapped because women as such are not concentrated nor do they control a particular social unit, organization, or institution. Further, women are not a homogeneous category with the same problems and conditions of life. Miners are concentrated in mines and mining towns where they share similar conditions and interests, and where their work and life-styles create social bonds; adolescents are in schools and colleges, a setting for the emergence of a cohesive peer culture. Women, however, are scattered in millions of households and thousands of places of employment, and are preoccupied with caring for their immediate kin. The isolation of women from each other is unfavorable for the growth of associations, leadership, networks, and solidarity that provide the basis for collective action.

This state of affairs changed in the 1960s (Freeman 1975). The women's movement had its origin in two independent chains of events that increased women's capacity to act in common, and that powerfully reinforced each other. In 1961 President Kennedy established the Commission on the Status of Women, chaired by Eleanor Roosevelt. Its 1963 final report and other publications documented the denial to American women of many rights and opportunities that men took for granted. State commissions were also established but governors and political parties assigned the commissions' work and recommendations low priority. In effect, the commissions' work was ignored. Many active, prominent, and professional women who served on the commissions developed an expertise on the topic, and in the course of their work met with other similar women from all over the country with whom they forged close ties. A communications network among like-minded professional women came into being.

The work of the commissions encouraged the expectation of their members that government would take measures against sex discrimination in the economy. Yet public agencies stalled. The Equal Employment Opportunity Commission (EEOC) did not enforce the sex discrimination provisions of the Civil Rights Act of 1964, as it had the race discrimination provisions. The matter came to a crisis in 1966 at the National Conference of Commissions on the Status of Women when officials refused to consider a resolution urging the EEOC to move against sex discrimination. Many women commission members decided that something like an independent civil rights organization for women was needed to pressure government agencies and legislators to act on behalf of women, and founded the National Organization of Women, NOW. Such was the first chain of events that increased women's capacity to act collectively.

NOW's activists were initially recruited from existing national and state commissions, and consisted of white professional women. Its organization structure of state chapters and a national headquarters, with boards of directors, bylaws, elected officers, and a formal membership, mirrored the commissions' structure. NOW lacked a mass base at first, and went largely unnoticed in the mass media. Its goal was to pressure the government to enforce existing gender antidiscrimination legislation and to eliminate employment and education discrimination. Even though President Johnson amended an executive order to bar sex discrimination and other forms of bias in hiring by federal contractors in October 1967, it took four years of pressure by NOW to get the Office of Federal Contracts Compliance in the Labor Department to start implementing the presidential order. NOW also carried on a war against the EEOC to enforce existing law. It organized a public feminist collective action in December 1967 with a national day of picketing against EEOC offices in major cities. In a similar vein, another newly formed feminist organization, the Women's Equity Action League (WEAL) pressured the Department of Health, Education, and Welfare to start enforcing Title IX of the 1964 Civil Rights Act prohibiting sex discrimination in education. The Justice Department also came under pressure from these women's organizations. Even though it had the authority under existing statutes do so, the Justice Department was at first reluctant to act on behalf of women. Prodded by them, Justice entered suits against employers where there appeared to be a pattern and practice of sex discrimination.

All of these goings on attracted little public attention and did little to create a visible women's movement with a participatory mass base. That occurred independently with the emergence of Women's Liberation, the other wing of the women's movement. During the 1960s' social movements, under-thirty college women had been activists in civil rights, antiwar, and New Left organizations, where they had acquired a political education and organization skills. As participants in these social and political action projects of the 1960s, and living often in the counterculture community, radical women had gotten to know each other, forged lasting ties, and developed a sense of solidarity. Just as the experience of professional women serving on the commissions had done, the political action experience of the 1960s increased the young women's capacity for collective action. The second chain of events leading to the women's movement was about to start. When these women sought to raise women's concerns within their radical organizations, however, they were ignored or ridiculed. At the 1967 National Conference for New Politics, a coalition of New Left and antiwar groups, the women's caucus was informed that its resolutions on women's rights were not significant enough to merit floor discussion. Activist women decided thereupon to form their own independent radical groups for pursuing women's issues and goals.

From the radical women the idea of women's groups spread by way of personal relationships to many college campuses and adjoining off-campus communities. In short order there occurred a proliferation of women's liberation groups of all types: rap groups, consciousness raising groups, sister groups, women's studies groups, women's centers. Without a central direction or a national organization, yet loosely tied by itinerant feminist speakers, newsletters, conferences, and interpersonal ties, these groups opened feminist bookstores, ran women's centers and hot lines, conducted rape protection classes, provided women's shelters, counseled on contraception and abortion, maintained child care centers, and organized women's studies circles. Thus there was built up a mass movement of like minded young women sensitized to each other's common problems and providing each other with social support.

For some women, Women's Liberation became a conversion experience that manifested itself in extreme hostility to men, the breaking of conventions about appropriate feminine behavior such as the use of obscene language and insistence on permissive sexual conduct. Public opinion and the mass media in turn ridiculed and condemned "women's libbers" and commented on their looks, home lives, and sex lives instead of on the broader issues of women's equality. Unhampered by daily family responsibilities because many were single and childless, these activists and transitory teams of young women devoted a great deal of time and energy to building a feminist community from which sustained collective action could be mounted. Nevertheless, though it fanned out from big cities and universities to smaller localities even in the hinterland, Women's Liberation did not penetrate into the black and Hispanic population, nor into the white working class. Why not? Probably because interpersonal ties through which recruitment took place did not bridge the major divisions in American society, because black women already were getting a voice as blacks in community action programs, and because working class women were not attracted by the emphasis on personal liberation.

Though Women's Liberation had no legislative program as had NOW and WEAL and others, and concerned itself with service projects and spreading a spirit of sisterhood, mass media coverage of the women's movement sharply increased as it became a hot issue. Women's groups took advantage by staging media events such as the protest of the 1968 Miss America pageant during which bras, girdles, and false eyelashes were thrown into a trash can and a sheep was crowned Miss America. As a growing number of women became sensitized to women's issues and the existence of the movement, they swelled the ranks of women's groups. NOW had become an influence to reckon with since, as far as the public was concerned, it spoke for a visible constituency. And as informed and articulate debate on gender equalities and discrimination spilled out from feminist groups and publications into legislative chambers and traditional women's magazines, an attentive conscience constituency of both men and women grew up and added its support to the women's movement.

The concrete manifestations of the women's movement were varied (*Ms.* 1979). (1) There were high profile protest actions such as the Women's Strike for Equality on 26 August 1970 when women were called upon to stay away from work, as many did, and to march in celebration of the 50th anniversary of women's suffrage, as about 50,000 did on Fifth Avenue in New York. Another such public action was the pro-abortion manifesto published in *Ms. Magazine* in 1972 and signed by prominent women who declared that they had had an abortion. (2) There was institution and organization building, such as the creation of a National Women's Political Caucus whose goal was to increase the number of women elected and appointed to public office, the establishment of women's centers as meeting places and information exchanges, the creation of battered women's shelters as a refuge from physical abuse. (3) Finally, there was lobbying and lawsuits against employers, such as the multimillion dollar lawsuit by stewardesses against TWA charging sex discrimination, a WEAL-sponsored sex discrimination suit against the University of Maryland, and the Justice Department sex discrimination suit against a major glass and chemical corporation and the unions with which it had labor contracts.

Soon the women's movement was achieving substantial victories, both symbolic and concrete. The University of Michigan became the first university to commit itself to an affirmative hiring and promotion policy. ATT signed a 35 million dollar settlement with EEOC and the Labor Department, to compensate its women employees for past wage inequity, and agreed to goals and timetables for increasing women in supervisory and management posts. The Supreme Court declared sex segregation in classified job advertisements unconstitutional. There were many firsts: Ella Grasso became the first woman governor elected on her own; the University of Minnesota admitted women into its marching band; the first women generals were commissioned in the armed forces; the first all-women's professional tennis tour was launched; women were appointed as pages in the U.S. Senate for the first time, and so forth. Some of these victories benefited women generally, even the free riders who hadn't participated in the women's movement.

Typical of loosely organized movements, the women's movement was chaotic, torn by internal dissent and speaking with contradictory voices. In the spirit of equality and sisterhood, it sought to provide a platform for all its constituent elements. Yet the active lesbian groups within the movement pushing for a hearing on the homosexual rights issue created a dilemma, because tolerance of lesbians and espousing their legislative goals would hurt the movement with the public at large. And it did. There was also the reformists versus the radicals split: reformists sought changes in legislation, public programs, and policy in employment primarily; radicals sought liberation from traditional constraints, demanding a fundamental restructuring of family and marriage, permissive sexual conduct, and alternate life-styles (Echols 1989). Some of the writings of the radicals promoted the ideal of households, jobs, education, and welfare services operated by and for women without male participation, and ridiculed and denigrated women who were attached to the traditional women's roles of housewife and mother. It was the pronouncements of the radicals, the activities of the lesbians, and the pursuit of abortion rights that occasioned the mobilization in 1973 of a countermovement of conservative, traditional women and men bent on protecting the traditional family and marriage threatened, as they saw it, by feminists and liberals. To conservative women, the collective "goods" sought by radicals and backed by other feminists for the sake of movement unity were collective "bads" that threatened their way of life and offended their moral sense.

The clash between conservative women and the women's movement was precipitated by the drive to ratify the Equal Rights Amendment (ERA). The proposed amendment to the United States Constitution states that "equality of rights under the law shall not be denied or abridged by the United States or by any state on account of sex." Feminist proponents considered the measure not only an important symbolic affirmation of equality for women, but necessary for protecting existing legislation barring sex discrimination and useful for challenging state laws that put women at a disadvantage on inheritance and property rights. Conservative opponents claimed that the amendment would eliminate alimony, legalize homosexual marriage, force women to be drafted and to serve in combat roles in the armed forces, and undermine the legal and cultural foundations of traditional marriage and family.

Unlike feminists who contend that nonphysical differences between men and women are due to culture, upbringing, the inertia of custom, and discrimination, conservative women believe that biological differences make equality between men and women inherently impossible and undesirable. In their view, the unique childbearing function of women calls for a safety net of legislation protecting women, whether or not they are married, divorced or widowed, to ensure the husband's obligation of financial support in marriage, and the mother's right to child custody and alimony in divorce. Religious beliefs in the sanctity of the traditional family are also an important part in the ideology and motivation of many conservative women.

Though the ERA was passed by the Congress in 1972, and thirrty-five states subsequently ratified, it was defeated in the summer of 1982 when the legislatures of Illinois, North Carolina, and Florida failed to pass it before the May 30 expiration date. The opposition to the amendment was led by long-time conservative activist Phyllis Schlafly, founder of STOP ERA, who had skillfully forged an alliance with the conservative wing of the Republican party, the New Christian Right, as well as a number of single-issue groups (Pro Life) and movements opposed to the permissive cultural changes of the previous two decades. This loosely structured conservative countermovement contributed to the Reagan victory in 1980, a contribution exaggerated by political analysts, columnists, and some scholars, and was consequently feared by legislators in excess of its actual power to deliver voters in elections. Defeat of ERA did not mean the end of the women's movement nor of the conservative opposition, for the cultural conflict over the redefinition of women's roles will continue on many fronts and won't be won or lost on any single issue.

By the mid-1970s, the original ferment of Women's Liberation had subsided, consciousness-raising groups had all but vanished, and institutionalization of the women's movement was well under way. Institutionalization consists of recognition of social movement leaders and organization as a legitimate voice in private associations and public agencies, and shifting the cost of movement goals to the polity and society at large. Recognition was symbolized by the prominence of leading feminists and of the feminist agenda at the 1977 National Women's Conference (Bird 1979). As for costs, the burden of maintaining services for women and of pursuing women's collective goals was being shifted to established associations, public bodies, and government agencies. Activist women placed in these organizations ensured that women's interests were represented, that women would have a voice in how these programs are run, and that part of their resources would be allocated to realizing women's goals. Women's studies formed by feminists in campus communities as a voluntary activity were being incorporated into the regular college curriculum. Women's centers and shelters first built on voluntary unpaid labor were being helped by funding from local government, federal programs, and foundations. Professional and scholarly organizations had established permanent organizational units for dealing with women's issues, as for example the Committee on the Status of Women in the Professions of the American Association of University Professors. Long established women's organizations— YWCA, League of Women Voters—were reviewing or introducing feminist goals in their activities. The Democratic and Republican parties introduced new rules for delegate selection to national and state contentions that ensured a better representation of women delegates. Women's interest groups and caucuses—such as Federally Employed Women and the Women's Division of the United Methodist Church—were growing in churches, voluntary associations, business, government, publishing, and education. The point is that the sum total of activity of behalf of women's goals was no longer sustained entirely by feminist activists. Government agencies, professional associations, established social units became contributors. With 800 chapters, 100,000 members, and a two million dollar annual income principally from membership dues, NOW was still exercising an overall leadership role within the movement, but institutional forces had become equally important for realizing women's objectives.

Nevertheless the women's movement is still far from success, measured by its own goals. After several years of vigorous enforcement of antidiscrimination statutes and of affirmative action programs, the median earnings of full-time, year-round women workers is still 70 percent of that of men's. And many more women are part-time and not year-round workers to begin with. This is no longer only a result of not paying men and women equally in the same jobs, nor of illegal discrimination. It is due to complex causes. Because new opportunities have but recently opened up for young women, it will take time for them to rise in their careers and for that to register in the occupation and income statistics (Fuchs 1988). Further, occupations dominated by female workers, such as office work, tend to have low salaries. Whether this is due to impersonal market forces alone or to discrimination as well is a complex question. Lastly, labor force attachment is strongly correlated with wages and authority in the job. Because many women take time out from work to bear and raise children in the crucial decade of young adulthood, and many do so as a matter of their own and their husband's choice, they inevitably suffer a career and wage penalty in comparison to men with a continuous record of labor force participation. It is debatable whether public policy and legislation ought to and can realistically be expected to deal with these last two sources of income inequality, as it has with discriminatory actions in labor markets.

As for the cultural dimension of women's roles, the easing of the double burden of work in and outside the family to make the two career family satisfactory for women will depend not only on cheaper and more accessible day care facilities and more flexible work schedules, but more importantly on fathers' and husbands' willingness to assume a much greater share of responsibility for homemaking and child care. Such attitudinal and behavioral changes are produced by the cumulative impact of socialization and cultural changes that are slow to take effect and probably require a new generation to grow into adulthood. One has therefore the sense that the women's movement has already won the "easiest" victories and that further gains will be more difficult to achieve. On noneconomic matters such as abortion, contraception, and tolerant and permissive attitudes towards sexual freedom, the women's movement is being strongly challenged by the pro-family and pro-life social movements that mobilized in the 1970s as a loose coalition of conservative women and men, conservative Republicans, and religious fundamentalists. In the 1990s, the women's movement will need to marshall all its forces in order to protect the gains it made since the 1970s.

13

The New Christian Right:
Culture Conflict in the Eighties

The counterculture of the 1960s and early 1970s pioneered by Greenwich Village and Bay Area artists, by hippies and rebellious adolescents, and which spread through the ranks of the students in the New Left, the Anti-Vietnam War movement and in women's liberation was permissive and promoted sexual liberation, drug use, freedom from traditional constraints ("doing one's own thing"), and new gender roles. It thumbed its nose at the office work ethic of the nine-to-five routine, the "my country right or wrong" sort of patriotism, conformity with authority in its bureaucratic and familial embodiments. The dress, manner, hair styles, conduct, and attitudes of counterculture youth and the adults who adopted elements of it (smoking pot, long hair, sexual liberation) offended and outraged the sensibilities of the cultural traditionalists in the United States whose thought-world is anchored in the "old time religion" and the fusion of piety, prosperity, and patriotism typical of earlier American moral and religious revivals as well (McLoughlin 1978). Spurred on by ultraconservative Republican strategists and fundamentalist preachers, a moral revival movement known as the "New Christian Right" (NCR) spread through the land (Liebman and Wuthnow 1983).

In the early 1980s, my students and I at the University of North Carolina continuously researched and monitored the New Christian Right and many of the associated groups, organizations, campaigns, revivals, and personalities active on the culture conflict battleground, on both sides of the issues, in North Carolina. We monitored the fundamentalist congregation that spearheaded the Moral Majority in the state; Pro-Life and Pro-Choice advocates; feminists campaigning for the Equal Rights Amendment and antiERA groups; the Christian Action League; Churches for Life and Liberty; church groups campaigning against sexually explicit and pornographic movies, head shops, school texts, and books in libraries that offended their religious beliefs and values; antidrinking and temperance activists, from Mothers Against Drunk Drivers (MADD) to an antiliquor referendum campaign in a small town; we joined a small Church of Christ congregation and attended a Pentecostal revival; we interviewed the antigay demonstrators at a "Miss Gay America Pageant," and attended the "Stand Up for America" multimedia extravaganza that launched the Reverend Jerry Falwell's Moral Majority in Raleigh. On the campus itself we observed Campus Crusade for Christ, the Fellowship of Christian Athletes, Intervarsity Christian Fellowship, and Bible study groups in dormitories. We collected mountains of publications, posters and pamphlets, and watched the Old Time Gospel Hour and several other religious broadcasts. In the fall of 1981 we undertook a statewide study of moral revival activity, with each student monitoring his or her home town and county and interviewing local opinion leaders and influentials on the issues and concerns that NCR leaders were promoting in the national news media and in their publications and broadcasts. Some of us were partisans of one or another cause; many had grown up in the cultural milieu of conservative Protestantism. All of that made for some lively debate, but also for a deeper understanding than novices to the subject matter could have accomplished. We found out that these groups and movements, the activists and the rank and file, as well as their opponents, were a great deal more complex and interesting than their one-dimensional stereotypes in the mass media and indeed even in some of the scholarly literature. Much of this chapter is based on the experiences and findings of our research, in addition to the literature cited. I will first account for the emergence of the New Right and of the NCR at the national level. Then I will turn to the grassroots battleground over morality and culture in North Carolina and how it was linked to the national arena. Without such concrete knowledge it is all too easy to theorize about the NCR in a simplistic fashion. I then turn to an exposition and critique of some social science explanations of the NCR, and close with a somewhat different theory and account of the NCR that views it in terms of a theory of culture change in the contemporary United States.

The New Right

The New Right, also referred to as the New Right Coalition or the ultraconservative right, was a group of younger conservative Republican activists who fervently promoted the capitalist market economy, deregulation, privatization, opposition to the welfare state, acceleration of the nuclear arms race, and a military-interventionist foreign policy in Third World countries against groups or movements that could be labeled liberal, left wing, reformist, or communist. The New Right had become disillusioned with the political compromises of the conservatives in the Republican party, with the likes of Senator Goldwater and President Nixon, and on the intellectual front, with William Buckley and the *National Review*, for not promoting conservatism vigorously and aggressively enough. A main item on the New Right agenda became the political mobilization of religious and cultural conservatives, especially white fundamentalist and conservative Protestants who had been bystanders in politics, behind the candidates and issues promoted by the New Right (NR). Their votes and political activism were needed to swing the Republican party to the right and to defeat the Democrats. The goals and activities of the New Right were many: electing its members and supporters to office, from the White House down to all levels of federal, state, and local government; the passage of legislation and constitutional amendments; getting its members and supporters appointed in the bureaucracy and the judiciary; a continuous, massive fund-raising campaign for financing NR publications, broadcasts, election campaigns, leadership recruitment and training seminars, and organization networks mobilizing the electorate behind NR candidates for elected office; influencing public opinion at large as well as the opinion makers in the media, in the intellectual world, in public affairs; and providing information, policy papers, technical expertise, and other resources for its politicians and publicists opposing the liberals.

Viguerie, a principal NR organizer, wrote that (1981, 8) "the New Right is the most important force to appear on the American scene in decades." Crawford (1980, 4) concurs that in the 1970s NR activists had built a political and organizational network that ranks fourth in the United

States, behind the Democratic party, the Republican party, and labor unions. There was the Committee for the Survival of a Free Congress (CSFC), founded with the financial help of Joseph Coors, the brewer, and headed by Paul Weyrich, an NR leader. CSFC seeks to unseat liberal incumbents and to elect conservatives and New Right candidates for Congress. There is Terry Dolan's National Conservative Political Action Committee (NCPAC), the largest conservative PAC in the country, helping the election campaigns of conservative and NR candidates running against liberals targeted for defeat. There is Jesse Helms' National Congressional Club (NCC), formerly the Congressional Club, with its affiliated tax-exempt foundations and other sister agencies, which has the same goals as NCPAC, and is very active in North Carolina elections. There is the Conservative Caucus (CC), launched in 1975, together with its sister tax-free educational and research foundations, headed by Howard Phillips, publishing *Congressional Report* and other political newsletters. CC's goal is to mobilize a congressman's constituents on behalf of NR positions and influence his voting record. There is Richard Viguerie's The Viguerie Company, the computerized, direct mail NR fund raiser, who also publishes the *Conservative Digest*. There is the Heritage Foundation, an NR think tank that publishes *Policy Review*.

These new 1970s' organizations were joined by the older National Right to Work Committee, an antitrade union lobby, by the American Conservative Union (which was founded by traditional conservatives in 1964 on behalf of Senator Goldwater's candidacy, and publishes *Human Events*) and by Young Americans for Freedom (YAF), founded by William F. Buckley in 1960 to constitute the New Right Coalition. In the news media, NR columnists Patrick Buchanan, Kevin Phillips, William Rusher and others promoted its philosophy, candidates, and positions.

In addition to fund raising and campaigning on behalf of NR politicians, opposing liberals, and helping NR incumbents with staff work, all of these organizations actively engaged in promoting the NR philosophy and its policies in numerous publications and on the various speakers' circuits (colleges, chambers of commerce, civic groups, etc.), in recruiting and grooming NR candidates for office, and in training NR political entrepreneurs, campaign managers and election workers in numerous seminars, leadership conferences, retreats, and luncheons. As Paul Weyrich, of the CSFC, stated in answer to critics (Crawford 1980, 77), "We spend money to recruit candidates, to train campaign managers, to analyze every vote cast in the House and the Senate, to publish newspapers and weekly reports, and none of this is reflected in the financial reports. People who look at what we spent and how much candidates actually got should look at our total program." The NR organizational and political entrepreneurial network was capable of bypassing the Republican party, when necessary, to mobilize public opinion and the voters for NR candidates and causes nationwide and in most states. When it worked on behalf of GOP candidates, it did so independently, collecting debts owed to it. According to Viguerie (1981, 10) "The Congressional Club, the Fund for a Conservative Majority, and NCPAC raised and spent over eight million dollars to help elect Reagan, completely independently of the official Reagan presidential campaign."

The NR was driven to action by what it saw as the Republican's ineptitude in taking advantage of the large defections over racial, cultural, and social issues from the Democratic party, the virtual falling apart of the New Deal coalition since the mid-sixties. Discontent in the country and disaffection with the Democrats was manifested in the successes of the Wallace campaigns, the taxpayers' revolts, the marches of the hard hats, the grassroots organizations mushrooming all over the country opposed to court-ordered busing, gay rights, the women's movement, abortion, to mention but the most vocal and visible protests. These were incentives for NR action.

Opportunities for success in the mid-seventies for the NR were the post-Watergate disarray of the mainline Republican Party, and the sweeping campaign finance reform laws that reduced, among other things, the role of the "fat cats" in elections with a one thousand dollar limit on individual contributions to any candidate in a primary or general election. Correspondingly, direct mail fund raising aimed at thousands of contributors by Political Action Committees (PACs) on behalf of or against candidates and causes gained in importance, and bypassed the established political parties. PACs may legally spend as much as they want for or against a candidate for office so long as the PAC runs an "independent expenditure campaign," with no direct ties to the candidate's own election campaign organization. The prominence of single-issue politics in the seventies, much of it over social issues, thus got a boost from the campaign reform law that unwittingly promoted single-issue PACs. Direct mail solicitation by PACs could be performed more cheaply and efficiently than ever by computers that consolidated and merged household lists, divided them up along geographical and election district lines, and kept track of responses by each household to each issue and candidate appeal.

In some ways, the New Right was not "new" at all, but a selective adaptation of the public philosophy and values of nineteenth-century small town, small business, conservative Republicanism and Southern states' rights advocates to the latter half of the twentieth-century, shorn of isolationism. As Viguerie (1981, 12) admits," except for supply side economics, there aren't that many new conservative ideas. Most of the ideas have been around for a long time. What is really new is that conservatives have learned how to recruit, how to organize, and how to successfully market ideas."

What was new about the NR was its innovative strategy for political power. It knew that its economic program and foreign policy were unpalatable to a majority of American voters, and that it therefore had to build an electoral majority about social and cultural issues, a "moral majority." Viguerie was quite explicit (1981, 186):

> For the past 50 years, conservatives have stressed almost exclusively economic and foreign policy. The New Right shares the same basic beliefs of other conservatives in economics and foreign policy matters, but we feel that conservatives cannot become a dominant political force in America until we stress the issues of concern to ethnic and blue collar Americans, born-again Christians, Pro-Life Catholics and Jews. Some of these issues are busing, quotas, crime, abortion, pornography, education and traditional Biblical moral values.

The notion of a silent majority, real majority, or just plain majority on cultural issues has been much commented on in connection with the break up of the Democratic coalition in the late sixties and seventies, only temporarily halted by Watergate (Scammon and Wattenberg 1972). Alabama Governor George Wallace had tried to build such a majority coalition in a succession of Democratic primary challenges and presidential candidacies. Wallace's image as a narrow-minded, single issue, Southern redneck racist and his lack of experience and qualifications in foreign affairs were, however, too heavy a burden for him to become a viable presidential choice. Yet it is noteworthy that Wallace won Democratic primaries in the North in 1964 and 1968, and 13.5 percent of the national presidential vote in 1968 on a campaign organization that was not much more than an extension of the Alabama governor's office in Montgomery and tens of thousands of small "nickels and dimes" contributions pouring into the governor's mansion through the mails (Lipset and Raab 1970). A gunman's bullet that partially paralyzed him at a suburban shopping center in Maryland in 1972 removed him from further presidential politics.

A decade after Wallace, Jerry Falwell characterized the coalition of voters the NR was trying to put together as a unified political force in the following manner (Viguerie 1981, introduction):

> hard working citizens sick and tired of high taxes and ever increasing inflation; small businessmen angry at excessive government regulations and federal red tape; born-again Christians disturbed about sex on TV and in the movies; parents opposed to forced busing; supporters of the right to life and against federal financing of abortions; middle class Americans tired of Big Government, Big Business, Big Labor, and Big Education telling us what to do and what not to do; Pro-Defense citizens alarmed by appeasement and weakness in U.S. foreign policy.

Such a coalition is the "backbone of our country—those citizens who are Pro-Family, Pro-Life, and Pro-American, who have integrity and believe in hard work, those who pledge allegiance to the flag and proudly sing our national anthem." At other times Falwell simply referred to all these groups as "moral Americans" or "Bible-believing Christians." With the help of the NR and other fundamentalist pastors and preachers, Falwell set out to organize these "Bible believing Christians" into what became known as the New Christian Right, or NCR.

The New Christian Right (NCR)

In the span of just a few years, the NR managed to organize a politico-religious movement appealing directly to conservative Protestants. The most important component of the NCR was the Reverend Jerry Falwell's Moral Majority, which became a household word and was often used as a generic name for the entire NCR phenomenon. First gaining national mass media visibility in the 1980 election, Moral Majority, according to Falwell (*Time*, 13 October 1980), claimed a "membership" of 72,000 ministers, and from three to four million lay members, with "chapters" in all fifty states. These figures were based on mailing lists and did not represent the size of paid-up members, which remained a closely guarded secret. Moral Majority was the secular-political arm of Falwell's Lynchburg, Virginia, fundamentalist ministry that spread out from a 17,000 member congregation, the Thomas Road Baptist Church, to Liberty Baptist College, the *Old Time Gospel Hour* (on 373 television stations at its peak) and several other short-lived campaigns and crusades, such as the Clean Up America Crusade (Fitzgerald 1981). Because Falwell openly advocated morality through legislation, coercive moralism, he drew critics not only from the liberal camp for mixing religion and politics in violation of the First Amendment separation of Church and state, but from fellow evangelists like Billy Graham and conservative columnist William Safire who was opposed on principle to the legislation of morality (*New York Times*, 18 November 1980).

Another major organization in the NCR was the Religious Round Table (RRT) founded by Ed McAteer in 1979. It organized public affairs briefings for conservative ministers and religious leaders, at which NR leaders addressed them. The most successful and publicized such assembly was the three day, August 1980 Dallas National Affairs Briefing attended by 18,000 religious leaders and addressed by a number of conservative and NR religious personages and politicians, including presidential hopeful Reagan. The RRT acted as a bridge between the NR and the NCR. Another NCR organization was the Los Angeles-based Christian Voice (CV). Founded in 1978, it was headed by the Reverend Robert Grant and claimed 37,000 clergymen from forty-five denominations among its 187,000 members (Viguerie 1981, 129). Claimed "membership" in these organizations, it should be noted, tended to be as broad and elusive a concept as the "audience" of Christian broadcasts. It appeared to refer to the number of addresses on a mailing list that regularly received newsletters and other materials, including solicitations for contributions. CV was, as were the other NCR organizations, an intertwined mesh of PAC, education foundation, congressional lobby, direct mail, and publisher and distributor of politico-religious materials, the most important of which was the *Congressional Report Card* that printed congressmen's votes on school prayer, abortion, and tuition exemption that had a religious dimension, as well as other issues like the Panama Canal treaty, foreign aid to Nicaragua, busing for desegregation, balanced budget, all of which were central NR political concerns, and for which CV identified a "correct" Christian position (Hill and Owen 1982, 57-63).

In addition to Jerry Falwell's *Old Time Gospel Hour*, the NCR included televangelists like Pat Robertson's Christian Broadcast Network, a relentless crusader against "secular humanism"; the Dallas-based evangelist broadcaster Reverend James Robison; writer-publicist-family counselor Tim LaHaye; the Plymouth Rock Foundation, an ultraconservative educational foundation disseminating materials for public and Christian schools that voiced the "correct" Christian position on American history, current public affairs, and social policy; advocates of scientific creationism in the public school curriculum; various Federations for Decency and Citizens for Decency, led by fundamentalist ministers such as Reverend Donald Wildmon who organized antipornography and clean-up-television campaigns and boycotts.

Although many of the NCR leaders were from independent Baptist fundamentalist churches, theologically and politically ultraconservative Southern Baptist pastors and fundamentalist ministers of other denominations also participated and pulled in part of their congregations. On college campuses, the Campus Crusade for Christ and the National Association of Evangelicals were on the fringes of the NCR (Hill and Owen 1982).

It is important to know that the New Right Coalition was instigated and engineered by the NR politicians. According to Viguerie's account (1981, 53), Paul Weyrich and Howard Phillips, two key NR political entrepreneurs, "spent countless hours with electronic ministers like Jerry Falwell, James Robison and Pat Robertson, urging them to get involved in conservative politics." They worked closely with Falwell in launching the Moral Majority (1981, 129); they invented and coined that term. The conservative Protestant churches and denominations, as a religious movement, were already gaining converts, starting new churches, training ministers, and exercising greater influence on theology and policy within denominations and in interdenominational bodies. It had a momentum of its own and would have prospered in any case, without political entanglements, whereas the NR could not hope to become an influential political party without the votes and organized support of conservative church members.

As a result of this alliance, the NR acquired a communications and broadcast network independent of the "liberal" networks and prestige newspapers that allegedly covered it in a negative, unflattering, exaggerated, and distorted manner. The NR also acquired viable church-centered communities that it mobilized as blocs, effectively and at low cost, by using existing religious organizations and networks, much the same way as the Anti-Saloon League used conservative and fundamentalist churches and pastors in the 1890–1920 period to push successfully for the prohibition of alcoholic beverages (Odegard 1927). Thus the NR was afforded a chance to politically socialize previously apolitical citizens, an easier task then to permanently wean away loyal followers from a political party and tradition.

How successful the politico-religious linkage was and how broad its reach is best illustrated by the list of signers of a telegram to President Reagan objecting to the appointment of Dr. James Wyngaarden to head the National Institute of Health because he was for "freedom of choice" on abortion. The list includes the heads of the PACs, foundations, publications, associations, lobbies, and support organizations of the NR, the NCR, and the Pro-Family, Pro-Life movements (*Moral Majority Report*, 24 May 1982, 7): Paul Brown, Life Amendment PAC; Howard Phillips, the Conservative Caucus; Paul Weyrich, Coalitions for America; Dr. Ronald S. Godwin, Moral Majority; Gordon Jones, United Families of America; Peter Gemma, National Pro-Life PAC; Forest Montgomery, National Association of Evangelicals; Connaught Marshner, National Pro-Family Coalition; Bill Billings, National Christian Action Coalition; Melanie Hoy, Christian Voice; Judie Brown, American Life Lobby; Jim Wright, Family Protection Lobby; Gary Bergel, Intercessors of America; Mary Jane Wright, Concerned Women of America; Fr. Paul Marx, O.S.B., Human Life International; Joseph Scheidler, Pro-Life Action League; Dr. Murray Norris, Christian Family Renewal; Michael Schwartz, Catholic League for Religious and Civil Rights; Lorraine Syms, No. Virginia Pro-Family Forum; Rosemary Stokes, Citizens Against Planned Parenthood; Joan Solms, Family Life League of Illinois; James Deger, Life Issues in Formal Education; Olga Fairfax, United Methodists for Life; John Mackey, Ad Hoc Committee in Defense of Life; Doug Badger, Christian Action Council; Earl Appleby, Americans for Catholic Values; and Phyllis Schlafly, Eagle Forum. These political and cultural entrepreneurs and their organizations form part of the core of the New Right Coalition. It was vocal, and on the offensive.

Despite these impressive assets, the NCR was not without organizational liabilities. Zald and McCarthy (1987, chap. 7) have noted that a public issue arena has financial, organizational, and supporter limits. It is much easier to attract adherents who are already favorably disposed to one's ideology than to reach and convert apathetic, disengaged persons or supporters from one's targets. After mobilizing one's constituency, one will necessarily compete with one's allies for the same limited human and material resources. Conservative Protestants, especially the Southern Baptists, are one of the best organized and most participatory religious groups. They are already active on most of the cultural, moral and religious issues that the NCR based its appeal on. The NCR crusaders thus ran into and antagonized an already well-greased, politically powerful, "old" religious establishment suspicious of an upstart muscling in on an already crowded moral turf, and with whom it had a long history of doctrinal, denominational, and personal disagreements and rivalries.

The fundamentalist camp itself, and especially the televangelist ministries, was intensely competitive for members, dollars and viewers (Hadden and Swann 1981). The vigor of fundamentalist and independent Baptist congregations, and their success, has always been due to the aggressive entrepreneurial style of pastors and preachers building a personal following. Success was measured by the tons of brick and mortar sunk into church buildings, the size of the parking lot, and the late model autos of congregation families, all symbols of the affluence and upward mobility of the faithful. The personal leadership style of the pastors militated against an effective bureaucratic organization for a social movement of national scope. A pastor will soon overreach his ability to lead his enterprises and his flock all at the same time. Though a television ministry does overcome some limitations with a pseudo-*gemeinschaft* of toll-free 800 numbers, "personalized" computer mail, and other electronic gimmicks, a technologically sophisticated operation and television production are very expensive to maintain. Organizational limits, factionalism, and personal rivalries have marked the NCR, and its competition with the powerful "Old" Right conservative Protestantism has limited its success more than its liberal and secular targets.

Morality and the NCR

Research on matters of religion, sexuality, drinking, drugs and morality supports the notion that in addition to the more narrowly circumscribed area of religious beliefs, devotion, and ritual, active membership in the conservative end of the Protestant religious spectrum has positive consequences on agreement with a Biblical view, and conformity with traditional morality and morals. More than others, conservative Protestants avoid some behaviors and negative effects on health when carried to excess, such as smoking and drinking, and avoid socially and physically harmful behavior, such as drinking and driving, sexual promiscuity that risks venereal disease, and marijuana smoking and drug abuse that risks running afoul of the law. The effects of conservative Protestantism are as, or more, powerful than the usual background variables examined by social scientists in studies of these topics such as race, education, gender, and socioeconomic standing of the family. Here are highlights of some findings.

Stark and Glock (1968) distinguish five dimensions of personal religiosity, (1) beliefs, such as belief in the supernatural; (2) ritual practice, such as church attendance; (3) devotion, such as praying and Bible reading; (4) knowledge, such as knowledge of the scriptures; and (5) experience, such as feeling the presence of God and being born again. When one classifies Protestant churches on their theology along a liberal to conservative dimension, starting with Congregational, through Methodist, Episcopalian, Disciples of Christ, Presbyterian, American Lutheran and American Baptist (the Northern Baptists), and ending at the conservative end with Missouri Lutheran, Southern Baptist, and Sects (which encompass Assemblies of God, Church of God, Church of Christ, Church of Nazarene, Seventh Day Adventist, Mennonites, in other words what is usually referred to as Pentecostals, Holiness churches, and Independent and other Baptists not part of the Southern Baptist Convention), one obtains a striking, consistent, and quite general set of findings, not limited to a particular sample, year of study, geographic location, investigator, and method used,

First, there is an even progression of greater adherence and greater consensus for the conservative Christian tenets, as one moves from liberal denominations to the Missouri Lutherans, Southern Baptist, and the Sects, with practically unanimous adherence (over 90 percent agreement) by Southern Baptists (SBs) and Sect members to the belief that Jesus is Divine and the Son of God, was born of a virgin, walked on water, will actually return to earth; further that there is life after death, the devil actually exists, and miracles happened as the Bible said they did; and that belief in Jesus Christ the Saviour is necessary for salvation.

Second, Southern Baptists and sect members are consistently highest on ritual participation, including attending church services on Sunday every week, saying grace at all meals, spending two or more evenings a week in church or with church activity groups.

Third, members of these conservative denominations are highest on regular Bible reading, prayer, and belief that prayers are answered (in the 85 to 92 percent range).

Fourth, they score highest on scriptural knowledge.

Fifth, they score highest, again in comparison with other denominations, on personally experiencing the presence of God, on certainty of being saved, and having been tempted by the devil.

Sixth, they also score highest on participation, involvement and support for their church community, such as having best friends in their congregation, and giving the highest weekly financial contribution to their church.

Seventh, they also tend to watch religious broadcasts more regularly than other Protestants, and are most confident of their religious faith, nine out of ten state that they have found the answer to the meaning and purpose of life.

Viewed sociologically, conservative Protestant church members form a religious community in the classic sense of shared beliefs and values, high level of support for and participation in the community's formal and informal institutions, common identity, and boundaries with other social units.

A viable community is the most favorable social structural condition for mobilization on behalf of a social movement and for effective collective action (Oberschall 1973). Also, a community that survives by demographic and cultural reproduction will be very sensitive to threats to its capacity to socialize children and youth to its world view and way of life, and to retain their loyalty and attachment to the community.

On matters of morals, sexuality, and morality, research findings are also consistent: church going among youth is positively correlated with less drinking, less smoking, less drug use, with the conservative Protestants scoring highest on conformity with traditional morality (Wechsler and McFadden 1979; Schlegel and Sanborn 1979; Rachal 1980; Bachman 1981). Also parental influence on youth about dating, courtship and premarital sex is strongest among frequent church goers so typical of conservative Protestants (DeLamater 1981). Though no single finding is huge in the statistical sense, the direction of findings is consistent, and supports Hill's (1966, 107) contention that for Southern Protestants sexual promiscuity, drinking, gambling, and the like constitute the essence of immorality, and that these churches "consistently expend far more energy attacking the passage of pornographic materials in the mail, the liquor industry, and the houses of chance than they do grappling with such issues as discrimination, disenfranchisement, poverty and ignorance." The energy has visibly paid off.

If one bears in mind the universal apprehension and concern of parents about their children growing up into productive, law abiding adults, without getting "messed up" and into trouble, and the enormous investment of time and effort spent by them, and churches, schools and civic groups on socialization and reproduction of the dominant culture, one cannot help but notice that conservative Protestants are rather more successful in doing so than other groups in the U.S. at the present time.

An explanation of the NCR and its forays into politics and public policy over moral issues must put the accent on the conflict that fundamentalist and conservative religious groups are engaged in with liberals, professional groups, feminists, counterculture groups, the courts, and government agencies over who will control the means of culture reproduction—especially the schools, the mass media, and the popular culture industry. If the institutions of culture reproduction come to mirror and reinforce the religious orientation and morality of conservative religious groups, the collective task of socialization will be greatly simplified for them, because government, schools, the mass media will then reinforce, and not challenge and contradict, the influences emanating from family, church, and conservative civic groups.

At the Grassroots

In North Carolina, it would be a mistake to interpret the political and moral confrontations of the 80s as a showdown pitting the ultraconservatives against the liberals. Liberals there were in North Carolina, both in churches and in politics, but they were few and weak. The main rival of the NCR were the Old Religious Right, that is, the majority of the Southern Baptists, United Methodists and other large Protestant denominations, prominent evangelicals and television personalities such as Billy Graham; and the conservative Democrats in the Sam Ervin tradition who dominated the Democratic Party. The NCR was not entering a moral vacuum or liberal cultural milieu, but a conservative state with an established, viable political and religious tradition. If the NCR was to succeed, it would have to muscle aside a powerful group that was not about to yield. The situation was ambiguous and complex, however, since many conservative Protestants agreed with the goals and diagnoses of the NCR, though they objected to its lack of tolerance and self-righteous theology. There was also the antagonism between upstart and establishment, and personal rivalries, which played an important role.

From reading direct-mail solicitations on moral issues put out by moral activists and their liberal opponents, one would think the United States was in the grip of a profound crisis, with the clock at five minutes before midnight, religious zealots about to establish a theocracy, or amoral "secular humanists" about to complete the destruction of the family and of the social order, depending on which side was speaking. This was far from the truth, so far as North Carolina was concerned.

North Carolina is basically a conservative state, in religion, in morality, in the fiscal sense, in labor relations, in welfare benefits and eligibility. Churches dot the landscape. Its congressional delegation votes on the conservative side of socioeconomic legislation, tax bills, and military spending. The unionized labor force is the lowest of all states. There are dry counties. Basketball and football, fishing and hunting, are the consummate passions of the citizenry. At the end of the week, newspapers are filled with coming church and religious activities that are well attended. You are more likely to find religious pamphlets in the public libraries than *Playboy*. Close to half the freshman class at the Chapel Hill campus call themselves "born again" Christians. If there are gays, swinging singles, radicals—and there are some—they keep a low profile. Life, liberty and the pursuit of happiness rest on a solid foundation, as does organized religion and family life. The racial tensions of the 1950s and 1960s have subsided, and the wounds are healing.

This view is not based on advertisements promoting tourism to the Tar Heel State, but on systematic monitoring of the press, on statistics published by state and voluntary agencies, and the research papers of undergraduates in the fall of 1981 on their home towns and counties based on interviews with community influentials on issues and controversies important locally. Moral decline and revival was not a major preoccupation compared to zoning, condominium conversion, tax assessments, soaring utility rates, annexation, the financing of a school building program, and chemical dumping. By far the most frequently mentioned social and moral problem was adolescent drinking and drug abuse, which means beer and marijuana. Though concerned, the principals, editors, bankers, businessmen, ministers, librarians, and teachers we interviewed do not interpret such youth behavior as a symptom of moral decline, but blame the boredom of small-town life, the universal problems of growing up, and the spread of national trends. Nor are law enforcement and preaching the only community reaction. Churches, parents, schools and civic groups organized outreach programs, invited reformed drug addicts and health professionals to speak and opened community centers to compete with the video arcade, and so on.

Homosexuality didn't rate a single mention as an issue and problem in our interviews. Homosexuality is one of the manifestations of sin and moral decay that the NCR actively opposes. Among some conservative Protestants there was a debate whether or not one can be a Christian and homosexual at the same time, and whether homosexuality is an "abomination to God." To the public, it was largely a nonissue, except for homosexual teachers. In conversations with antihomosexual demonstrators it appears that their folk view of homosexuality is that of an illness acquired through contagion in youth, like an infectious childhood disease, that can be cured by an act of will and discipline, and especially by religious conversion. This explained both the extreme sensitivity and the lack of tolerance of the public in national opinion polls to homosexuals in occupations dealing with youth and to homosexuals adopting children, and its relative indifference and greater tolerance of homosexuality in other settings.

For the public homosexuality was not a religious issue, but a matter of prudence, of protecting children and adolescents. For the NCR, homosexuality, as all issues involving sexual conduct and standards, was a central preoccupation, not because there was any of it among "good" Christians, but because it was "closing in" from without, unless it was checked. When I interviewed Reverend Chambers, organizer of the Citizens for Moral Decency rally against the Miss Gay America Pageant in Charlotte in September 1982, he assured me that gays were not a problem in his city. But he didn't want it to become another San Francisco, and wanted that message to go out loud and clear. A Gastonia preacher picketing the Legislative Building in Raleigh at a fundamentalist STOP-ERA demonstration in June 1982, told me he was against the ERA because it would legalize homosexual marriage and force his Christian academy to hire homosexual teachers. The ERA to him meant abolition of gender differences, and thus a legitimation of homosexuality, a sort of third sex. When I expressed astonishment that gay teachers had applied for teaching posts in his school, he replied, "Oh no, it hasn't happened yet," but it would if the ERA passed. Again, the outside threat to the, as yet, safe Christian refuge. However, outside of the Christian Right, homosexuality was not a public issue in North Carolina.

Pornography was a more visible issue in the state, but again it was highly localized in large cities and around military bases. Much of North Carolina consists of small towns. The typical response from one such place in our survey was that of a Baptist minister who stated that pornography was not controversial because "no X-rated movies are shown in the county." A newspaper editor recalled that "a few years ago the county interministerial alliance organized a drive to eliminate pornographic magazines [meaning *Playboy*, *Hustler*, etc.] from public display in newsstands and convenience stores . . . an ordinance was passed . . . everyone complied," and there the matter rested. In fact, without the help of state laws on obscenity, and irrespective of Supreme Court decisions, much of North Carolina enforces "contemporary community standards," as it always has, by means of social pressures exercised through church leaders and concerned citizens' committees, and by means of local ordinances, a combination that is quite effective. Here was a typical example: when a downtown cinema started screening X-rated films in a county seat, a citizens' group led by ministers organized a petition campaign and picketed the cinema at show time. The theater closed shortly for lack of business since potential patrons couldn't afford to defy public opinion. From a small town, we had a report of an adult book store owner who was "converted" by the local ministers. They got him to "change his way of life" and to close his store.

In cities there are isolated downtown cinemas screening X-rated films, a few adult book stores, massage parlors, an occasional drive-in showing soft porn, a few "head shops"—a meager fare by big city and international standards. The areas around the big military bases, Fort Bragg and Camp LeJeune in particular, are a different story. Hay Street in Fayetteville, also known as Combat Alley, rivaled Las Vegas and New Orleans. A student researcher counted twenty-two topless bars. Prostitutes solicited openly. The action was heavy after payday when some of the 82nd Airborne and the Green Berets from Fort Bragg celebrated. The same applied for the burgeoning pornography industry in Jacksonville catering to the Marines at Camp LeJeune. These military bases and their civilian fringes were experiencing drug traffic in heroin, cocaine, PCP, and so on. Captain Collins, Chief of Detectives of the Jacksonville Police Department, explained to us that the magnitude of the law enforcement problem there overwhelms his department's capabilities, despite the help he gets from military police. The scale of drug abuse and drinking at these military bases makes the problems in high schools and on college campuses pale by comparison. When a unit of the 82nd Airborne joined the Sinai peacekeeping force in March 1982, 150 of the 800 soldiers showed traces of drugs in urine samples. It was ironic that because the NCR views the military as the front line of our defense against communism, it ignores these manifestations of "moral decay" that it attacks in other settings.

Pornography affords an interesting comparison of how the Old and New Christian Right deal with a moral issue. For the NCR, following Falwell's line in *How You Can Help Clean Up America*, pornography and "smut" are promoted by Hugh Heffner, Norman Lear, the ACLU, and other "secular humanists." The Old Right, led by the Christian Action League, knows that its opponents are small businessmen out to make a buck. Since the "Miller" Supreme Court decision in 1973 which set a new test for obscenity ("whether the average person, applying contemporary community standards, would find that the work, taken as a whole, appeals to the prurient interest..."), the Old Right has been lobbying the legislature to beef up obscenity legislation that would make prosecution cheaper and more effective, and has been pressuring the prosecutors and law enforcement agencies to go after the small pornography businesses and prostitution. It has achieved limited success, and avoids rhetorical flights and media grandstanding that characterize the NCR on these issues.

The Old Right's campaign against alcoholic beverages took the form of opposing liquor referenda. In the early 1980s their efforts to raise the legal drinking age and to promote new tougher drinking and driving laws and their enforcement, had the support of the Democratic governor. Led by the Christian Action League (CAL), the successor to prohibition and temperance organizations in North Carolina, the Old Christian Right stressed instrumental arguments rather than sin and morality. The CAL knows full well that it is the restaurants and supermarkets, the Chambers of Commerce, the promoters of local tourism and real estate that seek changes in liquor laws for business reasons, and were trying to sell it to the public as a means of raising revenues and of keeping local taxes down. The CAL answered these arguments in kind, and linked liquor sales with traffic fatalities. Its methods, as we observed them in a small-town ABC store referendum campaign, were a copy of the turn of the century temperance movement. A church-based citizens' committee forms, led by the local ministers; they organize subcommittees on finance, publicity, transportation, and the like, place advertisements in the local papers and radio, distribute information on handbills, hold mass meetings that feature prominent citizens, and register dry voters. All of it is capped by the ministers preaching against liquor from the pulpit on the Sundays prior to the referendum. This formula was successful in small towns and rural counties, where the wets have been defeated on a number of referenda by two to one.

Our study also encompassed the creationism versus Darwinism controversy, sex education, and family life courses in public schools, groups objecting to material in textbooks, recommended readings, books in school libraries and public libraries, on religious, moral, and patriotic grounds. Such issues did not create much controversy in North Carolina. The main reason was that public institutions minimized content that might be offensive and objectionable, and went out of their way to satisfy parents and the local citizenry. A few quotations will give an idea on how this worked: A high school principal told us that "the curriculum [of the high school] covers Darwinism in evolutionary theory...[The biology teacher] tries to explain Darwinism so it does not contradict the Bible because there are certain religious groups within the community whose beliefs conflict with Darwinism." A biology teacher described how he covered evolution in ninth grade biology, "I do not get too involved in a heavy discussion of the subject. . . . I stress these are just theories, nothing has been proven." A principal said, "Sex education is not taught because the staff feels human reproduction is covered well enough in Advanced Biology," which very few students took. A teacher: "Before a student views a film concerning this topic [sex education], he or she has to have a signed permission from his or her parents." Listen to a public librarian: "I stay on the ball and attend workshops. The Joy Christian Church surveyed my books and okayed them." Here's the decision of a school superintendent's Media Committee after a parent objected to a required book: "The M.C. does not recommend *The Confessions of Nat Turner*, and it cannot be used for required reading. The M.C. recommends that the book be put on closed library shelves so that students must ask for it."

The pattern is clear. Controversial material was avoided, and the professionals' decisions were screened and reviewed by citizens' advisory boards. Complaints by parents and citizens were complied with. Pupils got routinely exempted from exposure to any material that their parents objected to on religious grounds. As far as libraries were concerned, there was no organized campaign on foot by any group, but only a trickle of complaints by conservative Christians, as well as feminists and blacks, objecting to gender and race stereotypes.

The four public issues in North Carolina that have led to grassroots mobilization on a substantial scale were school prayer, the Christian academies, the ERA, and abortion. How did the NCR and the established conservative Protestant churches deal with these issues? The grassroots base of the Old Religious Right is the mainline denominations and churches, principally the Southern Baptist Convention and the United Methodists. Its leadership and organizational arms are the elected leaders and prominent committee members of the convention, the editors of major religious publications, the ministers of the largest congregations, prominent evangelicals like Billy Graham, and the interdenominational legislative lobby, the Christian Action League, closely tied to the Southern Baptists. The NCR is based on fundamentalist churches, some independent Baptists, and Christians for Life and Liberty, an association of Christian academies.

The Moral Majority, the rising national star of the NCR, was not a factor in North Carolina. Like the secular humanists it decried, the Moral Majority was a creation of the mass media and of NCR fund-raisers. It basked in the halo of Jerry Falwell's national standing as the symbol and principal spokesman of the NCR. Despite the fact that Falwell helped launch the state organizations with a rousing "Stand Up for America Rally" at the Raleigh Municipal Auditorium in September 1981, MM Inc. of North Carolina (MMNC) never took off. The state leader was Reverend Lamar Mooneyham, an alumnus of Falwell's Liberty Baptist College in Lynchburg and pastor of the fundamentalist Tri-City Baptist Temple in Durham. Aside from his own congregation and a handful of other Liberty Baptist alumni and Falwell followers, there was no grassroots membership and organization. The mailing list of MMNC, variously put at 8, 10, and 14,000, was no more than just that, a direct-mail list out of Lynchburg through which funds for the national MM were solicited and an occasional newsletter and "Congressional Update" was mailed out, consisting of reprints from the *Moral Majority Report* and other right-wing PAC publications. Mooneyham's office at Tri-City Baptist doubled as state headquarters. He himself was too busy in his own congregation to devote time to MM, aside from answering queries from the mass media and press releases on the Moral Majority position. MMNC had no lobbyist in Raleigh. Its one collective action was the release of a critical twenty-eight-page review of a dozen public school textbooks and teaching materials, based on the work of a few study groups, in the spring of 1981. Although Mooneyham and MMNC reaped a rich harvest of media publicity, their report had no impact whatsoever on the State Textbook Commission and on school boards. Local and state polls indicated in the early 1980s that only half the respondents knew of the MM, and of those who had, the public was split close to 50-50 between those who supported and opposed its activities and goals. Viewers of the *Old Time Gospel Hour* in North Carolina were too few to be reported in the Nielsen and Arbitron audience ratings. By all measures, MMNC was a flop.

Christians for Life and Liberty (CLL) was the statewide organization of and legislative lobby for the Christian academies that became active in the early 1980s in the campaign against the ERA. CLL was formed over the Christian academies issue that antedated the rise of the NCR and the Moral Majority by two decades. In North Carolina, about five percent of the state's pupils are enrolled in private schools. Half are fundamentalist Christian academies, the other half are private country day schools, Catholic parochial schools, Quakers, with a long tradition of private education. Some of the Christian academies were founded after the 1963 public school prayer ban by the Supreme Court; others were a response to desegregation and court-ordered busing in the 1960s and early 1970s. In the early 1980s, they were no longer the segregated academies they originally were, except for Goldsboro Christian, which still excluded blacks, and whose federal tax exemption was being litigated before the Supreme Court. Christian academies were created at considerable financial sacrifice and a tremendous investment of time and resources by parents and pastors of fundamentalist congregations, and made a heavy demand on parents and church members. They stressed discipline, strict dress codes, the old time religion and morality. The CLL was forged when the Christian academies battled the Internal Revenue Service, the Department of Health, Education, and Welfare, the Justice Department, and the North Carolina Department of Public Instruction, and won by astute lobbying, mass mobilization and petition campaigns. The major victory was achieved in 1979 when a state law exempted religious schools from state teacher certification, curriculum review, high school competency tests, standard length of school days and terms, and other such requirements. They remained subject only to health, fire, and safety regulations. A little later they were exempted from participating in the state unemployment fund and from state taxes. Disputes continued over church day care centers. No one or group is at present contesting the newly won status of the religious schools in North Carolina.

The Christian academies' and fundamentalist congregations' participation in the anti-ERA and antiabortion movements coincided with the national emergence of a Pro-Family movement with strong linkages to the NCR. In North Carolina, the ERA was defeated in the state legislature in June 1982, in what proved to be a bitter fight. Both Pro-ERA and STOP ERA carried out a massive grassroots campaign in their effort to influence the legislative outcome. The Senate vote defeating ERA reflected the deep cleavage over moral and social issues between city and small town constituencies and their legislators in the state. STOP ERA was a coalition of ultraconservative Republican women and Christians for Life and Liberty. Before the crucial June 4 vote in the State Senate, over 1,000 fundamentalists descended upon the General Assembly, brought in from all over the state on church school buses. This rally was organized on three days notice through a CLL pastors' telephone network. Other STOP ERA campaign costs, such as newspaper ads, were covered by contributions from the conservative political right.

The fundamentalist women I interviewed at the STOP ERA rally were all in favor of nondiscrimination in wages, in employment, in family law, which they maintained were already protected by legislation, though they spoke without much conviction. However, to offset these advantages, the Phyllis Schlafly scare about homosexual marriage and young women drafted in the army and service in combat had made inroads among them. Still, that wasn't the crux of the matter. In their minds, the best protection of their economic status, of their marriages, of the future of their children, was a "good Christian husband." The ERA was perhaps useful for divorced women, for women with shaky marriages, and irrelevant for women who were "well off." But the demonstrators didn't fall into any of these categories. For them, a likely consequence of the ERA would be to undermine marriage, for men, even "good Christian husbands," would lose respect for women. So why take a chance? A Pro-ERA stance was tantamount to a no-confidence vote in their husbands and an attempt to undermine his God-sanctioned authority in the family. Further, in their view, the ERA was being pushed and supported by "libbers," liberals, lesbians and others whom they mistrusted and opposed on other issues, such as on abortion and school prayer. To be sure, the North Carolina Pro-ERA movement was not made up of such women, as was plain to see when they rubbed shoulders on the sidewalk outside the General Assembly and in the visitors' galleries with their opponents. But it was true for the National ERA campaign, as they perceived it in the mass media and through the Schlafly STOP ERA literature. Thus underneath the obvious religious position justified by the usual Biblical quotations on the patriarchal family was a more complex set of beliefs, perceptions and apprehensions that the women's movement hadn't effectively dealt with.

The same groups that faced each other on ERA were also confronting each other over abortion, plus or minus some allies and defectors. This issue was clearly the most explosive in North Carolina. Abortion necessarily involves sex, and premarital teenage sex at that, aside from the obvious Pro-Choice and Pro-Life debate on the rights of the fetus and the rights of the mother. Thus it hits the conservative Christian nerve, Catholic and Protestant alike, at its most exposed spot, for everything that the NCR and many other conservative Christians think has gone awry in the United States, the sexual revolution, the rebellion of youth, the redefinition of sex roles, the undermining of marriage, rampant immorality, hedonism, irreligion, venereal disease, and welfare mothers come together in female, teenage, premarital sexual intercourse. To opponents, abortion is a license that invites all these evils, and lets the culprits off the hook, at the taxpayers' expense. In North Carolina in recent years, about 30,000 abortions were performed annually, one quarter of all reported pregnancies. Other studies on venereal disease and teen pregnancies confirm that the sexual revolution had reached the state, and that it had done so in rural counties and small towns, not only the cities.

In the early 1980s, the National Right to Life PAC and the National Committee for a Human Life Amendment were beefing up North Carolina Right to Life, with funding and technical resources and advice on how to run Pro-Life voter identification projects and Pro-Life campaigns to back conservative Republicans. Grassroots Pro-Life activists were starting to picket abortion clinics, hospitals providing abortion services and family planning offices throughout the state. Opposing them was North Carolina Coalition for Choice, a Pro-Choice federation of some forty organizations consisting of North Carolina NARAL, North Carolina Religious Coalition for Abortion Rights, and other feminist, health professional and liberal church groups. Pro-Choice was also getting active at the grassroots. In 1982 it organized a petition with over 10,000 signatures and delivered it to Senators Helms and East in Washington as a protest to their support of Pro-Life bills and constitutional amendments. The situation was complex and fluid throughout the 80s. Both sides know that the abortion issue will be decided in Washington by the Supreme Court, the Congress, and presidential vetos. Meanwhile, they are fighting skirmishes over state funding for abortion for poor women.

A grassroots assessment of the NCR in North Carolina remains inconclusive. It never got rooted principally because some of the moral ills it diagnosed were local non-issues, and others that the public was concerned with were being successfully dealt with by traditional proven methods under mainline Baptist and Methodist leadership. The protection of Christian academies from government regulation, which was the most important issue for fundamentalists, was successfully handled by CLL even before the NCR hit the national scene. Nevertheless the NCR and its political allies stimulated a conservative ideological swing that spurred fundamentalists and other conservative Protestants to activism on issues beyond what they would have done otherwise, as we observed in the STOP ERA campaign. Yet STOP ERA in turn stimulated an active Pro-ERA countermobilization. What the net effect of their confrontation was on the North Carolina legislature is impossible to assess with any precision. Some observers, myself included, doubt that the ERA ever had a chance to be ratified in 1982 in this conservative state.

The principal check to NCR organization growth and influence was not from its liberal targets, but from the main Protestant churches. The Southern Baptists with 1.3 million adherents are by far the largest group, followed by the United Methodists with 600,000, the black General

Baptists, the AME Zion Church, with about 300,000 each, followed by the Presbyterians, Lutherans, Catholics and Episcopalians. Independent Baptists, Assemblies of God, Pentecostals, and other sects do not report membership figures but are sizeable in the state, and were more susceptible to NCR appeals. The Baptists opposed the NCR not on values, but on the principle of church-state separation, and on style of action.

Baptists have a long established tradition of participating in the political arena over liquor and pornography. This they do with the Christian Action League, by far the largest, most effective moral activist organization in the state. But on issues on which church leaders themselves are divided, the CAL stands aside. That is how the NCR had an opportunity to enter the moral arena, on abortion, the ERA, public school prayer, yet it failed.

The relationship between fundamentalists in the NCR and the mainline Protestants was competition, rivalry, and suspicion mixed with hostility based on the accumulation of past conflicts. Billy Graham said in a 1982 interview that "I told [Jerry Falwell] to preach the Gospel. That's our calling. I want to preserve the purity of the Gospel and the freedom of religion in America . . . it would disturb me if there was a wedding between the religious fundamentalists and the political Right. The Hard Right has no interest in religion except to manipulate it." The editor of the *Biblical Recorder*, the state Baptist newspaper, voiced the dominant sentiment of the mainline Baptist in an interview,

> I think the Moral Majority has some very legitimate concerns. I share many of their concerns, but I think they're trying to accomplish their concerns in the wrong way. . . . The Moral Majority has operated in such a way that it appears it wants to capture the machinery of government and then use that machinery of government to implement its value system. . . . No church should try to capture candidates to implement through law what they cannot implement through preaching of the Gospel.

Billy Graham and the editor of the *Biblical Recorder* represented and still represent the majority in North Carolina.

Interpretation: The NCR, Symbolic Politics, and Secularization

The attraction and influence of an ideology to adherent and bystander publics is commonly explained in terms of interest and strain, and so it has also been for the NCR. In Geertz's words (1973, 20),

> There are currently two main approaches to the study of the social determinants of ideology, the interest theory and the strain theory; for the first, ideology is a mask and a weapon; for the second, a symptom and a remedy. In the interest theory, ideological pronouncements are seen against a background of a universal struggle for advantage; in the strain theory, against a background of a chronic effort to correct sociopsychological disequilibrium. In the one, men pursue power; in the other, they flee anxiety . . . the two theories are not necessarily contradictory.

As Geertz and a growing number of sociologists (Snow et al. 1986; Gamson 1988) have stressed, and as I myself have underscored elsewhere in this volume (see chaps. 1, 2, 5, and 6), interest and strain theories are incomplete and flawed. An ideology, or thought-world as I prefer to call it, and especially a religious ideology, possesses a cognitive, moral, and emotional structure expressed in terms of frames and symbols without which it could not be persuasively comprehended, argued, communicated, learned, remembered, and believed. A thought-world invests ordinary life routines with meanings, legitimizes social roles and institutions, and provides answers to fundamental questions about life and death, justice and injustice, right and wrong. It enables human beings to plan life jointly, sustain adversity, and to build an identity for individuals and groups. Attachment to a thought-world results from socialization in a particular milieu and keeps being renewed through group membership, social ties, shared life experiences, and social control. The religious symbols and frames of conservative Christianity have survived for two millennia and have spread to the five continents. They are embedded in our culture, in the very language of everyday life. It is doubtful that attachment to variants of conservative Christianity can be explained in terms of changing interests and relief from stress.

I will first discuss some explanations of the NCR based on interest and strain, and then circumvent social reductionism with a more comprehensive structural and cultural explanation. To be sure no single explanation or analyst of such a complex and varied movement as the NCR reduces its ideology and its influence to a single cause, be it interest, strain, or any other factor. It is a matter of where the emphasis is put.

Before the NCR, the scholarly literature on American moral revivals and right-wing conservative movements has used a fairly definite body of ideas to explain them. The historian Hofstadter (1964, 99) preferred the term "cultural politics" to characterize a broad class of issues and movements in U.S. history:

> In our political life there have always been certain types of cultural issues, questions of faith and morals, tone and style, freedom and coercion, which become fighting issues . . . prohibition was an issue of this kind . . . the issue mobilized religious and moral convictions, ethnic habits and hostilities, attitudes toward health and sexuality. There are always such issues at work in any body politic.

In Daniel Bell's (1976, 77) view as well, political and value conflicts in the United States have been of two kinds, class and economic conflicts, and culture conflicts pitting "tradition" against "modernity," or rural, small town, Protestant America against cosmopolitan, urban, liberal groups:

> The traditionalist defends fundamentalist religion, censorship, stricter divorce and antiabortion laws; the modernist is for secular rationality, freer personal relations, tolerance of sexual deviance, and the like . . . this is the realm of symbolic or expressive politics.

For Lipset and Raab the loss of status and power (actual or threatened) is the source of anxiety and strain that underlies these movements (1970, 23–24):

> certain groups still among the more socially prominent and economically privileged may feel that prevailing trends in society threaten them with loss of status and privileges, as in the case of doctors who feel the weight of growing government controls, or working class whites who feel the pressure of Negro demands on their schools and neighborhoods.

According to Lipset and Raab, problems of status loss are particularly acute in the United States because it is a fluid, open society without a means for insulating groups from status challenges, whereas Hofstadter points to American cultural, religious, and ethnic pluralism as the source of "cultural politics." Bell (1977) attributes these conflicts to the growth of a hedonist ethic and life-styles fostered by the logic of mass consumption in mature capitalism, which clashes with the earlier Protestant moral asceticism and work ethic of an emerging capitalist economy.

The most sophisticated sociological formulation of the status and symbolic politics idea is provided by Gusfield on the temperance movement (1966). Gusfield distinguishes class movements pursuing instrumental goals ("bread and butter") and status groups competing to change or defend social prestige by pursuing symbolic goals. For Gusfield, moral reform legislation (gambling, prohibition, birth control, prostitution) is valued by proponents for its symbolic, status legitimizing and conferring aspects more than for its effectiveness for changing deviant behavior (actually decreasing alcohol consumption, prostitution). He distinguishes further between the disinterested reform impulse of socially dominant groups that seek to reform the character and conduct of deviant individuals (drinkers) and the coercive reform of status threatened groups reacting to a sense of declining dominance by imposing their morality on others through legislation. Gusfield is mindful that temperance activists also perceived drinking in its instrumental dimension as a road to ruin (poverty, family breakdown, and health). He rejects a reductionist mode of thinking that would explain belief in the sinfulness of drinking as a mere cloak for status interests and preoccupations. Yet he does emphasize the symbolic politics of moral revival movements.

One reason a cultural and status loss and symbolic politics interpretation of the NCR is doubtful is that the small-town Protestant fundamentalists active in the NCR are by and large an upwardly mobile group who never had it so good in the material sense (Fitzgerald 1981) and that their political allies tend to be upper-middle-class, affluent conservative Republicans, as we observed in North Carolina during the STOP ERA campaign. Further, the notion of a cultural misfit between mass consumption capitalism and traditional Victorian sexual morality can also be doubted. Banning abortion, curbing pornography, reducing premarital sexual intercourse, tightening divorce laws, reciting prayer in public schools, and so on are just as compatible with the health of the American economy as their very opposite: it does not make American auto manufacturers any more or less competitive with Japanese imports, nor does it have an impact on the rate of inflation, the national debt, energy conservation, and so on. What is "tradition" and "modern" in family life, in private sexual behavior and public morals, are value-laden descriptive labels; they are not backed by a body of proven social science theory about the inevitable directionality of culture change. The notion of a lack of fit between culture and economy producing strain and conflicts that some counter with moral revival raises questions about interest and strain explanations. Is it any less strain to change and adapt culture when it no longer fits an economic logic than it is to remain attached to one's culture and fight a series of losing battles? Isn't it more in one's interest to change and adapt culture to economic necessity than to resist it? Such questions cannot be answered with a social reductionist explanation of culture.

Religious values have the character of what Max Weber called the "ethic of ultimate ends." Devout Christians may be opposed to premarital sex and abortion because these are sinful according to their religious beliefs, regardless of any instrumental benefits and costs (such as higher welfare rolls), just as leaders of the ACLU support the right of the American Nazi Party to march in Skokie, Illinois, despite anticipated political harm and resignations from the ACLU. Commitment to a set of "ultimate ends," for example, those of fundamental Protestantism, and undergoing a religious experience such as being "born again" may be the product of a particular tragic or psychologically disturbing experience, but it is more likely to be simply the result of routine socializing experiences in a religious milieu which is surprisingly resilient to changes in the collective experience (affluence, more education, downward mobility, recession) of the group as well as the personal experience of its members (Wood and Hughes 1984). Fervor and activism by a moral community to impose its morality on others with legislation and other forms of pressure can be the result of a variety of motives. It may be, as Gusfield found for the latter stages of the temperance movement, due to a sense of declining prestige and political influence that seeks relief in a symbolic, public reaffirmation of one's values and norms. But it may also be the consequence of devotion to a religious creed that compels missionary activity and subordinates the secular to the religious. According to Max Weber (1958, 119, 336):

> By the Sermon on the Mount, we mean the absolute ethic of the gospel . . . this ethic is no joking matter . . . it is all or nothing. This is precisely the meaning of the gospel if trivialities are not the result. . . . Puritanism . . . interprets God's will to mean that the revealed commandments of God should be imposed upon the creatural world by the means of this world.

That is, active proselytizing, political action, coercive morality.

These doubts raised by a social reductionist explanation of moral revivalism suggest that one examine the cognitive and moral structure of conservative Christianity, and of fundamentalist Protestantism in particular, for a key to its persistence and to its attraction for some. Without going back to early and medieval Christianity for the metaphors, symbols, personifications, and moral tales that it has used to frame its message so persuasively, one does well to ponder the unusual hold of Christian thought on American culture and politics since the first years of English colonization in the seventeenth century. Viewed in this light, the thought-world and coercive moralism of the NCR is not an unusual, extremist, deviant culture phenomenon, but a variant of American culture, a subculture, off the center of the cultural spectrum, but not way off.

In comparing the United States with European countries, Gary Wills observed (quoted in Benson 1981):

> There are of course changes in the manifestations of American piety . . . but they are less important than the larger steadiness and energy of the religious instinct among us. American religion is, even now, not a marvel of rebirth but of vigorous old age. It is not Lazarus, but Methuselah.

Compared to Europe, the American people report a much higher percentage of belief in God, church attendance, life after death, the importance of religion in one's life. Nor are these manifestations of religion confined to ritual, devotion, social church activity; they encompass also beliefs about the natural and supernatural, such as, for instance, that the devil is a physical being, hell and heaven are physical places where physical rewards and punishment are meted out, that supernatural forces and miracles are real (in contrast to symbolic), and not least the belief that the Bible is the actual word of God. These religious beliefs are shared by many conservative Christians and constitute the staple tenets of fundamentalists (Gaustad 1972). These findings are all the more striking because the United States has a higher proportion of secondary school graduates and of college graduates than European countries, and has been the recognized world leader in science and technology. Education and science have been thought to be chiefly responsible for a decline of religion in the modern age, and to be the chief instruments of secularization. Why hasn't it happened in the United States?

One answer is a variant of the strain explanation of culture. Religion provides therapeutic, psychological relief from the stresses of modern life. It is used as a prop enabling many to "get their act together."

Much of the substance of television evangelism, evangelical revivals, religious tracts, and sermons stress the instrumental benefits of religion for inner peace, psychological and physical health, success in career, harmonious social relationships. For instance, in the course of my research, I was handed the following quite typical message on a leaflet at an evangelical rally:

> Yes to . . . Alcohol, dope, speed, downers, acid and junk?
> Parties, sex, and one-night stands?
> Hangovers, addiction, and withdrawal? . . .

Rejection, loneliness and self hatred?
Self-destruction...perhaps suicide?
Or Yes to...Real freedom and happiness
Peace, satisfaction and fulfillment...
Pure and perfect love
A reason for living
Jesus

Drug addicts, homosexuals, criminals, and alcoholics who have been reformed by religious conversion are paraded before the public in the popular religious media and at crusades as living proof that Jesus, prayer, and religion "work."

It has also been argued that membership in a church and active participation in its activities provides a great many social benefits in a mass society with high social and geographical mobility, especially for couples with growing children. But, so the argument goes, although psychological and social functions have preserved it, religion has been privatized and reduced to but a pale shadow of its former predominant role in shaping American culture, social institutions, and public discourse. Despite the outward manifestations of religion, the United States has become a secular society, much as other Western societies have.

However well the theory of secularization and privatization fit other countries, there is good reason to be skeptical of it when applied to the United States. American values, political institutions, the free enterprise market economy, foreign policy, and much else, have had a religious justification, and particularly of the Calvinist Protestant variety. According to the historian McLoughlin (1978, xiv):

> At the heart of our culture are the beliefs that Americans are a chosen people; that they have a manifest destiny . . . to lead the world to the millennium; that their democratic-republican institutions, their bountiful natural resources, and their concept of the free and morally responsible individual operate under a body of higher moral law (to transgress which is to threaten our destiny); and that the Judeo-Christian personal and social ethic . . . cause the general welfare to thrive.

Throughout the nineteenth century, according to John Schaar writing in *The New York Review of Books* (28 October 1976), people believed that "Piety, patriotism, and prosperity advanced hand in hand," and "that the first of the three great things was the foundation of the others." And, Schaar adds, "That view is still held by many." Listen to Senator Jesse Helms (*Time*, 14 September 1981): "this land of ours was divinely inspired. Thomas Jefferson and all the rest were not smart enough to come up with this system. They got on their knees and prayed for it. That's what makes our country unique." These are rock-bottom sentiments in fundamentalist circles and were unremittingly repeated by NCR leaders. Public discourse and debate have not been secularized, or only partially so. Religion has not been privatized in the United States. It has never been that.

Though the Founding Fathers, with the First Amendment to the Constitution, did not establish an official religion in the new American Republic, they did not establish a secular state either. The First Amendment provided an extraordinary protection and encouragement to all forms of organized religion, which flourished in America as nowhere else. The First Amendment in principle favored all religions, though in practice at first and for quite some time Protestantism enjoyed a near-monopoly and privileged standing. In time other major religions got equal time, rather than all religions getting no time.

Given the religious temper of the American people, Congress and Presidents gave at least lip service, and often much more than that, to Christian symbols and ritual, in addition to public displayed of personal piety. According to Bellah (1967), "God is mentioned or referred to in all inaugural addresses but Washington's [very short] second," though early presidents tended to refer to God obliquely as "Almighty Being," "Providence," or "Supreme Being." Leo Pfeffer, an authority on the constitutional history of the separation of church and state, writes that (1970, 335)

> While the American people have been committed to separation in principle, they have in practice not merely permitted but insisted on public manifestations of religiosity on the part of government and government officials. Thus, of all the Presidents, only Jefferson and Jackson refused to issue proclamations for thanksgiving and prayer and even the former found it politic occasionally to attend religious services in the Capitol. In the privacy of his notebook, Madison wrote that congressional chaplaincy was unconstitutional, but as a member of the first Congress, he offered no objection.

There is still much recognition to religion in the U.S.: tax exemption for contributions to religious organizations and tax exemptions enjoyed by churches; the opening of legislative sessions with prayer; the chaplains in Congress, the armed forces, the military academies, and religious holidays. The list could be lengthened. Since the early decades of the Republic, religious symbols and the recognition of religion in public life have increased, not diminished. An act of Congress in 1864 granted the

Treasury the power to mint coins with the motto "In God We Trust," and a 1955 law required it on all U.S. currency. The words "under God" were added to the Pledge of Allegiance by a joint act of Congress as recently as 1954. The tolerance for religion in the United States meant that for a long time Protestantism enjoyed a privileged position, since it was already entrenched at the beginning of the American Republic, not as the official state religion to be sure, but in social and public life, in public ceremonies, in legislation, in the religious underpinnings of private and public morality, and countless other ways. When tax supported public education was introduced in the Jacksonian era, the curriculum and instruction retained its earlier Protestant religious content. This led to bitter religious controversies and civil strife in the 1830s and 1840s when Irish Catholic immigrants arrived in large numbers for the first time in East Coast cities.

The secularization of higher education in the United States was also a long, controversial, and conflict-ridden process. Freedom of thought and inquiry did not extend to the open advocacy of atheism and antireligious points of view. Even if the courts, and many political and civic leaders have increasingly interpreted the first amendment as ensuring neutrality of the state in matters of religion, many citizens have not gone along. In a nationwide study of tolerance and civil liberties in the early 1950s, Samuel Stouffer (1955) found that 60 percent of the citizenry gave a negative answer to the question "If a person wanted to make a speech in your community against churches and religion, should he be allowed to speak, or not?" Stouffer's study also helps clarify why there has been so much apprehension about communism in the United States, a country where communism as an organized political force has been a negligible quantity. Stouffer found that the most salient fact about communism, to much of the American public, was that it is atheist, against God and religion. Opposition and fear of communism was based on its atheism.

It wasn't only the Radical Right and evangelical revivalists who framed American foreign policy in the Cold War era as a Holy War or Crusade against atheistic communism; it was also presidents, secretaries of state, and congressmen. When Dean Rusk, McGeorge Bundy, Walt Rostow, and others justified American military intervention in Indochina, they framed it in terms of falling dominos: if Indochina fell to communism, in short order Thailand, Burma, Malaysia, Indochina, and the Philippines would fall, like dominos, in succession. Falling dominos and the road to ruin have long been standard metaphors of fundamentalists in their battle against irreligion, liberal theology, alcohol consumption, and other forms of moral depravity (Sinclair 1962). Marsden (1980, 173) reproduces a drawing from a fundamentalist tract captioned "The Descent of the Modernists." In it, a stairway is shown, lit at the top and plunged in darkness at the bottom. These captions are written on each stair, starting at the top: Christianity; Bible not infallible; Man not made in God's image; No Miracles; No Virgin Birth; No Deity; No Atonement; No Resurrection; Agnosticism. The bottom floor of the cellar is marked in capital letters "ATHEISM." Protestant temperance advocates framed their message with a "road to ruin" imagery: yielding to the temptation of even one drink is fatal, because it will lead to another, and then another drink, and so on, and end in physical and spiritual ruin.

The metaphors, language, and symbols of American culture and politics are steeped in the Biblical thought-world of Christianity. History and our field work in North Carolina confirm that the Old Time Religion and folk views on moral conduct and deviance—for many they are the same—are alive and well, especially in the South where the NCR was so active. That is after all what the term Bible Belt refers to. When not checked by some powerful countervailing influences, moral crusades and coercive moralism are the age-old, proven reaffirmation of one's beliefs and morality when they are challenged.

Interpretation: The NCR and Social Movement Theory

In the theory of social movements, four sets of questions have to be dealt with (Oberschall 1973), the first two on the demand side, and the last two on the supply side of collective action:

1. What changes in life conditions are likely to produce dissatisfactions and public controversies, and why the usual ways of providing relief and of handling problems are not working?

2. What are the beliefs, values, expectations, thought-worlds, ideologies for filtering, framing, communicating and responding to dissatisfactions, problems, and public controversies?

3. What is the capacity to act collectively, such as freedom of association, communications, solidarity, leadership, size of challengers, and the like?

4. What are the opportunities for success, such as effectiveness of social control, support from public opinion and allies, success of other challengers, a favorable international situation, and the like?

Looking at the NCR, the Pro-Family movement and moral revivals of the eighties, there are few surprises on the supply side. Let us dispose of it first.

The Supply Side

In the early twentieth-century battle between modernists and fundamentalists among Protestants, the modernists won out in every denomination (Marsden 1980). The fundamentalists retrenched behind doctrinal and social barriers and built up a viable and encapsulating form of socioreligious organization, high levels of commitment and participation by the faithful in active local congregations, summer camps, retreats, Bible colleges, revival circuits. This Old Time Religion remained the conventional religion of much of the working-class Southern population. The typical congregation was led by a pastor-preacher whose success in building a large church and in achieving high status depended on his oratorical and entrepreneurial talents. Many a mill owner supported him and backed religious revivals since they so obviously promoted orderly work habits, stable family, and an otherworldly orientation hostile to trade unions. Congregations were small, participatory, cohesive, and loosely linked through the revival circuit, Bible colleges and camps, and personal links among pastors. Many an ambitious, talented young man of modest education and class background rose on the fundamentalist mobility escalator, as others did in the military, because economic opportunities were less in the South than elsewhere in the United States.

What is less well known is that the Old Time Religion adapted quite successfully to post-World War II urbanization and material prosperity. It thrived on the familism and baby boom of the late 1940s and 1950s. New congregations were formed or were transplanted into growing cities. Yet the emotional, participatory style of worship, the "*gemein-schaft*" character of the congregation, the theology and religious message remained much the same (Fitzgerald 1981). Indeed the more secure material level of living made it possible to expand and beef up the encapsulating socioreligious organization. As well, the new social security benefits enabled older folk to contribute more to religion.

The fundamentalist and conservative religious message blended well with the commercial, materialist, achievement oriented aspects of American culture, the culture of capitalism. Prosperity was a manifestation of God's blessing to the Saints. This successful adaptation of the Old Time Religion to ecological, demographic, educational, and economic changes in these decades was impressive and a testimony of its continuing vitality. Theories about secularization have a problem explaining it (Wilson 1982).

All this is of central importance for the supply-side factors in collective action. A key hypothesis of social movement theory is that a group with an encapsulating organization, yet cut off (segmented) from higher social strata has a great capacity and strong incentives for both rapid and wide-ranging mobilization (Oberschall 1973). Leadership and members are trapped within the group. Exit is discouraged and difficult. Established leaders have legitimacy and enjoy the backing of followers for defending and promoting group values and interests. The small size of congregations discourages free riding as informal social sanctions are effective. Solidarity incentives for participation are strong. Preexisting organization cuts down on opportunity and organization maintenance costs. Shared beliefs and values cut down on transaction costs, reaching agreement about goals and strategies of action comes easily. Further, on top of this favorable capacity to act, the NCR received help on how to enter the national political arena in which it had little experience and sophistications from the conservative wing of the Republican Party that was building an electoral majority on cultural issues since the mid 1970s, as described above. Opportunities were favorable. As far as supply-side factors are concerned, the pattern of NCR mobilization accords well with social movement and collective action theory.

The Demand Side

The demand side of the NCR story is more complex and interesting. The usual explanation runs as follows: the NCR and the conservative Pro-Family movement were a response to the 1960s' sexual revolution, feminism, counterculture, gay rights, the secularizing and liberalizing trends and their excesses and failures, all of which outraged cultural traditionalists. Groups defend their cultural heritage as they defend their material and political interests. The moral crusade was a cultural coun-terrevolution.

Such an explanation has much merit but is incomplete. What has to be explained more specifically is why the NCR was more immune and less receptive to the 1960s' and 1970s' cultural changes than other groups, and why its reaction was coercive moralism. The answer requires a structural analysis and an ideological analysis, neither of which can be derived from the other, as I have already argued.

Just as there are means of material production and conflict over who controls them, there are means of culture production, principally the schools and the mass media, but including peer group settings from Boy Scouts to rock concerts, and there is conflict over who controls them. Whose values and moral codes are transmitted in these institutions makes a great deal of difference for socialization and social control. These are expensive, time-consuming, labor-intensive activities that are reduced when the burden is widely shared with like-minded others and when institutions uphold group values and norms. Suppose parents seek to teach a restrictive sexual code of conduct to their children. They will find the task easier if there is visible public support for it, among their neighbors, in the schools, in the mass media, in youth activity groups. If restrictions are placed on popular culture role models, films, magazines, television programs, school texts and curricula, peer activities not under adult control that advocate a permissive, hedonist sexual morality, or indifference to sexual conduct, the parents' job will be easier and more effective. The visibility and especially advocacy and glorification of a permissive morality creates external costs to the adherents of conven-tional morality. The result is cultural conflict. Even though the instru-mental aspects of this conflict are stressed here, much of it is over symbols. Symbols frame legitimacy, and legitimacy makes it easier to enforce conformity.

What are a group's external costs of socialization and social control from alternative moralities and life-styles? An upper status group, into which people seek entry, can rely on anticipatory socialization, the costs of which are borne by the upwardly mobile. The upper class erects social and economic barriers that insulate it from unwanted influences: zoning of neighborhoods, private schools, exclusive clubs and resorts, a pro-tected environment. All this makes for low vulnerability to alternate moralities. Lower- and middle-class groups can't afford these barriers, or have to make great sacrifices, as the fundamentalists did with Christian academies. These groups then are more vulnerable to unwanted cultural and moral challenges.

Family-centered groups, such as fundamentalists and conservative Protestants more broadly, will be especially sensitive to socialization and social control in interpersonal relationships, gender, and family roles. Affluent, educated people tend to invest in big corporations, secure careers, pension plans and individual achievement for getting them through life, and they have a big stake in how efficiently and honestly these organizations and programs are run. Their access to the political and the legal system provide effective social control for these. Other groups have less access to the political, economic, and organizational mainstream. They may instead invest in stable, interpersonal relationships, in other people, especially kin, neighbors, a church congregation, for getting them through life. For that to be successful, a solid consensus on mutual rights and obligations is necessary, and much attention devoted to harmonious interpersonal relations. Such consensus and stability has to be provided from within the group, through socialization and social control and stable expectations, and disposes them to be conservative on family and gender norms. Such groups become vulnerable if the younger generation does not adopt the culture of their parents, and does not remain cohesive and supportive of it. These groups are exposed to the risk of downward mobility and drift. One lives in a social milieu near to others caught up in chaotic, disorderly, violent life-styles and interpersonal relationships. Moral barriers and social encapsulation protect the group and its members against downward drift.

The expanded role of mass media and popular culture in socializing young people intensify concern with socialization and social control. Corporate culture production and marketing have become divorced from accountability and social control. Those who produce, market, and profit from popular culture and the mass media (e.g., fostering new life-styles and a rebellious disposition towards adults) do not pay for its negative consequences, whereas failure in interpersonally produced socialization in one's proximate social milieu will have immediate, tangible, costly consequences. Thus popular culture and the mass media have no incentives to foster traditional values and role models, as parents and families do. Interpersonal socialization then becomes more and more burdensome as youth become plugged into popular culture and mass media.

Socialization and social controls become a salient issue when cultur-ally diverse groups, once isolated from each other, have to share common culture production institutions: consolidation of small schools into a large district, or rural folk coming to live in the big city are typical examples (Page and Clelland 1978). Another trend is the professionalization of the teachers making them less subject and responsive to local groups, espe-cially low status groups, on values and norms taught in public schools. To sum it all up, a structural analysis concludes that lower SES, family-oriented groups will be more likely than other groups to invest in traditional family and gender roles, and will increase their interpersonal socialization and social control efforts when they lose their grip on cultural production institutions (schools, popular culture, mass media) they come to share with other, nontraditional groups. Thus the attraction of the NCR, which led and organized socialization and social control on traditional lines.

How does such an explanation compare with the symbolic politics interpretation of conservative culture movements? It may well be that conflicts over values and morality are partly a cover in the contest for social prestige, respect, esteem, and influence (Gusfield 1966). Esteem and prestige accrue to those conforming to the moral principles that are publicly recognized. Parents earn respect if their children turn out "right." Alternative values erode this source of respect and self-esteem. What was selfless devotion comes to be seen as wasted exertion, or perhaps merely quaint and old fashioned, but no longer worthy of merit. Changing values erode prestige in much the same way as inflation erodes the value of money. Thus one would expect groups to defend their values much as they defend their savings. Public affirmation of values is akin to an antiinflationary policy. This explanation is appealing, but does not an-swer the further question of why investment in morality is chosen as the means of achieving respect when other means are available, for instance material and occupational success. Let me suggest again that this avenue is less open for lower and middle social strata where the NCR was strong than for the upper-middle and upper strata. Seen from this angle, sym-bolic politics and status defense theory turns out to be one dimension of a more comprehensive culture conflict explanation. But it is not neces-sary to link status defense with status decline (Lipset and Raab 1970).

Structural analysis of the NCR needs to be complemented by a cultural analysis. Culture is a design for social organization and prescribes conduct. Culture is shared, public, and authoritative (Douglas 1982). Culture is more rigid than private beliefs, which are flexible and tolerant of ambiguity. Cultural categories are not easily accommodating, and easily subject to revision. They cannot neglect the challenge of aberrant forms, that is, what is deviance from their vantage point. Culture requires action validation. If deviance were ignored it would represent a collective admission of the culture's irrelevance. Culture would then be viewed as empty formality and would no longer be an effective design for living and for social organization. Indifference to deviance is not a neutral act, it undermines the authority of culture. What has to be explained in the case of the NCR is not its condemnation of deviance, but the intensity of opposition, and why the NCR singled out deviance from traditional gender roles and sexual conduct for such particular attention.

The NCR's reaction has roots that go back to early Christianity, have been passed down from generation to generation, and keep being revived in the conservative wings of Protestant and Catholic Christianity (McLoughlin 1978). Their religious thought-world is a product of so-cially shared learning and experiences; it is a symbol system that provides coherent answers to core existential questions that confront every human being and group, about life and death, the meaning of suffering, injustice, the human condition (Bell 1976). Three thought-bundles of this conser-vative Christian belief system are particularly important for understand-ing the NCR's coercive moralism (Gaustad 1972; Marsden 1980):

1. Men and women are born sinful; human nature is destructive; extraordinary efforts have to be made to control destructive impulses. A corollary is a domino theory of backsliding, it is the road to ruin. Little transgressions rapidly become dangerous vices, unless checked. The domino principle also operates at the cognitive level, small deviations from orthodoxy lead to skepticism, agnosticism, atheism. Satan, an ever present force, actively encourages all this backsliding in order to undermine God's design. Extraor-dinary vigilance against deviance is required lest it get out of hand.

2. Morality and social institutions are not man made, nor adaptations to ecolog-ical, demographic, technological imperatives. There are moral absolutes, there is one correct answer to every moral question; there is only one correct form of social organization for mankind. These have been revealed by God in the Bible. God's moral and institutional design works well, it is plain to see. As I already indicated, the NCR rallies and pamphlets are full of examples of people who led dissolute, destructive, unhappy lives (drug addicts, alcoholics, gamblers, homosexuals, womanizers . . .) who become

transformed into exemplary, productive, successful, happy individuals after submitting to God's design and plan. There is a corollary. Because God's design has been revealed and works, those who repeatedly ignore it and oppose it are malevolent and evil, and they deserve harsh treatment.

3. Just as deviance is not just harmful, but sin, there is no such thing as "victimless" deviance and victimless crime. God showers his blessing on peoples and nations that submit to his design, and God punishes collectively the peoples and nations that tolerate deviants and harbor sin. Private morality is a contradiction in terms. It is a public matter since it affects collective welfare. Checking deviance thus ought to be a matter of public policy. When America closes its eyes to sin, it is a weak, ineffective country; when America punishes sin and follows God's path, it is a successful superpower, respected by all.

The consequences of these three thought-frames is coercive moralism, opposition to moral relativism, extraordinary vigilance against deviants, and "criminalizing" deviants.

Why did the NCR react with "coercive moralism" to deviance and nonconformity especially in gender roles, family roles, sexual conduct, that is, the sphere of family, marriage, sexuality and parent-adolescent relations? I have argued that certain groups invest in family and in lifelong personal relationships within a community composed of family units. The NCR appealed to such people. The unrestrained quest for sexual fulfillment is a major source of marital instability and conflict between parents and their adolescent children and men and women. Conflict over gender roles—how to reconcile the aspirations of women within a family framework—has also been a major source of marital instability and family disruption. Stable family and culture reproduction from within, by transmission of parental values to children, is the core foundation of the NCR. For the NCR, traditional gender roles and sexual morality have worked out well for ensuring stable families and community. Any departures from these time-proven formulas is a big collective risk, with no benefits. The Biblical thought that buttresses these pro-family, gender specific, patriarchal norms and attitudes is self-serving, to be sure, but close to two millennia old, and not a crisis response to family disorganization within conservative Protestant congregations. On the contrary, by all indices ranging from divorce rate to teenage pregnancies and drug abuse, as we have seen, fundamentalists do better than any other denomination or secular group. This conservative ideology has existed in mainstream Christianity in lean years and in fat years. The norms and attitudes that follow from it are salient and familiar in the context of the family life experiences and the social milieu of NCR adherents. The protective net the NCR weaves about the traditional family is not only directed at subversive influences emanating from New York and San Francisco. It is also protection against internal change.

An illustration from a STOP ERA demonstration will make these statements more concrete. Two women held up a banner that read, "In my family, my husband wears the britches." I fell into conversation with them, during which they explained what makes for a good marriage. They echoed Biblical doctrine and norms. Marriage, as they described it, is a bargain over gender norms. Men, they said, were by nature sexually promiscuous, drank with their buddies, were reckless and irresponsible with money, difficult to tie down into family roles. To make them into responsible providers, good partners and faithful husbands, you had to give them authority, respect, obedience within the family. Put them in charge. That will tame their wandering, destructive impulses and commit them to marriage, spouse, and children. That meant sharp gender role distinctions and boundaries, and a woman's subordination to her husband. "Christian" husbands will not exploit their authority because they in turn are responsible to God. Women's quest for equality will simply undermine the family, and women like them will be the big losers. If women don't hold to their side of the bargain, men will not either, they will become wanderers, run around with sexually liberated women, spend recklessly instead of bringing the paycheck home. That was their view, and those were the reasons they opposed ERA.

Far from expressing unreasonable fears, these two women were voicing apprehension about present cultural trends that were far wider held than NCR circles. No one knows for sure just how much change the conventional family can absorb, and what long-term societal consequences follow should the family not adapt. Whosoever reflects on the NCR and the conservative pro-family movement and its chances of success should realize that these movements are raising very basic issues about social relations, culture and the viability of social order, and that the solutions they advocate make sense from within their own encapsulated social world and experience, and from a two-thousand-year-old religious tradition.

Epilogue

A social movement will decline when successful, its work accomplished and its policies and programs institutionalized, and when unsuccessful, deserted by its constituency or simply drifting away from it. The NCR faded from the national limelight in the late 1980s, for both reasons. The conservative politico-religious alliance has been successful. The political temper of the United States had become conservative. To be a liberal had become a liability. Three successive Republican administrations in Washington had put on the bench a conservative federal judiciary, all the way up to the Supreme Court. More voters, even among young adults, were Republican than Democrat. The economy was deregulated, patriotism was rekindled; communism unravelled worldwide, even in the Soviet Union; the capitalist market economy was spreading worldwide.

On the cultural and moral front, the record is mixed and the jury is still out. The Moral Majority was disbanded by Jerry Falwell in August 1989. According to the *Wall Street Journal* (25 September 1989), its annual revenue fell from a peak of 11 million dollars in 1984 to a bare three million dollars in 1988, to the point where its fund raising by direct mail wasn't covering its expenses. The conservative crusade had spawned so many competing professional reformers and SMOs that it had over-saturated its constituency. As our North Carolina research showed, the conservative mainline Protestants on their home turf blocked out the Moral Majority. Without grassroots organization, moral activists drifted to the likes of Randall Terry's Pro-Life Operation Rescue that picketed and invaded abortion clinics and family planning offices. In coalition with others, the NCR had helped block the ERA. Many states raised the drinking age and toughened drunk driver laws and enforcement. It had contributed to the conservative political swing, as Viguerie and other political strategists had hoped a decade earlier. But its broader cultural goal of reversing the sexual revolution and of restoring the traditional family and gender roles must be judged a failure. On all indices of social disorganization, the American family weakened in the 1980s; drug abuse continued at high levels; with the inner cities a combat zone. The public schools continued their academic decline and refused to get involved in a Christian moral crusade. Feminism, homosexuality, pornography are about. The NCR has protected its religious enclaves from outside cultural invasion, and the faithful have once more beat a retreat to their encapsulating communities, the Christian academies and Liberty universities that dot the fundamentalist landscape, whence they shall sally forth once again, unexpectedly, in yet another moral revival movement, as has happened repeatedly in American history.

Glossary

ACTIVIST. Person who is actively and intensely participating in a social movement over a period of time.

ADAPTIVE BEHAVIOR. Specific behavior chosen from a set of alternatives, when it is expected to yield the most gain for the least cost.

ADHERENTS. Leaders, activists, transitory teams, conscience constituency, and on the edges, sympathizers.

BREAKDOWN THEORY. The theory that explains the origin and growth of social movements by emphasizing rapid social change, dislocation and uprooting, all of which creates widespread and intense dissatisfactions conducive to both individual deviance and collective protests.

BYSTANDER PUBLIC. Those who have no initial stake in the outcome of an issue under dispute, but who are in danger of suffering some loss from confrontation.

CHALLENGER. SMO, with the help of adherents and allies.

COLLECTIVE ACTION. Actions based on the voluntary pooling of resources and efforts by many people for the purpose of realizing shared goals or benefits.

COLLECTIVE BEHAVIOR. A form of voluntary, purposive, episodic collective action, in relatively unstructured situations. The benefits and costs of participants' choices usually differ from those in other situations, and the usual norms of conduct may be temporarily replaced by other norms.

COLLECTIVE GOOD. A good or benefit accessible to all members of a group or category of people, regardless of whether or not they contributed to attaining it.

CONSCIENCE CONSTITUENCY. People drawn to a social movement by the justness of its cause, even when it does not provide them tangible, bread and butter, benefits.

CONSTITUENCY. Group or social category that movement leaders and activists claim to represent and speak for.

CONVERGENCE. The coming together, by a process of self-selection, of similarly disposed persons in a crowd, audience, assembly or organization, resulting in some uniformity of attitudes, dispositions and behavior.

COUNTERMOVEMENT. A social movement whose main target is another social movement.

DIRECT PARTICIPATION COSTS. Costs, such as ridicule, arrest or injury, incurred from participation in collective action.

FREE RIDER. A person who benefits from a collective good, but did not contribute to its attainment.

INSTITUTIONALIZATION. The process by which social movement leaders and organizations are recognized as legitimate voices for a constituency, and come to be represented on official bodies, public agencies, and in voluntary associations, which then gradually contribute to obtaining some movement goals.

MOBILIZATION. The process whereby activists build loyalty and commitment for their cause and assemble followers, funds and resources, all of which increases the capacity to act collectively.

NORMATIVE BEHAVIOR. Behavior that conforms to law, convention, rules of conduct, and notions about what is right and appropriate.

OPPORTUNITY COSTS. Cost of the opportunities that people forego when they contribute scarce resources, such as time and money, to collective action.

PROFESSIONAL SOCIAL MOVEMENT. A social movement characterized by full time leaders who draw resources largely from outside their constituency, small or "paper" membership base, and relying on media manipulation to achieve movement goals.

SELECTIVE INCENTIVE. Benefit or good that results from participation in collective action, and which is not obtained by nonparticipants.

SOCIAL MOVEMENT. A challenger that seeks collective goods and benefits for a constituency by means of a variety of strategies, some of which may entail nonroutine, even illegal, means of pressuring targets.

SOCIAL MOVEMENT ORGANIZATION (SMO). An organized group or association with a distinct name and identity, controlled by activists, whose proclaimed goal is to provide a collective good for a constituency.

SOLIDARITY THEORY. The theory that social movements originate and grow when social bonds, attachments, shared identity, leadership and organization exist in a group, all of which contribute to its capacity to act collectively.

SYMPATHIZER. Person who openly sympathizes with a social movement, but does not otherwise contribute to or participate in it.

TARGET. Authorities and/or other organizations and groups, whose inaction, actions, and opposition blocks the achievement of social movement goals.

TRANSITORY TEAMS. Part-time activists who donate mostly their labor and time to a social movement.

Bibliography

Africa Report. 1966. 11 (November).

Anonymous (n.d.) *Der Kelheimer Hexenhammer (1487). Verlag Konrad Kopbl* (new edition reprint): Grunwald.

Bachman, Jerald et al. 1981. "Smoking, drinking and drug abuse among American high school students." *American Journal of Public Health* 71 (1).

Balazs, Etienne. 1964. *Chinese Civilization and Bureaucracy.* New Haven, Conn.: Yale University Press.

Barnet, R. 1973. *Roots of War.* Baltimore: Penguin Books.

Bell, Daniel. 1976. *The Cultural Contradictions of Capitalism.* New York: Basic Books.

Bell, Daniel. 1977. "The return of the sacred?" *British Journal of Sociology* 28 (December).

Bell, Wendell, ed. 1967. *The Democratic Revolution in the West Indies.* Cambridge, Mass.: Schenkman.

Bellah, Robert. 1967. "Civil religion in America." *Daedalus* (Winter).

Benson, John. 1981. "The polls: A rebirth of religion?" *Public Opinion Quarterly* 45: 576-85.

Berelson, B. and G. Steiner. 1964. *Human Behavior.* New York: Harcourt, Brace and World.

Bird, Caroline. 1979. *What Women Want.* New York: Simon and Schuster.

Blanksten, George. 1963. "Transference of social and political loyalties." In B. Hoselitz and W. Moore (eds.), *Industrialization and Society.* Paris: UNESCO.

Blauner, R. 1966. "Whitewash over Watts." *Transaction 3* (March/April).

Boudon, Raymond. 1986. *L'Ideologie, ou l'Origine des Idees Recues.* Paris: Gallimard.

Boulding, K. 1963. *Conflict and Defense.* New York: Harper Torchbooks.

Brimmer, A. 1974. "Economic developments in the black community." *Public Interest* 34: 146-63.

Brinton, C. 1957. *The Anatomy of Revolution.* New York: Vintage.

Brown, Roger. 1965. *Social Psychology.* New York: Free Press.

Buechler, Steven. 1990. *Women's Movements in the U.S.* New Brunswick, N.J.: Rutgers University Press.

Cantril, Hadley. 1965. *The Pattern of Human Concerns.* New Brunswick, N.J.: Rutgers University Press.

Carden, Maren Lockwood. 1974. *The New Feminist Movement.* New York: Russell Sage.

Caute, David. 1986. *Sixty-Eight: The Year of the Barricades.* London: Hamish Hamilton.

Chafe, W. 1980. *Civilities and Civil Liberties*. New York: Oxford University Press.

Chan, Anita, Stanley Rosen, and Jonathan Unger. 1980. "Students and class warfare: The social roots of the Red Guard conflict in Canton." *China Quarterly* 83 (September): 397–446.

Civil Disorder Digest 1, 1, 15 September 1969.

Cohen, J. and W.S. Murphy. 1966. *Burn, Baby, Burn*. New York: Dutton.

Cohn, Norman. 1975. *Europe's Inner Demons: An Enquiry Inspired by the Great Witch-Hunt*. New York: Basic Books.

Coleman, J.S. 1957. *Community Conflict*. New York: Free Press.

Coleman, James. 1990. *Foundations of Social Theory*. Cambridge, Mass.: Harvard University Press.

Collins, R. 1975. *Conflict Sociology, Towards an Explanatory Science*. New York: Academic.

Commons, J.R. 1918. *History of Labour in the United States, II*. New York: Macmillan.

Commons, J.R. 1935. *History of Labour in the United States, IV*. New York: Macmillan.

Conot, R. 1967. *Rivers of Blood, Years of Darkness*. New York: Bantam.

Coser, L. 1956. *The Functions of Social Conflict*. New York: Free Press.

Coser, L. 1967. *Continuities in the Study of Social Conflict*. New York: Free Press.

Crawford, Alan. 1980. *Thunder on the Right*. New York: Pantheon Books.

Crozier, Michel. 1973. *The Stalled Society*. New York: Viking.

D'Andrade, Roy. 1984. "Culture." In Richard Schweder and Robert Levine (eds.), *Culture Theory*. Cambridge: Cambridge University Press.

Dahrendorf, R. 1959. *Class and Class Conflict in Industrial Society*. Palo Alto, Cal.: Stanford University Press.

Daniels, S. 1974. "The Weathermen." *Government and Opposition* 9: 430–59.

Darvall, F. 1934. *Popular Disturbances and Public Order in Regency England*. London: Oxford University Press.

de Sola Pool, Ithiel. 1966. "Communication and development." In Myron Weiner (ed.), *Modernization*. New York: Basic Books.

de Sola Pool, Ithiel. 1966. "Communication in the process of modernization and technological change." In B. Hoselitz and W. Moore (eds.), *Industrialization and Society*. Paris: UNESCO.

de Tocqueville, A. 1955. *The Old Regime and the French Revolution*. New York: Doubleday Anchor.

Dean, E. 1966. *The Supply Response of African Farmers*. New York: Columbia University Press.

DeLamater, John. 1981. "The social control of sexuality." *Annual Review of Sociology* 7: 263-90.

Dellinger, D. 1975. *More Power Than We Know*. Garden City, NY: Doubleday Anchor.

DeNardo, J. 1972. "The diffusion of civil disturbances." Unpublished manuscript, Yale University, Sociology Department.

Deutsch, Karl. 1961. "Social mobilization and political development." *American Political Science Review* 55 (September): 493–514.

Deutsch, M. 1973. *The Resolution of Conflict*. New Haven, Conn.: Yale University Press.

Douglas, Mary. 1982. "The effects of modernization on religious change." *Daedalus* (Winter): 1–19.

Douglas, Mary. 1986. *How Institutions Think*. Syracuse, N.Y.: Syracuse University Press.

Downs, Anthony. 1972. "Up and down with ecology—the "issue-attention cycle." *Public Interest*, 28 (Summer).

Duesenberry, James. 1959. *Income, Savings, and the Theory of Consumer Behavior*. Cambridge, Mass.: Harvard University Press.

Dumont, Louis. 1966. *Homo Hierarchicus*. Paris: Gallimard.

Dumont, Louis. 1977. *Homo Aequalis I*. Paris: Gallimard.

Durkheim, Emile. 1981 [1895]. *Les Regles de la Methode Sociologique*. Paris: Paris University Press.

Echols, Alice. 1989. *Daring to Be Bad: Radical Feminism in America, 1967–1975*. Minneapolis: University of Minnesota Press.

Eckstein, H. 1964. *Internal War*. New York: Free Press.

Erikson, Kai. 1966. *Wayward Puritans*. New York: Wiley.

Finkel, Steven, Edward Muller, and Karl Dieter Opp. 1989. "Personal influence, collective rationality and mass political action." *American Political Science Review* 83, 3 (September).

Fireman, B. and W. Gamson. 1979. "Utilitarian logic in the resource mobilization perspective." In M. Zald and J. McCarthy (eds.), *The Dynamics of Social Movements*. Cambridge, Mass.: Winthrop Publishers, Inc.

Fitzgerald, Frances. 1981. *Cities on a Hill*. New York: Simon and Schuster.

Fleck, Ludwig. 1980 [1935]. *Entstehung und Entwicklung einer Wissenschaftlicher Tatsache*. Frankfurt: Suhrkamp.

Foster, J. and D. Long. 1970. *Protest: Student Activism in America*. New York: Morrow.

Foucault, Michel. 1979. *Discipline and Punish*. New York: Vintage.

Free, Lloyd. 1964. *The Attitudes, Hopes and Fears of Nigerians*. Princeton, N.J.: The Institute for International Social Research.

Freeman, Jo. 1975. *The Politics of Women's Liberation*. New York: Longman.

Friedan, Betty. 1963. *The Feminine Mystique*. New York: Dell.

Friedl, Ernestine. 1964. "Lagging emulation in post-peasant society." *American Anthropologist*, 66, 3, 1 (June).

Frohlich, N., J.A. Oppenheimer, and O.R. Young. 1971. *Political Leadership and Collective Goods*. Princeton, N.J.: Princeton University Press.

Fuchs, Victor. 1988. *Women's Quest for Economic Equality*. Cambridge, Mass.: Harvard.

Gamson, William. 1975. *The Strategy of Social Protest*. Homewood, Ill.: Dorsey Press.

Gamson, William. 1988. "Political discourse and collective action." *International Social Movement Research*, 1: 219–44.

Gamson, William. 1990. *The Strategy of Social Protest* (second edition). Belmont, Cal.: Wadsworth.

Gamson, W. and B. Fireman. 1978. "Utilitarian logic in the resource mobilization perspective." In M. Zald and J. McCarthy (eds.), *The Dynamics of Social Movements: Resource Mobilization, Tactics, and Social Control*. Beverly Hills, Cal.: Sage. In press.

Gamson, William and Andre Modigliani. 1989. "Media discourse and public opinion on nuclear power: A constructionist approach." *American Journal of Sociology*, 95 (July): 1–37.

Gaustad, Edwin. 1972. "The structure of a fundamentalist Christian belief-system." In Samuel Hill, Jr. (ed.), *Religion and the Solid South*. Nashville: Abingdon Press.

Geertz, Clifford, ed. 1963. "The integrative revolution." In *Old Societies and New States*. New York: Free Press.

Geertz, Clifford. 1973. *The Interpretation of Cultures*. New York: Basic Books.

Gerlach, Luther and Virginia Hine. 1970. *People, Power, Change: Movement of Social Transformation*. Indianapolis: Dobbs-Merrill.

Gerschenkron, A. 1964. "Reflections on economic aspects of revolutions." In H. Eckstein (ed.), *Internal War*, New York: Free Press.

Gerschenkron, A. 1966 *Bread and Democracy in Germany*. New York: Fertig.

Gilchrist, G.A. 1983. "Voice interview." *The People's Voice* (October 5–18), Weldon, N.C.

Goldin, Claudia. 1990. *Understanding the Gender Gap: An Economic History of American Women*. New York: Oxford University Press.

Granovetter, M. 1978. "Threshold models of collective behavior." *American Journal of Sociology 83*, 6 (May): 1420–43.

Green, R.H. and S.H. Hymer. 1966. "Cocoa in the gold coast." *Journal of Economic History* 16, 3 (September).

Greer, Donald. 1935. *The Incidence of the Terror During the French Revolution*. Cambridge, Mass.: Harvard University Press.

Grimshaw, A. 1960. "Urban racial violence in the U.S." *American Journal of Sociology* 66 (September): 109–20.

Gurr, T.R. 1967. *The Conditions of Civil Violence*. Princeton, N.J.: Center for International Studies, Research Monograph 28.

Gurr, T.R. 1968. "A causal model of civil strife." *American Political Science Review* 62, 4: 1104–24.

Gurr, T.R. 1969. "A comparative study of civil strife." In H. Graham and T. Gurr (eds.), *Violence in America*, New York: New American Library.

Gurr, T.R. 1970. *Why Men Rebel*. Princeton, N.J.: Princeton University Press.

Gusfield, Joseph. 1966. *Symbolic Crusade: Status Politics and the American Temperance Movement*. Second edition, Urbana, Ill.: University of Illinois Press.

Gusfield, Joseph. 1967. "Tradition and modernity: misplaced polarities in the study of social change." *American Journal of Sociology* 72 (January).

Gutkind, Peter. 1962. "African urban life." *Cahiers d' Etudes Africaines*, 3, 3.

Hadden, Jeffrey and Charles Swann. 1981. *Prime Time Preachers*. Reading, Mass.: Addison Wesley.

Halberstram, D. 1969. *The Best and the Brightest*. New York: Random House.

Halpern, Joel M. 1967. *The Changing Village Community*. Engelwood Cliffs, N.J.: Prentice Hall.

Harris, Richard. 1965. "Nigeria: Crisis and compromise." *Africa Report* 10 (March).

Heath, G.L. 1976. *Off the Pigs*. Metuchen, N.J.: Scarecrow Press.

Heberle, R. 1945. *From Democracy to Nazism*. Baton Rouge: Louisiana State University Press.

Heberle, R. 1951. *Social Movements*. New York: Appleton-Century-Crofts.

Hechter, M. 1975. *Internal Colonialism: The Celtic Fringe in British National Development, 1536 - 1966*. Berkeley: University of California Press.

Heirich, M. 1971. *The Spiral of Conflict: Berkeley 1964*. New York: Columbia University Press.

Helmreich, W.B. 1973. *The Black Crusaders*. New York: Harper and Row.

Henningsen, Gustav. 1980. "The greatest witch-trial of all: Navarre, 1609–1614." *History Today* 30 (November): 36–39.

Hicks, J.D. 1961. *The Populist Revolt*. Lincoln: Nebraska University Press.

Hill, Samuel Jr. 1966. *Southern Churches in Crisis*. New York: Holt, Rhinehart and Winston.

Hill, Samuel Jr. and Dennis Owen. 1982. *The New Religious Political Right in America*. Nashville: Abingdon Press.

Hirschman, A.O. 1970. *Exit, Voice, and Loyalty*. Cambridge, Mass.: Harvard University Press.

Hirschman, Albert. 1982. *Shifting Involvements*. Princeton, N.J.: Princeton University Press.

History Today. 1980. 30 (November): 23–39.

Hobsbawm, E.J. 1959. *Primitive Rebels*. New York: W.W. Norton.

Hodgkin, T. 1957. *Nationalism in Colonial Africa*. New York: New York University Press.

Hofstadter, Richard. 1964. "Pseudo-conservatism revisited—a postscript." In Daniel Bell (ed.), *The Radical Right* Garden City, N.Y.: Doubleday Anchor.

Hopkins, Terrence. 1967. "Politics in Uganda: The Buganda question." In H. Castagnio and J. Butler (eds.), *Boston University Papers in African Politics*. New York: Praeger.

Huntington, S. 1962. "Patterns of violence in world politics." In S. Huntington (ed.), *Changing Patterns of Military Politics*. Glencoe, Ill.: Free Press.

Huntington, S. 1968. *Political Order in Changing Societies*. New Haven, Conn.: Yale University Press.

Hyden, Goran. 1968. *Political Development in Rural Tanzania*. UNISKOL: Lund.

Inglehart, Ronald. 1990. *Culture Shift in Advanced Industrial Society*. Princeton, N.J.: Princeton University Press.

Jacobs, P. and S. Landau. 1966. *The New Radicals*. New York: Vintage Books.

Janis, Irving. 1972. *Victims of Groupthink*. Boston: Houghton Mifflin.

Journalist M. 1970. *A Year is Eight Months*. New York: Doubleday.

Karsch, Irving. 1980. "Demonology and science during the scientific revolution." *Journal of the History of the Behavioral Sciences* 16: 359-68.

Kerr, C. and A. Siegel. 1954. "The inter-industry propensity to strike." In A. Kornhauser, R. Dubin and A. Ross (eds.), *Industrial Conflict*. New York: McGraw Hill.

Kieckhefer, Richard. 1976. *European Witch Trials: Their Foundation in Popular and Learned Culture, 1300–1500*. Berkeley: University of California Press.

Killian, L. 1964. "Social movements." In R. Faris (ed.), *Handbook of Modern Sociology*. Chicago: Rand McNally.

Killian, L. 1975. *The Impossible Revolution: Phase II*. New York: Random House.

Killian, L. 1984. "Organization, rationality and spontaneity in the civil rights movement." *American Sociological Review* 49, (6): 770–83.

Kilson, M. 1971. "Politics of black ethnicity." *Dissent* (August): 333–45.

Kindleberger, Charles. 1963. "The post war resurgence of the French economy." In Stanley Hoffmann (ed.), *In Search of France*. Cambridge, Mass.: Harvard University Press.

King, M.L., Jr. 1964. *Stride Toward Freedom*. New York: Harper and Row.

Klandermans, Bert. 1984. "Mobilization and participation: Social psychological expansions of resource mobilization theory." *American Sociological Review* 49, (5): 583–600.

Klandermans, Bert and Dirk Oegema. 1987. "Potentials, networks, motivations, and barriers: Steps toward participation in social movements." *American Sociological Review* 52, (4): 519–31.

Kravetz, Marc, ed. 1968. *L'Insurrection Etudiante*. Paris: UGE.

Kriesberg, L. 1973. *The Sociology of Social Conflicts*. Englewood Cliffs, N.J.: Prentice Hall.

Kriesi, Hanspeter. 1989. "New social movements and the new class in the Netherlands." *American Journal of Sociology* 94 (5): 1078–1116.

Kuhn, Thomas. 1962. *The Structure of Scientific Revolutions*. Chicago: Phoenix Books.

Laqueur, W. 1976. *Guerilla, A Historical and Critical Study*. Boston: Little Brown.

Laue, J. 1965. "The changing character of Negro protest." *The Annals of the American Academy of Political and Sociological Science*, 357.

Leach, Edmund. 1976. *Culture and Communication*. New York: Cambridge University Press.

Le Bon, Gustave. 1960. *The Crowd*. New York: Viking Press.

Lee, A.M. and N.D. Humphrey. 1943. *Race Riot*. New York: Dryden.

Lee, S. 1951. "Agrarianism and social upheaval in China." *American Journal of Sociology* 56 (May): 511–18.

Leites, N. and C.J. Wolf. 1970. *Rebellion and Authority*. Chicago: Markham.

Lerner, D. 1963. "Toward a communication theory of modernization." In Lucian Pye (ed.), *Communication and Political Development*. Princeton, N.J.: Princeton University Press.

Lerner, Daniel. 1964. *The Passing of Traditional Society in the Middle East*. New York: Free Press.

Lewontin, R.C. 1989. "Bookreview." *New York Review of Books* (April 27).

Liang, Heng and Judith Shapiro. 1984. *Son of the Revolution*. New York: Vintage.

Liebman, Robert and Robert Wuthnow. 1983. *The New Christian Right*. New York: Aldine.

Lindblom, Charles. 1968. *The Policy Process*. Englewood Cliffs, N.J.: Prentice Hall.

Lipset, S.M. 1963. *Political Man*. New York: Doubleday Anchor.

Lipset, Seymour, M. and Philip Altbach, eds. 1969. *Students in Revolt*. Boston: Beacon Press.

Lipset, Seymour M. and Earl Raab. 1970. *The Politics of Unreason*. New York: Harper Torch Books.

Littell, Robert, ed. 1969. *The Czech Black Book*. New York: Avon.

Liu, Allen. 1976. *Political Culture and Group Conflict in Communist China*. Santa Barbara, Cal.: Clio Press.

Liu, Guo Kai. 1986/1987. "A brief analysis of the Cultural Revolution." In *Chinese Sociology and Anthropology* 19 (Winter).

Lomax, L. 1963. *The Negro Revolt*. New York: Signet.

Lorwin, V. 1957. "Reflections on the history of the French and American labor movements." *Journal of Economic History* 17 (March): 25–44.

Macfarlane, Alan. 1970. *Witchcraft in Tudor and Stuart England: A Regional and Comparative Study*. London: Routledge and Kegan Paul.

Mair, Lucy. 1963. *New Nations*. Chicago: Chicago University Press.

Major, R. 1971. *A Panther is a Black Cat*. New York: Morrow.

Mandrou, Robert. 1968. *Magistrats et Sorcieres en France au XVII Siecle*. Paris: Plon.

Mansbridge, Jane, ed. 1990. *Beyond Self-Interest*. Chicago: Chicago University Press.

Marriott, McKim. 1963. "Cultural policy in the new states." In C. Geertz (ed.), *Old Societies and New States*. New York: Free Press.

Marsden, George. 1980. *Fundamentalism and American Culture*. New York: Oxford University Press.

Martin, J.B. 1957. *The Deep South Says Never*. New York: Ballentine Books.

Marx, G. 1974. "Thoughts on a neglected category of social movement participant: The agent provocateur and the informant." *American Journal of Sociology* 80: 402–44.

Matossian, Mary K. 1989. *Poisons of the Past.* New Haven, Conn.: Yale University Press.

McAdam, D. 1982. *Political Process and the Development of Black Insurgency, 1930–1970.* Chicago: Chicago University Press.

McAdam, D. 1983. "Tactical innovation and the pace of insurgency." *American Sociological Review,* 48, 6: 735–54.

McAdam, Doug. 1986. "Recruitment to high risk activism: The case of freedom summer." *American Journal of Sociology* 92 (July): 64–90.

McCarthy, J. 1974. "Note on competition and cooperation among social movement organizations." Unpublished paper, Vanderbilt University, Department of Sociology and Anthropology.

McCarthy, J.D. and M.N. Zald. 1973. *The Trend of Social Movements in America: Professionalization and Resource Mobilization.* Morristown, N.J.: General Learning Press.

McCone Report, Governor's Commission on the Los Angeles Riots, *Violence in the City. An End or a Beginning,* 2 December 1965.

McLoughlin, William. 1978. *Revivals, Awakenings and Reform.* Chicago: Chicago University Press.

McNeely, J. 1966. "Origins of the Zapata revolt in Morelos." *Hispanic-American Historical Review* 46 (May): 153–69.

McPhail, C. 1971. "Civil disorder participation: A critical examination of recent research." *American Sociological Review,* 36, 6: 1058–72.

Meier, A. and E. Rudwick. 1973. *CORE.* New York: Oxford University Press.

Merton, Robert K. 1957. *Social Theory and Social Structure.* Glencoe, Ill.: The Free Press.

Michels, Robert. 1959. *Political Parties.* New York: Dover.

Midelfort, H.C. Erick. 1972. *Witch Hunting in Southwest Germany, 1562–1684.* Stanford, Cal.: Stanford University Press.

Mitchell, G and W. Peace. 1962. *The Angry Black South.* New York: Corinth Books.

Monter, E. William. 1976. *Witchcraft in France and Switzerland: The Borderlands During the Reformation.* Ithaca, NY: Cornell University Press.

Moore, B. 1966. *Social Origins of Dictatorship and Democracy.* Boston: Beacon.

Morris, A. 1981. "Black Southern student sit-in movement: An analysis of internal organization." *American Sociological Review* 46 (December): 744–67.

Morris, A. 1984. *The Origins of the Civil Rights Movement.* New York: Free Press.

Ms Magazine. 1979. "The Decade of Women" (December): 60–94.

Murphy, R. and H. Elinson, eds. 1966. *Problems and Prospects of the Negro Movement.* Belmont, Cal.: Wadsworth Company.

Naipaul, Shiva. 1981. *Journey to Nowhere*. New York: Simon and Schuster.

National Advisory Commission. 1968. *Report of the National Advisory Commission on Civil Disorders*. New York: Bantam.

Newfield, J. 1966. *A Prophetic Minority*. New York: Signet Books.

Nicholls, David. 1980. "The Devil in Renaissance France." *History Today* 30 (November): 25–30.

Oberschall, A. 1973. *Social Conflict and Social Movements*. Englewood Cliffs, N.J.: Prentice Hall.

Oberschall, A. 1978. "The decline of the 1960s social movements." In L. Kriesberg (ed.), *Research in Social Movements; Conflict, and Change*. JAI Press. Reprinted in this volume.

Oberschall, A. 1979. "Protracted conflict." In M. Zald and J. McCarthy (eds.), *The Dynamics of Social Movements*. Cambridge, Mass.: Winthrop Publishers, Inc. Reprinted in this volume.

Oberschall, A. 1980. "Loosely structured collective conflict." In L. Kriesberg (ed.), *Research in Social Movements, Conflict and Change*, 3: 45–68. Greenwich, Conn.: JAI Press. Reprinted in this volume.

Odegard, Peter. 1927. *Pressure Politics: The Story of the Anti-Saloon League*. New York: Columbia University Press.

Oliver, P. et al., n.d. "Group heterogeneity, interdependence, and the production of collective goods." Department of Sociology, University of Wisconsin. Unpublished manuscript.

Oliver, Pamela. 1984. "If you don't do it, nobody else will." *American Sociological Review* 49 (5): 601–10.

Olson, Mancur, Jr. 1963. "Rapid economic growth as a destabilizing force." *Journal of Economic History* 23 (December): 529–52.

Olson, Mancur, Jr. 1968. *The Logic of Collective Action*. New York: Schocken Books.

Olson, Mancur, Jr. 1982. *The Rise and Fall of Nations*. New Haven, Conn.: Yale University Press.

Opp, Karl-Dieter. 1988. "Grievances and participation in social movements." *American Sociological Review*, 53 (6): 853–64.

Oppenheimer, M. 1963. *The Genesis of the Southern Negro Student Movement*. Ann Arbor, Mich.: University Microfilms.

Orum, A., n.d. *Black Students in Protest*. Washington, D.C.: American Sociological Association.

Page, Ann and Donald Clelland. 1978. "The Kanawha County textbook controversy." *Social Forces* 57: 265–81.

Paige, J. 1975. *Agrarian Revolution*. New York: Free Press.

Patrick, C. 1960. "Lunchcounter desegregation in Winston Salem, N.C." The Mayor's Goodwill Committee (July).

Peterson, R. 1968. *The Scope of Organized Student Protest in 1967–1968*. Princeton, N.J.: Education Testing Service.

Pettee, George. 1938. *The Process of Revolution*. New York: Harper and Brothers.

Pheffer, Leo. 1970. "The right to religious liberty." In N. Doren (ed.), *The Rights of Americans*. New York: Random.

Pike Report, U.S. Commission on Civil Rights, California Advisory Committee, *Police Minority Group Relations in Los Angeles and the San Francisco Bay Area* (August 1963).

Piven, Frances Fox and Richard Cloward. 1977. *Poor People's Movements*. New York: Pantheon.

Postgate, R. 1962. *Revolution From 1789 to 1906*. New York: Harper Torchbook.

Pride, R. and D. Clarke. 1973. "Race relations in television news: A content analysis of the networks." *Journalism Quarterly* 50: 318-28.

Pride, R. and B. Richards. 1974. "Denigration of authority?. Television news coverage of the student movement." *Journal of Politics* 33: 638-60.

Proudfoot, M. 1962. *Diary of a Sit-In*. Chapel Hill: University of North Carolina Press.

Pye, Lucian, ed. 1963. *Communications and Political Development*. Princeton, N.J.: Princeton University Press.

Rachal, Valley J. 1980. "The extent and nature of adolescent drug use: The 1974 and 1978 national sample studies," p. 21. Research Triangle Park, NC: RTI (October).

Raines, Howell. 1977. *My Soul is Rested*. New York: Bantam.

Redfield, Robert. 1953. *The Primitive World and Its Transformation*. Ithaca, N.Y.: Cornell University Press.

Reed, John. 1967. *Ten Days That Shook the World*. New York: Signet.

Richardson, L. 1960. *Statistics of Deadly Quarrels*. Chicago: Quadrangle.

Rothchild, Donald and Michael Rogin. 1966. "Uganda." In Gwendolyn Carter (ed.), *National Unity and Regionalism in Eight African States*. Ithaca, N.Y.: Cornell University Press.

RPS, Los Angeles County Probation Department, *Riot Participation Study*, Research Report No. 26 (November 1965).

Rubin, J. 1970. *Do It*. New York: Simon and Schuster.

Rude, George. 1959. *The Crowd in the French Revolution*. New York: Oxford University Press.

Rude, George. 1964. *The Crowd in History*. New York: John Wiley.

Ruffin, B. 1985. "Black man's ice, black man's coal." *The North Carolina Independent* (January 18-31): 12.

Russell, Jeffrey. 1980. *A History of Witchcraft*. London: Thames and Hudson.

Sale, K. 1973. *SDS*. New York: Vintage Books.

Salert, B. 1976. *Revolutions and Revolutionaries*. New York: Elsevier.

Scammon, Richard and Ben Wattenberg. 1972. *The Real Majority*. New York: Berkeley.

Schama, Simon. 1989. *Citizens*. New York: Knopf.

Schelling, T. 1963. *The Strategy of Conflict*. New York: Oxford University Press.

Schlegel, Ronald and Margaret Sanborn. 1979. "Religious affiliation and adolescent drinking." *Journal of Studies on Alcohol*, 40 (7).

Schlesinger, A., Jr. 1973. *The Imperial Presidency*. New York: Popular Library Edition.

Schlosser, J. 1985. "Sit-ins." *News and Record*, Greensboro, NC (January 27): A7.

Schramm, Wilber. 1964. *Mass Media and National Development*. Stanford, Cal.: Stanford University Press.

Seale, Patrick and Maureen McConville. 1968. *Red Flag, Black Flag*. New York: Ballentine.

Simon, Herbert. 1969. *The Sciences of the Artificial*. Cambridge, Mass.: MIT Press.

Sinclair, Andrew. 1962. *Era of Excess, A Social History of the Prohibition Movement*. New York: Harper Coliphon Books.

Skocpol, Theda. 1979. *States and Revolutions*. New York: Cambridge University Press.

Skolnick, J. 1969. *The Politics of Protest*. New York: Ballantine Books.

Smelser, N.J. 1963. *Theory of Collective Behavior*. New York: Free Press.

Smelser, N.J. 1964. "Collective behavior and conflict." *Sociological Quarterly* 5 (Spring): 116–22.

Smelser, N.J. 1968. "Toward a theory of modernization." In N. Smelser (ed.), *Essays in Sociological Explanation*. Englewood Cliffs, N.J.: Prentice Hall.

Smith, Adam. 1809. *The Theory of Moral Sentiments*, 12th Edition). Glasgow.

Snow, David et al. 1986. "Frame alignment processes, micromobilization, and movement participation." *American Sociological Review* 51, (4): 464–481.

Snow, David and Robert Benford. 1988. "Ideology, frame resonance and participant mobilization." *International Social Movement Research* 1: 197–217.

Southern Regional Council (SRC. 1961. "The student protest movement." Atlanta (September 29).

"Special Census Survey of the South and East Los Angeles Areas: November 1965." *Current Population Report*, Technical Studies, Series P-23, 17 (23 March 1967).

Spilerman, S. 1970. "The causes of racial disturbances: A comparison of alternative explanations." *American Sociological Review* 35, 4:627–49.

Spilerman, S. 1976. "Structural characteristics of cities and the severity of racial disorders." *American Sociological Review* 41, 5:771–93.

Stark, Rodney and Charles Glock. 1968. *American Piety*. Berkeley: University of California Press.

Stark, Rodney and William Bainbridge. 1980. "Networks of faith: Interpersonal bonds and recruitment to cults and sects." *American Journal of Sociology* 85 (6) (May): 1376–95.

Stone, L. 1965. "Theories of revolution." *World Politics* 18 (January): 159–76.

Stouffer, Samuel. 1955. *Communism, Conformity and Civil Liberties*. New York: Doubleday.

Suleiman, Ezra. 1978. *Elites in French Society*. Princeton, N.J.: Princeton University Press.

Taft, P. 1966. "Violence in American labor disputes." *Annals of the American Academy of Social and Political Science* (March): 127–40.

Tallman, Irving and Louis Gray. 1990. "Choices, decisions and problem-solving." *Annual Review of Sociology* 16: 405–33.

Tarrow, Sidney. 1989. *Democracy and Disorder*. Oxford: Oxford University Press.

Tchou, ed. 1968. *Les Murs Ont la Parole, Mai 68*. Paris: Tchou.

Thomas, Keith. 1971. *Religion and the Decline of Magic*. New York: Scribner.

Tilly, Charles. 1964. *The Vendee*. Cambridge, Mass.: Harvard University Press.

Tilly, Charles. 1975. "Revolutions and collective violence." In F.I. Greenstein and N.W. Polsby (eds.), *Handbook of Political Science* 3:483–555. Reading, Mass.: Addison Wesley.

Tilly, Charles. 1978. *From Mobilization to Revolution*. Reading, Mass.: Addison Wesley.

Tilly, Charles. 1985. "Models and realities of popular collective action." *Social Research* 52 (4): 717–47.

Tilly, C. and J. Rule. 1965. *Measuring Political Upheaval*. Princeton, N.J.: Center of International Studies, Research Monograph 19.

Tilly, C., L. Tilly, and R. Tilly. 1975. *The Rebellious Century, 1830 to 1930*. Cambridge, Mass.: Harvard University Press.

Tocqueville, Alexis de. 1955. *The Old Regime and the French Revolution*. New York: Doubleday Anchor.

Trotsky, L. 1959. *The Russian Revolution*. New York: Doubleday Anchor.

Turner, R. 1964. "Collective behavior and conflict." *Sociological Quarterly* 5 (Spring): 122–32.

Turner, Ralph and Lewis Killian. 1957. *Collective Behavior*. Englewood Cliffs, N.J.: Prentice Hall.

Turner, Ralph and Lewis Killian. 1987. *Collective Behavior*. 2d ed. Englewood Cliffs, N.J.: Prentice Hall.

U.S. Senate, Select Committee to Study Government Operations with Respect to Intelligence Activities. 1976. *Final Report: Book II, Intelligence Activities and the Rights of Americans*. Washington, D.C.: U.S. Government Printing Office.

Ullman-Margalit, Edna. 1977. *The Emergence of Norms*. Oxford: Clarendon.

United Nations. 1957. *Report of the Special Committee on the Problem of Hungary*. New York: General Assembly, Eleventh Session, Supplement Number 18 (A/3592).

Useem, Bert. 1980. "Solidarity model, breakdown model and the Boston anti-busing movement." *American Sociological Review* 45 (3): 357–69.

van den Berghe, Pierre, ed. 1965. *Africa, Social Problems and Change and Conflict*. San Francisco: Chandler.

Viguerie, Richard. 1981. *The New Right: We're Ready to Lead*. Falls Church, Va.: The Viguerie Company.

Viorst, Milton. 1979. *Fire in the Streets*. New York: Simon and Schuster.

Wagley, C.C. 1959. *Crops and Wealth in Uganda*. Kampala, Uganda: East African Institute of Social Research.

Walder, Andrew. 1986. *Communist Neo-Traditionalism*. Berkeley: University of California Press.

Walker, D.P. 1981. *Unclear Spirits: Possessions and Exorcism in France and England in the Late 16th and Early 17th Century*. Philadelphia: University of Pennsylvania Press.

Wallerstein, Immanuel, ed. 1966. *Social Change*. New York: John Wiley.

Waskow, A. 1967. *From Race Riot to Sit-In, 1919 and the 1960s*. New York: Doubleday Anchor.

Weber, Max. 1947. *The Theory of Social and Economic Organization*. Glencoe, Ill.: Free Press.

Weber, Max. 1921 [1956]. *Wirtschaft und Gesellschaft*. Tübingen: Mohr.

Weber, Max. 1956. *Wirtschaft und Gesellschaft*, vol. 1. Tübingen: Mohr.

Weber, Max. 1958. *From Max Weber: Essays in Sociology*, H. Gerth and W. Mills (eds.). New York: Oxford University Press.

Weber, Max. 1964. "Uber Einige Kategorien der Verstehenden Soziologie." *Soziologie, Analysen, Politik*. Kröner Verlag.

Wechsler, Henry and Mary McFadden. 1979. "Drinking among college students in New England." *Journal of Studies in Alcohol* 40 (11).

Wehr, P. 1960. "The sit-down protests." Department of Sociology, University of North Carolina. Unpublished Masters Thesis.

White, Lynn III. 1989. *Policies of Chaos*. Princeton, N.J.: Princeton University Press.

Wilson, Bryan. 1982. *Religion in Sociological Perspective*. Oxford: Oxford University Press.

Wilson, J.Q. 1961. "The strategy of protest: Problems of Negro civic action." *Journal of Conflict Resolution* 5:291–303.

Wood, Michael and Michael Hughes. 1984. "The moral basis of moral reform." *American Sociology Review* 49, (1): 86–99.

WRA, Bureau of Criminal Records, Department of Justice, State of California, *Watts Riot Arrests* (June 1966), Sacramento, California.

Young, M. Crawford. 1966. "The Obote Revolution." *Africa Report* 11 (June).

Zald, Mayer and John McCarthy. 1987. *Social Movements in an Organizational Society*. New Brunswick, N.J.: Transaction Books.

Zeman, Z.A.B. 1969. *Prague Spring*. New York: Hill and Wang.

Zinn, H. 1965. *SNCC, The New Abolitionists*. Boston: Beacon Press.

Index

Anti-war movement, 270-271, 295-296, 318-320.

Black Panthers, 268-270, 319.
Bloc recruitment, 24, 37,74.

Civil rights movement, 114-115, 213-237, 267-270, 319.
Collective action, 1-3, 12, 68-77, 221-226, 326-327, 383.
Collective behavior, 3-16, 68-69, 239-264; and rationality, 68-69; as ritual, 13, 21.
Collective goods, 3, 20, 57, 68, 97, 383.
Conciliation, 100-103, 112-113.
Cultural revolution in China, 303-308.
Culture, 201-211, 364; truth value of, 188, 203-204; and metaphor, 202-203, 367; reality test of, 206; social construction of, 203; and symbolic politics, 364-366, 377. *See also* Ideology.
Conflict, 39, 98-109, 152, 157; definition of, 39; dimensions of, 40; and derivative issues, 99, 104; dynamics of, 60-65, 97-124; and polarization 64-65.
Countermovements, 20, 323, 335, 338, 384.
Crowd. *See* Collective behavior.

Diffusion, 37, 63, 73-77, 88-94, 213-226, 284, 302; and mass media, 225, 232-233, 253, 283-284.
Discontent, 16-19, 46-52, 54, 153, 157-164, 179, 191, 321, 326-328, 372; of rioters, 240, 247-251, 259-260. *See also* Relative deprivation and revolution of rising expectations.

Equal Rights Amendment (ERA), 335-336, 360-362.
Erratic reformism, 152-153, 155-156, 294.

European witchcraze 187-212; and feminist theory, 192, 199-200; and functionalism, 197-198; and interest theory, 191-192, 198-199; and labeling theory, 198; and modernization theory, 200; and psychological theory, 196; and the scientific revolution, 207-210.

Framing, 38, 202. *See also* Culture.
Free riders, 20, 24, 35, 37, 57, 68, 74, 384.
French revolution of 1968, 313-318.

Grievances. *See* Discontent.

Identification move, 73, 275.
Ideology, 188-189, 275; and interest theory 188-190, 192, 364; of the New Christian Right, 364-372, 377-379; of the 1960's movements, 277-278; in the witchcraze, 192-194; of the women's movement, 329, 335-337. *See also* Culture.
Irish Republican Army (IRA), 102, 107-109.

Mass media, 126, 135-136, 167, 225, 276, 279; and the anti-war movement, 280-284; and media stars, 280-281; and the New Christian Right, 346-349, 377; and rioting, 240-241, 253-254.
Methodological individualism, 33-34, 36-37, 187.
Mobilization, 20-31, 43, 46, 55-59; in the anti-war movement 274-278; in the Los Angeles riot, 252-253; in the New Christian Right, 342-349, 351, 373-374; and the production function, 70-72; in the women's movement, 330-332.
Moral majority, 340, 345-346, 358-359.